Learn Python by Building Data Science Applications

Science Applications

A fun, project-based guide to learning Python 3 while building real-world apps

Philipp Kats
David Katz

BIRMINGHAM - MUMBAI

Learn Python by Building Data Science Applications

Commissioning Editor: Richa Tripathi
Acquisition Editor: Chaitanya Nair
Content Development Editor: Tiksha Sarang
Senior Editor: Afshaan Khan
Technical Editor: Romy Dias
Copy Editor: Safis Editing
Project Coordinator: Prajakta Naik
Proofreader: Safis Editing
Indexer: Rekha Nair
Production Designer: Nilesh Mohite

First published: August 2019

Production reference: 1300819

Published by Packt Publishing Ltd.
Livery Place
35 Livery Street
Birmingham
B3 2PB, UK.

ISBN 978-1-78953-536-5

www.packt.com

Packt.com

Subscribe to our online digital library for full access to over 7,000 books and videos, as well as industry leading tools to help you plan your personal development and advance your career. For more information, please visit our website.

Why subscribe?

- Spend less time learning and more time coding with practical eBooks and Videos from over 4,000 industry professionals

- Improve your learning with Skill Plans built especially for you

- Get a free eBook or video every month

- Fully searchable for easy access to vital information

- Copy and paste, print, and bookmark content

Did you know that Packt offers eBook versions of every book published, with PDF and ePub files available? You can upgrade to the eBook version at www.packt.com and as a print book customer, you are entitled to a discount on the eBook copy. Get in touch with us at customercare@packtpub.com for more details.

At www.packt.com, you can also read a collection of free technical articles, sign up for a range of free newsletters, and receive exclusive discounts and offers on Packt books and eBooks.

Contributors

About the authors

Philipp Kats is a researcher at the Urban Complexity Lab, NYU CUSP, a research fellow at Kazan Federal University, and a data scientist at StreetEasy, with many years of experience in software development. His interests include data analysis, urban studies, data journalism, and visualization. Having a bachelor's degree in architectural design and a having followed the rocky path (at first) of being a self-taught developer, Philipp knows the pain points of learning programming and is eager to share his experience.

I would like to thank my wife, Anna, and son, Solomon, for their support and patience.

David Katz is a researcher and holds a Ph.D. in mathematics. As a mathematician at heart, he sees code as a tool to express his questions. David believes that code literacy is essential as it applies to most disciplines and professions. David is passionate about sharing his knowledge and has 6 years of experience teaching college and high school students.

I would like to thank my wife, Dina, for her support and help.

The authors would also like to thank the administration of the Kazan Federal University IT-Lyceum, and its director, Timerbulat Samerkhanov, for the opportunity to conduct a course that laid the foundation for this book. Our special thanks go to our students for their help and feedback:

- *Azat Davletshin*
- *Danis Saifullin*
- *Evdokimov Alexandr*
- *Kasatkin Alexander*
- *Kirill Kaidanov*
- *Nikolai Plantonov*

About the reviewers

Sri Manikanta is an undergraduate student pursuing his bachelor's degree in computer science and engineering at SICET under JNTUH. He is a founder of the Open Stack Developer Community at his college. He started his journey as a competitive programmer and he always loves to solve problems that are related to the filed of data science. He has worked on a couple of projects on deep learning and machine learning. He has published many articles regarding data science, machine learning, programming and cyber security in top publications such as Hacker Noon, freeCodeCamp, Towards Data Science, and DDI. He completed his Python specialization at the University of Michigan, through Coursera.

I would like to express my deepest gratitude to my spiritual and biological parents for everything that they have done for me.

A special thanks to my friends and well-wishers for supporting me, and to Packt Publishing for giving me the opportunity to review this book.

Richard Marsden has 25 years of professional software development experience. After starting in the field of geophysical surveying for the oil industry, he has spent the last 15 years running the Winwaed Software Technology LLC, an independent software vendor. Winwaed specializes in geospatial tools and applications including web applications and operates the Mapping-Tools website for tools and add-ins for geospatial applications such as Caliper Maptitude, Microsoft MapPoint, Android, and Ultra Mileage.

Richard has been a technical reviewer for a number of Packt publications, including *Python Geospatial Development* and *Python Geospatial Analysis Essentials*, both by Erik Westra; and *Python Geospatial Analysis Cookbook*, by Michael Diener.

Packt is searching for authors like you

If you're interested in becoming an author for Packt, please visit authors.packtpub.com and apply today. We have worked with thousands of developers and tech professionals, just like you, to help them share their insight with the global tech community. You can make a general application, apply for a specific hot topic that we are recruiting an author for, or submit your own idea.

Table of Contents

Preface

There are no separate systems. The world is a continuum. Where to draw a boundary around a system depends on the purpose of the discussion.

– Donella H. Meadows, Thinking in Systems: A Primer

Python has become one of the most popular programming languages in the world, according to multiple polls and metrics. This popularity is, to no small extent, a direct result of the simplicity of the language, its power, and scalability, allowing it to run even large-scale applications, such as Dropbox, YouTube, and many others. It becomes even more valuable with the rise in the adoption of machine learning techniques and algorithms, including state-of-the-art algorithms on the edge of scientific advancements.

Consequently, there are hundreds of books, courses, and online tutorials on different aspects of programming, machine learning, data processing, and more. Many sources highlight the importance of learning-by-doing and building your own projects. Connecting the dots and structuring all this vast knowledge into one big picture is not an easy task. Seeing the big picture, in our opinion, is critical for the completion of any project. Indeed, there are plenty of options and decisions to take at every step. It is the grand schema of a project as a whole that helps you make those decisions, focus on what matters, and spend your time wisely.

This book is designed to be an entry point for any newcomer or novice developer, aiming to cover the whole life cycle of a data-driven application. By the end of it, you will be able to write arbitrary Python code, collect and process data, explore it, and build your own packages, dashboards, and APIs. Multiple notes and tips point to alternative solutions or decisions, allowing you to alternate code for your specific needs.

This book will be a useful resource if any of the following apply to you:

- You have just started to code.
- You know the basics but struggle to build something handy.
- You know your specific domain well—whether it be statistics, machine learning, or development—but lack experience in other parts of building a project.
- You're an experienced developer with little exposure to Python, trying to learn about the Python package's ecosystem.

If you feel you fall into any of those categories, or want to build a project from scratch for other reasons, please join us on this journey.

Who this book is for

This book is aimed at new Python developers with little to no prior programming skills beyond basic computer literacy. The book doesn't require any previous background in data science or statistics either. That being said, it covers a variety of topics, from data processing to visualization, to delivery—including dashboards, building APIs, **Extract, Transform, Load** (ETL) pipelines, or a standalone package. Thus, it is also suited to experienced data scientists interested in productizing their work. For a complete novice, this book aims to cover all major parts of the data application life cycle—from Python basics to scripts, data collection and processing, and the delivery of your work in different formats.

What this book covers

This book consists of three main sections. The first one is focused on language fundamentals, the second introduces data analysis in Python, and the final section covers different ways to deliver the results of your work. The last chapter of each section is focused on non-Python tools and topics related to the section subject.

Section 1, *Getting Started with Python*, introduces the Python programming language and explains how to install Python and all of the packages and tools we'll be using.

Chapter 1, *Preparing the Workspace*, covers all the tools we'll need throughout the book—what they are, how to install them, and how to use their interfaces. This includes the installation process for Python 3.7, all of the packages we'll require throughout the book, how to install all of them at once in a separate environment, as well as two code development tools we'll use—the Jupyter Notebook and VS Code. Finally, we'll run our first script to ensure everything works fine! By the end of this chapter, you will have everything you need to execute the book's code, ready to go.

Chapter 2, *First Steps in Coding – Variables and Data Types*, gives an introduction to fundamental programming concepts, such as variables and data types. You'll start writing code in Jupyter, and will even solve a simple problem using the knowledge you've just acquired.

Chapter 3, *Functions*, introduces yet another concept fundamental to programming—functions. This chapter covers the most important built-in functions and teaches you about writing new ones. Finally, you will revisit the problem from the previous chapter, and write an alternative solution, using functions.

Chapter 4, *Data Structures*, covers different types of data structures in Python—lists, sets, dictionaries, and many others. You will learn about the properties of each structure, their interfaces, how to operate them, and when to use them.

Chapter 5, *Loops and Other Compound Statements*, illustrates different compound statements in Python—loops—`if`/`else`, `try`/`except`, one-liners, and others. These represent core logic in the code and allow non-linear code execution. At the end of this chapter, you'll be able to operate large data structures using short, expressive code.

Chapter 6, *First Script – Geocoding with Web APIs*, introduces the concept of APIs, working with HTTP and geocoding service APIs in particular, from Python. At the end of this chapter, you'll have fully operational code for geocoding addresses from the dataset—code that you'll be using extensively throughout the rest of the book, but that's also highly applicable to many tasks beyond it.

Chapter 7, *Scraping Data from the Web with Beautiful Soup 4*, illustrates a solution to a similar but more complex task of data extraction from HTML pages—scraping. Step by step, you will build a script that collects pages and extracts data on all the battles in World War II, as described in Wikipedia. At the end of this chapter, you'll know the limitations, challenges, and the main solutions of the scraping packages used for the task, and will be able to write your own scrapers.

Chapter 8, *Simulation with Classes and Inheritance*, introduces one more critical concept for programming in Python—classes. Using classes, we will build a simple simulation model of an ecological system. We'll compute, collect, and visualize metrics, and use them to analyze the system's behavior.

Chapter 9, *Shell, Git, Conda, and More – at Your Command*, covers the basic tools essential for the development process—from Shell and Git, to Conda packaging and virtual environments, to the use of makefiles and the Cookiecutter tool. The information we share in this chapter is essential for code development in general, and Python development in particular, and will allow you to collaborate and talk the same language with other developers.

Section 2, *Hands-On with Data*, focuses on using Python for data processing analysis, including cleaning, visualization, and training machine learning models.

`Chapter 10`, *Python for Data Applications*, works as an introduction to the Python data analysis ecosystem—a distinct group of packages that allow simple work with data, its processing, and analysis. As a result, you will get familiar with the main packages and their purpose, their special syntaxes, and will understand what makes them work substantially faster than normal Python for numeric calculations.

`Chapter 11`, *Data Cleaning and Manipulation*, shows how to use the `pandas` package to process and clean our data, and make it ready for analysis. As an example, we'll clean and prepare the dataset we obtained from Wikipedia in `Chapter 7`, *Scraping Data from the Web with Beautiful Soup 4*. Through the process, we'll learn how to use regular expressions, use the geocoding code we wrote in `Chapter 6`, *First Script – Geocoding with Web APIs*, and an array of other techniques to clean the data.

`Chapter 12`, *Data Exploration and Visualization*, explains how to explore an arbitrary dataset and ask and answer questions about it, using queries, statistics, and visualizations. You'll learn how to use two visualization libraries, Matplotlib and Altair. Both make static charts quickly or more advanced, interactive ones. As our case example, we'll use the dataset we cleaned in the previous chapter.

`Chapter 13`, *Training a Machine Learning Model*, presents the core idea of machine learning and shows how to apply unsupervised learning with the k-means clustering algorithm, and supervised learning with KNN, linear regression, and decision trees, to a given dataset.

`Chapter 14`, *Improving Your Model – Pipelines and Experiments*, highlights ways to improve your model, using feature engineering, cross-validation, and by applying a more sophisticated algorithm. In addition, you will learn how to track your experiments and keep both code and data under version control, using data version control with `dvc`.

`Section 3`, *Moving to Production*, is focused on delivering the results of your work with Python, in different formats.

`Chapter 15`, *Packaging and Testing with Poetry and PyTest*, explains the process of packaging. Using our Wikipedia scraper as an example, we'll create a package using the `poetry` library, set dependencies and a development environment, and make the package accessible for installation using `pip` from GitHub. To ensure the package's functionality, we will add a few unit tests using the `pytest` testing library.

`Chapter 16`, *Data Pipelines with Luigi*, introduces ETL pipelines and explains how to build and schedule one using the `luigi` framework. We will build a set of interdependent tasks for data collection and processing and set them to work on a scheduled basis, writing data to local files, S3 buckets, or a database.

Chapter 17, *Let's Build a Dashboard*, covers a few ways to build and share a dashboard online. We'll start by writing a static dashboard based on the charts we made with the Altair library in Chapter 12, *Data Exploration and Visualization*. As an alternative, we will also deploy a dynamic dashboard that pulls data from a database upon request, using the panel library.

Chapter 18, *Serving Models with a RESTful API*, brings us back to the API theme—but this time, we'll build an API on our own, using the fastAPI framework and the pydantic package for validation. Using a machine learning model, we'll build a fully operational API server, with the OpenAPI documentation and strict request validation. As FastAPI supports asynchronous execution, we'll also discuss what that means and when to use it.

Chapter 19, *Serverless API Using Chalice*, goes beyond serving an API with a personal server and shows how to achieve similar results with a serverless application, using AWS Lambda and the chalice package. This includes building an API endpoint, a scheduled pipeline, and serving a machine learning model. Along the way, we discuss the pros and cons of running serverless, its limitations, and ways to mitigate them.

Chapter 20, *Best Practices and Python Performance*, is comprises of three distinct parts. The first part showcases different ways to make your code faster, by using NumPy's vectorized computations or a specific data structure (in our case, a k-d tree), extending computations to multiple cores or even machines with Dask, or by leveraging performance (and, potentially, GIL-release) of just-in-time compilation with Numba. We also discuss different ways to achieve concurrency in Python—using threads, asynchronous tasks, or multiple processes.

The second part of the chapter focuses on improving the speed and quality of development. In particular, we'll cover the use of linters and formatters—the black package in particular; code maintainability measurements with wily; and advanced, data-driven code testing with the hypothesis package.

Finally, the third part of this chapter goes over a few technologies beyond Python, but that are still potentially useful to you. This list includes different Python interpreters, such as Jython, Brython, and Iodide; Docker technology; and Kubernetes.

To get the most out of this book

This book is designed for complete beginners and people who have just started to learn to code. It does not require any specific knowledge besides basic computer literacy.

...tion of the code examples provided in this book requires an installation of Python ... or later on macOS, Linux, or Microsoft Windows. The code presented throughout the book makes use of many Python libraries. In each chapter, a list of required libraries is given at the beginning. A full list of libraries is stored in the GitHub repository, in the `environment.yaml` file. The same file can be used to install Python and all of the required libraries in bulk—full instructions are given in `Chapter 1`, *Preparing the Workspace*.

The code for this book was developed in and extensively uses two development environments—VS Code editor with its Python bundle, and Jupyter. We recommend using both for better alignment with the book's narrative.

The code for `Chapter 6`, *First Script – Geocoding with Web APIs*, `Chapter 7`, *Scraping Data from the Web with Beautiful Soup 4*, `Chapter 11`, *Data Cleaning and Manipulation*, and `Chapter 16`, *Data Pipelines with Luigi*, requires an internet connection.

The first chapter will provide you with step-by-step instructions and some useful tips for setting up your Python environment, the core libraries, and all the necessary tools.

Download the example code files

You can download the example code files for this book from your account at `www.packt.com`. If you purchased this book elsewhere, you can visit `www.packt.com/support` and register to have the files emailed directly to you.

You can download the code files by following these steps:

1. Log in or register at `www.packt.com`.
2. Select the **SUPPORT** tab.
3. Click on **Code Downloads & Errata**.
4. Enter the name of the book in the **Search** box and follow the onscreen instructions.

Once the file is downloaded, please make sure that you unzip or extract the folder using the latest version of:

- WinRAR/7-Zip for Windows
- Zipeg/iZip/UnRarX for Mac
- 7-Zip/PeaZip for Linux

The code bundle for the book is also hosted on GitHub at `https://github.com/PacktPublishing/Learn-Python-by-Building-Data-Science-Applications`. In case there's an update to the code, it will be updated on the existing GitHub repository.

We also have other code bundles from our rich catalog of books and videos available at `https://github.com/PacktPublishing/`. Check them out!

Download the color images

We also provide a PDF file that has color images of the screenshots/diagrams used in this book. You can download it here: `https://static.packt-cdn.com/downloads/9781789535365_ColorImages.pdf`.

Code in Action

Visit the following link to check out videos of the code being run: `http://bit.ly/2MIb3Pn`

Conventions used

There are a number of text conventions used throughout this book.

`CodeInText`: Indicates code words in text, database table names, folder names, filenames, file extensions, pathnames, dummy URLs, user input, and Twitter handles. Here is an example: "As you can see, `pi` is a float, `name` is a string, `age` is an integer, and `sky_is_blue` is a Boolean."

A block of code is set as follows:

```
import pandas as pd

for word in 'Hello Word!'.split():
    print(word)
```

When we wish to draw your attention to a particular part of a code block, the relevant lines or items are set in bold:

```
pi = 3.14159265359     # Decimal
name = 'Philipp'       # Text
age = 31               # Integer
sky_is_blue = True     # Boolean
```

Often code will be shown as a print of an interactive console, with both code and the output being mixed. In this case, all input code lines will start with a triple "greater than" sign. Lines with no such sign represent the output:

```
>>> import pandas as pd
>>> for word in 'Hello Word!'.split():
>>>     print(word)

Hello
Word
```

Any command-line input or output is written as follows:

```
> conda install <mypackage>
> conda install -c <mychannel> <mypackage>
```

Bold: Indicates a new term, an important word, or words that you see onscreen. For example, words in menus or dialog boxes appear in the text like this. Here is an example: "Just use the **Clone or download** button on the right-hand side (1), and select **Download ZIP** (2)."

Warnings or important notes appear like this.

Tips and tricks appear like this.

Get in touch

Feedback from our readers is always welcome.

General feedback: If you have questions about any aspect of this book, mention the book title in the subject of your message and email us at customercare@packtpub.com.

Errata: Although we have taken every care to ensure the accuracy of our content, mistakes do happen. If you have found a mistake in this book, we would be grateful if you would report this to us. Please visit www.packt.com/submit-errata, selecting your book, clicking on the Errata Submission Form link, and entering the details.

Piracy: If you come across any illegal copies of our works in any form on the internet, we would be grateful if you would provide us with the location address or website name. Please contact us at copyright@packt.com with a link to the material.

If you are interested in becoming an author: If there is a topic that you have expertise in and you are interested in either writing or contributing to a book, please visit authors.packtpub.com.

Reviews

Please leave a review. Once you have read and used this book, why not leave a review on the site that you purchased it from? Potential readers can then see and use your unbiased opinion to make purchase decisions, we at Packt can understand what you think about our products, and our authors can see your feedback on their book. Thank you!

For more information about Packt, please visit packt.com.

Section 1: Getting Started with Python

This section focuses on becoming familiar with general-purpose Python, making use of existing libraries, writing our first scripts, learning the basics of Git, and using the IDE. In this section, we will also lay the foundation for our projects, building pipelines to process (project 1), collect (project 2), and simulate (project 3) data.

This section comprises the following chapters:

- Chapter 1, *Preparing the Workspace*
- Chapter 2, *First Steps in Coding – Variables and Data Types*
- Chapter 3, *Functions*
- Chapter 4, *Data Structures*
- Chapter 5, *Loops and Other Compound Statements*
- Chapter 6, *First Script – Geocoding with Web APIs*
- Chapter 7, *Scraping Data from the Web with Beautiful Soup 4*
- Chapter 8, *Classes and Inheritance*
- Chapter 9, *Shell, Git, Conda, and More – at Your Command*

Preparing the Workspace 1

Welcome! We're very excited to start learning and building things with you! However, we need to get ourselves ready first.

In this chapter, we'll learn how to download and install everything you'll need throughout the book, including Python itself, all the Python packages that we'll need, and two development tools we will be using extensively: Jupyter and **Visual Studio Code (VS Code)**. After that, we'll go through a brief overview of Jupyter and VS Code interfaces. Finally, you will run your very first line of Python, so we need to ensure that everything is ready before we dive in.

In this chapter, we'll cover the following:

- The minimum computer configuration required
- How to install the Anaconda distribution
- How to download the code for this book
- Setting up and getting familiar with VS Code and Jupyter
- Running your first line of code to ensure everything runs smoothly

By the end of this chapter, you will have learned about the hardware requirements for Python and this book, and what you can do if you don't have a sufficiently powerful computer. You will also learn how to install Python 3.7.2 and all required packages and tools using the open source Anaconda distribution.

Technical requirements

Python can be very humble and does not require an advanced computer. In fact, you can run Python on a $10 Raspberry Pi or an Arduino board! The code and data we use in this book do not require any special computational power, any laptop, or any computer made after 2008. At least 2 GB of RAM, 20 GB of disk space, and an internet connection should suffice. Your **operating system (OS)** shouldn't be a problem either, as Python and all the tools we will use are cross-platform and work on Windows, macOS, and Linux.

Throughout the book, we'll use two main tools to write the code: Jupyter and VS Code. Both of them are free and aren't demanding.

All the code for the book is publicly available and free to access at `https://github.com/PacktPublishing/Learn-Python-by-Building-Data-Science-Applications`.

Installing Python

There are multiple Python distributions, starting with the original, vanilla Python, which is accessible at `https://www.python.org/`. Data analysis, however, adds unique requirements for packaging (`https://www.youtube.com/watch?v=QjXJLVINsSAfeature=youtu.bet=3555`). In this book, we use **Anaconda**, which is an open source and free Python distribution, designed for data science and machine learning. Anaconda's main features include a smooth installation of data science packages (many of which run C and Fortran languages under the hood) and `conda`, which is a great package and environment manager (we will talk more about environments and `conda` later in `Chapter 9`, *Shell, Git, Conda, and More – at Your Command*). Conveniently, the Anaconda distribution installs all the packages (`https://docs.anaconda.com/anaconda/packages/pkg-docs/`) we need in this book and many more!

In order to install Anaconda, follow these steps:

1. First, go to the Anaconda distribution web page at `https://www.anaconda.com/distribution/`.

2. Select the Python 3.7 graphical installer for your platform and download it (at the time of writing, there is no graphical installer for Linux, so you'll have to use the one for the command line). The following screenshot shows what the interface looks like—we've marked the link we're interested in with dotted lines:

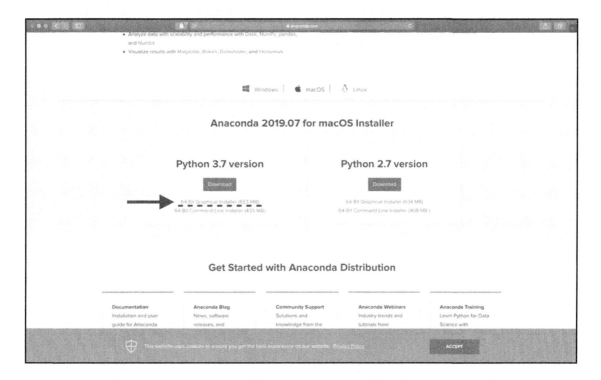

3. Run the installation. Keep all settings as default. When you're asked if you want to install PyCharm, select no (until you personally want to, of course, but we won't use PyCharm in this book):

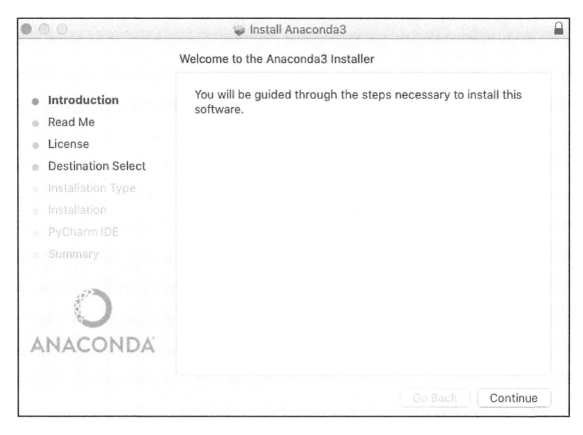

Voila! Now we have Python up and running! Next, let's download all the materials for this book.

 We use Anaconda build 3-2018.12, which is the most recent version at the time of writing this book. Until a new version is released, this build will be accessible at https://repo.anaconda.com/archive/.

Downloading materials for running the code

All code in this book is also available as a separate archive of files—either Python scripts or Jupyter notebooks. You can download the full archive and follow along with the book using the relevant code from GitHub (`https://github.com/PacktPublishing/Learn-Python-by-Building-Data-Science-Applications`). Everything is stored on GitHub, which is an online service for code storage with version control. We will discuss both Git and GitHub in `Chapter 9`, *Shell, Git, Conda, and More – at Your Command*, but in this case, you won't need version control, so it is easier to download everything as an archive. Just use the **Clone or download** button on the right side (**1**), and select **Download ZIP** (**2**):

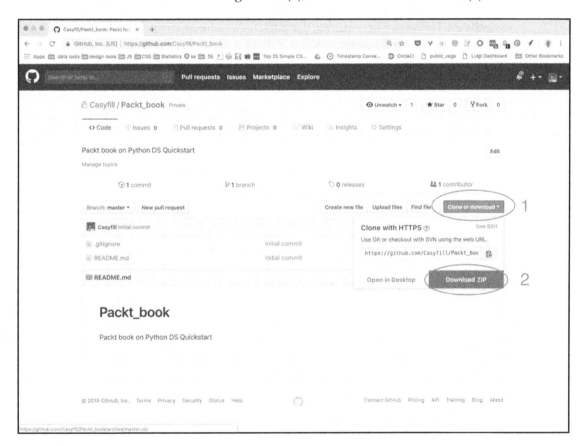

Once the download is complete, unzip the file and move it to a convenient location. This folder will be our main workspace throughout the book.

Installing Python packages

Many of the chapters in this book teach you how to make use of specific packages. Most of them are included in the standard Anaconda distribution, so if you installed Python using the Anaconda distribution, then you will have them already. Some packages might not be installed though, so we'll have to install them separately as per our requirements for every chapter. This is totally fine, and we'll specify which packages will be used at the beginning of each chapter.

In order to install a specific package, you have two options:

- Installing via Anaconda by running either of the following commands. Specifying a channel is required if a package is rare and not present on the default channels of Anaconda and conda-forge:

```
> conda install <mypackage>
> conda install -c <mychannel> <mypackage>
```

Some packages are not present in conda at all. You can search for packages through the channels at https://anaconda.org/.

- Most packages can be installed using pip:

```
> pip install <mypackage>
```

Generally speaking, we recommend using conda over pip for installation.

Alternatively, there is a single specification in the root of the repository that you can use to install everything at once. To do so, you need to go in your Terminal, and then to the repository's root (we will explain how to do that in Chapter 9, *Shell, Git, Conda, and More – at Your Command*, but VS Code's Terminal will open in the root of the given folder automatically). Once there, run the following command:

```
conda env update --name root -f environment.yml
```

Then, follow the instructions. Here, conda uses the environment.yml specification file as a list of packages to install.

Now, let's install our main development tools: VS Code and Jupyter.

Working with VS Code

VS Code is invaluable for Python development and experimentation. VS Code—not to be confused with Visual Studio, which is a commercial product—is a sophisticated, completely free, and open source text editor created by Microsoft. It is language-agnostic and will work perfectly with Python, JavaScript, Java, or any other language. VS Code has hundreds of built-in features and thousands of great plugins to expand its capabilities.

In order to install VS Code, head to its main web page, `https://code.visualstudio.com/`, and download the package for your OS. The installation is pretty straightforward; there is no need to change any of the default settings. Assuming you installed VS Code as part of the previous steps, you now need to open the VS Code application. Next, switch to the plugin marketplace menu (as shown in the following screenshot), type `Python`, and install the plugin. Python binding for VS Code provides plenty of Python-specific features and will prove very useful for us throughout the book.

In the following screenshot, **1** represents the plugin marketplace. Once switched, type `Python` in the search form (**2**), select the plugin (**3**), and hit install (Python was already installed in this screenshot, hence it offers to uninstall it instead):

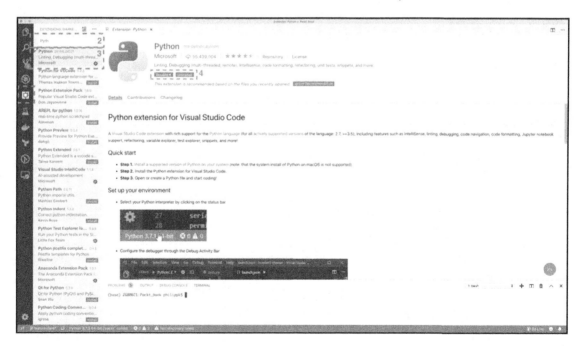

Once that's done, let's briefly review the interface of the tool.

The VS Code interface

Let's go over the VS Code interface. In the following screenshot, you can see five distinctive sections:

Section **1** of VS Code has six icons (more will appear after installing certain plugins). The last one at the bottom of the toolbar, which is a gear symbol, represents the settings. All the others represent different modes, from top to bottom:

1. Explorer mode, which allows us to look for the files that are open in the given workspace
2. Search mode, which allows us to look for a particular text element throughout the whole workplace

3. A built-in Git client (more on that in `Chapter 3`, *Functions*)
4. Debugger mode, which halts and inspects code in the middle of the execution in order to understand what's happening under the hood
5. VS Code's plugin marketplace

Every mode changes the content of section **2**. This is as an area that is dedicated to working with the workspace as a whole, which includes adding new files, removing existing ones, working with the workspace, or traversing through variables in debugging sessions.

Section **3** is the main one. Here, we actually write and read the code. You can have multiple tabs or even split this window into many: vertically, horizontally, or both. Most of the time, each tab represents one file in the workspace.

If you don't have section **4** open, then go to **View | Terminal** or use the *Ctrl + `* shortcut. You can also drag this section out from the upper edge of section **5** using your mouse, if you prefer.

Section **5** has four subsections. In **PROBLEMS**, VS Code will point you to some potential issues in the code. The **OUTPUT** and **DEBUG CONSOLE** tabs' roles are self-explanatory, and we won't use them much. The most important tab here is **Terminal**: it duplicates the Terminal built into your OS (hence, it does not directly relate to VS Code itself). Terminals allow us to run system-wide commands, create folders, write to files, execute Python scripts, and run any software, which is essentially everything you can do via your OS graphical interface, but done just using code. We will cover the Terminal in more depth in `Chapter 9`, *Shell, Git, Conda, and More – at Your Command*. Conveniently, VS Code's Terminals open in the root directory of the workspace, which is a feature we will constantly utilize throughout the book.

Lastly, section **5** is an information bar that shows the current properties of the workspace, including the interpreter's name, Git repository and branch names (more on that in `Chapter 3`, *Functions*), and cursor position. Most of those elements are interactive!

One more feature that is hidden from the newcomers, but is an extremely powerful feature of VS Code, is its command palette, as shown in the following screenshot:

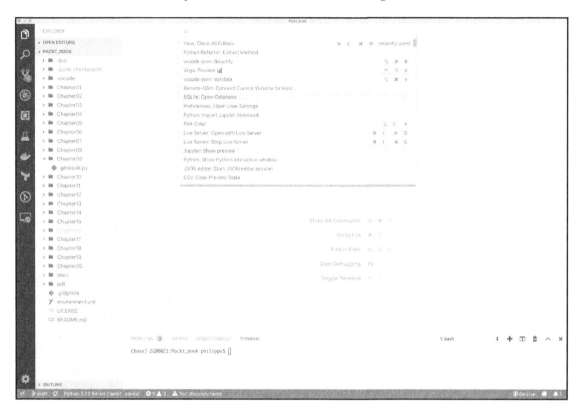

You can open the command palette using the *Ctrl* (*command* on macOS) + *Shift* + *P* shortcut. The command palette allows you to type in, select, and execute practically any feature of the application, from switching the color theme to searching for a word, to almost anything else. This feature allows programmers to avoid using a mouse or trackpad, and once mastered, it drastically increases productivity.

For example, let's create a new file (*Ctrl/command + N*) and type `Hello Python!`. Now, in order to switch that text to uppercase, all we need is to do the following:

1. Select all of the text by using *Ctrl/command + A*.
2. Open the command palette (*Ctrl/command + Shift + P*) and type `Upper`. Select the **Transform to Uppercase** command (note that the command palette also shows shortcuts).

Spend some time learning VS Code's features! One great place for that is the Interactive Playground: you can jump straight into it by typing the name into the command palette.

 Another great feature of VS Code is that it can use the key bindings that you use in other editors, including Vim, Sublime, and Atom. If you're used to their bindings, then switch to them, as they will save you a lot of time and frustration.

Beginning with Jupyter

Another development environment we'll use is Jupyter. If you have installed Anaconda, then Jupyter is already on your machine, as it is one of the tools that come with Anaconda. To start using Jupyter, we need to run it from the Terminal (you might need to open a new Terminal to update the paths). The following code will run a newer version of the tool's frontend face, and that is what we'll use:

```
$ jupyter lab
```

Alternatively, it also supports an older version of the frontend via `Jupyter Notebook`. The two have their differences, but we'll stick with the lab.

The app's behavior depends on the folder from which it was started; it is more convenient to run it directly from the project's root folder. That's why it is so handy that VS Code's Terminal opens in a workspace folder by itself, as we don't need to navigate there every time. But why do we need another developer tool, anyway? That's what the next section is all about.

Notebooks

As we mentioned earlier, Jupyter is designed with a different approach to programming than VS Code. Its central concept is so-called *notebooks*: files that allow the mixing of actual code, text (including markdown and LaTeX equations), as well as plots, images, videos, and interactive visualizations. In notebooks, you execute code interactively, one cell after another. This way, you can experiment easily—write some code, run it, see the outcomes, and then tweak it again.

The outcomes are shown along with the code so that you can open and read the notebook, even without executing it. Because of that, notebooks are especially useful in scientific/analytical contexts, as on the one hand, they allow us to describe what we're doing with text and illustrations, and on the other hand, they keep the actual code tied to the narrative so that anyone can inspect and confirm that your analysis is valid. One great example of that is LIGO notebooks, which represent the actual code that was used to discover gravitational waves in the universe (this research won the Nobel Prize in 2017).

Notebooks are also great for teaching (as in the case of this book), as students can interact with each and every part of the code by themselves. However, while Jupyter is good for exploration, it feels less convenient when your code base starts to grow and mature. Because of this, we will switch back and forth between Jupyter and VS Code throughout the course of this book, picking the right tool for each particular job.

Let's now look at Jupyter's interface.

The Jupyter interface

Let's get familiar with Jupyter's interface. This software works differently to VS Code: Jupyter works as a web server that is accessible through a browser. To make it run, just type `jupyter lab` in VS Code's Terminal window and hit *Enter*. This will start the server. Depending on your OS, either a link will be printed in the Terminal (starting with `localhost://...`), or your default web browser will just open the page automatically. You can stop the Jupyter server by hitting *Ctrl + C* within the Terminal and typing `yes`, if prompted, or by closing the window.

Jupyter's layout, as shown in the following screenshot, is somewhat similar to that of VS Code:

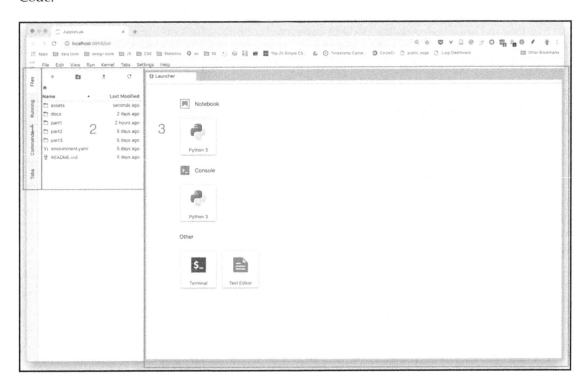

Here, again, the tabs in section **1** show all the modes available for section **2**, including a file browser, a list of running notebooks, a list of available commands, and tabs. The second section represents one of the modes previously described. Finally, the main section, section **3**, shows all open tabs, similar to section **3** in VS Code. The default tab is **Launcher**. From here, we can create new notebooks, text files (such as classic code or data files), Terminals, and consoles.

Note that the launcher explicitly states **Python 3** for both notebooks and consoles. This is because Jupyter is also language-agnostic. In fact, the name Jupyter comes from the **Julia-Python-R** triad of analytical languages, but the application supports many others, including C, Java, and Rust. In this book, we'll only use Python.

If everything went smoothly with Jupyter, then we're ready to go! But before we dive into coding, let's do one last pre-flight check.

Pre-flight check

Before we proceed to the content of this book, let's ensure our code can actually be executed by running the simplest possible code in Jupyter. To do this, let's create a test notebook and run some code to ensure everything works as intended. Click on the **Python 3** square in the **Notebook** section. A new tab should open, called `Untitled.ipynb`.

First, the blue line highlighted represents the selected cell in the notebook. Each cell represents a separate snippet of code, which is executed simultaneously in one step. Let's write our very first line of code in this cell:

```
print('Hello world')
```

Now, hit *Shift + Enter*. This shortcut executes the selected cells in Python and outputs the result on the next line. It also automatically creates a new input cell if there are none, as shown in the following screenshot. The number on the left gives a hint as to the order in which cells are executed, so the first cell to be executed will be marked with 1. The asterisk means the cell is under execution and computation is underway:

If everything worked properly, and you see `Hello world` in the output, then congratulations—you are ready for the following chapters!

Cells can also include markdown, which is useful for including explanations, images, or equations. For that, just switch from **Code** to **Markdown** by using the dropdown at the top.

Summary

In this chapter, we prepared our working environment for the journey ahead. In particular, we installed the Anaconda Scientific Python Distribution with Python 3.7.2, which includes all the packages we'll need throughout the course of this book. We also installed and learned about the basics of VS Code, which is a sophisticated and interactive development environment that will be our primary tool for writing arbitrary code, and Jupyter, which we use for experimentation and analysis. Finally, we discussed and even ran some code already! We did this in Jupyter, which is a coding environment that is perfect for prototyping, experimentation, analysis, and educational purposes.

In the next chapter, we'll begin our introduction to Python, learning about variables, variable assignment, and Python's basic data types.

Questions

1. What version of Python do we use?
2. Will it work on a Windows PC?
3. Do I need to install any additional packages?
4. What is a Jupyter Notebook?
5. When and why should I use Jupyter Notebooks?
6. When should I switch to VS Code?
7. Can I run the code from this book on my smartphone/tablet?

Further reading

- *Python for Beginners: Learn Python Programming (Python 3) [Video]* (https://www.packtpub.com/application-development/python-beginners-learn-python-programming-python-3-video)
- *Data Science Projects with Python* (https://www.packtpub.com/big-data-and-business-intelligence/data-science-projects-python)
- *The Scientific Paper Is Obsolete* (https://www.theatlantic.com/science/archive/2018/04/the-scientific-paper-is-obsolete/556676/)

First Steps in Coding - Variables and Data Types

2

Having set up all the tools, you're now ready to dive into development. Fire up Jupyter—in this chapter, we will get our hands dirty with code! We'll start with the concept of variables, and learn how to assign and use them in Python. We will discuss best practices on naming them, covering both strict requirements and general conventions. Next, we will cover Python's basic *data types* and the operators they support, including integers, decimal numbers (floats), strings, and Boolean values. Each data type has a corresponding behavior, typing rules, built-in methods, and works with certain operators.

At the end of this chapter, we will put everything we learned into practice by writing our own vacation budgeting calculator.

The topics covered in this chapter are as follows:

- Assigning variables
- Naming the variables
- Understanding data types
- Converting the data types
- Exercise

Technical requirements

You can follow the code for this chapter in the `Chapter02/first_code.ipynb` notebook. No additional packages are required, just Python.

You can find the code via the following link, which is in the GitHub repository in the `Chapter02` folder (`https://github.com/PacktPublishing/Learn-Python-by-Building-Data-Science-Applications`).

 Important note: In this and many other chapters, we'll include both snippets of code and interactive shells, similar to what your code will look like in Jupyter. In order to distinguish the code we ran from the output, in every code block that has an interaction, the running code will start after a triple *greater than* sign (>>>), similar to how it is present in Python consoles. By the way, you still can copy and paste the code—Jupyter will simply ignore this symbol and will run correctly.

Assigning variables

At the end of the previous chapter, we ran a simple Python function for the sake of testing:

```
print('Hello world!')
```

Here, "`Hello world`" is an argument, that is, a data point used as an input for the function. In this particular case, we used a raw data value. However, this approach won't get us far—what if we need to change this value, or use it in some other code? This can be done by using variables!

Variables are one of the most basic and powerful concepts in programming. You can think of them as aliases, similar to variables in math equations. Variables are representations of the actual underlying data in the code, which allow us to write operations and describe relations without knowing the exact values the code will operate on. This allows us to write generalized code, which can be used multiple times and in different situations.

In order to assign any value to the variable, we use the equals sign (=), as shown in the following line of code:

```
<variable_name> = <value>
```

Take a look at these examples showing the equals sign used to assign any type of value to variables:

```
pi = 3.14159265359      # Decimal
name = 'Philipp'        # Text
age = 31                # Integer
sky_is_blue = True      # Boolean
```

 Note the text after the # sign on the same lines as code. Those are comments. They are ignored by the code (because of the symbol before them) and are very useful for explaining the code, jotting an idea, or commenting on specific solutions. Most editors, including VS Code and Jupyter, comment and uncomment whole lines with the *command/Ctrl +* / shortcut key.

Once a variable is assigned, it is stored in the machine's memory for the entire session, until script execution is over or the notebook's kernel is shut down. Now we can use them in our code:

```
>>> print(pi)
3.14159265359
```

Sometimes, it is convenient to assign a few variables on the same line by using packing, which makes the code more readable:

```
>>> x, y = 10, 5
>>> print(x)
10

>>> print(y)
5
```

We can always reassign the variable by using the same process:

```
>>> pi = 'Philipp'
>>> print(pi)
Philipp
```

 Reassignment can be also done with packing, like this: x, y = y, x.

If a variable is not defined, then Python will raise an error. This is a classic Jupyter rookie mistake: people tend to skip cells with variable assignment in the notebooks. The following is an example code block for this:

```
>>> print(non_existent_variable)
```

```
---------------------------------------------------------------------------
NameError                                  Traceback (most recent call last)
<ipython-input-1-4e13ec8d6c49> in <module>()
----> 1 print(non_existent_variable)
NameError: name 'non_existent_variable' is not defined
```

In addition to the notation used in the preceding snippet, integers and floats have additional ways to be defined. Integers can use an underscore (_) to mark the number of thousands for readability purposes, for example, `ten_million = 10_000_000`. Floats do not need this first zero if the value is lower than one, for example, `small = .25`. On top of this, floats support scientific notations, for example, `sci_thousand = 10e3`.

Naming the variable

Naming variables may seem to be a minor topic, but trust us, adopting a good habit of proper naming will save you a lot of time and nerves down the road. Do your best to name variables wisely and consistently. Ambiguous names will make code extremely hard to read, understand, and debug, for no good reason.

Now, technically there are just three requirements for variable names:

- You cannot use reserved words: `False`, `class`, `finally`, `is`, `return`, `None`, `continue`, `for`, `lambda`, `try`, `True`, `def`, `from`, `nonlocal`, `while`, `and`, `del`, `global`, `not`, `with`, `as`, `elif`, `if`, `or`, `yield`, `assert`, `else`, `import`, `pass`, `break`, `except`, `in`, or `raise`. You also cannot use operators or special symbols (`+`, `-`, `/`, `*`, `%`, `=`, `<`, `>`, `@`, `&`) or brackets and parentheses as part of variable names.
- Variable names can't start with digits.
- Variable names can't contain whitespace. Use the underscore symbol instead.

On top of that, there are also some general naming conventions. You don't have to, but it is strongly recommended to follow them:

- Name your variables meaningfully and consistently, so that readers will understand what they are meant to be. Some examples are `counter`, `car`, and `today`.
- Apply `snake_case` for naming: Use lowercase letters that are joined by an underscore. Some examples are `my_car`, `app_counter`, and `get_settings`.

For broader recommendations on naming and coding style in general, please read *PEP8 -- Style Guide for Python Code* (`https://www.python.org/dev/peps/pep-0008/#function-and-variable-names`).

Understanding data types

Every data point in programming has a type. This type defines how much memory is allocated, how the value behaves, what operations Python will allow you to do with it, and more. Understanding the properties of different data types is vital for effective programming in Python.

You can always check the value's type with another built-in function, `type()`:

```
>>> type(pi)
float

>>> type(name)
str

>>> type(age)
int

>>> type(sky_is_blue)
bool
```

As we can see, `pi` is a float, `name` is a string, `age` is an integer, and `sky_is_blue` is a Boolean value. These four types represent the most popular data types that are built into Python. The fifth one is `None` (of the `NoneType` type): the data type of one value that represents, well, nothing (a non-existent value). There are a few more data types, such as complex numbers, but we won't use them in this book.

Floats and integers

Floats and integers represent rational numbers with and without a decimal part, respectively. Those types are quite intuitive to use, as they can be added, subtracted, multiplied, divided, and more. Let's take a look at the following example. First, we assign two variables:

```
A = 6
B = 5
```

Now, let's go over some possible operations:

```
>>> A + B
11

>>> A - B
1

>>> A / B
1.2

>>> A * B
30
```

You can also raise numbers to a power by using double asterisks:

```
>>> 2**3
8

>>> 3**2
9
```

You might have noticed that the division of two integers will result in a float. This happens even if the remainder is zero:

```
>>> 10 / 2
5.0
```

If you need to keep the integer division result as an integer (rounded, if needed), then use a double slash instead; this operation has significantly higher performance. However, if any of the two values is a float, then it will keep the result as a float, although rounded. The following code shows this:

```
>>> 9 // 4
3

>>> 10.0 // 4
2.0
```

Finally, you can also get the remainder (or modulus) by using a percentage sign:

```
>>> 10 % 3
1
```

 Starting with Python 3.5, the @ symbol is reserved for matrix multiplication. Core Python does not have a notion of matrices, and therefore can't use it. Multiple third-party libraries, however, respect and accept this symbol.

Operations with self-assignment

Most operators can be modified to allow variable self-assignment. For example, if we want to update the count variable by adding 1 to it, then we can write a simpler notation:

```
count += 1 # instead of cound = count + 1
```

The same approach works with other operators as well:

```
count -= 1
count *= 2
count /= 2
count //= 2
count **= 2
count %= 4
```

As you can see, operators with self-assignment are useful, should we ever have to make a repetitive operation on one variable.

Order of execution

The order of execution works as in standard arithmetic calculations. This means we can use parentheses in our code:

```
>>> (2 + 10) / 2
6.0

>>> 10 / (1 + 1)
5.0
```

There could be any number of nested parentheses.

Strings

Strings represent text of any kind. As Python needs to distinguish between code (what it should execute) and strings (data), strings have to be wrapped with quotes: single quotes, double quotes, or triple single quotation marks. This last option can be used with multiline text, while the first two options will only work on the same line.

Let's see some examples. Here is a string that is surrounded by single quotes. In this case, you can use double quotes within your text string, and this won't break the parsing mechanism:

```
text1 = 'This is a so-called "speakeasy"'
```

Here is a similar example with double quotes. In this case, we can use single quotes in the text without breaking the code:

```
text2 = "This is Sam's Tavern"
```

Finally, triple single quotes allow us to write multiline text:

```
text3 = ''' This is Sam's Tavern.
 "Welcome everyone!" - is written on the door.'''
```

Another way to enter text that will be multiline in representation is to use a special newline symbol (\n) within your text, on the same line:

```
>>> print('Hello\nWorld!')
Hello
World!
```

Strings don't work with most operators. The only exceptions are addition and multiplication. The addition will concatenate two strings, while multiplication (by an integer) will repeat the string:

```
>>> 'Hello' + ' World!'
'Hello World!'

>>> 'Hello' * 3
'HelloHelloHello'
```

However, strings do have multiple built-in methods. Methods are essentially functions that are attached to a particular object, and whose behavior often depends on this object. Methods are defined by the data type or object's class. The following are the most useful methods of strings. The upper, lower, and title methods help us to change the casing of the strings:

```
>>> "Hello World".upper()
'HELLO WORLD'

>>> "Hello World".lower()
'hello world'

>>> "hello world".title()
'Hello World'
```

Another method, replace, returns the string with the matching values replaced:

```
>>> "Hello world".replace("world", "planet")
'Hello planet'
```

Similarly, the find and rfind methods provide a convenient way to find the index of the first occurrence for the matching string in the initial string. find provides the index starting from the beginning, while rfind finds it from the end:

```
>>> 'To be or not to be'.find('be')
3

>>> 'To be or not to be'.rfind('be')
16
```

Finally, the `startswith` and `endswith` methods will return `True` or `False` (more on those values later in this chapter) depending on whichever your base string starts or ends with:

```
>>> 'To be or not to be'.startswith('T')
True

>>> 'To be or not to be'.startswith('t')
False
```

There also are some other methods that are supported by strings.

Formatting

There are a number of ways to format strings to how you desire.

For example, `.rjust` and `.ljust` format the length of the string, adding symbols—if needed—to the right and left, respectively:

```
>>> 'hello'.rjust(10, ' ')
'     hello'

>>> 'hello'.ljust(10, ' ')
'hello     '
```

Similarly, `.zfill` adds zeros at the beginning of the string:

```
>>> '999'.zfill(10)
'0000000999'
```

Another important option is to embed values into an existing string using formatting. Indeed, this is very handy as it allows us to embed any type of values without converting them to strings explicitly, and furthermore, defining representation rules and putting them in place. There are a few ways to do that. Let's take a look!

Format method

A string's format method will inject its arguments into the string, replacing the fields defined by curly braces. A specific field can be defined either by the number (in this case, you just should keep arguments in the same order) or by using keywords. Here are some examples:

1. The following example has no placement strategy and simple curly brackets:

```
>>> 'Hello {} world and our blue {}'.format('beautiful', 'planet')
'Hello beautiful world and our blue planet'
```

2. The following example uses a numeric order (note the change of order and the repetition in the template):

```
>>> '{0} {2} {1} and our {2}
{3}!'.format('Hello','World','Beautiful', 'Planet')
'Hello Beautiful World and our Beautiful Planet!'
```

3. The following example uses keywords:

```
>>> 'Hello {adj} world!'.format(adj='beautiful')
'Hello beautiful world!'
```

Personally, we prefer the last one, as it is explicit and prevents any mistakes with the position of the arguments. However, there is one more way to format strings on the go: via F-strings.

F-strings

F-strings are relatively new features of Python. They were released in version 3.6 and are both elegant and faster to execute because everything is computed on the go. Here is one example (note the letter f before the starting single quote symbol):

```
>>> adj = 'beautiful'
>>> f'Hello {adj} world!'
Hello beautiful world
```

Everything inside the curly brackets is actually executable code. Inside this brackets, you can use arithmetic or even run functions:

```
>>> N = 99
>>> f'{N-1} bottles of milk on the wall.'
'98 bottles of milk on the wall.'

>>> name = 'pHILIPP'
>>> f'Hello mr{name.title()}'
'Hello mr. Phillipp'
```

Legacy formatting

Lastly, we want to show a *legacy* way to format, which uses percentage symbols. This approach predates Python 3. Don't use it—just be aware that it exists and can be seen in some old code bases. There is nothing particularly wrong with this approach, of course, but it is considered a legacy. Subjectively, we think that it is less readable, but that is our personal view:

```
>>> name = 'David'
>>> print('Hello mr. %s' % name)
Hello mr. David
```

Formatting mini-language

In all cases, you can format injected values along the way by using Python's **formatting mini-language**. Just add a colon after your expression in the curly brackets, and then write the mini-language notation. Take this example:

```
>>> pct = .345
>>> value = 45500
>>> f'Price grew by {pct:.1%} or ${value:,}'
'Price grew by 34.5% or 45,500'
```

More information on the Python formatting language can be accessed via the official documentation (https://docs.python.org/3/library/string.html#formatspec).

Strings as sequences

Python also treats strings as sequences. We'll cover sequences in depth in Chapter 4, *Data Structures*, and in Chapter 5, *Loops and Other Compound Statements*. Generally speaking, strings can be seen as ordered arrays of characters that allow us to traverse through, get characters one by one, use slicing to get substrings, and check whether it includes a substring.

All indices in Python are integers, starting with zero. If we want to get the first symbol of a string, then we should use index 0:

```
>>> "Hello World"[0]
'H'
```

Here, square brackets after the value indicate **slicing**. We can also specify a subsequence of characters to retrieve by using a colon (:), and a subsequence for the start and finish indices. In this case, the character corresponding to the first index will be included, but the last one will not:

```
>>> "Hello World"[0:5]
'Hello'
```

Finally, because strings are sequences, we can find out whether one string contains another one by using the in keyword:

```
>>> "World" in "Hello World!"
True
```

Booleans

Booleans can have only one of two values: either False or True. They are used to describe logical operations, for example, tests or conditions. There are a few operations that result in Boolean values:

- First, you can use the equality test for any type of data:

  ```
  >>> 'World' == 'World'
  True

  >>> pi == pi
  True
  ```

- In the previous section, we ran into another example, which was inclusion test:

  ```
  >>> "World" in "Hello World!"
  True
  ```

- != is the opposite of equal, not equal:

  ```
  >>> pi != pi
  False
  ```

There are more test operators, including greater than (>), less than (<), greater than or equal to (>=), less than or equal to (<=), and nonequal (<>). Those tests will also work with strings by comparing them lexicographically. Python will compare the order of the first elements of each string. If they are equal, then Python will go to the next pair, and so on. If any pair is not equal (not the same character), or one string is shorter than another, then this will define the outcome.

Logical operators

There are four logical operators that work specifically on Boolean values:

- !—the NOT keyword (inverse of the resulting value):

  ```
  >>> not (5 > 4)
  False
  ```

  Jupyter interprets cells with an exclamation mark at the beginning as Terminal commands, so we can't use it there.

- |—the OR keyword (one or another, or both the values):

  ```
  >>> (5 > 4) | (6 < 5)
  True
  ```

- &—the AND keyword (one and another value):

  ```
  >>> (5 > 4) & (6 < 5)
  False
  ```

- ^—the XOR keyword (either one or another, but not both of the values):

  ```
  >>> (5 > 4) ^ (5 < 6)
  False
  ```

The following are built-in functions that work on Boolean arrays:

- all(): Will return true only if all elements are True
- any(): Will return true if at least one element is True

Python has strong typing—it does not convert data types implicitly. The only exception is tests for True/False: any data type will work as a Boolean in any test, following these general rules: While using variables like that in tests looks nice, be careful; it often introduces bugs, for example, if you mean variable to be None in the tests, but it was returned as an empty string. If you're not sure, better check for a specific value.

Zero (both float and int), empty string, and None behave in tests as False. Anything else behaves as True. Consider this example:

```
>>> not ''
True
>>> bool('')
False
```

We will cover working with arrays and other structures in Chapter 4, *Data Structures*.

Converting the data types

Quite often, there is a need to convert one data type to another, such as a float to an integer, or a string into a number and back. No worries! It is easy to achieve using built-in functions. However, there are some conversion rules to be learned. A string to a float is as follows:

```
>>> float ("2.5")
2.5
```

A string to an integer is as follows:

```
>>> int ("45")
45
```

A float to an integer and vice versa are as follows:

```
>>> int (4.521)
4

>>> float (5)
5.0
```

Booleans to integers, floats, and strings are as follows:

```
>>> int(True)
1

>>> float(False)
0.0

>>> str(True)
'True'
```

If Python cannot convert values, then it will raise an error:

```
>>> int("2.5")
File "<ipython-input-11-cf753495344d>", line 1
    int("2.5")
        ^
SyntaxError: invalid character in identifier
```

 Python data types are strong. Python does not convert them implicitly under the hood, as some other languages, such as JavaScript, do. There is one exception to that: Booleans can behave as integers, specifically 0 (False) and 1 (True). This is a direct result of a not-so-hidden secret.

Exercise

As a practical exercise, let's solve a simple, yet annoying, problem: converting the temperature from Celsius to Fahrenheit and back. Indeed, the formula is easy, but every time we need to do it in our head, it takes some time. The formulas are as follows:

$$T(°F) = T(°C) \times 9/5 + 32$$

$$T_{(°C)} = (T_{(°F)} - 32) \times 5/9$$

Let's calculate the Celsius equivalent of 100°F!

First, let's store the constants and our input as variables:

```
CONST = 32
RATIO = 5/9

T_f = 100
```

Now, let's do the conversion:

```
>>> T_c = (T_f - CONST) * RATIO
>>> T_c
37.77777777777778
```

Now, let's convert it back:

```
>>> T_f2 = (T_c / RATIO) + CONST
>>> T_f2
100.0
```

What is the simplest way to compute the following code for a different temperature? It seems that the easiest way is to change the initial value of the variables, and everything else should follow. Let's run the code for 70°F:

```
>>> T_f = 70
>>> T_c = (T_f - CONST) * RATIO
>>> T_c
21.11111111111111
```

Pretty neat! In the next chapter, we'll learn how to make this calculation even more convenient and easy to reuse by writing it as a function.

Summary

In this chapter, we learned about the concept of variables. We now know how to assign and update variables, and use them as function arguments. Next, we learned about Python's basic data types, which represent text, numerical, and logical values. Each data type behaves differently and works with different operators. We had to review each of them on their own and execute snippets of code. That included numerical operations, the order of computation, string methods, and logical operations. As a result, in the last section of this chapter, we were able to compute the answer to a specific problem and generate a simple textual report as a result.

In the next chapter, we'll start by reviewing our solution and discuss how we can make it better by introducing functions.

Questions

1. Why do we need to use variables in code?
2. What is the recommended way to name variables? Why does it matter?
3. What do data types mean and why do they matter for computation?
4. What are the four most popular data types in Python?
5. What does the @ operator stand for? Why doesn't it work?
6. What are the two operators that will work with strings?
7. How would you combine the results of two tests if we need to return a `True` value, but only when both of them return `True`? What about when at least one returns `True`? What about if only one (but not both) returns `True`?

Further reading

Everything you need to know to become a developer can be found here: `https://docs.python.org/3/library/string.html#formatspec`.

3
Functions

At the end of the previous chapter, we solved a simple conversion problem, and while the problem was solved, it can be argued that the code we used wasn't exactly perfect; of course, it allowed us to change variable names (for instance, update hotel pricing), but it was still hard to read and error-prone. In addition, some particular elements of the code were repetitive, as we performed the same operations on different values.

This is exactly the opposite of one measure of code quality employed by programmers—**Don't Repeat Yourself! (DRY)** code—code that has no repeating parts. In other words, operations that we use multiple times should be articulated and defined once. This will allow us to keep the code short, concise, and expressive. It will be easier to maintain, debug, and change when needed. But how can this be achieved? First of all, it is necessary to use functions.

In this chapter, we will understand the concept of functions, review those functions built into Python, and learn how to build our own ones, including, as usual, strict technical requirements, common design patterns, and general conventions. In the process, we will rewrite our solution from `Chapter 2`, *First Steps in Coding – Variables and Data Types*, and practice on other practical examples.

In particular, we will cover the following topics:

- Built-in functions
- Defining the function
- Refactoring the budget code
- Anonymous (lambda) functions
- Recursion

Technical requirements

This chapter requires no additional packages to install. All the code is available in the `Chapter03` folder on GitHub, `https://github.com/PacktPublishing/Learn-Python-by-Building-Data-Science-Applications`.

To access and run example notebooks for this and other chapters, open the folder you cloned from GitHub in your VS Code, then switch to its Terminal window (that way, you're guaranteed to be in the correct folder) and type `jupyter lab`. On running, the application will either open a JupyterLab Notebook in your default browser or print a link. Via this link, go to the `Chapter03` folder and run the `Functions` notebook. Once the notebook is running, you're ready to proceed!

Understanding a function

What is a function anyway? In programming, a function is a named section of code that encapsulates a specific task and can be used relatively independently of surrounding code. Most (but not all) functions are stateless—their outcome depends solely on the function's explicit inputs.

Functions are ubiquitous in Python code. In fact, we have used some functions already; `print` is one example. Those functions are part of Python's default arsenal of built-in functions. There are 69 built-in functions in total in modern pandas. Before we start writing functions on our own, let's review these built-in functions first.

In the following sections, we will discuss just a handful of functions that we'll use frequently throughout the book; some others we'll discuss later. We have grouped all functions into four groups depending on the topic, starting with the interface.

Interface functions

Here, we have put together two functions that help us to interact with the code in a more convenient way.

The input function

A function that is basically the opposite of `print`, is `input`. This function takes some sort of question/statement as an argument, prints it, and requires a user to give an answer—this answer will be returned as a result of the function. It does work in Jupyter, but is mostly used in standalone scripts.

Let's have a look at the following example:

```
>>> name = input('Your name?')
Your name? Guido

>>> name
Guido
```

As you can see, when we run the `input` function, it halts the whole computation, waiting for the operator to type in the value; once a value is added, the program resumes.

The eval function

The `eval` function takes a string as an argument and attempts to parse and execute it as Python code. This can be used if you get the code from external sources (although this is potentially dangerous from the security standpoint).

Here is an example:

```
>>> problem = "2 + 2"
>>> answer = int(input(problem + ' = '))
2 + 2 = 4

>>> eval(problem) == answer
True
```

What is happening here? First, we store the operation `"2 + 2"` as a string. On the next line, we use that string, concatenating the equals sign, to ask the user for an answer. Once input is received, the value is converted to an integer. Finally, we evaluate this string, as if it was a Python code, and check whether the result matches the typed-in answer.

Using that approach, you could generate dozens of arithmetic puzzles and create a simple educational game to train math skills, and all without knowing the answers yourself!

In the next section, we'll go meta, talking about functions allowing us to inspect the properties of variables.

Variable properties

As we have learned already, variables are a critical part of any code. Sometimes, however, they can be confusing, as we won't be sure what type of value is hiding behind the alias, and what properties it has. The functions explained in the following sections help us to inspect the values, look at the documentation, and explore their types, methods, and attributes.

The help function

Most obvious, and perhaps most useful for a novice, the help function provides the information on a given value type, function, or other entity. Let's get meta and see how the help function works by itself. If you type help(help), this is what you'll get in VS Code (press q to exit):

```
Help on _Helper in module _sitebuiltins object:

class _Helper(builtins.object)
 |  Define the builtin 'help'.
 |
 |  This is a wrapper around pydoc.help that provides a helpful message
 |  when 'help' is typed at the Python interactive prompt.
 |
 |  Calling help() at the Python prompt starts an interactive help session.
 |  Calling help(thing) prints help for the python object 'thing'.
 |
 |  Methods defined here:
 |
 |  __call__(self, *args, **kwds)
 |      Call self as a function.
 |
 |  __repr__(self)
 |      Return repr(self).
 |
 |  ----------------------------------------------------------------------
 |  Data descriptors defined here:
 |
 |  __dict__
 |      dictionary for instance variables (if defined)
 |
 :
```

In Jupyter, there is a similar built-in command—the question mark (?). Here is an example using a question mark in Jupyter—`help?`:

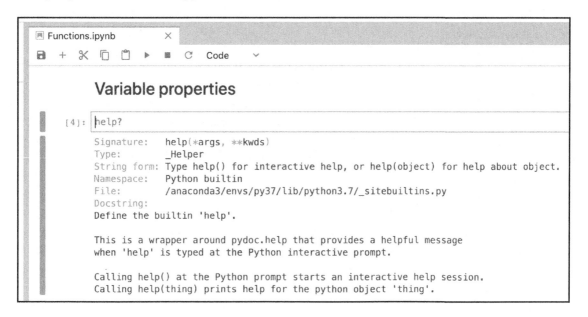

Generally speaking, `help` provides a longer description and works everywhere, but the question mark works on variables as well.

In the most recent versions of JupyterLab (versions 1 and above), you can open a window called **Contextual Help** next to your code. Once opened, the window will show the documentation for the closest function or variable automatically.

The type function

The `type` function returns the type of variable that was passed to it. As in the following example, for the string variable, it will return `str`; for the number variable, `int` or `float`, and so on and so forth:

```
>>> type('Hello world')
str
```

Here, the function returns the type of the `Hello world` value, which is a string. This function allows us to differentiate between values, even if this is not very clear. Take a look at the following example:

```
>>> type(101)
int

>> type('101')
str
```

Here, `type` identifies the fact that similar looking values are an integer and a string. Often, however, we don't need to know the specific type of the value, but rather whether the value is of a certain type (and adjust our methods accordingly). For this, there is `isinstance`.

The isinstance function

Similar to `type`, `isinstance` checks whether a variable is of a particular data type, structure, or class. This makes it very useful for testing purposes, or if you want to check arguments for the correct type:

```
>>> isinstance('Hello world', str)
True
```

Here, we checked whether the value is a string—and indeed it is! We can also pass multiple variable types, in which case `isinstance` will return `True` if the value matches any of the given types:

```
>>> isinstance(1, (int, float))
True
```

Note the second parenthesis, surrounding two value types we pass in. This parenthesis represents a tuple, one of the data structures, which we'll discuss in the next chapter.

Finally, there is `dir`, which is invaluable if we need to work with obscure, badly documented code.

dir

When run, `dir` will return all the corresponding values and methods, connected to the given object, as an array of strings. This is a convenient way to drill down and investigate all the methods and values of the particular variable:

```
>>> dir('Hello world')

['__add__',
 '__class__',
 '__contains__',
 '__delattr__',
 '__dir__',

...

 'rsplit',
 'rstrip',
 'split',
 'splitlines',
 'startswith',
 'strip',
 'swapcase',
 'title',
 'translate',
 'upper',
 'zfill']
```

We removed some lines in order to save some space in the book in the preceding code. Feel free to execute that function yourself. As you can see, the list includes all the methods we described in the previous chapter—including `title`, `upper`, and `zfill`, and many others besides.

Let's now take a look at the built-in mathematical functions.

Math

Of course, there are a few functions dedicated to math. In fact, quite a few are stored in dedicated `math` and `statistics` built-in libraries. The most frequent ones, though, are incorporated directly into the language. Let's cover them in the following sections.

abs

The `abs` function's name stands for *absolute*. As you may expect, it returns an absolute (positive) representation of the passed number by removing the negative sign, if there is one. For example, if we pass –1 or 1 as an argument, we'll get 1 as a result, as you can see in the following code:

```
>>> abs(-1)
1

>>> abs(1)
1
```

Another function is `round`, and it is also easy to guess what this does

The round function

The `round` function takes a float and an integer as its arguments. The second value defines the desired number of digits after the decimal point. This second value is optional—if nothing is passed, the function will return an integer as a result. The following is an example for the `round` function:

```
>>> round(3.14159265359, 2)
3.14

>>> round(3.14159265359)
3
```

In accordance with standard procedure, the function rounds the values up if the next digit is equal to 5 or above; otherwise, it rounds it down.

The following section is focused on functions that work with iterables—collections composed of multiple values.

Iterables

We will talk about iterables and other data structures, in the next chapter. For now, you can imagine iterables as collections composed of many values. The following functions operate on such collections.

The len function

The `len` function expects a collection as input and returns the length of this collection—in other words, how many elements it consists of.

We measure the length of the string object in the following code, which is also iterable—you can think of it as a collection of characters:

```
>>> len('Hello')
5
```

Indeed, there are five characters in this word!

The sorted function

This function takes an iterable as an input and returns it, sorted. This function can take two additional arguments—`reverse` (Boolean) and `key` (iterable). The `reverse` argument allows us to get the values in reverse order, from big to small. `key`, if specified, is expected to be of the same length as the first one and will be used to sort by.

Let's look at the following example:

```
>>> sorted('Hi there!')
[' ', 'H', 'e', 'e', 'h', 'i', 'r', 't']

>>> sorted('Hi there!', reverse=True)
['t', 'r', 'i', 'h', 'e', 'e', 'H', '!', ' ']
```

The next function does not expect you to pass an iterable—instead, it generates one.

The range function

The `range` function generates a sequence of integers. It takes from one to three arguments, and each of those is expected to be an integer. If only one is defined, it will be treated as a right-hand limit of the range and will be not included. If two are defined—the first one will be the left-hand limit, and included in the range, while the second will take the role of the right-hand limit. If a third value is specified, it will be used as a step—the default step is equal to `1`.

 The range function returns a generator—a special type of iterable that computes its values on the fly. That is why, in order to see the actual result, we need to convert it to a list.

Let's look at the following example. Here, we generate a range of three values. We convert the outcome to a list in order to show the values:

```
>>> list(range(3))
[0, 1, 2]

>>> list(range(2, 5))
[2, 3, 4]
```

In the second example, we pass two arguments instead. In this case, the first argument defines the starting value, and the range will go up until the second argument.

The all and any functions

all and any both take an array as their input and are logical expansions of & and | for more than two variables. Essentially, they are equal to repeating & or | for all the elements of the array. Here is an example:

```
>>> all((True, False, True))
False

>>> any((True, False, False))
True
```

In the first case, the function returns False, as there is at least one False instance in the iterable. In the second case, there is at least one True instance, so that function returns True as well.

The max, min, and sum functions

The max, min, and sum functions all take an array of numbers and return the maximum, minimum, or sum value as a result. Here are some examples:

```
>>> T = 1,2,3
>>> min(T)
1
>>> max(T)
3
>>> sum(T)
6
```

As you can see, a tuple can be assigned to a variable without any brackets. All three results are expected—of values 1, 2, and 3, 1 is the minimum, 3 is the maximum, and the sum of those three values is equal to 6.

So now that we know what a function is and its properties, let's see how we can define them and why defining is important.

Defining the function

Now that we have reviewed built-in functions, you probably have some understanding of how to use them as a consumer. But how can a custom function be created? It's very simple! You just have to observe the following structure:

```
def function_name(arguments):
    '''Documentation string'''
    # code inside, using arguments
    return  result
```

Let's break this down. Here, `def` is a reserved keyword that tells Python that we are going to create a function. After that comes the name of the function—following the same rules as variables. The name is followed by a parenthesis. If the function requires any argument we should state them here by name (you can think of them as new variables). If you don't anticipate any arguments, a parenthesis should be kept empty.

 Functions do have access to variables and functions outside—so you can use variables defined somewhere else in your function, even without defining them as arguments. The context will be preserved—the function will use those variables even if imported into another context. This approach is, however, regarded as a bad practice, since it makes code less readable and transparent.

The colon after the parenthesis marks the start of the function's inner scope. Note that when you hit *Enter*, both Jupyter and VS Code adds an indentation of four white spaces on the next line – stick with it! This indentation is important; in contrast to other languages, in Python, it is part of the syntax and directly impacts the computation. Everything within the same indentation stays in the same scope, for example, in our case – a function's internal level. Variables assigned here, including function arguments, will be dropped once we get out of this indentation.

On the first line of the function's internal scope, we usually define docstring – a small note on what functions achieve and how to use it. The docstring is not required, but we really, really recommend that you write them up; you will thank yourself later.

Both `help` and `?` print out a docstring of the function. VS Code will show the docstring in a tooltip, whenever you start typing the function name if the function is declared in this space.

Finally, we can write the actual code of the function, also preserving the indentation. Inside this code, we can use the function's arguments as variables, even though there is no value in them yet.

To exit the function and return a value, use the `return` keyword – it will return whatever variable is stated after. Once the function executes `return`, Python exits the function, and no code after the `return` statement will be executed, ever. Of course, functions do not have to return anything. For example, a function that creates a new folder on a filesystem won't need to return any result within Python.

Here is an example. Imagine we want to compute a negative value v to the power of p. Here is how we should define our function:

```
def negative_power(v, p):
    '''Return negative value v in to the power of p'''
    return -1 * (v**p)
```

Here, we first declare the function with the `def` keyword. Next, we state the name of the function—`negative_power`. Then, we declare two required arguments—v and p. On the next line, we define a docstring, explaining the meaning of this function. Lastly, we define the actual code that that function runs—in this case, it will return a negative value of v to the power of p.

Let's try this function out. The value of 2 to the power of 3, multiplied by -1, is -8. This seems correct, and the same for 3 to the power of 2—the outcome is -9:

```
>>> negative_power(2, 3)
-8

>>>negative_power(3, 2)
-9
```

So far, Python has assigned v and p by their order. We can also specify them explicitly, by assigning them as arguments. This way, the order does not matter. The following is an illustration of that – we assigned the arguments in reverse order, and everything works fine:

```
>>> negative_power(p=2, v=3)
-9
```

The named (explicit) assignment is arguably more desirable as the code is then easier to read and more prone to human errors.

 Actually, functions always return something. Even if you don't use `return` in your function, it will just return `None`. Jupyter does not print or show `None`, and, because of that, it seems nothing was returned, but you can store it in the variable if you want.

In many cases, functions require a lot of arguments, many of which could be optional and tedious to restate on every function call. To avoid that, there is a way to state the argument's default value. In the next section, we will cover how to do that.

Default values

In some cases, it is convenient to have a default value for a specific argument, so that we won't need to state it explicitly every time. For example, we can assume that most of the time, we need to get a negative square root (depending on the case, of course), and it would be a waste of time to explicitly define p=2 every time. In this case, we'll have to modify our code just a bit, by p=2 within the parentheses. Here is how the code would appear:

```python
def negative_power(v, p=2):
    '''Return negative value v in power p'''
    return -1 * (v**p)
```

We still have to define v every time, but p is now optional – if we don't state it explicitly, it will be assumed to be equal to 2. The following code illustrates the case. Once we don't explicitly state the value of p, the function falls back to p=2; therefore, every value (2 in this case) of v will be squared and returned with a negative sign:

```python
negative_power(2, 3)
>>> -8

negative_power(2)
>>> -4
```

There is an important rule to follow here. According to Python syntax, arguments with the default values have to be defined after all the others with no default values, otherwise Python will raise a syntax error:

```python
>>> def negative_power(p=2, v):
        '''Return negative value v in power p'''
        return -1 * (v**p)

File "<ipython-input-9-9a12e59bef45>", line 1
```

```
def negative_power(p=2, v):
                       ^
SyntaxError: non-default argument follows default argument
```

There is some logic to that – the important parameters should be kept both first and required (to avoid any possibility of forgetting to state them), and the optional ones kept in the end.

Var-positional and var-keyword

In some cases, we don't know beforehand the exact number of arguments that will be passed to the function. For example, the `print` function will take and print any number of arguments. The same can be done for our custom function, using `*args`. In this case, `args` itself is not a keyword, but rather a conventional name of all those multiple values, packed – technically, you can use any name you want. All of the actual job is done by the asterisks – it indicates that all passed values will be packed into one tuple (we'll discuss tuples in `Chapter 4`, *Data Structures*). Within the function's scope, you can use `args` as a tuple variable, or pass it using the same asterisks.

Similarly, in some cases, those multiple values are named. In order to pass multiple name arguments, use `**kwargs` (which stands for *keyword arguments*). As with `args`, the name itself is a mere convention; all the heavy lifting is done by the double asterisks, which groups those arguments into a dictionary (another type of data structure that will be explained in the next chapter). Within the function, `kwargs` can be used as a single entity (dictionary), or passed down using similar double asterisks. Both `args` and `kwargs` should be defined after all normal arguments. Consider this example:

```
def f(a, b, *args, **kwargs):
  return a + b
```

This function simply adds two arguments. It will, however, accept any number of additional arguments without any effect on its result. Here is an illustration.

Here, we pass two first arguments as 1 and 2, respectively. After that, we pass 10. Lastly, we pass one more, a named argument. As we specified both `*args` and `**kwargs` in the function, both these parameters won't raise any errors on the execution. In fact, they will be completely ignored, as we use neither `args` nor `kwargs` in the function code, as shown here:

```
f(1,2, 10, other_argument=0)
>>> 3
```

args and kwargs are indeed very useful. One frequently encountered case is when your function runs an external function within your code, with plenty of optional parameters. Instead of declaring all of them one more time in your function, you can just pass kwargs. This way, the code will remain both concise and flexible (also, you won't need to change your code if the external function's interface changes). Consider the following example:

```
# sets up plotting in jupyter
%matplotlib inline

import pylab as plt


def draw_scatter(x, y, color='k', **kwargs):
    plt.scatter(x, y, color=color, **kwargs)
```

In the preceding code, we use pylab – one of the interfaces for matplotlib, a data visualization library. Like most of the visualization functions, plt.scatter (which, you guessed, is here to draw a scatter plot) has dozens of optional parameters, defining the title, title font, title size, the same for the *x* axis title, and the *y* axis title, as well as color, shape, opacity, size, position of the markets, and many other parameters besides. It would be insane to replicate all those options (and their documentation) within your code. Instead, we can pass kwargs as a set of the arguments you want to pass to the scatter function.

Here is an example of function usage. As you can see, we can pass any variable that the original scatter function accepts – and it will be passed, and used:

```
draw_scatter([1,2,3], [3,2,1], s=[10, 100, 300])
```

As a result, we get the following diagram. Obviously, the data is meaningful, but the size argument we passed is reflected in the resulting chart:

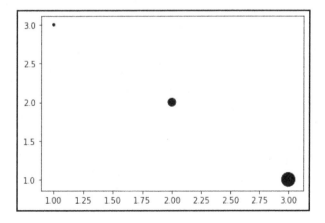

In the preceding example, we imported the `pylab` library, one of the interfaces for the `matplotib` plotting language. The particle as in the import line, `import pylab AS plt`, allows us to define alias names for the libraries. While the name of the alias is arbitrary and could be anything you want, most popular libraries, including `pylab`, have widely adopted, near-standard aliases. It makes sense to stick with the popular ones to make the code easier to read and understand. Some other libraries with well-known aliases are `pandas` (pd), `numpy` (np), and `seaborn` (sns).

We'll cover import in depth in the following chapters.

Docstrings

As with naming, docstrings might seem to be a minor issue – but they are not. Always add a docstring to your code; it will double your productivity! Also, it will help you to keep good relationships with your colleagues and clients.

As we mentioned before, docstrings are short explanation texts bound to specific module (`.py` file), function, or class. All you need is to write it as a string at the beginning of the corresponding scope – beginning of the file, function, or class. At the execution time, those strings are stored as a __docs__ variable. What's even more important is the fact that all coding environments, including VS Code and Jupyter, understand docstrings and how to handle them.

As we mentioned previously, in Jupyter, adding a question mark before or after any class, module, or function, will print out corresponding documentation. This will work for any function – including the ones you declared. The following is an example of a function declaration that includes a docstring:

```
def myfunction(a, b):
    '''this is my favorite function!

    it uses arguments:
    a: argument a
    b: argument b
    '''
    return a + b
```

Once the function is declared (or imported), we can pull the documentation by using the question mark – similar to how we approached the `print` function before:

```
>>> myfunction

Signature: myfunction(a, b)
Docstring:
this is my favorite function!
it uses arguments:
a: argument a
b: argument b
File: ~/<ipython-input-2-a0cabd3ba678>
Type: function
```

VS Code will do even more – it will show docstrings in a tooltip while you're typing.

But that is not the only thing you can use your docstrings for! Using the `sphynx` package, you can generate full stack documentation such as a static website, PDF, or an EPUB electronic book, which extracts all the information from the docstrings. If you are wondering why there are so many similar cookie-cutter documentation websites around, that's why! An enhanced version even encourages you to add example code within the docstring – and there are packages that will test and validate this code-within-the-docstrings!

There is no standard format for the docstrings. Instead, there are a few style formatting conventions used in different companies and groups. Among the most popular ones are the REST, Google Style, and `numpydoc` styles. For example, here is an example of a docstring defined according to Google Style:

```
"""
This is an example of Google style.

Args: parameter1: This is our first parameter.
      parameter2: This is our second parameter.

Returns:
    This is a description of what is returned.

Raises:
    KeyError: Raises an exception.
"""
```

It does not really matter which style to use. If you like restructured text, use REST. If you don't, use the Google Style or NumPy style. There are plugins that help to generate docstring templates from your function arguments on the fly – they save some time. Further time can be saved using type annotations.

Type annotations

Starting with version 3.6, Python introduced type annotations – these hint at what data types the function expects to get, and what data type it will return.

Let's look at the following example. Here is the negative power function we declared already. This time, however, we added the type annotations both for the function arguments and the outcome:

```
def negative_power(v:int, p:int)-> int:
    '''Return negative value v in power p'''
    return -1 * (v**p)
```

First of all, those additional characters *do not* affect code execution in any direct way. Those are type annotations – merely hints at the function's expected data types for arguments and return value, stored within the function – in the same way docstrings are.

While there is no effect on the code itself, those annotations can be used for testing purposes and raise an error, if the function is fed with the wrong data. The most popular tool for that testing is called mypy, developed at Dropbox. Once installed, mypy can run through your code and test whether any of the operations with data type annotations are used inappropriately.

There are other use cases as well. For example, a FastAPI web framework that we'll use in Chapter 18, *Serving Models with a RESTful API*, of this book, uses type annotations to validate inbound API calls, while Cython and Numba, which we'll discuss in Chapter 20, *Best Practices and Python Performance*, can use type annotations to efficiently compile Python into optimized C code.

Type annotations are not bound to basic variable types either. You can describe more complex requirements using the standard typing package; for example, you can explicitly describe *any type* using the Any class, or state that you expect a tuple, filled with string variables. Nevertheless, type annotations are a very recent phenomenon, not widely adopted, and have limited support throughout the libraries. In this book, we will use them only in Chapter 18, *Serving Models with a RESTful API*.

This concludes the main body of information that you'll need in order to write effective functions. Given all that, let's revisit our budgeting example!

Refactoring the temperature conversion

In Chapter 2, *First Steps in Coding – Variables and Data Types*, we've performed a simple exercise by converting temperature from Fahrenheit to Celsius, and back. The approach was similar to how we'd use a calculator, except that we were able to store parameters beforehand, and then rerun the calculations for the new inputs. At this point, you can probably see that this is a great case for a separate function. So, let's refactor our code into a pair of functions:

```
def fahrenheit_to_celsius(temp):
    CONST, RATIO = 32, 5/9
    return (temp - CONST) * RATIO

def celsius_to_fahrenheit(temp):
    CONST, RATIO = 32, 5/9
    return (temp/RATIO) + CONST
```

Let's now test these function as follows:

```
>>> fahrenheit_to_celsius(100)
37.77777777777778

>>> celsius_to_fahrenheit(37.77777777777778)
100.0

>>> fahrenheit_to_celsius(70)
21.11111111111111
```

Sweet! Everything seems to work as it should. Be aware that now, we don't need to reassign variables—all we need in order to get a new computation is to call this function with a new argument. While this particular function is rather simple, it is still better than having raw code around. For one, having a function reduces the cognitive complexity of the code – you don't need to remember the code that is stored inside, nor distinguish it from the other. In a broader sense, functions also add modularity – if needed, you can change the behavior and features of the function, without the need to change any code that uses this function. Last but not least, having your code wrapped in functions reduces the chance of human error – you can't mess with code you're not working with.

Now, let's talk about a special type of functions – anonymous functions.

Understanding anonymous (lambda) functions

In some cases, it is convenient to declare simple one-time functions in place; for that, we can use lambdas – anonymous functions (they are anonymous in the sense that you won't store them in-memory, so there is no name for them). Lambdas use simplified syntax:

```
lambda <arguments>: <code>
```

Note that there is no `return` keyword – `lambda` will return the result of the code automatically. It also does not accept multiline code.

Take a look at this example:

```
models = [
    'Bimbus-3000',
    'Nimbus-1000',
    'Timbus-2000'
]

sort(models, key=lambda x: x[-4:])
```

The output for the preceding code would be as follows:

```
>>> ['Nimbus-1000','Timbus-2000', 'Bimbus-3000']
```

Here, the array of strings are sorted – however, the string's alphanumeric order is only applied to the last four characters, as we use `lambda` to return them as keys.

 Technically, you can store `lambda` to a variable, and then use it as a regular function. Don't do it! This is really bad practice.

After learning about anonymous functions and how they work, let's move on to what recursion means for a function.

Understanding recursion

Recursion is a process of internal, nested repetition. A well-known example of recursion are fractals, for example, the Sierpiński carpet – shapes repeat themselves while you keep zooming in. In the context of programming, recursion represents an ability of the function to call itself from its body. In some cases, this makes your code shorter and more expressive, as you can split complex problems into sets (Russian dolls?) of simple ones.

Consider an example of a factorial function (*N!* in math). A factorial of a value is a multiplicative of all numbers from *1* to the given one – for example, for *3*, it will be *6: 1 * 2 * 3*. The following is one way to compute a factorial through recursion:

```
def factorial(n):
    if n == 1:
        return n

    return n * factorial(n-1)
```

Here, the factorial of 1 will always return 1. For any other positive *N*, the function will return *N*, multiplied by the factorial of *(N-1)*.

Because of recursion, this will happen again and again – the function will keep calling itself on a smaller value until the sequence reaches 1. From that moment, it will start returning the values, multiplying, returning again – going all the way back up the stack. Finally, it will return the value we're looking for. For us, though, the entire process will appear fast and simple:

```
>>> factorial(4)
24
```

The factorial of *4* is *24 = 1*2*3*4*.

In the preceding function, we used the `if` statement for the first time. We will look at all types of statements in `Chapter 4`, *Data Structures*. Here, the statement checks whether the test value is true – in this case, if `n` is equal to 1, and, if yes, executes all the indented code. As `return` exits the function, none of the following code will be executed in this case. As you can see, indentations are also used here as well, and can be nested.

Another (more real-live) case for recursion is traversing over a complex structure. Take, for example, a website. If we need to collect all (or some) data from the site, we'll have to go to the main page, collect the info here, collect a number of links, and then start going over those links, and so on.

For an arbitrary website, we don't know the links and the overall number of pages. So, this is a good place to use recursion. We can run a data collection function on the main page. This function can then find the links, and, for each link, call itself. In their turns, those instances of the function will call more and more functions. While the overall process could be long and complicated, the code, in this case, will be short – and we won't need to know or even store the links in the process!

Summary

In this chapter, we learned one of the main pillars of code – functions. Functions allow us to write concise and expressive code that can be reused multiple times. Functions serve as building blocks of our programs – be it report generation, interaction with the APIs, or training the model. We discussed how to declare both standard and anonymous functions, how to set arguments, and their default values, and how to use `args` and `kwargs` for more flexible interface design. We also learned how to write good quality documentation strings and add type annotations. Finally, we did rewrite our code from the previous chapter, using functions, which made it slightly more expressive and error-prone.

In the last section, we defined recursion – an approach where a function is called from within itself, and which allows us to solve rather complex tasks with simple, chained snippets of code.

In the next chapter, we will talk about data structures. Data structures are the way in which the program can compose many data values into collections. There are quite a few different ways to structure your data – some variants are good for general-purpose cases, while others are better for specific tasks. Knowing data structures is an essential part of programming.

Questions

1. What are functions, and when should we use them?
2. How can data be provided to functions?
3. What does indentation mean? Is it required?
4. What should be covered in the docstring function? How can I read the docstring function?
5. When could it be useful to use type annotations?
6. How can a function be designed if I don't know the exact number of arguments or their names beforehand?
7. What does *anonymous function* mean? When should they be used?

Further reading

- *Functional Python Programming – Second Edition*, by Steven F. Lott, published by Packt (https://www.packtpub.com/application-development/functional-python-programming-second-edition)
- *Functional Programming in Python*, by Sebastiaan Mathôt, published by Packt (https://www.packtpub.com/application-development/functional-programming-python-video)
- *Python Type Checking*, by Geir Arne Hjelle (https://realpython.com/python-type-checking/)

4
Data Structures

In the previous chapters, we worked with single variables. It is not hard to see the limitations of this approach—many tasks involve repetitive processes and rich data structures. In fact, the actual number of values can often vary, so our code should be able to work with values in bulk. Of course, Python has a handful of built-in data structures to meet those requirements!

In this chapter, we will discuss the most popular data structures and each of their APIs, benefits, and shortcomings. Data structures are essential to programming skills, as they are required for most tasks and their behaviors. The pros and cons of each specific type of structure are deeply rooted in their underlying mechanisms, which significantly affect the performance of their code. Understanding data structures allows us to write shorter and more expressive code.

In this chapter, we will go through the following topics:

- What are data structures?
- More data structures
- Using generators
- Useful functions to use with data structures
- Comprehensions

Technical requirements

This chapter does not require any additional packages; all the code is available in the `Chapter04` folder of the GitHub repository (`https://github.com/PacktPublishing/Learn-Python-by-Building-Data-Science-Applications`).

What are data structures?

What exactly do we mean by data structures? Generally speaking, they are objects capable of storing and retrieving an arbitrary number of values of any type in a systematic way. In other words, data structures are similar to basic data types: they can be stored via variables, removed, changed, and more.

Built-in data structures provide a standard and highly performant way to work with bulk data. However, there is simply no silver bullet or one-size-fits-all data structure. The benefits and shortcomings of each are built-in and inseparable from the general design. Let's go through the main data structures and discuss both the pros and cons of each one. The following sections will go over the main data structures in Python, starting with the most popular one: lists.

Lists

Lists are probably the most frequently used type of data structure in Python. A list is a simple and ordered 1D array of elements. Each element has its own index number, starting with 0, so the last element always has an index of *L*-1, where *L* is the number of elements in the list. Lists can store any mix of data types. They can also store any other data structure. For example, a matrix (2D array) can be represented as a list of lists, or a 3D matrix can be represented as a list of lists of lists. Lists are dynamic, which means you can add or drop items in any number, or even change their order in place, without rebuilding the list from scratch.

You can create a new list by using the `list()` function, or by using square brackets, with the elements separated by commas:

```
fruits = ['banana', 'apple', 'plum']
```

If needed, you can create an empty list as well:

```
basket  = []
another_basket = list()
```

As with strings, we can check the length of the list by using the built-in `len` function:

```
>>> len(fruits)
3

>>> len(basket)
0
```

We can always add new elements to the end of the list via the .append method:

```
>>> fruits.append('pineapple')
>>> fruits
['banana', 'apple', 'plum', 'pineapple']
```

Alternatively, we can insert them into a specific position:

```
>>> fruits.insert(2, 'orange')
>>> fruits
['banana', 'apple', 'orange', 'plum', 'pineapple']
```

We can also merge them with another list by using .extend:

```
>>> fruits.extend(['melon', 'watermelon'])
```

In some cases, you may want to retrieve one element and also remove it from the list. One such example is if you need to process elements one by one. For that, the .pop() method is ideal, as it will return the element from the end of the list and remove it from the list at the same time. In the following example, we pop (remove) the last value from the list. After that, unsurprisingly, the length of the list is decreased by one:

```
>>> len(fruits)
7

>>>fruits.pop()
'watermelon'

len(fruits)
>>> 6
```

Finally, you can use the in statement to check whether the list contains a certain element. This will also work with any other iterables:

```
>>> 'melon' in fruits
True
```

Now, let's talk about an important property of lists, strings, and many other data structures: slicing.

Slicing

As with strings, in order to get a single value from the list, you need to use its index in the square brackets after the value, as shown in the following code snippet:

```
>>> fruits[0]
'banana'
```

You can also obtain a subset of list values by using slices: intervals of indexes that are defined by two numbers and separated by a colon. The numbers represent start and end indices; the former number is inclusive, but the latter number is not. If one or both numbers are missing, then Python assumes those to be the ends of the list. Here is an example:

```
>>> fruits[0:2]
['banana', 'apple']

>>> fruits[:2]
['banana', 'apple']
```

In both cases, we're pulling the first two elements. In this case, it doesn't matter whether we include 0 or not.

This is exactly the same interface we used with strings. As with strings, we can use negative indices. For example, -1 will represent the last element in the list, no matter what is the actual index of the value. One more feature of slicing is its ability to define the step of the increase. By default, the step is equal to 1. However, if you state it as 2, only even elements will be retrieved:

```
>>> fruits[::2]
['banana', 'orange', 'pineapple']
```

Similarly, -1 will retrieve all elements, but in the reverse order:

```
>>> fruits[:2:-1]
['melon', 'pineapple', 'plum']
```

Slicing is widespread across data structures. Apart from lists and strings, it can be used with tuples (see the next section) and a few other types, so it is a good idea to master the skill of slicing.

Tuples

Tuples often stay in the shadow of lists. On the surface, they are very similar: they are also 1D arrays, can mix different types, use the same indices, and can be sliced. Similar to lists, tuples can be created using the `tuple()` function, or by only using parentheses:

```
breakfast = ('oatmill', 'scrambled eggs', 'orange juice')
```

There is one major difference that makes tuples work better for some tasks, but less so for others. As we mentioned before, lists are dynamic and can be modified in place. Tuples are not; once built, tuples remain static and cannot be changed (therefore, they don't have append and extend methods). This property is known as immutability.

Immutability

Immutable objects can't be changed in place; without creation of a new variable, you have to create a new object. In of itself, this is inconvenient, but it also implies that none of the internal values can be changed, which—by definition—means that tuples cannot contain lists or any other dynamic objects.

They are made like this on purpose, and this has serious merits. First, the dynamic nature of lists comes with a price: in order to be both dynamic and highly performant, they reserve more memory than they need. Tuples, by comparison, use up to two times less memory! Secondly, and this is the most important part, as tuples are guaranteed to be static, they *can* be used as an immutable part of other data structures, such as sets or dictionaries. Essentially, once we guarantee that the value cannot change, we can use it to generate its unique ID—hash—and to retrieve either itself or other data, using this hash as a key.

Dictionaries

Dictionaries are a different type of structure. Instead of being ordered arrays, they are key-value storage types. Dictionaries do not have any order, per se. Instead, they store everything as key-value pairs. As physical keys, the dictionary's keys have to be unique and unambiguously static. In other words, immutable. Hence, there cannot be two keys of the same value, and lists cannot be used as keys, but tuples can. Frequently, however, keys are strings, as they allow us to add some sort of semantics to the structure:

```
person = {'name': 'Jim',
 'surname': 'Hawkins',
 'age':17
 }
```

As you can see, dictionaries are defined by the curly brackets, with key-value pairs separated by the colon and split by the comma. Once the dictionary is assigned, you can retrieve values by using square brackets. This is the same as for lists and tuples, but it uses keys instead of indices:

```
>>> person['age']
17
```

Note that dictionaries do not support slicing. You can't push two keys at once, or reverse dictionary, as there is no order to start with.

Similarly, you can add key-value pairs to the dictionary, like this:

```
person['hair'] = 'red'
```

As there cannot be two keys of the same value, another assignment will override the previous value with no warnings:

```
person['hair'] = 'ginger'
```

As with lists, you can merge two dictionaries. One way to do that is through the .update method:

```
additional_info = {
    'gender': 'male',
    'nationality': 'british',
    'age': 16
}

person.update(additional_info)
```

Similar to lists, dictionaries have a .pop() method. But in this case, the .pop() method requires a specific key, for which the value will be retrieved and removed:

```
>>> person.pop('age')
16
```

On top of the preceding methods, dictionaries have a couple of handy methods up their sleeve. First, you can get either keys or values as list-like structures by using .keys() or .values(), respectively. Sometimes, it is convenient to get iterables of key-value pairs. This can be achieved by using the .items() method:

```
>>> print({'name':'Jim', 'surname': 'Hawkins'}.items())
dict_items([('name', 'Jim'), ('surname', 'Hawkins')])
```

When you try to get values by submitting a key that is not in the dictionary, `KeyError` is raised. In cases where you don't want this behavior, use the `.get()` method. It takes two values: the first value is for the key and the second value is for the default value. The default value is one that `.get()` will return if there is no data in the dictionary:

```
>>> person.get('eye color', 'brown')
'brown'
```

Lastly, dictionaries can behave as iterables, as you can loop through them (more on that in `Chapter 5`, *Loops and Other Compound Statements*) or check whether an element is in them. However, both of these cases work with keys, but not values:

```
>>> 'name' in person
True

>>> 'Jim' in person
False
```

Sets

Sets are—in a way—dictionaries without values. First, they use the same curly brackets, and second, their members cannot be duplicated, which are both similar to dictionary keys. Because of that, they are handy to use for deduplication or membership tests. On top of that, sets have built-in mathematical operations, unions, intersections, differences, and symmetrical differences:

```
>>> names = set(['Sam', 'John', 'James', 'Sam'])
>>> names
{'James', 'John', 'Sam'}

>>> other_names = {'James', 'Nikolai', 'Iliah'}
>>> names.difference(other_names)
{'John', 'Sam'}

>>> names.symmetric_difference(other_names)
{'Iliah', 'John', 'Nikolai', 'Sam'}
```

Sets don't have an order and, compared to dictionaries, do not guarantee that the order of representation and the order of retrieval will be equal to the order of insertion.

As sets are based on hash tables, it is way faster to check for membership with sets, rather than lists, especially when a lot of elements are present. Let's use Jupyter's *magic* to compare the performance. Using `%timeit` for a specific line or `%%timeit` for a whole cell will estimate the time that it takes to compute this code on your machine:

```
>>> l = ['apple', 'banana', 'orange', 'grapefruit', 'plum', 'grape',
'pear']
>>> s = set(l)

>>> %timeit 'pear' in l
84.9 ns ± 1.99 ns per loop (mean ± std. dev. of 7 runs, 10000000 loops
each)


>>> %timeit 'pear' in s
31.6 ns ± 1.21 ns per loop (mean ± std. dev. of 7 runs, 10000000 loops
each)
```

As you can see, even for the shorter array, the performance is essentially more than two times better (faster). This difference will only increase on the larger arrays. Next, let's move on to learning about data structures in more depth.

More data structures

Lists, tuples, dictionaries, and sets are the most popular and widespread data structures in Python. However, they are not the only ones, and—even in the barebone Python distribution—there are many more. As these data structures are way more niche, we'll cover each of them with a brief overview. You can find additional information in the Python documentation (https://docs.python.org/3/tutorial/datastructures.html).

frozenset

`frozenset` lives in Python itself, so there is no need to import anything. They are 100% similar to ordinal sets, except that they are immutable. Just like tuples, you cannot change them, and they can be used as dictionary keys, among other similarities:

```
>>> frozenset('Hello')
frozenset({'e', 'H', 'l', 'o'})
```

defaultdict

defaultdict lives in the built-in collections module. It has a default value set upon creation, and if a missing key is passed, it will return this default value instead of raising KeyError. While this behavior can be achieved through the get method of an ordinary dictionary, defaultdict performs twice as quickly as those that have missing values. In the following snippet, we define a dictionary that will return an empty string if the key value is missing:

```
from collections import defaultdict
d = defaultdict(str) # returns empty string as default value

d['name'] = 'John'
```

Now, let's get the values out:

```
>>> d['name']
John

>>>d['surname']
>>> ''
```

As you can see, defaultdict does not raise KeyError if the key is missing. Instead, it passes a default value that is defined by the function we added upon initiation (in our case, str).

Counter

The Counter structure from the collections module is designed to count the values. You can create it from an iterable. In this case, it will count the frequency of all values. Alternatively, you can feed it a dictionary with values that are all integers, and it will consider keys as elements to count and values as corresponding frequencies. It's easy to add to or subtract from the Counter structures one by one. You can also feed them more iterables, update them with dict, or with another Counter instance:

```
>>> from collections import Counter

>>> Counter('Hello')
Counter({'l': 2, 'H': 1, 'e': 1, 'o': 1})

>>> c1 = Counter({'banana': 2, 'apple': 1})
>>> c1['apple'] += 1
>>> c1
Counter({'banana': 2, 'apple': 2})
```

If treated as an iterable, counter will go over all the encountered elements—counter with frequencies of `'a':2`, `'b':3` will iterate as if was a list of `['a', 'a', 'b', 'b', 'b']`.

Queue

The `Queue` module provides a set of queue structures, which are efficient at adding and releasing values. A classic `Queue` object, also known as **first-in, first-out** (**FIFO**), provides a convenient way to manage things such as tasks. You don't need to worry about order of instances, as the first submitted task will be retrieved first, and so on.

Queues have a `maxsize` argument and will raise an exception if you try to add more elements than the `maxsize` value. They also have the `.task_done()` method, which you can run from your code, indicating that the task is done and allowing `Queue` to safely drop it, thus decreasing the number of tasks in the queue.

 As queues are designed with multithreading in mind (multiple tasks running at the same time), queues also support waiting for the *vacant space* in the queue on `put` and `get` methods, maximum wait time can be defined by a timeout argument—infinite by default.

Let's have a look at the following example. First, we are creating a queue and adding two *tasks* into it. We can see the number of tasks by using the `qsize` method:

```
>>> from queue import Queue
>>> Q = Queue(maxsize=2)

>>> Q.put('wash dishes')
>>> Q.put('water flowers')

>>> Q.qsize()
2
```

As our `Queue` has a maximum size of 2, it is now full and if we attempt to add one more task it will wait (in our case, forever) for the existing tasks to be removed. We could, however, override this by adding another task with the `put_nowait` method if we wanted to. Now, let's pull tasks from the queue. The first task will be `wash dishes`, as it was the first to enter the queue:

```
>>> Q.get()
'wash dishes'
```

Once we have pulled the task, we can pretend that it is done and tell the queue. We can further check the number of tasks that need to be done via the following commands:

```
>>> Q.task_done()
>>> Q.qsize()
1
```

As the number is now smaller than the maximum, we can push new tasks without needing to wait for tasks to be removed from Queue:

```
>>> Q.put('check mail')
>>> Q.qsize()
2
```

A **last-in, first-out (LIFO) queue**, also known as a **stack**, works the same way, except that it releases the last submitted task first, so that the first submitted task will be retrieved last. A **priority queue** manages the order of tasks by the corresponding priority value.

Starting with Python 3.7, the Queue module also has SimpleQueue, which is a simpler FIFO data structure that cannot track tasks and, hence, does not have the .task_done() method.

deque

Another similar data structure, deque, also lives in the collections module and is similar to queues, but with one nuance. As they are **double-ended queues**, which is what the name refers to, they can efficiently add and release values from both sides, rather than from one end.

Let's have a look at the following code:

```
from collections import deque
D = deque(['wash dishes', 'water flowers', 'check mail'])
```

As we mentioned, deque can efficiently remove values both from the right and the left end of the queue. In the following code, pop represents the rightmost end, while popleft pulls the value from the left side:

```
>>> D.pop()
'check mail'

>>> D.popleft()
'wash dishes'
```

Similar to `.pop_left()`, deque has the `.append_left()` and `.extend_left()` methods. They also support rotation, where items move from the left end to the right, either in one direction or the opposite direction.

Queues, stacks, and dequeues are highly performant data structures for very specific tasks. For example, dequeues are used in certain task scheduling algorithms, where different workers can add tasks for themselves on one side and—if their job is done—*steal* another worker's job from the other side. Still, these kind of problems are very low-level and specific. Throughout this book, we will not use any of them, but it is still important to know about them.

namedtuple

The `namedtuple` collection makes it convenient to store data in an expressive way. You can think of them as a hybrid of tuples and dictionaries, as they get the small memory footprint and immutability from the former and keyword access from the latter. They are very effective if you work with multiple data points of the same structure that have no bound logic, for example, users or goods in the eShop. Before we actually create an instance, we'll have to specify the properties of our future record (immutability, remember?). In the following code snippet, we create a data structure for users that contains the `name`, `surname`, and `age` properties. Once a named tuple is defined, there is no way to change it:

```
from collections import namedtuple
user = namedtuple('User', 'name, surname, age')
```

Now, we can add the instances, which are based on the previously defined tuples:

```
peter = user(name='Peter', surname='Pan', age=13)
wendy = user(name='Wendy', surname='Darling', age=13)
```

One of the reasons `namedtuple` is efficient is that its argument structure is stored once, rather than for every instance. Once we have instances, their properties can be retrieved by using an index, slicing, or the name of the property:

```
>>> peter[0]
Peter

>>> peter[:2]
('Peter', 'Pan')

>>> wendy.surname
'Darling'
```

If for any reason, we need to retrieve a property by its name as a string value or test whether such an argument exists, we can use Python's built-in `getattr` and `hasattr` functions:

```
>>> hasattr(wendy, 'age')
True

>>> getattr(wendy, 'age')
13
```

A `namedtuple` collection is a class that inherits from a tuple; the resulting instances of the tuple are 100% normal class instances. You can see the code under the hood by passing a `verbose=True` argument. With that being said, Python 3.7 introduces data classes, which are pure Python classes that can solve a somewhat similar set of problems. They are a little more descriptive and flexible, although they take more memory than the earlier data classes.

Enumerations

Enumerations are somewhat less popular data structures in Python. They are quite similar to named tuples, as they are immutable and their attributes are named. Enumerations also have one interesting property: they are always singletons. In other words, you can't have more than one instance of an `Enum` class at the same time. With that, enumerations work well as semantic layers (aliases) for a set of specific values; for example, for categories, we can define colors in the palette, aliasing specific implementation. The singleton property means that the value will always be exactly the same throughout the code.

In the following example, we define an `Enum` class for the color theme. Our `Enum` object supports three colors: MAIN, SECONDARY, and ACCENT. Note how we alias the values:

```
from enum import Enum

>>> class Colors(Enum):
...     MAIN = 'darkblue'
...     SECONDARY = 'lightgrey'
...     ACCENT = 'teal'
```

 In this example, we indeed use the `class` keyword, and, in this case, the `Colors` class inherits from the `Enum` class. We'll talk more about classes and inheritance in `Chapter 8`, *Simulation with Classes and Inheritance*.

As a result, we have a clear representation of the color palette (theme) in the code. Now, we can access the values without explicitly stating them. In the following code, we define a function that generates a `div` HTML object that is colored with the SECONDARY color. This level of semantics allows us to swap color themes later, with no need to adjust the code. Note that we don't need to create an instance of the class here:

```
def mainblock(content):
    return f"<div style='color:{Colors.SECONDARY.value}'>{content}</div>"

>>>  mainblock('Hello!')
<div style='color:lightgrey'>Hello!</div>
```

While `Enum` can be useful in certain cases, it was rarely used in code until recently. With the new feature of a type annotation being introduced in Python 3, enumerations have turned out to be a useful structure to represent an argument to be within a set of possible values. In particular, we will use `Enum` as a type hint in Chapter 18, *Serving Models with a RESTful API*, where it will help us to define a correct endpoint for the API we will build.

Next, after data structures, let's move on to generators and see what they are like.

Using generators

Generators are not exactly data structures—they are functions. However, while *normal* functions compute their results and return them at once, generators can be stopped and resumed on the fly, resulting in an iterable-like behavior. In other words, you can loop over a generator, retrieving one value at a time. Unlike classic iterables, however, generators are lazy. They compute values once we ask for them, but not before we do. As a result of that, there are a few significant differences in their behavior as compared to iterables:

- First, generators use a fixed amount of memory. Even if you ask one to compute zillions of values, a generator will produce and store just one value every time you ask, which is great! In fact, generators can produce an infinite number of values with no memory issues.
- Second, as generators do not store the values, there is no way to retrieve values by their index. In order to get the third element, you need to compute the first two, first. Similarly, there is no way to get *back* to the previous element. If you didn't store it, the value is lost. Also, there is no way to estimate the length of the generator other than computing all the values, but again, generators can be infinite.

For a function to work as a generator, it needs to emit multiple `yield` statements instead of `return` statements. Once the function is called, you can loop over it as if it were a list or a tuple, or retrieve one value at a time by using Python's built-in `next()` function:

```
def my_generator(N, power=2):
    # for loop, which we'll cover in depth in the next chapter.
    # note that loops require another level of indentation
    for el in range(N):
        yield el**power

N = my_generator(4, power=2)

next(N)
>>> 0

for el in N:
    print(el)
>>> 1    # zero was computed already
>>> 4
>>> 9
```

In the preceding example, we used the `range()` function, which takes one to three integer arguments, with only 1 required. If 1 is provided, `range` will return a generator of numbers from 0 to this number, excluding it. If 2 is provided, the former will become the starter, and the latter, which is at the end of the generator will, again, be excluded. If 3 is provided, it will be used as a step. There are plenty of other functions within Python that return **generators**. Don't worry if you need a list or tuple as a result—just convert them:

```
list(range(5))
>>> [0, 1, 2, 3, 4]
```

The `range` object has some *syntactic sugar* functionality. For example, it *can* check for inclusion without actually calculating the values (which is a very easy thing to do, if you think about it thoroughly):

```
20346 in range(0, 100_000_000, 2)  # even numbers
>>> True
```

Useful functions to use with data structures

There are a few functions and interfaces that are useful for working with data, from simple ones such as `sum`, `max`, and `min`, to complex ones such as `zip`, `map`, `filter`, and `reduce`.

The sum, max, and min functions

These functions are pretty much self-explanatory: they will try to summarize or compare values in iterables. Just remember that for the dictionary, its keys—not values—will be used:

```
sum({1:'A', 2:'B'})
>>> 3
```

Note that `min` and `max` don't require elements to be integers or floats:

```
max({'A':1, 'B':2})
>>> 'B'
```

The all and any functions

`all` and `any` are self-explanatory as well. Simply put, they are extended `and` and `or` operators, and work with multiple values at once:

```
all([False, True, True])
>>> False

any([False, True, False])
>>> True
```

The zip function

`zip` is useful when you have *N* lists of *M* elements, and you need to transpose them, so as to get *M* lists of *N* elements. Similar to `range`, it will return a generator object:

```
data1, data2 = (1, 2, 3, 4, 5), ('A', 'B', 'C', 'D', 'E')

result = list(zip(data1, data2))

result
>>> [(1, 'A'), (2, 'B'), (3, 'C'), (4, 'D'), (5, 'E')]
```

`zip` can also be done in reverse by using the `result` variable as `args`:

```
list(zip(*result))
>>> [(1, 2, 3, 4, 5), ('A', 'B', 'C', 'D', 'E')]
```

`zip` can also be used to create data structures:

```
dict(zip(data1, data2))
>>> {1: 'A', 2: 'B', 3: 'C', 4: 'D', 5: 'E'}
```

The map, filter, and reduce functions

Other functions that you might find useful with data structures are `map`, `filter`, and `reduce`. These are very useful in conjunction with other functions, such as lambdas.

`map` runs given functions on every element of the iterable, returning a generator:

```
>>> data1, data2 = (1, 2, 3, 4, 5), ('A', 'B', 'C', 'D', 'E')

>>> list(map(lambda x: x**2, data1))
# converting to list in order to seE results
[1, 4, 9, 16, 25]

>>> list(map(lambda x: x.lower(), data2))
['a', 'b', 'c', 'd', 'e']
```

Similarly, `filter` returns a subarray of elements for which the function returns a true or truthy value:

```
list(filter(lambda x: x > 3, data1))
>>> [4, 5]
```

Finally, `reduce`—which was moved to the `itertools` package in Python 3—runs given functions on pairs and in cascades, with the expectation to get one value as a result so that all the values will triple down to one. For example, the `sum` function can be seen as a specific case of `reduce`.

While it is useful to know that those functions exist, there is another more expressive method that can achieve the same results—comprehensions.

Comprehensions

Comprehensions are a nice and expressive way to work with data structures. Let's start with a simple example:

```
{el**2 for el in range(3)}
>>> {0, 1, 4}
```

Here, the curly brackets define our result. We use `range` to create the initial iterable, and then loop over its values, computing the square value of each. This is not a real loop, though. List comprehensions are actually faster than loops and even `map`, as there are no lambdas, and thus, no additional costs for stack lookups:

```
>>> %%timeit
... s = set()
... for el in range(10):
...     s.add(el**2)
3.35 µs ± 134 ns per loop (mean ± std. dev. of 7 runs, 100000 loops each)

>>> %timeit set(map(lambda x: x**2, range(10)))
3.72 µs ± 207 ns per loop (mean ± std. dev. of 7 runs, 100000 loops each)

>>> %timeit {el**2 for el in range(10)}
3.11 µs ± 309 ns per loop (mean ± std. dev. of 7 runs, 100000 loops each)
```

On top of that, comprehensions can be nested, use `if` statements (thus, replace the `filter` function), and operate on different data structures. In the following example, we use a comprehension to run over a list of dictionaries, and create a new list that contains character names, but only for characters with an age that is below 15 (only they can go to *Neverland*, you know):

```
>>> characters = [
    {'name': 'Peter Pan', 'age': 13, 'type': 'boy'},
    {'name': 'Wendy Darling', 'age': 14, 'type': 'girl'},
    {'name': 'Captain Cook', 'age': 45, 'type': 'pirate'}
     # just guessing
]

>>> [el['name'] for el in characters if el['age'] < 15]
['Peter Pan', 'Wendy Darling']
```

We can even use the comprehension to swap keys and values of the dictionary that way. In the following code, we create a new dictionary by using the values of the existing one as keys, and by using keys as values:

```
D = {'A':1, 'B':2 }

{v:k for k, v in D.items()}
>>> {1:'A', 2:'B'}
```

This concludes our exposé into data structures. In the following chapters, we'll be using everything we just learned more extensively.

Summary

In this chapter, we learned about the basic and more advanced data structures in Python. We covered how to create, interact with, and operate on those structures. In addition to structures, we covered generators, which are functions that *pretend* to be iterable structures, and comprehensions, which are a concise and fast way to create and work with data structures. We also briefly touched on loops and `if` statements and learned how they work.

In the next chapter, we'll discuss different types of loops and statements, which will allow us to operate on datasets dynamically and embed logic into our code.

Questions

1. How do we retrieve one element from a list? How do we retrieve the last element of the list without computing its length explicitly?
2. How do we get all elements of a list—except the first one and the last one—in the reverse order?
3. How do we merge two dictionaries, and what happens if some of the keys are the same in both of them?
4. What is the best data structure to check for membership?
5. Can we get the last element of the generator without getting all the others?
6. How do we combine elements from *N* triplets into three arrays of *N* one by one?
7. What is the shortest way to generate a list of specific dictionary properties—which are retrieved from a list of dictionaries—if a certain other property of each dictionary is in the set?

Further reading

Python Data Structures and Algorithms (https://www.packtpub.com/application-development/python-data-structures-and-algorithms)

Loops and Other Compound Statements

5

In the previous chapter, we learned how to create and operate on data structures. Now, let's discuss how to operate on them effectively.

We will first cover loops—a special type of compound statement (code that compounds other code, just like functions)—that allows the same code to be run over and over—any number of times, or even indefinitely. After loops, we will discuss if-else statements—logical forks that allow us to split code execution based on test results. Finally, we will cover two less popular, but still very useful, clauses—`try`, which helps to save the day if something goes wrong (an error is raised) within the code, and `with`, which helps to close the context safely (for example, close the file correctly).

Hence, this chapter will cover the following topics:

- Understanding `if`, `else`, and `elif` statements
- Running code many times with loops
- Handling exceptions with `try/except` and `try/finally`
- Understanding `with` statements

Technical requirements

The code in this chapter does not require any additional packages. All the code is available in the `Chapter05` folder in the repository (`https://github.com/PacktPublishing/Learn-Python-by-Building-Data-Science-Applications`).

Understanding if, else, and elif statements

Conditional execution is one of the cornerstones of programming. It allows us to execute one code, but not the other, depending on the condition. This condition is described in Python as an `if` statement. It is pretty self-explanatory: code within the scope will be executed if the condition is met:

```
if rain is True:
    agenda = 'Stay Home'
```

Here, if the `rain` variable is true, the agenda is to stay at home.

This statement can make functions more flexible. In the following example, if `b` is equal to `0`, we can't use it as a denominator, so we can check the value, and return `None` instead. As `return` terminates all the code of the function, the division does not happen:

```
def percentage(a, b):
    if b == 0:
        return None

    return round(a / b, 2)
```

On many occasions, there could be more than one outcome of the logical fork. If you need an alternative code to run if the statement is false, you can use the `else` keyword. The following code checks whether the name is equal to `Annie`. If the name matches, the code would print a greeting. If, and only if, it does not (which is the case here), an alternative statement (`I don't know you...`) will be printed:

```
name = 'Adrian'

if name == 'Annie':
    print('Hello Annie!')
else:
    print("I don't know you...")
```

Since the name is not `Annie`, this code will print the `I don't know you...` phrase.

We are not just bound by two options either! You can have more than two logical branches, using the `elif` keyword (which works like an `else-if` statement).

Consider the following code. Here, we have four logical branches! First, if the name is in the first set of people we know, the code will print a greeting. If not, but the name is in another set, the greeting will be different. The third option checks whether the name is in our *blacklist*, in which case we'll ignore the person by passing on execution. Finally, as a last resort, the code will state that we don't know the person:

```
if name in {'Adrian', 'Annie'}:
  print('I know you!')

elif name in {'Agnus', 'Angela'}:
    print("Hi! I thing we've met somewhere...")

elif name in {'Boris', 'Brunhilde'} :
    # don't talk with them
    pass
    # pass can be used in code when sintaxis requires some code,
    # but none is needed

else:
    print("I don't think I know you...")
```

While that is absolutely feasible, we generally don't recommend writing more than one or two `elif` branches—they are verbose and hard to read and debug; very often, there are better options in terms of structuring the logic.

So far, we have used `else`/`if` statements with indentation, but we also can use them on the same line. In the next section, we'll cover how to use `if` in inline statements.

Inline if statements

In some cases, you just want to assign (or reassign) variables. Bad practice would involve doing the following:

```
name = name or 'Sigizmund'
```

Here, `name` will have a value of `Sigizmund` if it was equal to `Sigizmund` before, or is *untruthy* (equal to `None`, `False`, or `zero`). This is fine in certain cases, but can lead to uncertainty due to ambiguity. A better solution would be to use `if` instead:

```
name = name if name is not None else 'Sigizmund'
```

Here, the logic is exactly the same—name will have a value Sigizmund if not None, but stated more explicitly. One key difference is that the preceding statement will not consider *untruthy* values as None—if name is equal to False or zero, it will not be overwritten. Perhaps counterintuitively, this is considered a better practice—if the value is somehow invalid, it is better to know this as soon as possible.

Another option is to use if as part of the comprehension—we actually did just that in the previous chapter. Let's revisit that example in the next section.

Using if in a comprehension

In the previous chapter, we discussed comprehensions, one-liner code expressions, which usually create iterable objects from one or a few other iterables. They do support the if condition as well. For example, the following comprehension loops over a list of dictionaries, and returns a list of character names, one per dictionary in the first list, if the surname of the corresponding character is equal to Rabbit:

```
>>> characters = [
    {'name': 'Peter', "surname": 'Rabbit'},
    {'name': 'Josephine', 'surname': 'Rabbit'},
    {'name': 'Michael', 'surname': 'McGregor'}
]

>>> rabbits = [el['name'] for el in characters if el['surname'] ==
'Rabbit']
>>> rabbits
['Peter', 'Josephine']
```

Using comprehensions with if is a great practice; most of the time, comprehensions are very expressive and easy to grasp, while short and performant—a rare win-win scenario.

One-liners are great, but they can't completely replace loops. Besides, there are different types of loops, and some are quite different from the one-liners in terms of what they do. Let's take a look.

Running code many times with loops

Loops are compound statements that repeat the code within them many times, a specific number of times, until a certain test is met, or even indefinitely. By doing so, loops enable us to incrementally update the values or traverse over a collection of values, computing something for each of them. For example, the factorization function we wrote at the end of the last chapter to illustrate recursing can be written with loops, multiplying the value by the next value in the row each time.

Python loops have two main forms—`for` and `while`. Let's now look at them in detail.

The for loop

The `for` loop is the classical form of the loop—it literally goes over an iterable (collection of values) and performs the same computation for each value, consecutively. The code within the loop may or may not be using the value for which it is computed.

For example, if we just need to run some specific code *N* times, we can run the loop over the range object that contains *N* values. Consider the following example:

```
>>> for i in range(3):
>>>     print(i)
0
1
2
```

Here, we execute a built-in range function (which we discussed in Chapter 3, *Functions*) and run a loop, printing each element in this loop.

Any other iterable would suffice as well, including strings, sets, lists, tuples, dictionaries, and generators. All the code in the scope of the loop will be repeated as many times as there are elements in the iterable. In the following code, we loop through the characters in a string, printing each of them:

```
>>> for char in 'Jack':
>>>     print(char)
J
a
c
k
```

Loops require indentation—just like functions. In contrast to functions, however, variables assigned in the loop (the last value they were assigned to), will be accessible from the outside of this indentation. The looping variable (`el` in the first example, and `char` in the second) can be named as you see fit.

In fact, we can pass more than one value using unpacking. Here is one example. We're iterating over a dictionary, using its `items` method. In the first line of the loop, we can define two variables, the first representing the key, and the second the value. Once defined, both variables can be used in the code—in this case, printed. If we were to state one argument instead, it would be assigned a tuple of key-value pairs:

```
>>> person = {
 'name':'Jim',
 'surname':'Hockins'
}

>>> for k, v in person.items():
        print(k, ':', v)

name : Jim
surname : Hockins
```

As a result, `key` and `value` are printed for each pair in the dictionary—`name : Jim`.

Any number of loops can be nested one within the other—as many as you like. In that case, an internal loop will require an additional level of indentation. Note, however, that loops are generally time-consuming, and nesting increases time exponentially. Typically, pay attention if you need to nest two or more loops; there may be a better way.

The power of loops can be expanded, leveraging built-in additional tools. Let's take a look.

itertools

There is a built-in library for working with iterations—`itertools`. This library provides a large set of sophisticated iterable constructors in three main categories:

- **Infinite iterators**: Iterators that allow us to loop an arbitrary number of times through the same collection until certain criteria are met.
- **Terminating on the shortest input sequence**: Functions that somehow group iterators, merging or filtering their elements.
- **Combinatoric iterators**: These combine multiple iterators, producing a combination of them.

There are a lot of functions, so be sure to check the documentation (`https://docs.python.org/3/library/itertools.html`). Here, we will discuss just a handful of them.

cycle

`itertools.cycle` allows the iterable to be gone through, repeating itself multiple times, or until the certain criteria are met. For example, if you have a plot with colors assigned by a category, and there is a chance there are more categories than colors in the style guide, you can make use of `cycle`. Consider the following example; we first initialize the `cycle` object, passing categories as arguments:

```
from itertools import cycle
colors = cycle(('red', 'green', 'blue'))
categories = (1, 2, 3, 4, 5)
```

Next, we loop over both iterators by using the `zip` function. As you know, generally, `zip` loops until the shortest collection ends. In this case, there are five categories but just three colors, so without cycling, the loop will only print the first three categories:

```
>>> for cat, color in zip(categories, colors):
>>>     print(cat, color)

1 red
2 green
3 blue
4 red
5 green
```

With cycling, however, `colors` is essentially an infinite iterable—so the shortest one is now *categories*.

chain

`chain` allows multiple iterables to be added together. This is especially useful if both iterables are generators, as `chain` does not execute them. Consider this example. First, we create two iterables—a generator and a string:

```
from itertools import chain

generator = range(3)
iterable = 'Python'
```

Now, we chain them together, and iterate over them:

```
>>> for el in chain(generator, iterable):
>>>     print(el)

0
1
2
P
y
t
h
o
n
```

As you can see, the two are merged together seamlessly. `chain` is a fast operation that can be extremely useful in certain cases.

product

`itertools.product` generates a Cartesian product (a set of all permutations), a concise equivalent of a nested `for` loop. Here is how it appears. First, we create three sets (`product` can take any number of iterables):

```
s1 = {'Peter', 'Benjamin'}
s2 = {'Flopsy', 'Mopsy', 'Cottontail'}
s3 = {'McGregor', 'Thomas', 'Bea'}
```

Next, we call a `product` function on all of them, printing the result:

```
>>> from itertools import product
>>> for el in product(s1, s2, s3):
        print(el)

('Peter', 'Mopsy', 'Bea')
('Peter', 'Mopsy', 'Thomas')
('Peter', 'Mopsy', 'McGregor')
('Peter', 'Cottontail', 'Bea')
('Peter', 'Cottontail', 'Thomas')
('Peter', 'Cottontail', 'McGregor')
('Peter', 'Flopsy', 'Bea')
('Peter', 'Flopsy', 'Thomas')
('Peter', 'Flopsy', 'McGregor')
('Benjamin', 'Mopsy', 'Bea')
('Benjamin', 'Mopsy', 'Thomas')
('Benjamin', 'Mopsy', 'McGregor')
```

```
('Benjamin', 'Cottontail', 'Bea')
('Benjamin', 'Cottontail', 'Thomas')
('Benjamin', 'Cottontail', 'McGregor')
('Benjamin', 'Flopsy', 'Bea')
('Benjamin', 'Flopsy', 'Thomas')
('Benjamin', 'Flopsy', 'McGregor')
```

As you can see, the `product` function generates all the permutations of the elements from three sets.

Enumeration

Sometimes, you want to keep the record of the iteration you're at while using an iterable. A naive approach would be to get the length of the iterable, use the `range` function, and then use each number to get values from the iterable—indeed, that is how loops work in other languages, such as Java and JavaScript. But don't do that! Indeed, this construct requires two function calls in its basic case, and more if we need to numerate iterations, starting from a number other than zero. In Python, there is a better solution! Just use `enumerate`—this will create a generator that will return an index and a corresponding value from the original iterable, as a tuple. This can be used even if you had tuples already—just use parentheses for the unpacking. Here is an illustration using the `person` data structure. All we need is to run the enumerator over our iterable. In this case, the iterable contains a number of key-value pairs as tuples. In order to name them, we unpack values, describing the entire composition after the `for` keyword; here, `i` is the index generated by the `enumerate` function, while `k` and `v` are the key-value pair. Number `1` in the enumerator indicates the beginning of the enumeration:

```
>>> person = { 'name':'Jim', 'surname':'Hockins'}
>>> for i, (k, v) in enumerate(person.items(), 1):
>>> print(f'{i}. {k}: {v}')

1. name : Jim
2. surname L Hockins
```

With that, we can use each element by its name within the loop—in our case, we use this to format each line properly.

The while loop

`while` loops are quite similar to `for` loops, with one major distinction: they don't need an iterable to run over—instead, they are driven by a simple Boolean value. While this value is true, the loop will continue to run, potentially an infinite number of times. Consider the following example. Here, we run a `while` loop until the `counter` value is less than 5. Once that is no longer the case, the loop stops. As the initial value of the variable is zero, it is easy to deduce that the loop ran five times:

```
counter = 0
while counter < 5:
    print(counter)
    counter += 1
```

Be careful! It is easy to make this loop infinite by accident. In some cases, however, that is exactly what we want, so we can make this explicit through the pattern:

```
while True:
    compute()
```

The preceding loop is explicitly infinite: it will run forever, or, realistically, until something stops the script—either from inside (code error), or outside (you terminating the script, or the computer rebooting). This pattern is useful for continuous tasks—for example, collecting data from the streaming endpoint.

Additional loop functionality – break and continue

At any point, the loop can be broken from inside. Using the `break` keyword, the loop will be terminated immediately. The following code loops over the string and halts the loop once the letter is equal to `t`. As `t` is the third letter, the loop is only able to print the first two letters:

```
>>> for letter in "Data":
>>>     if letter == 't':
>>>         break
>>>     print(letter)
D
a
```

The `break` keyword is especially useful for *infinite* loops, which can be triggered to stop if a certain condition is met.

Alternatively, if you just need to skip one round without stopping the entire loop, you can use the `continue` keyword. We execute the same example—except this time, if the letter is equal to `'t'`, the loop will skip one round of execution and jump to the next one for the letter `'a'`:

```
>>> for letter in "Data":
>>>     if letter == 't':
>>>         continue
>>>     print(letter)
D
a
a
```

`break` and `continue` will work with both types of loops. Both are relatively rare, but could prove invaluable in specific cases; for example, when you need to stop the traverse on a certain condition. It could be because you need it as part of your algorithm, or if you want to halt/pass on an invalid case, which can cause errors.

Our next compound statement is designed specifically to handle the errors so that your code will survive and adjust accordingly. Let's see how this is done.

Handling exceptions with try/except and try/finally

`try/except` is here to save the day if some code fails. We've seen errors before. In Jupyter, they appear as text highlighted in red when we do something wrong. In many cases, however, it is hard to predict whether an error will occur—for example, if we're working with an external database or service, there is no guarantee that everything will work as it should all the time. Before we learn how to mitigate those potential exceptions, let's briefly review what the exception is and why we should create our own ones.

Exceptions

But what are the exceptions? You can think of them as warning messages letting us know about computation issues and halting the computation. For example, when we're trying to divide by zero, the computer knows it's wrong and raises a corresponding ZeroDivisionError type error, stopping the process. We can raise exceptions from within our own code by using the raise keyword. There are a handful of built-in exception types, such as KeyError, ValueError, and IndexError. The only significant difference between these is the name, which helps us to understand and differentiate between issues. All those exceptions inherit from the base exception type—Exception. Each exception can be raised with supporting text if you so desire. Consider the following example. Here, we declare a function, which checks whether a given instance is of a certain type, using the isinstance function. If it is not, the function will raise a ValueError exception. Predictably, the function won't raise anything when we pass Hello and str as its arguments—indeed, Hello is a string:

```
def _check_raise(inst, type_, text=None):
    text = text if text is not None else f'Wrong value: requires {type}
format, got {type(inst)}'

    if not isinstance(inst, type_):
        raise ValueError(text)

>>> _check_raise('Hello', str)
```

But when we replace str with int, this throws the error, as intended:

```
_check_raise('Hello', int)
-------------------------------------------------
ValueError          Traceback (most recent call last)
<ipython-input-50-145b6e9f288c> in <module>
----> 1 _check_raise('Hello', int)

<ipython-input-49-b95b042dc54b> in _check_raise(inst, type_, text)
      3
      4     if not isinstance(inst, type_):
----> 5         raise ValueError(text)

ValueError: Wrong value: requires <class 'type'> format, got <class 'str'>
```

In many cases, it makes sense to create our own exceptions—we'll do that in Chapter 8, *Simulation with Classes and Inheritance*.

Many new learners consider exceptions as a bad thing, and which should be resolved immediately in situ. Not only is it hard to do and adds a lot of additional code, but also makes your program obscure and hard to debug. So, don't run from exceptions—instead of trying to resolve all possible issues in situ (within each script or function), let them occur—and do raise them yourself, adding a helpful message. This will help your code to fail fast, as well as help you to detect and resolve the issue at its root and handle issues at the right level.

Now that we know about exceptions, let's circle back to the `try` clause.

try/except

The `try/except` construct allows you to handle the errors within and fall back on alternative code if something goes wrong. You can use it for an exception as an umbrella case (any error), or specify precise exceptions to catch. In the following code, we're trying to run a *bad* code, dividing by zero. In this case, Python raises a specific exception—ZeroDivisionError. Knowing that, we add an except ZeroDivisionError clause, printing a string in it:

```
>>> try:
>>>     result = 1 / 0
>>> except ZeroDivisionError:
>>>     print('something is wrong!')
something is wrong!
```

Because we are catching specific ZeroDivisionError exceptions, everything else will still raise an exception. As it is precisely the exception that was raised, we caught it, a print statement was executed, and the code continued the execution. If necessary, we can specify multiple types of errors, use caught exceptions in our code, and even add different behavior for a different type of issue.

Let's illustrate this with another example, using a built-in example for warnings. Warnings are a more explicit way to catch attention, as opposed to printing, and won't halt the code, as exceptions do. In the following code, we define a function that calculates the percent, taking the value and the total arguments. It handles ZeroDivisionError as the preceding code. In addition, it handles TypeError and KeyError (the latter was added just to illustrate how to pass multiple exceptions in the same statement). Finally, there is a fallback scenario for all other types of exceptions:

```
import warnings
# built-in library that helps warning people - similar to exceptions, but
```

```
won't halt code,
# you can also set up filter for different warning types

def percentage(value, total):
    try:
        return 100 * (value / total)

    except ZeroDivisionError:
        warnings.warn('Total cannot be zero!')

    except (TypeError, KeyError) as e:
        # Keyerror here would never occur - just used it for example
        warnings.warn(f"Something with the wrong: {e}")
    except Exception as e:
        raise Exception(value, total, e)
```

Let's test it in practice. In the following code, we run a function for a proper set of values, for `total` equal to `0`, and, finally, for two strings. In all cases, a proper exception (or lack thereof) was used:

```
>>> percentage(1, 10)
10.0

>>> percentage(10, 0)
/Users/philippk/anaconda3/envs/py36/lib/python3.7/site-
packages/ipykernel_launcher.py:10: UserWarning: Total cannot be zero!

>>> percentage('Hello', 'world')
/Users/philippk/anaconda3/envs/py36/lib/python3.7/site-
packages/ipykernel_launcher.py:14: UserWarning: Something with the wrong:
unsupported operand type(s) for /: 'str' and 'str'
```

try/except/finally

The `try` statement supports yet another option – the `finally` clause. When added, `finally` represents the code that will be executed, irrespective of which branch of `try`/`except` actually did run in the end. It is usually used to release external resources—a close connection to the file or the database. Consider this example. Here, we're attempting to open the file and perform certain computations:

```
try:
    file = open("test.txt")
    # some operations on file
finally:
    file.close()
```

No matter what happens within `try`, the file will be properly closed. This *on the way out* principle will work with other events as well, including `break`, `continue`, and `return`.

 Note that the `as` variable assigns the raised exception to the `e` variable, but it will be deleted once we're out of the `except` clause.

`try`/`except` statements allow us to dodge an exception if something goes south. This is a great solution in terms of adding some fault tolerance to the code. The danger with this approach is being overly fault tolerant, meaning that the code will keep working OK in a situation where you'd ideally want to intervene and halt it. Let's now talk about our last statement for today—the `with` statement.

Understanding the with statements

Last but not least, the `with` statement is usually used with any kind of connections or managed resources such as file handles. Consider the following example:

```
with open('./text_file.txt', 'r') as file:
    data = file.read()

print(data)
```

Here, we use a `with` clause together with the `open()` function. The `open` function returns a file-like object that has __enter__ and __exit__ methods, representing the opening and closing of the file. Both can be used directly, but the file needs to be closed properly once it is opened. The `close()` function along together with the `with` clause does exactly that – it opens an object, and makes sure it is closed (using those two methods) at the end. Essentially, it is the equivalent of the following `try`/`finally` statement:

```
try:
    file = open('./text_file.txt', 'r').__enter__()
    data = file.read()
finally:
    file.__exit__()
```

You can see that this statement is quite similar to `try`/`finally`, but definitely more expressive and clean. As always, with Python, `with` is designed around the *duck typing* principle (if it quacks like a duck and walks like a duck, consider it a duck): if any arbitrary object has __enter__ and __exit__ methods, it can be used in the `with` clause as the statement does not care what actually is happening in those functions. Most database connections and cursors support this feature.

Summary

In this chapter, we covered a wide spectrum of compound statements. In particular, we covered the `if` clause, which allows us to build logical forks – parts of code that are executed if a condition is met. We also discussed two types of loops, which allow us to run the same code multiple times, in repetition. Lastly, we covered `try`/`except`/`finally` and `with` clauses, which gives us options in terms of catching errors on the fly, without halting execution of the script, and guaranteeing that given connections, such as open files, are handled properly.

This chapter concludes our tour of the basics of the language. By no means have we covered it all! However, from now on, we will depart from the sandbox example and start writing code that is actually useful.

In the next chapter, we'll start communicating with external APIs and process data. See you there!

Questions

1. Can the `if` clause work with multiple (more than two) logical branches?
2. What is the difference between `for` and `while` loops?
3. How can I loop through multiple (two or more) arrays of the same length? Or of different lengths?
4. Why do we need exceptions? How can I catch one?
5. What is the difference between `finally` and `except`?
6. When should the `with` clause be used?
7. How can I use `with` on a custom object?

Further reading

- *Python Data Structures and Algorithms* (`https://www.packtpub.com/application-development/python-data-structures-and-algorithms`)
- *Errors and Exceptions* (`https://docs.python.org/3/tutorial/errors.html`)

First Script – Geocoding with Web APIs

6

Now that we know how to write functions, let's apply that knowledge to a practical task. In this chapter, we will build a function that will communicate with a web service via a REST API in order to get the latitude and longitude of a given address. Furthermore, we'll discuss how to use built-in Python libraries to read and write data from and to files. Finally, we will wrap this functionality into a standalone script, so that it can be used from the command line, with no Jupyter Notebook attached.

In this chapter, we will learn how to do the following:

- Work generally with Python's built-in libraries and `requests` in particular
- Communicate with web services via APIs
- Read and write data using the CSV file format
- Wrap code into a standalone script with the command-line interface, using the built-in `sys.argv` library, and import functionality back into a Jupyter Notebook

Technical requirements

In this chapter, we will use two third-party libraries—`requests` and `tqdm`. Both are included in Anaconda Distribution, so if you use Anaconda, they are already installed. Otherwise, please install them.

To install a new package, type the following:

- If you have `conda` installed, use `conda install requests`.
- Otherwise, if you have `pip`, use `pip install requests`.

You will also need an internet connection, as we'll be working with a web service API.

The code for this chapter is available in the GitHub repository, specifically the `Chapter06` folder (`https://github.com/PacktPublishing/Learn-Python-by-Building-Data-Science-Applications`).

Geocoding as a service

Often, the data we work with requires preprocessing; sometimes, that includes gathering additional information to add context or transform existing information. Typical examples of that are geocoding and reverse geocoding—the processes of converting an address into geocoordinates and vice versa, respectively. Converting an address into coordinates allows us to visualize data on a map, measure distances, and check membership (seeing things such as what country, neighborhood, or school district an address belongs to).

This is actually a hard task, as it requires you to have a large hierarchical database of relevant addresses and a complex parsing engine to make sense of semi-structured, often misspelled and ambiguous, addresses. Realistically, a service like that requires a large investment of time and resources.

The good news is that we can use some existing services to do this job. In fact, every mapping service—including Google Maps, Apple Maps, Bing Maps, Yandex Maps, **OpenStreetMap** (**OSM**), and Esri—has geocoding services; the chances are you used one of them when you last typed an address into the search bar of a browser-based map. But how can we connect to geocoding services from Python? Via a web API.

 Some services are paid for. Most of them are free—at least, for a limited number of requests. Beware: they still have a corresponding license and—often strict—requirements and limitations. Here, we will be using the Nominatim API, which allows the use of data under the **Open Database License** (**ODbL**). Any usage for educational/informational purposes (such as the use of the code in this chapter) will fall under the fair trade/fair deals policy. As well as only using it for demonstration/education purposes, let's try to *play nice* and not flood the server with lots of requests in a short period. Adding a short delay between each request is often advisable. OSM can and will block access for certain users if they find they're flooding their servers (this also includes the tile server).

So, now let's move on to our next topic, which is on web APIs.

Learning about web APIs

First, what is an API? Well, an **Application Programming Interface** (**API**) is an interface for working with a specific application programmatically—that is, via code. Think of Twitter bots or email clients—all of them use APIs to work with their corresponding applications (Twitter and email servers, respectively).

An API does not have to involve the web—many local applications on your computer have APIs of their own, so we can interact with them through Python or any other language. In our case, however, we need to work with a web API. Those APIs operate via HTTP requests and responses. Many contemporary APIs follow REST guidelines—a set of six design constraints that were put forward by Roy Fielding. You can learn more about REST architecture via *REST API Tutorial* (`https://restfulapi.net/`) or the Packt books cited at the end of this chapter. We will also talk about REST APIs in more detail in `Chapter 18`, *Serving Models with a RESTful APIs*, when we'll actually build one ourselves.

All REST APIs communicate with the consumer via the HTTP protocol—the same protocol we're using in our browsers. Let's briefly discuss them now.

Working with HTTPS

Hypertext Transfer Protocol (**HTTP**) and modern HTTPS (**S** for **Secure**) requests have three parts: the required **request** line, and the optional **body** and **headers**. Every request has a certain **method**—the most popular are `GET` and `POST`. The specific usage of different methods can vary for specific API endpoints. Most web APIs have parameters defined within their URLs.

HTTP **responses** have a similar structure, but also a universal HTTP status code, representing the request status. The most frequently used codes are 200 (success), 403 (forbidden, bad authentication), and 404 (URL not found). You can read more on different status codes at Mozilla's MDN website (`https://developer.mozilla.org/en-US/docs/Web/HTTP/Status`).

With this general understanding of APIs and HTTP requests, let's take a look at a particular geocoding service—Nominatim.

Working with the Nominatim API

In this particular case, we are going to use OSM's Nominatim service. Its API is simple, free, does not require authorization, and has a relatively open license. Moreover, as OSM is open source, we theoretically can add and improve its content, if that is necessary for our project.

In order to work with an API, we first need to read its documentation. Often, documentation includes example snippets of code to use with the service in question—the code is usually in Python. Nominatim's documentation can be found at `nominatim.openstreetmap.org`. According to it, to get information for a given address, we should send a request to the following URL:

```
https://nominatim.openstreetmap.org/search?
```

All our parameters—the address, response format, geographic limitations, and so on—need to be added using standard URL escaping (don't worry—Python will take care of it for us). For example, to receive information on the Eiffel Tower in Paris as a JSON object, you could use the following URL:

```
https://nominatim.openstreetmap.org/search.php?q=Eiffel+tower%2C+Paris&form
at=json
```

If we drop the last parameter—`format`—the response will be a valid HTML page, showing the search results. This might be useful for debugging purposes.

Now, let's write some Python code to work with this API!

The requests library

As in many other cases, Python has a built-in library to deal with HTTP requests—`urllib`. It is a great package that allows the handling of requests via a low-level technical interface. We will, however, use `requests`—a third-party library with a high-level (simpler) interface that uses `urllib` under the hood. As a third-party library, `requests` requires separate installation. However, if you have Anaconda Distribution installed, don't worry—`requests` is already installed!

The library supports many advanced options, including sessions, authentication, and **Secure Sockets Layer (SSL)** certificates. In this case, however, the only thing we need is the `get` method of `requests`, which takes the request URL and optional parameters as arguments. Let's now try using `requests`.

Starting to code

Let's try to put into practice everything we've learned so far in code.

First, our request will go to a specific URL. It makes sense to store that URL as a variable:

```
base_url = 'https://nominatim.openstreetmap.org/search?'
```

Nominatim requires us to add at least two parameters:

- `format`: This will define the format of the data we'll get in return.
- q: This stands for the address query—in other words, the address we want to geocode.

Due to the way requests work, we need to store those parameters in a dictionary:

```
params = {
 'format':'json',
 'q': 'Eiffel Tower'
}
```

Finally, as we have everything we need now, we can send our request and get the answer. In the following snippet, we import the library and pass a GET request (using the get method of the library) to the URL we stored, passing the parameters we defined. We also store the response in a new variable:

```
import requests

result = requests.get(base_url, params=params)
```

Once we get the response, we can check the status code. 200 means that everything went well:

```
>>> result.status_code
200
```

Success! Now, let's take a look at the result. As we explicitly specified that we need the result to be in JSON format, we can safely convert it into a Python structure, and `requests` can do that easily. All we need to do is call the response's `json` method:

```
>>> result.json()
[{'place_id': '69121935',
  'licence': 'Data © OpenStreetMap contributors, ODbL 1.0.
https://osm.org/copyright',
  'osm_type': 'way',
  'osm_id': '5013364',
  'boundingbox': ['48.8574753', '48.8590465', '2.2933084', '2.2956897'],
  'lat': '48.8582602',
  'lon': '2.29449905431968',
  'display_name': 'Tour Eiffel, 5, Avenue Anatole France, Gros-Caillou, 7e,
Paris, Île-de-France, France métropolitaine, 75007, France',
  'class': 'tourism',
  'type': 'attraction',
  'importance': 0.653772102971417,
  'icon':
'https://nominatim.openstreetmap.org/images/mapicons/poi_point_of_interest.
p.20.png'},
  ...
]
```

The response is a list that contains 10 data points, representing different locations associated with the Eiffel Tower, sorted by their `importance` scores. The original tower is first—but there are many replicas built all over the world, as well. Those are also returned but have a smaller `importance` score, and so are placed lower on the list. Every single one has `osm_id`, coordinates, `display_name`, a link to the icon, a class, and a type. Here, 10 is a default limit of points to return—we can explicitly change it. Note that if Nominatim fails to find the address, it will return an empty list:

```
>>> params = {
    'format':'json',
    'q': 'Cair Paravel, Narnia', 'limit':1
    }
>>> requests.get(base_url, params=params).json()
[]
```

Now that we know the code is working, let's wrap all that into a clean and flexible function. As we don't want to hit the limits and cause trouble for OSM, we will delay our requests using a built-in function, `time.sleep`. Here is how we'll approach it. First, we'll import all the libraries we need, and store the base URL:

```
import requests
from time import sleep

base_url = 'https://nominatim.openstreetmap.org/search?'
```

Next, we can declare the function itself. As its arguments, we'll need an address itself, the format (that can be defaulted to JSON), the limit of points to return (we defaulted it to 1), and `kwargs` (keyword arguments)—those will be passed to parameters, as Nominatim has quite a few additional parameters for this API endpoint; in some cases, we might need them. In the function itself, we add a docstring (note that we added a link to the documentation in the function's docstring—this might save you tons of time in the future!):

```
def nominatim_geocode(address, format='json', limit=1, **kwargs):
    '''thin wrapper around nominatim API.
    Documentation: https://wiki.openstreetmap.org/wiki
    /Nominatim#Parameters
    '''
```

Next, we set the parameter dictionary, based on the function arguments. Note how we used unpacking to pass the key-value arguments of `kwargs` to this new dictionary. With that dictionary, we send a request and store the answer in a new variable—the same as how we did it previously. In order to be sure that the interaction went well, we use the `raise_for_status` method of `requests`, which will raise an exception if something goes wrong (that is, if the status code is not 200):

```
params = {"q": address, "format": format, "limit": limit, **kwargs}

response = requests.get(base_url, params=params)
response.raise_for_status()
```

Finally, we set the function to sleep for a second (that is more than enough, and we can adjust it to fit Nominatim's limitations properly in the future). Once that is done, we can finally return the result as parsed JSON. Here is how the code looks as a whole:

```
import requests
from time import sleep

base_url = 'https://nominatim.openstreetmap.org/search?'

def nominatim_geocode(address, format='json', limit=1, **kwargs):
    '''thin wrapper around nominatim API.
```

```
Documentation: https://wiki.openstreetmap.org/wiki
/Nominatim#Parameters
'''
params = {"q": address, "format": format, "limit":
          limit, **kwargs}

response = requests.get(base_url, params=params)
response.raise_for_status()
sleep(1)
return response.json()
```

Now, let's try our new function:

```
nominatim_geocode('Eiffel Tower')
```

```
>>> [{'place_id': '69121935',
'licence': 'Data © OpenStreetMap contributors, ODbL 1.0.
https://osm.org/copyright',
'osm_type': 'way',
'osm_id': '5013364',
'boundingbox': ['48.8574753', '48.8590465', '2.2933084', '2.2956897'],
'lat': '48.8582602', 'lon': '2.29449905431968',
'display_name': 'Tour Eiffel, 5, Avenue Anatole France, Gros-Caillou, 7e,
Paris, Île-de-France, France métropolitaine, 75007, France',
'class': 'tourism',
'type': 'attraction',
'importance': 0.653772102971417,
'icon':
'https://nominatim.openstreetmap.org/images/mapicons/poi_point_of_interest.
p.20.png'}
]
```

Perfect!

Remember how, at first, Nominatim gave us 10 different Eiffel Towers in different places around the world? Often, the addresses we have on hand are all in the same country or even city, and we'll know that—but, by default, Nominatim won't. In this case, we can make sure Nominatim looks in the specific area by specifying a countrycodes parameter, which represents one or multiple (joined with a comma) country codes, as in countrycodes='fr'. With a city, the situation is slightly different—Nominatim offers a structured address search, which means that you need to provide an address as a set of parameters, including the street (house number and street name), city, and additional information such as the county, state, country, and postal code.

The API documentation also states that this structured address should not be mixed with a query parameter, which totally makes sense, but makes it a little harder for us to use the preceding function. Luckily, `requests` will not add an argument to the URL if the value is `None`, so we can use `None` as a default value. In the following, we explicitly state the address as `None`, while passing a structured address (split into a set of parameters: country, city, and street):

```
nominatim_geocode(address=None, street='221B Baker Street', city='London',
country='Great Britain')

>>> [{'place_id': '50843439',
  'licence': 'Data © OpenStreetMap contributors, ODbL 1.0.
https://osm.org/copyright',
  'osm_type': 'node',
  'osm_id': '3916613190',
  'boundingbox': ['51.5237104', '51.5238104', '-0.1585445', '-0.1584445'],
  'lat': '51.5237604',
  'lon': '-0.1584945',
  'display_name': 'The Sherlock Holmes Museum, 221B, Baker Street,
Marylebone, City of Westminster, London, Greater London, England, NW1 6XE,
UK',
  'class': 'tourism',
  'type': 'museum',
  'importance': 0.5209999999999999,
  'icon':
'https://nominatim.openstreetmap.org/images/mapicons/tourist_museum.p.20.pn
g'}]
```

Perfect!

Now that we can work with the Nominatim API, we can start collecting some data. But how do we store it—and how would we read some addresses from another file? Let's see how that's done in the next section.

Caching with decorators

As you can see, geocoding takes time—working with a server takes time, as does being nice and waiting between requests. Thus, we probably don't want to waste time asking the same questions over and over again. For example, if many records within the same sessions have the same address, it makes sense to pull that data once, and then reuse it. Specifics may depend on the nature of the data. Namely, if we're checking air ticket availability, we shouldn't cache the results—the data might change any second. But for geolocation, we don't anticipate any changes any time soon.

The process of storing data we've pulled locally and then using it instead of getting the same data again is called caching. For example, all modern browsers do this—they cache some secondary elements of the web page for you to use and they're kept for a certain period of time. Caching can have different forms. We can store information in memory for the current session, or store it to a disk to be able to retrieve it in other sessions (or by other processes).

Here, we'll go with the first option—especially as everything we need is built into Python itself. All hail the `lru_cache` function, part of the `functools` standard library. The name **LRU** represents a specific algorithm we use and stands for **Least Recently Used**. `lru_cache` stores N last requests, starting with the most recent one (so that it will be retrieved faster). Once the limit is surpassed, the oldest values will be thrown out.

But how can we neatly intervene in the request process to pull local data or cache the new result? Here, we'll use one more trick from up Python's sleeve—**decorators**. Consider the following example:

```
def title(f):
    def _title(*args, **kwargs):
        return f'<h1>{f(arg)}</h1>'
    return _title
```

Here, `title` is a decorator function that wraps a given function, `f`, and returns another function that executes `f` from inside. Here is how it can be used:

```
>>> def mytext(x):
        return str(x)

>>> MyTitle = title(mytext)
>>> MyTitle('hello')
<h1>hello</h1>
```

In other words, we inject our function inside another one that can run something else before and/or after running it! The preceding operation is a little clumsy (and long)—that's why Python has decorators, which are merely a syntactic sugar to make this pattern shorter. Here is exactly the same code, using decorator:

```
>>> @title
>>> def MyTitle(x):
        return str(x)

>>> MyTitle('hello')
<h1>hello</h1>
```

As you can see, the actual function we're running is _title, which is using MyTitle inside—and we don't need to create this "initial" function. Neat! But when is it useful?

Actually, quite often! Decorators are usually nice when you need some sort of framework to take your code and run within a certain context. We'll see this pattern quite often in Chapter 17, *Let's Build a Dashboard*, and Chapter 18, *Serving Models with a RESTful APIs*—for many web-related frameworks, it is easy to decorate your code with the application, which will then route and execute a given function when needed.

Now, how is that connected to caching? Simple: because it follows the same pattern. For a given function, we can initiate a caching data store, and then on any invocation of a function, check whether the corresponding values are pulled already and use them if they are. If they are not, we can run the function, store data in the cache, and return the values. See? It is exactly the decorator pattern. And, indeed, here is how it might look (we show only the first lines of the function to keep it short):

```
from functools import lru_cache

@lru_cache(maxsize=2000)    # lru decorator added
def nominatim_geocode(address, format='json', limit=1, **kwargs):
    '''thin wrapper around nominatim API.
    ...
```

As you can see, using the cache required just two lines here: one to import the function, and another right before the function declaration. Here, maxsize means the maximum number of values to store before starting to drop the old ones. The great part is that we—or anyone using the code—don't need to change anything in the external code; everything looks like it was an ordinary function with no caching.

> lru_cache will only store results for the time of the session. If your script timed out or exits with an exception, everything is lost. If you want to store cached data to disk, consider using third-party tools, such as joblib or python-diskcache. Both can store information to disk and retrieve it from any session, as long as the files are intact.

Reading and writing data

Now that the function works, we can put it to work using any address, or an array of addresses using loops. For that, addresses could be copied and pasted into Jupyter, but that is not a sustainable solution. Most of the time, our data is stored somewhere in a database or a file. Let's learn how to read addresses from a file and store the results to another file.

CSV is a popular text-based format for tabular data, where each line represents a row and cells are separated by separator symbols—usually commas, but it could be a semicolon or a pipe. Cells containing separator or newline symbols are usually "escaped" using quotes. This format is not the most efficient, but it is widespread and easy to read using any text editor.

Python has a built-in library for dealing with .csv files—it is called csv. It has two ways to parse files: representing each row as a list or as a dictionary. We'll use the second approach:

```
from csv import DictReader, DictWriter
path = './cities.csv'

with open(path, 'r') as f:
    data = list(DictReader(f))
```

Here, DictReader is a generator that treats the first row of the CSV file as the header (which would be the column names) and uses it to create an ordered dictionary (which is just a standard dictionary with the order ensured) for each row. Its content requires the file to be open, so we need to either convert it to a list (storing all the data in memory) before closing the file or run all our geocoding within the scope of the open file. The second approach can handle a file of any size, storing only one row at a time in memory, but is more complex. So, for now, we'll stick with the first, simpler approach, which is still sufficient in the vast majority of cases.

Let's wrap this code into another function, and, since we're working with files, write another one to write CSV files:

```
def read_csv(path):
    '''read csv and return it as a list of dictionaries, one per row'''
    with open(path, 'r') as f:
        return list(DictReader(f))

def write_csv(data, path, mode='w'):
    '''write data to csv or append to existing one'''
    if mode not in 'wa':
        raise ValueError("mode should be either 'w' or 'a'")
    with open(path, mode) as f:
        writer = DictWriter(f, fieldnames=data[0].keys())
        if mode == 'w':
            writer.writeheader()

        for row in data:
            writer.writerow(row)
```

The preceding `store_csv` function is capable of writing a new file or appending data to an existing one, assuming it is similarly structured, without adding a header a second time. With this code, we can now read and write data!

For testing purposes, we prepared a tiny CSV file called `cities.csv`, which covers the top 10 largest cities in the world, according to the ArchDaily website (`https://www.archdaily.com/906605/the-20-largest-cities-in-the-world-of-2018`). Here is what the first two rows of the data look like:

Name	Population	Country
Tokyo	38.05	Japan
Jakarta	32.27	Indonesia

Before we start geocoding, let's test our reading function on this sample. We use the function we just wrote to read the file in the following sections.

Once it's done, we check the first element in the resulting list (the one representing the first row in the CSV file):

```
cities = read_csv('./cities.csv')
cities[0]
>>> OrderedDict([('name', 'Tokyo'), ('population', '38.05'), ('country', 'Japan')])
```

Again, for the sake of testing, let's try writing the data into another file:

```
write_csv(cities, './my_cities.csv')
```

Once the operation is done, feel free to check the new file. Having read all the addresses into memory, we are now ready to geocode!

Geocoding the addresses

Now we know how to read and write data, let's now loop over the addresses from the file and store the results into another `.csv` file. For that, we'll create another function that loops over the addresses and geocodes them one by one. One reason to do so is to make the code more robust; currently, if something goes wrong with a specific request (say, the address is not found), our geocode function will raise an error, halting the whole process and, potentially, leading to the loss of all previously geocoded data. Arguably, a better way would be to keep the script running and store the dataset, reporting issues and the corresponding rows of the original dataset separately. So, let's catch errors and append them and the corresponding rows to another list. If there are no issues but no results either, we'll print the address and go to the next one.

The process will take some time—at least a second for each row, and then some. To keep us informed and entertained while we wait, let's add a progress bar. For that, we'll use another popular library, `tqdm`, that does exactly that. The library is very easy to use. To get our progress bar, the only thing we need is to loop over a `tqdm` object, initiated with our original iterable as an argument. Take a look at the following:

```
>>> from tqdm import tqdm:
>>> collection = ['Apple', 'Banana', 'Orange]

>>> for fruit in tqdm(collection):
>>>     pass

100%|███████████████| 3/3 [00:1<00:00, 0.20s/it]
```

Here, we have a collection of three strings. To add a progress bar over a loop, we initiate a `tqdm` object to our collection and loop over it instead, as if it was the original collection. Easy!

Now, let's break the function we want to write into chunks and go over it. First of all, we declare the function itself, specifying the data; the `column` property in each dictionary to use as an address; and lastly, a Boolean argument, `verbose` (that is, if we want the function to be verbose on what is happening under the hood). After a docstring, we create two lists—one for the good geocode, and one for the errored values:

```
def geocode_bulk(data, column='address', verbose=False):
    '''assuming data is an iterable of dicts, will attempt
        to geocode each, treating {column} as an address.
        Returns 2 iterables - result and errored rows'''
    result, errors = [], []
```

Now we can build the loop. As we planned, let's wrap data into a `tqdm` object to get the loop. Within the loop, we'll try to run the geocode and check the result. If no result is found, and we're in `verbose` mode, the event can be printed and the row can be added to the results list. If Nominatim found something, we can merge the first result with our initial information and also store it in our results:

```
try:
    search = nominatim_geocode(row[column], limit=1)
    if len(search) == 0: # no location found:
        result.append(row)
        if verbose:
            print(f"Can't find anything for {row[column]}")
```

As we don't want to lose all our progress because of an error, we use `except` so that errors for a particular address (troubles with the internet connection, for example) will lead to an empty result for this specific address but won't cause the whole of the code to fail. In this case, we'll add an error message to the record and pass it to the `errors` list:

```
except Exception as e:
    if verbose:
        print(e)
    row['error'] = e
    errors.append(row)
```

Finally, we report the total number of errors, if in `verbose` mode, and return two lists. Here is the function as a whole:

```
from tqdm import tqdm

def geocode_bulk(data, column='address', verbose=False):
    '''assuming data is an iterable of dicts, will attempt to
        geocode each, treating {column} as an address.
        Returns 2 iterables - result and errored rows'''
    result, errors = [], []

    for row in tqdm(data):
        try:
            search = nominatim_geocode(row[column], limit=1)
            if len(search) == 0: # no location found:
                result.append(row)
                if verbose:
                    print(f"Can't find anything for {row[column]}")
            else:
                info = search[0] # most "important" result
                info.update(row) # merge two dicts
                result.append(info)
        except Exception as e:
            if verbose:
                print(e)
            row['error'] = e
            errors.append(row)
    if len(errors) > 0 and verbose:
        print(f'{len(errors)}/{len(data)} rows failed')

    return result, errors
```

Shall we try it out? It seems that it is working: it took us 13 seconds to geocode the cities by their name:

```
result, errors = geocode_bulk(cities, column='name', verbose=True)

100%|████████████████████| 10/10 [00:14<00:00,  1.40s/it]
```

As a result, we now have two lists: one with successfully geocoded addresses—including the latitude and longitude of each—and another with problematic entries. If there are any errored rows, we can make one more attempt to geocode them or investigate the causes and tweak either the code or the data.

The code we just wrote is rather opinionated, as we made many assumptions. For example, it uses only one column for geocoding, takes only the first geocode result, and can be very verbose; you might want to tailor it to your own needs or write different versions for different projects.

Let's now talk about how to store those useful functions so that we can use them (and we will) in the future.

Moving code to a separate module

Now we have everything to process data and get the coordinates in bulk. In the Jupyter Notebook, this could be something as short as the following three lines, assuming we have the path_in and path_out variables predefined (of course, here we don't actually do anything with the errors):

```
path_in = './cities.csv'
path_out = './geocoded.csv'

data = read_csv(path_in)
result, errors = geocode_bulk(data, column='address', verbose=True)
write_csv(result, path_out)
```

It is not very convenient, however, to fire up Jupyter and run through all the cells every time just to load the functions we write. Instead, we can store our functions in a separate module—a text file with the .py extension—and import the functions from there.

Let's create a new text file using Visual Studio Code (which is what we recommend). Here is what you should do:

1. Create a new file and call it geocode.py in the same folder as that for the notebooks we run.

2. Once the file is open, copy and paste all the functions we created so far in the file. Visual Studio Code will highlight all possible mistypes and list code issues in the **PROBLEMS** section for you.

3. Once the file is ready, we can return back to Jupyter and import the code from this file (no need to use the extension) just as if it was a library:

```
from geocode import nominatim_geocode
result = nominatim_geocode('Eiffel Tower')
```

 This is important! For the preceding code to work, `geocode.py` needs to be in the same folder as a Jupyter Notebook. If you want to call this module from somewhere else, you need to either copy (or `symlink`) the code, or (better) create a package, which we'll do in Chapter 15, *Packaging and Testing with Poetry and PyTest*.

Of course, you can also import specific functions—or even variables, if you want. This ability to use Python files as modules is very useful. All the generic code that can be used for a broad range of applications, and all the code that is too long and not as relevant for the notebooks, should be moved into Python files and imported. This will improve notebook readability and helps you reuse existing code in other projects.

Now that we know how to move the code, let's see how to collect the data in the next section.

Collecting NYC Open Data from the Socrata service

In Chapter 12, *Data Exploration and Visualization*, Chapter 16, *Data Pipelines with Luigi*, Chapter 17, *Let's Build a Dashboard*, Chapter 18, *Serving Models with a RESTful API*, and Chapter 19, *Serverless API Using Chalice*, we'll be working with the New York City 311 complaints (a non-urgent version of the 911 service) dataset. This data is available via a public portal (https://data.cityofnewyork.us/Social-Services/311-Service-Requests-from-2010-to-Present/erm2-nwe9), both via a web interface and programmatically via an API. The code for pulling this data via the API is rather dull and similar to what we've written already, so we won't cover it in detail. In Chapter 16, *Data Pipelines with Luigi*, we'll discuss how to pull this dataset systematically and on a scheduled basis. If you want, however, feel free to check out the code—we added a corresponding file to this chapter's folder.

So, that is all there is for collection.

Summary

We've done a lot in this chapter. First, we learned about geocoding in general, including geocoding services and their web APIs. We also discussed how you can interact with web APIs programmatically, from Python, using the `requests` library. Then, we experimented with a specific API from Nominatim and wrote a thin wrapper function that geocodes any arbitrary address. On top of that, we wrote another function to geocode addresses in bulk that keeps working even if a specific request fails or no location was found for some addresses. We used the built-in `csv` library both to read data from and write to CSV files. Finally, as the code we used seemed as though it might be useful in the future, we moved it from a notebook into a dedicated Python file, which can be used as a standalone script with its own interface or as a module to import functions from.

In the next chapter, we'll go even further, covering cases when there is no simple API so data has to be scraped from raw HTML pages.

Questions

1. What is an API? Why would we use it?
2. What do the various HTTP response status codes mean?
3. Is there a built-in library for dealing with HTTP? Why do we use `requests` instead?
4. How do you define command-line interface parameters for Python scripts?
5. What does `if __name__ == '__main__'` mean and why do we need it at the end of a script?

Further reading

- *Hands-On RESTful API Design Patterns and Best Practices* by Pethuru Raj, Harihara Subramanian, Packt Publishing (`https://www.packtpub.com/application-development/hands-restful-api-design-patterns-and-best-practices`)
- *What is REST?* (`https://restfulapi.net/`)

7
Scraping Data from the Web with Beautiful Soup 4

In the previous chapter, we wrote a piece of code that communicates with the Nominatim web service in order to collect information. Frequently, however, there is no API in place, and data could be scattered throughout hundreds of web pages, or, even worse, files with a complex structure (PDFs). In this chapter, we'll explore another data collection path—scraping raw HTML pages. In order to do so, we will use another library, Beautiful Soup 4, which can parse raw HTML files into objects, and help us to sift through them, extracting bits of information. Using this tool, we will collect a relatively large dataset of historic battles of World War II, which we will, in the chapters to come, process, clean, and analyze.

In this chapter, we will cover the following topics:

- When there is no API
- Scraping WWII battles
- Beyond Beautiful Soup

Technical requirements

In this chapter, we'll make use of `requests` and `BeautifulSoup` libraries—both are included in the Anaconda distribution. If you don't use Anaconda, make sure to have them both installed. Given that you will scrape data from the web, an internet connection is also required. As usual, the code for this chapter is stored in `Chapter07` folder in the GitHub repository, `https://github.com/PacktPublishing/Learn-Python-by-Building-Data-Science-Applications`.

When there is no API

As with API services, web pages have their owners, and they may or may not be open to the idea of scraping their data. If there is an API in place, this is always preferred over scraping, for the following reasons:

- First, it is usually way better and simpler to use, and there are a number of guarantees that API owners will retain its structure, or at least let you know of upcoming changes in advance. With HTML web pages, there is no guarantee whatsoever; the website will often change, and they won't tell you ahead of time, so expect lots of emergency breaking changes!
- Second, being a good citizen, it is substantially cheaper, computation-wise, to serve raw data than a full-blown HTML page, so the service owners will be thankful.
- Lastly, some data (for example, historic changes) will not be available via the web page.

However, there are plenty of examples of web pages with no API. Some information is not intended for sharing (for example, electronic shops are not excited about their prices being tracked), and many organizations simply don't have the capacity to maintain them.

As a practical exercise, we will now scrape data from Wikipedia, which is, paradoxically, both an extremely good and extremely bad example of a website to scrape. It is a great example because Wikipedia fully supports scraping; in fact, it openly shares the whole dataset, so we can download and work with it if we want. At the same time, it is a bad example, because, by its very nature, Wikipedia has no strict template and data structure – every page can be unique in its structure and layout, and even a raw dataset won't change that. Most of the websites are pre-generated using the same templates, so data scraping, on average, is easier. But it is always dirty, semi-manual hard work.

But before we dive into coding, let's discuss what HTML is and how to work with it.

HTML in a nutshell

You are probably aware that web pages are written in three main languages – HTML, CSS, and JavaScript, of which only the latter is an actual language. In this triad, CSS is used to style objects visually, for example, set the color or font of the elements. JavaScript is a language that runs on the client's machine, and allows basic interactions on the website – for example, sending information back to the server, and selecting elements from the drop-down menu.

The main body of a page is described with HTML. Its goal is to present the hierarchy and the layout of the page. HTML is a subset of XML, a general-purpose markup language, designed specifically for web pages. Like XML, HTML describes the document via nested series of objects, defined with tags. It has a large nomenclature of those objects, each describing specific behavior. For example, the `<ol>` tag describes an ordered list; its children elements, `<li>`, will be enumerated. Similarly, `<table>` describes a table (duh), and the `<a>` element represents links. Each element can have the following:

- Internal text.
- Child elements.
- An ID attribute – unique identification for a specific element.
- A class attribute – non-unique type identification. One or more classes and IDs help to apply specific designs and interactions to the right elements.
- Any other attribute. For example, `<a>` elements encode their link as an `href` attribute (a hyperlink reference).

For the sake of scraping, we don't really need to understand how elements behave and differ from one another. Scrapers usually use a combination of element names, properties (IDs, classes, and so on), their relative position, and the content to find specific elements. As pages tend to differ slightly both in structure and content, in order to scrape, we have to understand the logic of the page builder, which might be tricky.

It is important to note that this approach works only with the pre-generated, static content on the page.

Most modern pages use JavaScript – client-side code, in order to execute some interactions; for example, to send a note to Google Analytics, or adjust the layout depending on the window size. Some, however, use JavaScript intensively; for example, for data acquisition (for example, the Facebook news feed). Beautiful Soup does not run JavaScript, so it won't work with these kinds of systems. There are ways to overcome this limitation, for example, by using special headless browsers. This approach, however, is significantly more complex and computation-demanding. We'll talk a little bit more about this topic and how to scrape JavaScript-intensive pages in the final section of this chapter.

Scraping with Beautiful Soup 4

Any publicly accessible HTTP can be pulled with a `requests` library. As you remember, if the resulting value is stored as a JSON, `requests` have a built-in parsing method. For HTML, it is different: parsing HTML is no simple task. It is much more complex than your ordinary JSON; HTML files are large and can be invalid (browsers will often still "fix" and render them).

In order to do so, we'll be using **Beautiful Soup 4 (BS4)**, one of the two main libraries for parsing HTML, together with **LXML**. Beautiful Soup also knows how to parse HTML, and can even repair invalid files. Once the document has Pythonic representation, we can drill down and retrieve specific elements we're interested in by using a combination of element ID, class, CSS properties, their order, and so on using either CSS selectors or the XPath mini-language.

CSS and XPath selectors

As mentioned previously, Beautiful Soup parses the HTML from string to a Python object. Even parsed, this structure is not an easy thing to navigate. This is especially true for bulk retrieval when we operate on multiple pages at once due to the dynamic nature of the web. Even the same page can change constantly, with some elements being added or removed, let alone different pages, even those with apparently the same structure. This is the moment when you'll start appreciating well-defined and stable APIs!

To navigate HTML document structures, also known as **Document Object Models (DOMs)**, two common and widely adopted techniques are used. The first one, CSS Selectors, is a pattern language built to work with HTML and identify elements using a combination of the element type, class, and ID properties, their nested structure, and a number of other options. Here is a full example of a CSS Selector for the main image on an arbitrary Wikipedia page:

```
body div#content.mw-body div#bodyContent.mw-body-content div@mw-content-
text.mw-content-itr div.mw-parser-output table.infobox.vevent tbody tr td
a.image img
```

As you can see, it is a very specific sequence of HTML elements – `div` tags, `table`, table body, table row, `image`, and so on.

Many of those elements have IDs – unique identifiers for the exact elements. IDs are defined after the element type, separated by the # symbol. Any element can have only one ID, and IDs are supposed to be unique, but that won't break the page.

Some elements have one or multiple classes – non-unique identifiers. Classes are not unique, so HTML elements can have any number of classes at the same time. Also, classes are separated by the dot (.) element.

The sequence of elements represents the required nesting structure for writing a code—for example, an element that fits the preceding pattern needs to be an image, nested within an a element with a class image, and nested within a td element.

This makes the preceding query extremely specific for scraping purposes; any change to this structure will break the retrieval, so we need to design a query that is as simple and general as possible so that it doesn't break, but specific enough to pull the correct information. Defining such queries is almost an art by itself. An example of an arguably better query for the same element could be something like the following:

```
table.infobox.vevent a.image img
```

This query is much shorter! The trick here is that the sequence does not require nesting to be direct or complete (for direct nesting, a > symbol can be used). We start by specifying that we're only interested in a table with two classes, infobox and vevent. In that table, we're looking at the a element with the image class, and pulling an image (img element) from it. Of course, there is a change here. There will be more than one image on the page. Inside that table, we can either decide to pull all of them, or just the first occurrence, by using a corresponding retrieval command in Python or adding :first-of-type to the CSS. There are many other properties and tricks of querying with CSS. To learn more, check out the Mozilla CSS documentation (https://developer.mozilla.org/en-US/docs/Web/css).

CSS attributes are at the core of navigation and the querying of HTML, but we don't have to use a CSS Selector to run a query. While CSS querying is usually short and readable, they don't provide advanced tooling for operating the structure of the document, for example, going *up* the document tree, or of the sibling elements. An alternative tool, one that can be used beyond HTML, is XPath, the XML path language. XPath has a lot of flexibility and power when it comes to locating objects.

XPath can sometimes look like a filesystem path – nesting is represented by a slash, while a double slash means recursive nesting (more than one level inside). Elements can be indexed with square brackets (similar to Python iterables). The existence of a certain attribute, or the matching of certain criteria (predicates), can also be specified within square brackets (we'll see a similar approach in Python, in `Chapter 11`, *Data Cleaning and Manipulation*). For example, here is the same query as earlier, but using XPath:

```
//table[contains(@class, 'infobox') and contains(@class,
'vevent')]//a[contains(@class, 'image')]//img
```

As you can see, this path is much longer! In fact, it has some problems as well – `contains` only checks for partial inclusion, so theoretically, `contains(@class, 'vevent')` will also match a class name such as `veventTest`. This may be a problem for some cases, but not in ours. Despite being verbose, on many other occasions, XPath works better than CSS, especially regarding the bulk retrieval of values. If you want more information on XPath, MDN (`https://developer.mozilla.org/en-US/docs/Web/XPath`) keeps you covered, again.

Both CSS Selectors and XPath are capable of retrieving almost any set of elements from a page. In addition, Beautiful Soup itself has quite a few tricks of its own. Here, we're using only CSS Selectors, as Beautiful Soup does not support XPath (LXML does, however).

Building a proper scraper requires a lot of testing and manual sifting through the web page to get the structure of HTML and CSS attributes just right. An invaluable tool at our disposal to this end is a browser developer console; both Chrome and Firefox have one. Let's have a look.

Developer console

Before we pull specific elements of a page, we first need to know where to search for them. In order to understand the page structure, we'll use the Chrome Developer console, which is built into the Chrome browser. Firefox has a similar tool – Firefox Developer Tools.

In order to see the HTML structure of any page, simply open it in Chrome, hover over any specific element of the page, right-click on the mouse button, and select **Inspect**—a new window will appear, showing a page's HTML centered on the element you just hovered over (refer to the following diagram):

Note that when you hover over other elements in this new window, corresponding elements on the page are highlighted. Now, go to the element you're interested in – find it in this new window. Notice the line following the window – it describes the path from the root of the document all the way to the element you see. This path is very important for us—we will use it to pull specific values from the path from Python.

Let's now see how all of this works in practice.

Scraping WWII battles

The goal of this chapter is to collect the information on all battles in WWII from Wikipedia. A corresponding list is provided: `https://en.wikipedia.org/wiki/List_of_World_War_II_battles`. As you can see, it contains links to a large set of pages, one for each battle, operation, and campaign. Furthermore, the list is structured, so battles are grouped according to the campaign or operation, which are, in turn, grouped by the theaters – it would be great to preserve this hierarchy! Most elements of the list also have a date. We'll work with those lists in a minute.

Now, if you check a couple of pages for specific battles, you may notice that they have a similar structure. For most of them, the large information card on the right has a set of similar subsections, including the main section with dates, locations, and outcomes, and a few additional sections, such as strengths, commanders, casualties, and belligerents. This is great news – we can use this structure to write generally applicable code, and collect specific information for each battle in a uniform fashion.

Given all that, the task can be executed in three steps:

1. First, we'll collect all the links and names from the initial list of battles, preserving the nested nature.
2. Next, we will create a scraper that will extract specific information, such as locations, dates, sides, leaders, and casualties from a page pertaining to a particular battle.
3. Finally, we will loop over all the links we collected in the first part and collect information for each.

In doing so, we will try to use several approaches that we have found to be useful:

- Write simple, universal functions first, moving all decisions and opinions to the functions of a higher level.
- Collect and store raw data – clean and process it afterward. Any exception or error might lead to the loss of the data.
- Don't clean data within the scraper – it will be way easier to do that afterward, in bulk, having the "raw" data as a reference.

Let's do it!

 The scraper we're building in this chapter does work at the time of writing. It may be broken in the future, however, by any design change in the Wikipedia page. This is the unfortunate nature of scrapers.

Step 1 – Scraping the list of battles

Let's start with scraping the main page. For that, let's go through a few steps.

First, we need to collect the main page as a string, using the `requests` library – the same way we pulled the information from Nominatim, using the HTTP `GET` request via the library's `get` method:

```
import requests as rq

base_url = 'https://en.wikipedia.org/wiki/List_of_World_War_II_battles'
response = rq.get(url)
```

We can access the raw content of the page via `response.content`.

Next, we need to parse this string into a Python representation of the page using BS4:

```
from bs4 import BeautifulSoup
soup = BeautifulSoup(response.content, 'html.parser')
```

Perfect! To structure the code, we create a new function, `get_dom` (**DOM** stands for **Document Object Model**), which encloses all the preceding code:

```
def get_dom(url):
    response = rq.get(url)
    response.raise_for_status()
    return BeautifulSoup(response.content, 'html.parser')
```

Next, once we have a parsed DOM, it is a good idea to specify the area of the page we'll be working in – the main content element. Using the Chrome Developer console, we can observe that the main text is stored within the `div` element with the `mw-parser-output` class, wrapped into another `div` element that has the `mw-content-text` ID. Let's now use that information to get it in Python, using BS4.

Beautiful Soup has three separate ways to search for an element – `find`, `find_all`, and `select`. The first and second approaches expect you to pass an object type and, optionally, attributes. A recursive argument defines whether the search should be recursive (deeper than one level in). The difference between these approaches is subtle – the first method will only retrieve the first occurrence. The second one, in contrast, will always return a list with all the elements. Finally, `select` will also return a list – and expects you to pass a single CSS Selector string. Because of that, it is easier to specify a nested element to retrieve:

```
content = soup.select('div#mw-content-text > div.mw-parser-output',
limit=1)[0]
```

The objects they return are similar to the root BS4 object, but only cover the corresponding section of the page.

In the next step, we need to collect the corresponding elements for each front, in our case, h2 headers. All fronts are organized as sections – each section has a title (the h2 element), but hierarchically, titles are not nested within the sections; all section content sits just below the corresponding title. There is also the last title that we don't care about – citations and notes. One way to filter would be just to drop the last element. Alternatively, we could use a CSS Selector trick, using the following predicate: :not(:last-of-type). To keep things simple and readable, we'll just drop the last element in the list in this case:

```
fronts = content.select('div.mw-parser-output>h2')[:-1]
```

Here, we are searching for all h2 headers in the content section, with no recursion. Did we collect all the correct titles? Let's check! To remove the [edit] element from the title, we simply remove the final six characters:

```
>>> for el in fronts:
>>>     print(el.text[:-6])
African Front
Mediterranean Front
Western Front
Atlantic Ocean
Eastern Front
Indian Ocean
Pacific Theatre
China Front
Southeast Asia Front
```

This looks correct. Now we have all the fronts!

But how can we get the corresponding ul lists for each header? This may seem like a problem – we need to retrieve elements that are based on, and associated with, other elements on the same level. Luckily, BS4 can take care of that using the find_next_siblings method. It works exactly like find_all, except that it won't look within the element but in the overarching document starting right after it. In other words, BS4 objects don't only store information on given HTML element – they are aware of the HTML document as a whole.

Take a look at the following code snippet, we're taking the first title by using 0 as an index, and then we run the method, passing the query properties—it should be a ul element within the first div with three classes: div-col, columns, and column-width:

```
>>> fronts[0].find_next_siblings("div", "div-col columns column-
width")[0].ul
<ul><li><a href="/wiki/North_African_Campaign" title="North African
Campaign">North African Campaign</a>.....
```

It worked! We asked BS4 to find all the div elements with the "div-col columns column-width" classes, after each header. There are many of them, but only the first div element is related to the header. Thus, we need to retrieve the first one and obtain the underlying ul element. And that is what we're going to do in the next section.

Unordered list

But how can we collect all the information from the nested list simultaneously? This seems like a proper task for recursion – for each element of the list, we will store the link and the date (where this exists), and, if it has some nested elements, we'll run the same function on them as well. To keep track of the nesting levels, we also add a level property. Consider the following example. It may seem overly complex at first, but all those try/else and if statements keep the code working if some values are missing—the function will still work if there is no date, or link, or nested elements. We're also using next as we don't want to get all the text elements (and waste time and memory on them); we only need the first two:

```
def dictify(ul, level=0):
    result = dict()
    for li in ul.find_all("li", recursive=False):
        text = li.stripped_strings
        key = next(text)
        try:
            time = next(text).replace(':', '').strip()
        except StopIteration:
            time = None
        ul, link = li.find("ul"), li.find('a')
        if link:
            link = _abs_link(link.get('href'))
        r ={'url': link,
            'time':time,
            'level': level}
        if ul:
            r['children'] = dictify(ul, level=(level + 1))
        result[key] = r
    return result
```

This function is not very elegant, but it does its job. Now, let's try running it on all the fronts:

```
theaters = {}

for front in fronts:
    list_element = front.find_next_siblings("div", "div-col columns column-
width")[0].ul
        theaters[front.text[:-6]] = dictify(list_element)
```

If you want, you can print the resulting data out – it works! Now, we have all the links – all that is left is to scrape them. But first, let's store what we have obtained so far as a JSON file. For that, we need to open the file as we did with the CSVs, in `'w'` (write) mode. Once that is done, we can use the `json` package to dump the dictionary into the file. Take a look at the following snippet:

```
import json

with open('all_battles.json', 'w') as f:
    json.dump(theaters, f)
```

That was easy! Now, let's parse the information from a specific battle's page.

 In this chapter, and generally throughout the book, we are trying to keep basic functions simple and universal – so that they can be used repeatedly without any change. All specific decisions are made on a higher level. This is not only helping to reuse the code; it also makes it more transparent and predictable. You won't need to remember all the decisions you made on the lower level.

Step 2 – Scraping information from the Wiki page

As we need to start from something, let's pick a battle page to test our code on – Operation Skorpion (`en.wikipedia.org//wiki/Operation_Skorpion`). The following is a screenshot of the page, with the areas in which we're interested highlighted in red:

The code for this part of the chapter is stored in the
`B_Scraping_part_2` notebook.

First, we can use the function we wrote in the earlier section to collect the page as a `dom` object:

```
url = 'https://en.wikipedia.org/wiki/Opeation_Scorpion'
dom = get_dom(url)
```

Next, as in the previous case, we select the larger container that stores all the information we're interested in – in this case, the info card (the larger, dotted red rectangle on the screenshot). All the information we're interested in (dates, location, outcomes, belligerents, and casualties) is there, below the map:

```
table = dom.find('table','infobox vevent')
```

Now that we have the card, all we need is to pull all the information out of it, which we'll do in the next section.

Key information

Key information is stored right below the map and includes dates, locations, and outcomes. Let's call this section the main one. As you can see via the developer console, this section is designed as a table with two columns – the first column representing a key (metric names), and the second, corresponding values. Indeed, it is very similar to how dictionaries are structured, so let's write a generic converter from this two-column table to a dictionary. Take a look at the following snippet. Here, we traverse through rows, adding the value of the first column as a key, and the second as a value, to the dictionary:

```
def _table_to_dict(table):
    result = {}
    for row in table.find_all('tr'):
        result[row.th.text] = row.td.get_text().strip()
    return result
```

Now, we can select the section and parse it. Again, we can find all rows in the info card and select this section by its order, but this approach will fail if there are a different number of sections or a different order. In contrast to the previous task, we cannot tolerate this now; given the dozens of links we have to hand, we have to write robust code that can work with any structure. So, instead of the order, let's search by the content – say, all sections containing the Location string. In the following code snippet, we do precisely that – traverse through all the tables within the info card, and pull only those with the Location word inside. Assuming that there is only one such table per page, we then pull the first one and transform it into a dictionary:

```
def _get_main_info(table):
    main = [el for el in table.tbody.find_all('tr', recursive=False) if
'Location' in el.get_text()][0]
    return {'main': _table_to_dict(main) }
```

Now, let's test it by running table we pulled from the Operation Skorpion page. As you can see here, it seems to work perfectly:

```
>>> _get_main_info(table)
{'main': {'Date': '26–27 May 1941', 'Location': 'Halfaya Pass, Egypt31°30′N
25°11′E\ufeff / \ufeff31.500°N 25.183°E\ufeff / 31.500; 25.183Coordinates:
31°30′N 25°11′E\ufeff / \ufeff31.500°N 25.183°E\ufeff / 31.500; 25.183',
'Result': 'Axis victory', 'Territorial': 'Axis re-captured Halfaya Pass'}}
```

Of course, the location string is a mess, but we should resist the temptation to parse it right now – *all parsing should be done once the data is collected!* Also, as you'll see, many pages won't have geocoordinates, so our attempt to parse those would fail in any case. Next, let's collect the supplementary information from each page.

Additional information

There is a lot of additional information on the page that we'd want to have in the dataset – sections such as belligerents, leaders, strengths, and casualties (refer to the lower rectangle on the screenshot in *Step 2 – Scraping information from the Wiki page* section, named **Supplemental info**). As you can see, each header here is a row in the table – and all the actual information sits beneath it – similar to lists after headers in the previous task. You will also observe that most of the sections are split horizontally into two cells, the first being on allies, and the second on the axis. In fact, in some cases (refer to the Vilnius Offensive page), Wikipedia adds third column for a third party involved in the event. For operation Skorpion, some sections have only one column, representing overall outcomes (for example, the total number of casualties), while for others (Operation Goodwood—https:// en.wikipedia.org/wiki/Operation_Goodwood), casualties are split between the two sides involved. This needs to be addressed as well.

All titles appear to be consistent throughout all the pages. Thus, we can search for specific headers – and if there are any, grab the corresponding data from the section beneath each. Here is the code snippet that does exactly that; it looks for a header, and if there is one, takes the next section:

```
def _find_row_by_header(table, string):
    header = table.tbody.find('tr', text=string)

    if header is not None:
        return header.next_sibling
```

Now that we know how to get each section, let's parse them. The following code checks for the number of rows in the table. If there is only one, it will be stored as total. If there are two or more, they will receive corresponding columns – allies, axis, and third party:

```
def _parse_row(row, names=('allies', 'axis', 'third party')):
    '''parse secondory info row
    as dict of info points
    '''
    cells = row.find_all('td', recursive=False)
    if len(cells) == 1:
        return {'total':cells[0].get_text().strip()}

    return {name:cell.get_text().strip() for name, cell in zip(names,
cells)}
```

The order of belligerents is assumed to be consistent within the same page. Unfortunately, the order of sides differs from page to page, and we failed to find any rationale for this. Thus, the column that we're calling `axis` may actually refer to the `allies` side – we will have to fix that during the data cleaning process in Chapter 11, *Data Cleaning and Manipulation.*

Let's now collect all the additional information together, using a predefined set of headers to look for:

```
def _additional(table):
    keywords = (
        'Belligerents',
        'Commanders and leaders',
        'Strength',
        'Casualties and losses',
    )
    result = {}
    for keyword in keywords:
        try:
            data = _find_row_by_header(table, keyword)
            if data:
                result[keyword] = _parse_row(data)
        except Exception as e:
            raise Exception(keyword, e)
    return result
```

Note that the exception here is used to show the keyword for which the issue is raised, thereby facilitating debugging.

Finally, let's wrap all the code for the page into one function that we'll run on all links:

```
def parse_battle_page(url):
    ''' main function to parse battle urls from wikipedia
    '''
    try:
        dom = _default_collect(url) # dom
    except Exception as e:
        warnings.warn(str(e))
        return {}


    table = dom.find('table','infobox vevent') # info table
    if table is None: # some campaigns don't have table
        return {}

    data = _get_main_info(table)
    data['url'] = url
```

```
    additional = _additional(table)
    data.update(additional)
    return data
```

The preceding `try/except` clause helps to catch an exception if there is no such page – we got one broken link in our database. You can find it on the initial page; it is highlighted in red.

Now, as an added bonus, all the operation and campaign pages have the same structure, so we collect all the info from them, using the same code. Nice!

To ensure that we have addressed most of the issues, test the code on a set of links, ideally, the most diverse and exotic ones. As the preceding code will be used in another notebook, it makes sense to copy it to a dedicated `.py` file.

Step 3 – Scraping data as a whole

Finally, we have all the links and code to scrape information from each one of them.

The code for this subsection can be found in the `C_Scraping_part3` notebook.

First, let's import all the code we will require, and read the file with links:

```python
import json
from wiki import parse_battle_page
import time

with open('./all_battles.json', 'r') as f:
    campaigns = json.load(f)
```

Once again, we need to write a recursive function that will scrape data for a given event and call itself for all nested events:

```python
def _parse_in_depth(element, name):
    '''attempts to scrape data for every
    element with url attribute – and all the children
    if there are any'''
    if 'children' in element:
        for k, child in element['children'].items():
            parsed = _parse_in_depth(child, k)
            element['children'][k].update(parsed)
    if element.get('url', None):
```

```
            try:
                element.update(parse_battle_page(element['url']))
            except Exception as e:
                raise Exception(name, e)
        time.sleep(.1) # let's be good citizens!
        return element
```

Note that we actively use the `try`/`except` clause as it helps to understand the specific page that needs to be resolved. Often, it is enough to look at the actual page to understand the problem.

Fronts and campaigns do not have links themselves. In order to pull information on all battles, we need to use a double loop. In the following code snippet, we loop over all fronts. For each front, we add a new key to the dictionary and start looping over the campaign links for this front. From here, our battle page parser can take over:

```
campaigns_parsed = {}

for fr_name, front in campaigns.items():
    print(fr_name)
    campaigns_parsed[fr_name] = {}
    for cp_name, campaign in front.items():
        print(f' {cp_name}')
        campaigns_parsed[fr_name][cp_name] = _parse_in_depth(campaign,
cp_name)
```

This process may take some time, mostly because we asked Python to sleep on each element. Note that scraping failed for one link – Operation Wotan. It seems that this operation is fictional, and the Wiki community decided to remove the page, which is fair enough, and the good part is that this didn't cause our code to stop, so all the other pages are collected.

Once it's done, let's check the overall quality of the data we just pulled. More on that in the next section.

Quality control

As we mentioned already, there are plenty of issues with this data, as web pages are very different in terms of their structure and offer different sets of information, formatted differently. There are a lot of issues in the code – cleaning all of it will take another chapter (and indeed, that's what we'll do in Chapter 11, *Data Cleaning and Manipulation*). It is good practice, however, to perform a modicum of basic quality control, verifying that all the pages have some minimal, requisite properties, and that they are not null. We could also add some other checks, ensuring, for example, that the additional fields are not empty, at least for a significant number of the pages.

The approach we'll be using is two-fold. First, we'll try to define a list of values we're assuming are required for each record. Second, we already know that some information will be missing for some of the pages, so let's at least calculate it. In order to do so, we define one dictionary to store all the information. At the start, it will contain only zeros. Consider the following example. Here, we cover all the battles we'll check (total), records with missing locations, outcomes, and territorial sections. In addition, we'll calculate a number of records with only total values for Casualties, Commanders, and Strength in the total section. Similarly, we will check how many records are devoid of those sections:

```
STATISTICS = {
    'battles_checked':0,
    'location_null':0,
    'result_null':0,
    'territorial_null': 0,
    'total': {
        'Casualties and losses':0,
        'Commanders and leaders':0,
        'Strength':0
    },
    'none': {
        'Casualties and losses':0,
        'Commanders and leaders':0,
        'Strength':0
    }
}
```

Once the data structure is defined, let's write a checking function. It is a rather simple one, in keeping with the others. It is recursive, as it calls itself on all the children of a given record.

Note that we check for required values at the outset. In the end, we only kept the `level` value as a required attribute:

```
def qa(battle, name='Unknown'):
    required = (
        # 'Location'
        # 'url',
        'level',
    )
    for el in required:
        assert el in battle and battle[el] is not None, (name, el)

    STATISTICS['battles_checked'] +=1
    for el in 'Location', 'Result', 'Territorial':
        if el not in battle or battle[el] is None:
            STATISTICS[f'{el.lower()}_null'] += 1
    for el in 'Casualties and losses', 'Commanders and leaders',
    'Strength':
        if el not in battle:
            STATISTICS['none'][el] += 1
            continue
        if 'total' in battle[el]:
            STATISTICS['total'][el] += 1
    if 'children' in battle:
        for name, child in battle['children'].items():
            qa(child, name)
```

With this function, we can now loop over the records and check our statistics:

```
for _, front in campaigns_parsed.items():
    for name, campaign in front.items():
        qa(campaign, name)
```

The preceding function, as defined, passes all the tests. But why did we remove `url` and `Location` from required? It transpires that some records do miss them – for example, `Battle of Lang Son` does not have a link at all, while a few others (for example, the French West Africa—https://en.wikipedia.org/wiki/French_West_Africa_in_World_War_II page) are missing `Location` and `Date`. In this case, we decided to relax our requirements but to add a note on those missing records. Feel free to modify the test – this will give you an insight into some of the different types of issues we'll have to mitigate with this dataset in the future.

Once the test is over, we can check the statistics:

```
>>> STATISTICS

{'battles_checked': 624,
 'location_null': 37,
 'result_null': 40,
 'territorial_null': 553,
 'total': {'Casualties and losses': 7,
  'Commanders and leaders': 3,
  'Strength': 2},
 'none': {'Casualties and losses': 83,
  'Commanders and leaders': 44,
  'Strength': 109}}
```

Most records are missing a territorial section – and quite a few don't have any information on the overall strength. Again, it is a good idea to collect that information for the future. For now, let's store the dataset we obtained to another JSON:

```
with open('_all_battles_parsed.json', 'w') as f:
    json.dump(campaigns_parsed, f)
```

And we're done! The three steps in this section will help you to scrape up the data and present it accordingly.

Beyond Beautiful Soup

In this example, we used the BS4 library to parse static HTML for us. Beautiful Soup is an invaluable library for dealing with occasionally messy HTML, but when it comes to large scales and dynamic pages, it simply won't suffice. For production scraping in large quantities, perhaps on a regular basis, it is a good idea to utilize the Scrapy (https://scrapy.org/) package. Scrapy is an entire framework for downloading HTML, parsing data, pulling data, and then storing it. One of its killer features is that it can run asynchronously – for example, while it is waiting for one page to load, it can switch to processing another, automatically. Because of that, Scrapy's scrapers are significantly faster on large lists of websites. At the same time, its interface is more expressive for a developer, as it is explicitly designed for scraping.

Depending on your goal, other alternatives may be available as well. For example, a marvelous package, newspaper (https://newspaper.readthedocs.io/en/latest/), can collect data (articles) from news websites – it has built-in configurations for the most popular ones, but also performs reasonably well on others with little guidance (for example, it can find the body of an article on the page).

Now, the elephant in the room is that in all those cases, we only use static content – HTML that is returned by the server when you get data from a URL. However, many modern sites actively add content after the initial page is loaded – for example, they add an infinite scroll by pulling new pieces of HTML while you scroll, a few steps ahead of you. If you need this information, none of those tools will suffice. In this case, you'll have to emulate the browser, rendering pages as if you were actually looking at them, running JavaScript, and so on. For this, people use Selenium – a browser automation system that can emulate a full-blown browser.

Selenium can pull a page, render the browser into an image, perform actions (for example, click on a button or scroll), and get you the resulting HTML. There is only one caveat – the process will be incredibly slow in this case. A more modern alternative is to use Splash, a JavaScript renderer written in the Lua language. It is somewhat faster than Selenium and does have integration with Scrapy, but is not as mature.

Scraping is no easy task. Ever-changing websites, data with no single structure, and developers trying to prevent you from scraping can make your work hard. In this environment, it is especially important to pick the right tool and design your code to be as clean and fault-tolerant as possible.

Summary

In this chapter, we learned the hard work of scraping data from HTML pages through the use of the Beautiful Soup 4 library. Using it, we were able to collect all the links from one page, preserving the hierarchy, and retrieve the information for each of the collected links. This skill is invaluable, as it allows you to collect information from the internet, for research, business, or as a personal hobby.

We also touched on Selenium, which emulates a full-blown browser, can interact with the page and execute JavaScript, giving us access beyond static content.

In the next chapter, we'll clean and use the data we collected, creating an interactive visualization of the war.

Questions

1. What does the term web scraping mean in this context?
2. What are the biggest differences between scraping and using an API? What are the challenges?
3. What exactly does Beautiful Soup do? Can we scrape without it?
4. Why did we use recursion here?
5. Should we clean data during scraping?
6. What is the right approach to dealing with missing data or broken links?

Further reading

- *Python Web Scraping – Second Edition*, by Richard Lawson and Katharine Jarmul, published by Packt (`https://www.packtpub.com/big-data-and-business-intelligence/python-web-scraping-second-edition`)
- *Python Web Scraping Cookbook*, by Michael Heydt, published by Packt (`https://www.packtpub.com/big-data-and-business-intelligence/python-web-scraping-cookbook`)

8
Simulation with Classes and Inheritance

In the previous chapters, we described the entities we derived from libraries as *objects* with no further explanation. For example, an entity describing a web page in our previous chapter was an object with its own *values* and *methods*—bound functions that seem to have access to objects internals.

In fact, we can create our own structures by defining *classes*. In this chapter, we'll do exactly that—learn how to define and make the most of classes and their properties. Along the way, we will use classes to create a rather complex system and monitor its behavior—something that classes are very good for. Because of that, classes are used extensively in games, computer graphics...in fact, any type of task where creating specific entities seems useful.

In this chapter, we will cover the following topics:

- Writing a class and generating its instances
- Using special methods of a class
- Class inheritance
- Build upon newly introduced syntaxes—data classes
- Demystifying the relationship between classes and functions in Python
- Creating a simplified dynamic model of an ecosystem using classes
- Learning the basics of visualization in Python with the Matplotlib library

Technical requirements

The code in this chapter requires one additional library to be installed—`matplotlib`. It is included in the default Anaconda distribution.

All the code is accessible via the GitHub repository, `https://github.com/ PacktPublishing/Learn-Python-by-Building-Data-Science-Applications`.

Understanding classes

You can think of classes as blueprints for their instances—for example, a `Car` class will describe the generic properties of a car, while a specific instance of this class will describe a particular car with its own characteristics. As such, classes provide a way to store information and related functions linked to the instances. In our example, the `Car` class can store a `drive` function in its body, which will rely on the `gasoline` value for each specific instance. This approach is extremely useful when we describe systems of entities, whether a representation of a physical object (`Car`), personal information (`Contact`), or some abstract entity (web page representation).

Let's start with the syntax. Take a look at this example:

```
class Person:
    '''person entity'''
    greeting = 'Hi {0}. My name is {1}!'
    def __init__(self, name, surname, age):
        self.name = name
        self.surname = surname
        self.age = age
    def __repr__(self):
        return f'Person(name={self.name}, surname={self.surname},
                    age={self.age})'
    def say_hi(self, name):
        print(self.greeting.format(name, self.name))
```

To declare a new class, we will start with the `class` keyword, followed by the class name—the same as we do for functions. As recommended in PEP8, class names are title-cased—they should start with an uppercase letter. The name is then followed by parentheses, if the class is based on (inherits from) another class (more on that later). You don't need them if it does not. Again, as with functions, this initial line needs to end with the colon, and all the following lines should start with an indentation.

 In some code samples outside of this book, you might notice that a class inherits from an object. This is a legacy style; there is no advantage in inheriting from an object in Python 3. This code was probably written to be compatible with Python 2.

Like functions, classes can (and should) contain a docstring. After that, you can describe its internals, such as the values and methods the class instance would have.

Right after the docstring, we can add class attribute—those will shared across all instances, until we overwrite them (in this case, a new value will be preserved for a specific instance). Using class attributes is a great practice to declare default values. Class attributes also save memory, as we store one value shared across all instances.

The functions within the class are called **methods**. While you can add any custom method or variable to a class, it is important to know the special values and methods that are bound to Python syntaxes and will change the class's behavior. To be easily distinguished, those special methods and attributes are enclosed by a double underscore and are therefore called **dunder** methods.

The __init__ method is used to initialize instances of each class. For example, when you call `Person('Pippi', 'Longstocking', 11)`, the __init__ function is called under the hood. The first argument—traditionally called `self` (although you can name it anything you want)—is the representation of the instance itself, so you can add, extract, or change any of its values. All class methods expect to add the object itself as a first argument (unless you set method to static using the `@staticmethod` decorator), but you won't need to actually pass this variable on execution—see the following example.

Similarly, the class will call the __repr__ method whenever the instance needs to be represented. For example, when you put a variable at the end of the cell in Jupyter, its __repr__ method is called under the hood, as you can see from the following example (note the `mood` attribute we just made up):

```
>>> P = Person('Pippi', 'Longstocking', 11)
>>> P
Person(name=Pippi, surname=Longstocking, age=11, mood=excited)
```

According to general Python philosophy (remember duck typing?), Python does not care much about what any of those functions are actually doing. There are some requirements, though—for example, __repr__ is required to return a string.

The say_hi function is one we have added. Note that it prints out the string using both internal and external data:

```
>>> P.say_hi('Kalle')
Hi Kalle. My name is Pippi!
```

Note that, even after initiation, we have full access to the properties and methods of a particular instance and are free to change and modify them, simply by overriding (assigning a new value):

```
>>> P.name, P.surname = 'Kalle', 'Blomkvist'
>>> P
Person(name=Kalle, surname=Blomkvist, age=11, mood=excited)
```

Special methods, such as __repr__ , can also be overridden, but they are defined on the class level, not by instance. In order to override it, you need to write this: P.__class__.__repr__ = lambda self: lambda self: f'mr. {self.name} {self.surname}, Detective'. Note that this will also override the behavior for other instances of the same class as well.

It may be a great feature, but also a total disaster if used unintentionally.

The power of classes is unleashed as you use the same class to describe and operate on multiple instances. We loop over a small dataset, initializing a Person object on every row of data:

```
data = [
    {'name':"Pippi", 'surname':'Longstocking', 'age':11},
    {'name':"Kalle", 'surname':'Blomkvist', 'age':10},
    {'name':'Karlsson-on-the-Roof', 'surname': None, 'age':12}
    # not sure of the age
]

characters = [Person(**row) for row in data]
for character in characters:
    character.say_hi('Reader')
```

The output should be the following:

```
>>> Hi Reader. My name is Pippi!
>>> Hi Reader. My name is Kalle!
>>> Hi Reader. My name is Karlsson-on-the-Roof!
```

As a result, we now have a list of objects, with every single one storing corresponding data and methods. Of course, objects can use and change global values, or interact with each other.

At the beginning of this section, we briefly mentioned two special methods for classes. Let's now go on a tour of other special methods we can use.

Special (dunder) methods

In the preceding example, __init__ and __repr__ are special methods—Python uses them in specific operations or if a special syntax is used. There are a lot of different methods out there! Let's review the most interesting ones, starting with __init__.

__init__

As we mentioned already, this method represents the initialization of a class instance. It is called any time you initialize a class. It is usually stored to add some properties you're passing upon initialization, and running any kind of initialization setup. During initialization, you can call any other method of the object. Here is an example:

```
class Animal:
    def __init__(self, age, diet):
        self.age = age
        self.diet = diet
```

In this example, we created an `Animal` class and stored two attributes, `age`, and `diet`, upon initialization.

__repr__ and __str__

These methods are assumed to return a string value that represents the object. The former is meant to be more strict and specific—ideally, you should be able to copy the outcome, run it as a code, and get an identical instance, like this:

```
class Animal:

    def __init__(self, age, diet):
        self.age = age
        self.diet = diet
    def __repr__(self):
        return f"Animal(age={self.age}, diet='{self.diet}')"
```

This is what the representation of this class will look like:

```
>>> Animal(1, 'worms')
Animal(age=1, diet='worms')
```

Indeed, if you copy that text and run it as a code, you'll get an identical copy. It should be noted, though, that far from all libraries follow that rule.

The latter method, __str__, is meant to be more human-readable. If this function is not defined, but __repr__ is, then it will be used instead:

```
>>> print(Animal(1, 'worms'))
Animal(age=1, diet='worms')
```

Now, let's take a look at Python operations.

Arithmetical and logical operations

In Python, when we add two numbers, what is happening under the hood is that one of them is calling its method on the other.

Consider the following example:

```
>>> 1 + 2
3
```

Here, under the hood, 1 is calling its __add__ method on 2. Inside, 1 is checking whether 2 is of a supported type, and runs the computation.

We don't want to mess with number behavior, but this process is exactly the same for any custom class as well. In other words, if you define the __add__ function of your class, you'll be able to add something to this class. In some cases, you might try to add something that your class doesn't know how to handle. It should then raise a built-in notImplemented exception. In this case, Python will try to run the __radd__ method of this second instance (which stands for *right add*, of course), and, if it won't work, it raises an exception.

Take a look at this snippet. Here, we define two classes—one for Fish and another one for a School. The School class is expecting to get multiple fish. The Fish class has an __add__ method that returns School of the two fish:

```
class School:
    def __init__(self, *fishes):
        self.fishes = list(fishes)

class Fish:
    def __add__(self, other):
        return School(self, other)
```

Let's see how it works:

```
>>> F1, F2 = Fish(), Fish()
>>> F1 + F2
<__main__.School at 0x104efdd68>
```

As you can see, the sum of two fish is now presented as a School object. Of course, this feature is not limited to addition. Take a look at the following table, which covers quite a few operations, both arithmetical and logical:

Basic function	"Right side" execution (if the element on the left does not support operation, method of the element on the right is used)	Corresponding symbol and arithmetical meaning
object.__add__(self, other)	object.__radd__(self, other)	+, addition
object.__sub__(self, other)	object.__rsub__(self, other)	−, subtraction
object.__mul__(self, other)	object.__rmul__(self, other)	*, multiplication
object.__matmul__(self, other)	object.__rmatmul__(self, other)	@, matrix multiplication
object.__truediv__(self, other)	object.__rtruediv__(self, other)	/, division

object.__floordiv__(self, other)	object.__rfloordiv__(self, other)	//, floor division
object.__mod__(self, other)	object.__rmod__(self, other)	%, modulo
object.__divmod__(self, other)	object.__rdivmod__(self, other)	divmod(), for numbers, returns the quotient and remainder
object.__pow__(self, other[, modulo])	object.__rpow__(self, other[, modulo])	**, power
object.__and__(self, other)	object.__rand__(self, other)	&, AND
object.__or__(self, other)	object.__ror__(self, other)	|, OR
object.__xor__(self, other)	object.__rxor__(self, other)	^, XOR

But where and when shall we use them? Wherever it feels natural. For example, a built-in library called `pathlib` uses division to concatenate two paths. It makes sense, because we use the slash symbol to add paths. Take a look at how it works:

```
>>> from pathlib import Path

>>> path = Path('.').parent / 'data'
>>> path.absolute()
PosixPath('/Users/philippk/Dropbox/personal_projects/Packt_book/Chapter08/d
ata')
```

 The preceding code works fine for Notebooks. Since scripts could be called from anywhere, they have a path to the file stored in the __file__ variable. Simply replace the dot with this variable and you're good to go.

The resulting path, in this case, will represent the relative path to the `data` folder, located next to the running script, and does not depend on the absolute location of both.

Another good example is how the visualization package Altair uses these operations. For Altair, the addition of two plots will overlay them, which seems intuitive (although it breaks the rule of symmetry—here, the order of charts does matter). Similarly, using a pipe (|) symbol (or) will put two charts side by side.

Equality/relationship methods

There are six equality/relationship methods. They represent what happens if an object is compared using any of the following symbols:

Function	Corresponding symbol and meaning
`object.__lt__(self, other)`	<, smaller
`object.__le__(self, other)`	<=, smaller or equal
`object.__eq__(self, other)`	==, equal
`object.__ne__(self, other)`	!=, not equal
`object.__gt__(self, other)`	>, larger
`object.__ge__(self, other)`	>=, larger or equal

Let's illustrate this function with an example based on our prior case—a `Person` class. We'll add a function that will allow us to sort characters by their age:

```
class Person:
    '''person entity'''

    def __init__(self, name, surname, age):
        self.name = name
        self.surname = surname
        self.age = age
    def __repr__(self):
        return f'Person(name={self.name}, surname={self.surname},
age={self.age})'

    def __lt__(self, other):
        return self.age < other.age
```

Now, let's use the same characters:

```
data = [
    {'name':"Pippi", 'surname':'Longstocking', 'age':11},
    {'name':"Kalle", 'surname':'Blomkvist', 'age':10},
    {'name':'Karlsson', 'surname': 'on-the-Roof', 'age':12}
]

characters = [Person(**row) for row in data]
```

Finally, we'll sort our characters. Under the hood, the sorting function uses the `smaller` method:

```
>>> sorted(characters)
[Person(name=Kalle, surname=Blomkvist, age=10),
 Person(name=Pippi, surname=Longstocking, age=11),
 Person(name=Karlsson, surname=on-the-Roof, age=12)]
```

__len__

Earlier, we built a `School` class that groups multiple fish together. There are a few special methods that can be used on classes if they represent a collection. The __len__ method, as you can guess, represents the length of the object, and runs whenever the built-in `len` function is called on the object. Let's modify our `School` class to return the number of fish:

```
class School:
    def __init__(self, *fishes):
        self.fishes = list(fishes)
    def __len__(self):
        return len(self.fishes)
```

Now, let's recreate `School` of two fish and see how it will work:

```
>>> S = School(Fish(), Fish())
>>> len(S)
2
```

__getitem__

This method runs under the hood when someone attempts to retrieve a specific value from an object using square brackets, as if it was a list or dictionary. Let's add one more section to our `School` class so that we'll be able to get specific fish by their index:

```
class School:
  def __init__(self, *fishes):
  self.fishes = list(fishes)

  def __getitem__(self, i):
  return self.fishes[i]
```

Now, let's test it:

```
>>> S = School(Fish(), Fish())
>>> S[0]
<__main__.Fish at 0x104d73d30>
```

Note that nothing prevents us from adding a different behavior—say, treating the object as a dictionary, and thus using the value in the square brackets as a key.

__class__

This is not a method, but rather an attribute—and there is no need to overwrite it. Python automatically stores the class that the instance is built upon under that alias. It comes in handy if you want to create a new instance of the same class from within the instance but don't want to explicitly specify the class itself:

```
>>> S.__class__
__main__.School
```

The great part is that if you'll later *inherit* from the class that uses this attribute, a new wrapping class will be returned. We'll use __class__ later in this chapter.

Here, we mentioned inheritance, but we haven't yet discussed it. Let's do that right now!

Inheritance

Another important property of the classes is their ability to inherit—some would say it is the most important feature of classes! What does inheritance mean? You can think of classes as Russian dolls—once you define one class, you can use it as a basis, *wrapping* another class around it. In this case, whenever there is a name collision, the new class will override the properties and methods but will keep all the other ones. This allows two main patterns of usage:

- First and foremost, we can define a base class (for example, Fish) describing some generic properties and logic that's relevant to the case. Once it is ready, we can start adding classes of specific fish—say, tuna, clownfish, and guppy —all inheriting from this base class, adding and modifying properties where necessary. This way, we explicitly share certain properties between those classes.

- Another pattern is similar, but with a twist: the base class could have some complex functionality and would be designed in such a way that it makes use of specific functions. When you inherit, you can override those functions, changing the behavior, while using the full potential of the base class's functionality—even without knowing how it works. This pattern is often used in frameworks. For example, Luigi, a data pipelining package that we'll cover in Chapter 16, *Data Pipelines with Luigi*, has a base class called `Task` that defines the job it needs to accomplish within its run function. By overriding this function, you create your own tasks for the system to run without knowing the details of the process.

To inherit from a class, we state the class in the parentheses after the new class's name, similar to an argument for a function. Consider the following example:

```
class Fish:
    weight = 5
    color = 'white'
    def __init__(self, w):
        self.weight = w


class ClownFish(Fish):
    color = 'red'
```

Here, we (yet again) define the `Fish` class, which will be used as a base class. Next, we define the `ClownFish` class, which inherits from the `Fish` class, by passing it as an argument within the parentheses. As a result, any instance of this new class has the default properties of the base class—for example, it has a default weight of 5. At the same time, the `color` property was overridden:

```
>>> c = ClownFish(w=15)
>>> c.weight
15

>>> c.color
red
```

But we won't stop there: Python has a rare capacity to inherit from multiple classes at the same time! In this case, properties with collided names will be overwritten by the latter class—but of course, most of the time you want to make sure they have different functionality. Consider the following example. Here, we declare another class, `Mammal`, that has a `produce` attribute. Another class, `Dolphin`, is then inheriting both from `Fish` and `Mammal`:

```
class Mammal:
    produce = 'milk'
```

```
class Dolphin(Fish, Mammal):
    pass
```

Thus, the `Dolphin` class gets properties from both classes. For example, it has a `produce` property, equal to `milk` from `Mammal`, and a `color` property, equal to `white`, inherited from the `Fish` class:

```
>>> d = Dolphin(w=20)
>>> d.produce
milk

>>> d.color
white
```

Mixing classes could be very helpful in certain cases. However, be careful with mixing, and inheritance in general! It is easy to make things complex and unpredictable that way. For example, it is very dangerous to inherit (especially in a sequence) from a class that is used itself—you might end up tweaking a class and getting different behavior in many others you didn't even think of. A safer approach is usually to create one or a few basic classes that are not meant to be used directly and then base multiple classes on them. Here is a discussion on the subject: https://softwareengineering.stackexchange.com/questions/312339/are-python-mixins-an-anti-pattern.

Using super()

Once in a while, you need to access parent class methods and attributes from within the instance—for example, when you initiate a new one and need to execute the parent class's initialization logic. For that, we can use a built-in function called `super`. It is very easy to use—just call it from within a class—and it will return a proxy object of a direct parent with access to all its methods and attributes. Take a look at the following snippet:

```
class Shark(Fish):

    def __init__(self, w=5000, teeth=121):
    self.teeth = teeth
    super().__init__(w=w)
```

Here, we create a new class called `Shark`, inheriting from `Fish`. This new class has its own custom initialization code, but it also utilizes the __init__ method of the `Fish` class via the `super` method. By doing so, this new class is storing the weight of the fish without writing the same code again:

```
>>> S = Shark()
>>> S.weight
50000
```

Data classes

Let's now discuss a new feature that was added in Python 3.7—data classes. First of all, data classes are just *syntactic sugar* (simpler syntax). The end result is just an ordinary instance of a class, and it can be achieved with *normal* classes, just in a few more lines. As the name implies, data classes are a simple way to write data-focused classes.

What do we mean by *data-focused*? Basically, data classes have the __repr__ and __init__ methods defined out of the box. By specifying additional parameters, such as `eq`, `order`, and `frozen`, we can make a data class generate additional boilerplate methods—such as equality (`eq`), smaller/greater (`order`), and add immutability (`frozen`). One caveat is that the default initiation function only assigns specified values. For any additional logic, you can write a __post_init__ method—it will be executed upon initiation.

Let's take a look at the following example. We're defining our `Person` class (yes, again) as a data class. For that, we need to import a `dataclass` object from the standard library. Next, we define the class, using the `dataclass` object as a decorator (remember, we discussed decorators in Chapter 3, *Functions*). In that class, we declare two variables, adding their data type (yes, it is required—but won't be enforced at runtime):

```
from dataclasses import dataclass

@dataclass
class Person:
    name:str
    age:int
```

That's it! This is way shorter than our previous solution. Let's try them:

```
>>> P1 = Person('Pippi', 11)
>>> P2 = Person('Pippi', 11)
>>> K = Person('Kalle', 10)

>>> P1 == K
False

>>> P1 == P2
True
```

Not only are we able to generate instances of the class, but they have a default, built-in equality mechanism! Data classes are a neat solution if you need to compare instances—they will save you quite a few lines of code (and, thus, reduce the chances of making an error).

Having learned so much about classes, let's now put our new skill to the test by using classes to simulate an ecosystem.

Using classes in simulation

Let's use this new knowledge for a fun project—modeling evolution. We are going to create a closed, simplistic representation of an ecosystem, containing *animals* that can age, breed, and survive (or not!) in harsh conditions. To test different scenarios, we will produce a few of those ecosystems, *islands*, each having different environmental conditions. We'll run the experiment by simulating the behavior of those systems and gather statistics on their dynamics over time. In order to do so, we will build a dedicated class for each of those entities.

Writing the base classes

Before we do any simulation, we should start by writing the basic classes we'll be using, describing the behavior of the system's elements. To make our code easy to navigate, let's write those classes in a dedicated file using VS Code, as we did in Chapter 6, *First Script – Geocoding with Web API*, and Chapter 7, *Scraping Data from the Web with Beautiful Soup 4*. Pay attention to the highlighting—VS Code is very helpful at spotting typos and other problems with the code.

Now, let's get to it. Let's first create a herbivore class. To keep it simple, our animals will breed without *mating*, they will just add another instance of the same class, with a certain probability. As we'll be dealing with certainty, we will use built-in `random` library, which is capable of generating random values. Our animal should carry a few variables—age (`max_age`), fertility (chance of breeding), and then we'll call `mutation_drift`—the level to which a baby animal's properties can diverge from the parent. The initiation method sets the age to `0` and allows us to pass a certain survival skill (an umbrella parameter for any evolutionary improvements):

```python
import random

class Herbivore:
    mutation_drift = 1
    fertility_rate = .25
    max_age = 4
    def __init__(self, survival_skill):
        self.age = 0
        self.survival_skill = survival_skill
```

Now we need to add a few other methods for those animals. In particular, they need to age and breed. The aging is simple—we just need to add `1` (we'll be running our simulation as a discrete system, once per year). The breeding is slightly more complex. First, we'll randomly pick a newborn's `survival_skill` as a function of its parent's `survival_skill` and a random value within a range between negative and positive `mutation_drift`. Lastly, we'll return a new instance of the same class (a baby), with the `survival_skill` we just calculated:

```python
    def _age(self):
        self.age +=1

    def breed(self):
        drift = random.randint(-1*self.mutation_drift,
                self.mutation_drift)
        mutation = self.survival_skill + drift

        return self.__class__(survival_skill=mutation)
```

Here, we used the __cls__ method, because, that way, we're not explicitly stating the class—if we'll want to inherit from that class later on, we won't need to tweak this function. Later, if you want, you'll be able to expand the system by adding other animals (say, carnivores, hunting our herbivores and hence both limiting and depending on their number).

Just in case, here is what the class looks like, overall:

```
import random

class Herbivore:
    mutation_drift = 1
    fertility_rate = .25
    max_age = 4
    def __init__(self, survival_skill):
        self.age = 0
        self.survival_skill = survival_skill

    def _age(self):
        self.age +=1
    def breed(self):
        drift = random.randint(-1*self.mutation_drift,
                self.mutation_drift)
        mutation = self.survival_skill + drift

        return self.__class__(survival_skill=mutation)
```

Writing the Island class

Next, let's describe the islands our animals will live on. Each island here is an isolated system that tracks all the changes, including the death and birth of all the animals, ever-changing conditions, and so on. For our purposes, these islands will also need to collect stats on the animals.

Let's start small by defining attributes of each island:

- A list of animals currently living on the island
- Current year (turn)
- Maximum population cap (integer)
- Umbrella object for all the statistics

The preceding attributes are defined in the following code snippet:

```
class Island:
 stats = dict()
 animals = list()
    max_pop, year = 0, 0

    def __init__(self, initial_pop=10, max_pop=2500):
        self.year = 0
        self.max_pop = max_pop
```

```
        self.stats = dict()
        self.animals = [Herbivore(survival_skill = random.randint(0,100))
    for _ in range(initial_pop)]
```

Upon initiation, we set up a maximum population on the island to the passed variable. We also generate some animals (`initial_pop`) with the survival uniformly random on the range from zero to a hundred.

Now, we need to create an overarching function to compute on each turn. Within computation, two steps should be executed:

1. If the population cap is not exceeded, animals will try to breed, until the cap is achieved.
2. All animals need to age. Old animals should be removed from the list.

This is what it will look like:

```
def _simulate(self):
    new_animals = list()
    pop = len(self.animals)

    random.shuffle(self.animals)
    for animal in self.animals:
        # step 1. breeding
        if pop <= self.max_pop:
            if random.random() <= animal.fertility_rate:
                new_animals.append(animal.breed())
                pop += 1
        # step 2. Aging and dying
        animal._age()
        if animal.age <= animal.max_age: # dies of age
            new_animals.append(animal)

    self.animals = new_animals
```

Note that we highlighted two functions here. First, we shuffled the animals before looping through it. It's subtle, but we don't want to introduce bias by letting the younger animals breed before the older ones until the cap is exceeded, do we? Another function we use is random.random, which, with default arguments, returns a random float in the range between 0 and 1. This is our *flip of a coin*—the higher the animal's fertility rate, the higher the chance it will breed. All the other code is rather trivial—we create a new list of animals and added the newborns and existing animals that didn't pass the max_age limit. In the end, we overwrite the existing list of animals with the new one.

Finally, we need to record the stats on the island. For that, we'll add yet another method that will also be run each turn. The metrics are rather simple—the number of animals (population), average age and survival skill, and the percentage of animals with a survival skill above 75. We could define `average` ourselves, but it is simpler to use the one from the built-in `math` library. Just don't forget to move it outside of the class:

```
from math import mean
```

Now let's write our method. All the metrics will be stored in a dictionary, which itself will be stored in the overall statistics dictionary of an object, with the corresponding year as a key. First, we'll calculate the overall population and store it in a dictionary. Next, if the population is non-zero, we will loop over all animals, pulling their age and survival skill into separate lists. To make it in one loop, and on one line, we will use the `zip` function. Once lists are there, we can run `mean` on each, storing the result in our dictionary.

Now, we will calculate the ratio of animals with good survival skills (above 75). Here, we're using a conversion trick—in the loop, we're computing Boolean values (whatever survival skill is above 75). Later, we run `sum` on this list; as the function expects numeric values, the Boolean values are converted, with `True` being mapped to `1` and `False` to `0`. Thus, the outcome of the function will represent the overall number of animals with this skill set. The only thing we'll need to do is to divide this value by the overall population:

```
def _collect_stats(self):
    '''run island statistics'''

    year_stats = {'pop': len(self.animals)}

    if len(self.animals) > 0:
        ages, skills, ss_75 = zip(*[(a.age, a.survival_skill,
            (a.survival_skill>75)) for a in self.animals])

        year_stats['mean_age'] = mean(ages)
        year_stats['mean_skill'] = mean(skills)
        year_stats['75_skill'] = sum(ss_75) / year_stats['pop']

        self.stats[self.year] = year_stats
```

Finally, we can combine the two functions into one function that will run them, step by step, through a number of turns/years. It is very simple—just loop over the given number of years, executing the simulation, collecting the stats, and incrementing the `year` value:

```
def compute_epoches(self, years):
    for _ in range(years):
        self._simulate()
        self._collect_stats()
```

```
        self.year += 1

    return self.stats
```

The core code is now complete. Let's see how it will work in action!

Herbivore haven

Let's open a new Jupyter Notebook. Before running a full-blown simulation, let's test whether our classes behave as we expect them to, starting with the `Animal` class. First of all, let's import both classes and initiate one instance:

```
import random
from animals import Herbivore, Island

A = Herbivore(10)
```

Now, let's run a few tests on it, checking how our ecosystem ages and breeds:

```
>>> A.age
0
>>> A._age()
>>> A.age
1
```

So far so good—the initial value of the animal's age should be 0, and incremented every time we run the `_age` method.

Now, let's check breeding. We used the `random.seed` method, which *pins* the following outcomes of the `random` functions in the package in the following code. This allows us to reproduce the exact results without compromising the randomness:

```
>>> random.seed(123)
>>> A2 = A.breed()

>>> A2.survival_skill
9
```

As you can see, the new animal has a survival skill of 9— one "skill" point away from it parent's; it seems to be correct.

Now let's create an instance of `Island` and test it. Take a look at the following snippet; here, we initiate an island with a population of `10` and a population cap of `100`:

```
I = Island(initial_pop=10, max_pop = 100)
```

Next, we check the initial year of the island and the number of animals on it:

```
>>> I.year
0

>>> len(I.animals)
10
```

Seems to be fine! We could add a few more tests, but let's cut straight to it and run the simulation. All we need to do is just run `compute_epoches` for a given number of years—we'll take `15`:

```
stats = I.compute_epoches(15)
```

Feel free to investigate the results. However, as we've built a probabilistic model based on random chance, we'd better simulate multiple systems at once and estimate the distribution of results, rather than one outcome, which may or may not be representative of the system as a whole. It is simple—all we need is to simulate multiple islands at once, with the same initial conditions and store all the resulting statistics together. In the following snippet we declare the parameters of the systems, and then simply create a list of islands (archipelago?) and store the statistics from each of them:

```
params = {'initial_pop': 10, 'max_pop':100}
years, N_islands = 15, 1000

islands = [Island(**params) for _ in range(N_islands)]
stats = [ island.compute_epoches(years) for island in islands]
```

The resulting statistics, *en masse*, should be more reliable for analysis. And, if anything, adding more islands to the simulation is very easy.

Later in this chapter, we will visualize and discuss those metrics. Before that, let's add a little more complexity to the system. In the default settings, `survival_skill` is declared, but never used—all the animals survive until they die of old age. In the following section, we'll add another type of island—harsh ones, where the weather conditions will constantly kill the animals whose survival skill is too low.

Harsh islands

Let's add harsh islands where, each turn, weather conditions change, killing animals below a certain level of skills. Hypothetically, that should add space for the luckier and more skillful ones, which, in turn, will result in a natural selection phenomenon—as baby's survival skill is dependent on the parent's survival skill, the survival skill of the entire population, on average, will start to grow. That's the theory—let's check if that will work, and if it will, how fast this improvement will be.

The good news is, we don't need to add much code. We only need to introduce this new type of island by inheriting from the original code and add just a few lines of code. Take a look at the following snippet. Here, we're inheriting from the `Island` object. As we have to add one more value to the initialization class, we use `**kwargs` and run the `super` method. By doing so, we are executing the `Island` object's initialization with all the corresponding values (passed via `kwargs`), but also storing the `env_range` as the object's attribute. This parameter will define the bounds of how harsh or peaceful the weather can be:

```
class HarshIsland(Island):
    '''same as Island, except
    has harsh conditions within [e_min,e_max] interval.
    Rabbits with survival skill below the condition die at the
    beginning of the epoch
    '''
    def __init__(self, env_range, **kwargs):
        self.env_range = env_range
        super().__init__(**kwargs)
```

One caveat is that the `init` function is now less readable and transparent—we won't see the original parameters upon calling the `help` function. It will suffice for now, but we shall keep that in mind for future class design.

Next, we will introduce the `weather` function. We compute the random integer within the range we passed earlier, representing weather severity, and keep only the animals with a survival skill equal to or greater than the result in the following code:

```
def _compute_env(self):
    condition = random.randint(*self.env_range)
    self.animals = [a for a in self.animals if a.survival_skill >=
                    condition]
```

Finally, we need to somehow incorporate this function into the flow. Here, we can again reuse `super`—all we need is to override the `_simulate` method, adding the function we just wrote—and only then execute the original simulation:

```
def _simulate(self):
    self._compute_env()
    super()._simulate()
```

But why are we overriding the existing method? Because it is already in use by the other methods—namely `compute_epoches`. Once we overwrote the method, `compute_epoch` will run it instead. In other words, our `HarshIsland` is ready.

> You might need to restart the Notebook to be able to import new code from the static `.py` files if you change them after the first import.

Now we can import this new class and run a simulation over hundreds of instances in the Notebook. As before, we specified the parameters (exactly the same, but with the addition of the `env_range` parameter). Everything else is also the same—except, of course, that we initiate the new class instead of the old one:

```
from animals import HarshIsland

params = {'initial_pop':10, 'max_pop':100, 'env_range':[20,80]}
years, N_islands = 15, 1000

h_islands = [HarshIsland(**params) for _ in range(N_islands)]
h_stats = [ island.compute_epoches(years) for island in h_islands]
```

It seems that the code runs without any issues. But what do we get as a result? And did the animals survive? Comparing statistics for 200 islands is tough. In order to have at least some understanding, we need to visualize them in charts in the next section.

Visualization

While we have all the stats for two types of islands, it is hard to make sense of the numbers. To help the case, let's visualize our data as a set of timelines. To do so, we'll use arguably the most popular (and one of the oldest) libraries for data visualization in Python, Matplotlib. We'll use Matplotlib extensively in the second part of this book, using more elegant interfaces, but, for now, let's keep it easy.

Here are the steps we need to take:

1. First, we'll import the library and prepare the Notebook to show plots within the Notebook itself, rather than in a separate window or as the library calls it, `inline`.

2. Next, we set up the `538` style for the visualization. This step is optional and the pick is arbitrary. Here is what it will look like in code:

```
# 1. sets jupyter to show plots within the notebook
%matplotlib inline

# 2. import matplotlib's most popular interface
from matplotlib import pylab as plt

# 3. (optional) style plots using "538" website style
plt.style.use('fivethirtyeight')
```

 In the preceding code, we set the plotting style to `538`. This step is completely optional—it merely changes the visual style (background and shapes colors) from the default style. There are plenty of built-in styles (`https://matplotlib.org/gallery/style_sheets/style_sheets_reference.html`) and we can always define our own one.

Now, Matplotlib is ready to visualize the data.

For the next step, we need to create the `chart` objects to draw on. We have four metrics to show—population, average age, average skill, and percentage of animals with a good skillset. We also have two sources—two kinds of islands. The way Matplotlib works, we'll need to iterate over the stats for each island and plot a line (remember, we're drawing timelines?) by passing a pair of arrays—one for years (*x* axis) and a given metric (*y* axis). To make code cleaner, let's prepare the data as a dictionary of two lists and make another one for the corresponding colors. This is how to do that:

```
datas = {"Heaven Islands":stats,
         'Harsh Islands':h_stats}

colors = {
    'Heaven Islands': 'blue',
    'Harsh Islands': 'red'
}
```

Finally, we can plot the visualization itself. The following needs to be in the same cell; we'll split the code in order to explain it, then show it as a whole, one more time:

1. On the first line, we are creating one chart with eight subplots—four rows (one per metric), and two columns (one per island type). The size of the chart is defined by the `figsize` argument. The `sharex` parameter sets the *x* axis to be shared across charts, thus, the axis will be shown only once. The `axes` variable is now a collection of four lists, representing rows, with two `axes` (subplot) objects in each. Having them, we can start adding marks and properties:

```
fig, axes = plt.subplots(4, 2, figsize=(10,10), sharex=True)
```

2. Next, we'll set a *y*-axis title for each chart, and specify their *x*-axis limits to 15 years:

```
for i, title in enumerate(('Population', 'Average age', 'Average
Survival Skill', '% with SSK > 75')):

    axes[i].set_ylabel(title)
    axes[i].set_xlim(0, 15)
```

3. Now, we will loop over two types of islands, and every string of statistics. For each, we will pull a pair of arrays, and send them to plot as a polyline. We'll also add titles to the plots in the first row. Using the `colors` dictionary, we'll pass a corresponding color to each line:

```
for i, (k, v) in enumerate(datas.items()):
    axes[0][i].set_title(k, fontsize=14)

    for s in v: # for each island
        years = list(s.keys())
        axes[0][i].plot(years, [v['pop'] for v in s.values()],
                        c=colors[k], alpha=.007)
        axes[1][i].plot(years, [v.get('mean_age', None)
            for v in s.values()], c=colors[k], alpha=.007)
        axes[2][i].plot(years, [v.get('mean_skill', None)
            for v in s.values()], c=colors[k], alpha=.007)
        axes[3][i].plot(years, [v.get('75_skill', None)
            for v in s.values()], c=colors[k], alpha=.007)
```

4. The following is the same code, pulled together:

```
fig, axes = plt.subplots(4, 2, figsize=(10,10), sharex=True)

for i, title in enumerate(('Population', 'Average age', 'Average
Survival Skill', '% with SSK > 75')):
```

```
                axes[i][0].set_ylabel(title)
                axes[i][0].set_xlim(0, 15)
                axes[i][1].set_xlim(0, 15)

        for i, (k, v) in enumerate(datas.items()):
            axes[0][i].set_title(k, fontsize=14)
            for s in v: # for each island
                years = list(s.keys())
                axes[0][i].plot(years, [v['pop'] for v in s.values()],
                                c=colors[k], label=k, alpha=.007)
                axes[1][i].plot(years, [v.get('mean_age', None)
                    for v in s.values()], c=colors[k], label=k, alpha=.007)
                axes[2][i].plot(years, [v.get('mean_skill', None)
                    for v in s.values()], c=colors[k], label=k, alpha=.007)
                axes[3][i].plot(years, [v.get('75_skill', None)
                    for v in s.values()], c=colors[k], label=k, alpha=.007)
```

5. Now, run the cell. If everything is fine, it will take a few seconds to execute. After that, you'll get your visualization. Here is what it looks like for us:

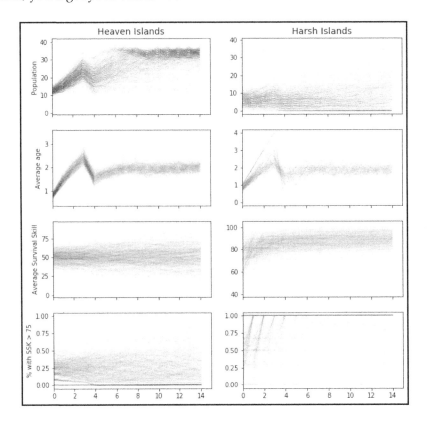

What can we get from this chart? Let's discuss every metric.

 Please use the graphic bundle list of the book for viewing all color images in the book.

As you can see on the first chart, **Heaven Islands** have no constraints but the maximum population gap—so the animal population quickly grows to the maximum. For the **Harsh Islands** population, this is not the case. In fact, many islands have no animals at all (see the thick red line at the zero, starting on year 4).

Next, the average age seems to behave similarly—in both scenarios, it seems to bump into the maximum age and then stay at half of the maximum age, which makes sense. Perhaps the trend would be different if the initial skill window was more narrow.

Both charts for average skill and percentage of animals with skill above a certain threshold tell us the same story. On the **Heaven Islands** there is no trend, but deviation starts to accumulate—on some islands, it even falls below 20 percent, as it has no impact on anything. For **Harsh Islands**, the picture is drastically different: it seems that in most cases, unskilled animals were killed in the first year (this can be confirmed by the decline in the population for the first two years). All those that survived started to breed—so the skill skyrocketed from the get-go. For most of the **Harsh Islands**, 100% of the population got survival skills beyond 75 after 1-2 years. In other words, our *natural selection* did indeed work.

Of course, the model we created is very simplistic. It is also driven by a number of arbitrary values and decisions—fertility rate, maximum age, harsh weather conditions, maximum population, `mutation_drift` level, initial conditions, as well as uniform integer distribution of weather conditions and order of computations on each stage. It is no surprise that the system worked as we expected. There is, however, room for deeper research and experimentation. For example, we could discuss the pace of improvement, or the probability of island extinction with different initial values and assumptions. Alternatively, we could create another type of animal (carnivores), whose survival depends on killing herbivores (say, by having a larger survival skill), and research the dynamics of the two species. We encourage the reader to play with this code, adding custom rules and characteristics.

In the meantime, let's proceed to the next chapter, where we'll talk about some non-Python tools that are essential for a productive workflow.

Summary

In this chapter, we have discussed the concept of classes and how we can use them to model entities with their properties and methods. Using classes, we created plenty of dynamic systems, illustrated the rules of natural selection, and explored their behavior. Finally, we discussed how to generate and collect a system's *telemetry* data and plot timelines in order to understand how systems behave.

In the next chapter, we'll review a few important technologies that are beyond Python, but that are extremely useful for productive programming.

Questions

1. What are classes? When should we use them?
2. Can we compare two instances of a class, or use arithmetic operations with them?
3. When should we use inheritance?
4. What is the use case for data classes?

Further reading

Check out the Python docs on class special methods (`https://docs.python.org/3/reference/datamodel.html`)

Shell, Git, Conda, and More – at Your Command

9

In this chapter, we will review a bunch of non-Pythonic tools that will make your life as a developer significantly easier, and that will help you communicate on the same terms with other developers. While this book is focused on teaching Python, nothing exists in a vacuum. Any developer (Python or not) uses multiple technologies and languages in their daily routine, knowing that at least some of them will improve their productivity significantly. Before we move on to building ever more complex substances, let's briefly review some tools beyond Python itself.

In this chapter, we will cover the following topics:

- Shell
- Running Python scripts and designing command-line interfaces
- Git and GitHub
- Reproducible virtual environments with `conda`
- Structuring your workflow with a Cookiecutter

Technical requirements

In this chapter, you'll need `git`, `conda`, and `cookiecutter` installed on your machine. The first two are included in the standard Anaconda distribution. To install `cookiecutter`, if you haven't already done so, run either of the following commands:

- `conda install -c conda-forge cookiecutter`
- `pip install --user cookiecutter`

The code for this chapter is available via the GitHub repository, in the `Chapter09` folder (`https://github.com/PacktPublishing/Learn-Python-by-Building-Data-Science-Applications`).

Shell

Every operating system, by definition, has some sort of interface to work with. Most people use the **graphical user interface (GUI)**, as it is easy to understand and navigate, and does not require any specific knowledge. However, graphical interfaces are complex, demanding, and not reproducible. Even before the GUI existed, programmers used code-based interfaces to interact with computers—shells. Both macOS and Linux systems are Unix-based and, hence, leverage the same shell interface, Bash. Windows, on the other hand, has two, a very basic command prompt, and a PowerShell (which we recommend using). There are also ways to install and use Bash on Windows. All those systems allow you to create, change, and delete files and folders, run programs and utilities, and so on. In addition, because those systems are based on textual commands (code, essentially), commands can be stacked, stored, and executed (and re-executed) together as scripts. As text requires minimum memory to exchange, this interface is used to operate remote servers.

You can access the shell on your computer in at least three ways:

- Open the original shell terminal. All three operating systems have built-in shell terminals.
- In Jupyter, open the terminal window via the launcher tab.
- Open the VS Code Terminal (window four in our interface overview).

Let's use VS Code for now—it has a handy feature for opening the terminal in the current project's folder, thereby saving us time. Note that some commands differ in terms of the name and interface between two systems, although many are similar. The following are a few of the most frequent commands, which are the same on both systems:

Operation	Bash command	CMD commands	Example (bash)
Change directory	`cd [path]`	`cd [path]`	`cd ../anotherproject/data/`
Move file/folders	`mv [current path] [new path]`	`move [current path] [new path]`	`mv data.csv ../data/dataset1.csv`
Copy file	`cp [current path] [new path]`	`copy [current path] [new path]`	`cp data/data.csv data/dataset2.csv`
Retrieve the content of a file	`cat [path]`	`type [path]`	`cat environment.yaml`
Remove file or folder	`rm [path]`	`del [path]`	`rm -r data/*.csv` (note: this will not move files to the trash bin. Once deleted, the files will not be available)
Show manual	`man [command]`	`help [command]`	`man rm` (use q to get out of the manual)
Show current position (the folder you're in)	`pwd`	`echo %CD%`	`pwd`
Show files and folders in the current folder	`ls [-l for table format]`	`dir`	`ls -l`
Create file	`touch [filename]`	`type NUL >> [filename]`	`touch .gitignore`
Create folder	`mkdir [folder_name]`	`mkdir [folder_name]`	`mkdir code`
Send the string to an output	`echo [options] [string]`	`echo [options] [string]`	`echo "Hello world"`
Filter multiple strings	`grep [pattern]`	`findstr [pattern] [filename]`	`echo -e "Hello\nworld"`

In the following examples, we use the double period as a representation of going one level up in the folders tree. Similarly, an asterisk (wildcard) can be used to specify all files/folders following the pattern (for example, where there are any letters/numbers in its place). For example, `data/*.csv` represents any CSV files in the data folder.

Pipes

Both systems allow commands to be combined in order to achieve even more complex processes using `pipes`. This works with main commands, but also any tools and utilities you use via the command line. The tree main pipes are as follows:

`|`	Sends the result of the previous command to the next one
`>`	Writes the result of the previous command to the file, overwriting it if it exists, and creating one if it doesn't
`>>`	Writes the result of the previous command to the file, creating a new one, or appending it if it exists already

You can add the preceding pipes after any command that has output – and then specify either a file or another command to be used.

For example, we can read, filter, and write a subset of addresses from Chapter 6, *First Script – Geocoding with Web APIs*, to a new file, based on the row, as follows:

```
cat ../Chapter06/cities.csv | grep ,2 > cities2.csv
```

Here, we retrieve all the text from the file, redirect it to filter for those with a population number that starts with 2, and store this text to another file.

Executing Python scripts

Python is no different to other tools—you can execute Python scripts via the command line, using a Python command):

```
$ echo 'print("Hello world!")' > script.py`
$ python script.py
Hello world!
```

In the preceding code, we first created a simple Python script and then ran it in the second line. Any Python script can be executed like that. In other words, you can write a program in Python and share it with others, or use it yourself via the command line, without going through the hassle of firing up Jupyter and executing cells one by one!

For learning purposes, let's modify the geocode.py file we wrote in Chapter 6, *First Script – Geocoding with Web APIs*, into a full-blown script that geocodes addresses one by one, or in batches.

First, let's copy it into a new folder (here, we assume we are in the chapter's folder):

```
cp ../Chapter06/geocode.py .
```

Now, the script has all functions, but there is no code that will be executed upon running: python Chapter09/geocode.py will return nothing. Let's add some code:

```
echo 'print(nominatim_geocode("13 Rue de la Chapelle, 70250 Ronchamp,
France"))' >> geocode.py
```

Of course, you can also add the same code via the VS Code editor.

Now, let's run the script:

```
$ python Chapter09/geocode.py
[{'place_id': 84388496, 'licence': 'Data © OpenStreetMap contributors, ODbL
1.0. https://osm.org/copyright', 'osm_type': 'way', 'osm_id': 34915920,
'boundingbox': ['47.7043284', '47.7045899', '6.6202675', '6.6207617'],
'lat': '47.7044779', 'lon': '6.62051522099271', 'display_name': 'Chapelle
Notre-Damedu-Haut, 13, Rue de la Chapelle, Ronchamp, Lure, Haute-Saône,
Bourgogne-Franche-Comté, France métropolitaine, 70250, France', 'class':
'amenity', 'type': 'place_of_worship', 'importance': 1.14130071139371,
'icon':
'https://nominatim.openstreetmap.org/images/mapicons/place_of_worship_unkno
wn3.p.20.png'}]
```

Perfect! However, we need to solve two issues in order for this script to be useful:

- First, the preceding code now runs every time you import from geocode.py.
- Second, we need to create some sort of interface to feed information—address or file paths—to our script.

First off, let's solve the first issue. Of course, we could separate the files we want to call from others, but that makes things too complex. Instead, there is a special pattern for this:

```
if __name__ == '__main__':
    print(nominatim_geocode('13 Rue de la Chapelle, 70250 Ronchamp,
France'))
```

In the preceding clause, __name__ is a special variable in the file's local namespace (Jupyter Notebooks don't have it). It is equal to __main__ if the file was called directly, and to other values if we import from it. Now, our geocoding will run from the command line, but not when we import from this file.

Command-line interface

Now, let's get back to the first issue. Essentially, we need to define a **command line interface** (CLI) for our script. There are a few packages for building complex CLIs, but for a simple one we can use the built-in argparse library. Let's design our interface so that we'll be able to pass the address from the shell:

```
python geocoder.py --address 'Kremlin, Moscow, Russia'
```

For that, we need to import the library and create a parser to parse the commands we call. We can add both to the beginning of the script:

```
import argparse
parser=argparse.ArgumentParser()
```

As a next step, we need to register the arguments we want to pass in with the parser object, using the add_argument method, and passing the argument name (usually beginning with a double dash) and a help test—it will be printed via the --help command provided by argparse. We can also pass a default value, which will be used if no value is passed:

```
parser.add_argument("--address", help="address to search for", default="13
Rue de la Chapelle, 70250 Ronchamp, France")
```

Once arguments are registered, we can parse them—and use the results in the code. Arguments will be stored as resulting object properties, returning None if the argument wasn't specified and no default value is defined:

```
args=parser.parse_args()
  print(nominatim_geocode(address=args.address))
```

Now, this script can be used as a standalone tool whenever you need to geocode anything. Perfect!

There are plenty of options for improvement—for example, we could add an interface to run geocoding in bulk, using the given CSV file as a source, and storing the results in another file.

Git

As you may have observed, the complexity of our code grows exponentially from chapter to chapter, it would be a pity to lose or break any code due to the incident. Of course, for any real-world business or service, this would be a disaster. That's why organizations make sure the code is kept safe via version control. Any time we need, we can revert the code to any of the previous versions—or even keep multiple versions of the same code, in parallel. Historically, there were a few technological solutions that allowed this, the most popular being **mercurial**, **subversion**, and **Git** systems. Currently, however, Git is by far the most popular – it is open source, fast, and distributed. You don't have to have the main server for the team to cooperate, but even for a single user, Git could be a life-saver!

In the following section, we will briefly discuss how Git works and where GitHub fits into this equation. We will also perform a small practical exercise.

Concept

The main idea behind Git is to store code in atomic snapshots—commits. Ideally, every commit should represent one logical step in development—say, an addition of one function. For each commit, you can add a message, explaining the change. They can also be tagged. This tag can be later used for ease of navigation between commits. When committed, files are archived in a special folder, named after the commit hash. Git keeps track of all the files that were changed, and stores a copy of only those in a new commit. You can always switch to another commit, revert code to the previous state, look at the history, or create "diffs," side-by-side comparisons of what changed between the two versions of the file.

Another important concept is branches. Technically, they are similar to tags. Imagine that you have a working project but want to add some features. To keep everything safe, you don't want to mix the current (working) code with the one you're working on. To do so, you can create another branch of the code base, and develop in parallel – all the new commits will be kept separate from the original branch (called the master) until you explicitly merge them. You can keep as many branches as you want at the same time; that way, two developers can work securely in parallel, without any interaction or conflicts; that is, until they decide to merge their branches, or merge them to the same third branch. In some cases, repositories maintain a few dedicated branches constantly, for example, with one code base for Windows machines, and a slightly different copy for Linux.

GitHub

It's easy to get confused between Git and GitHub, but there is a simple difference. Git is an open source tool, while GitHub is a web service that can function as a remote host for Git repositories. There is no strict dependency between the two, and you don't have to use GitHub or any other remote service (there are some others, such as BitBucket and GitLab) at all. Having said that, GitHub is a great way to store your code, collaborate on projects, and learn best practices. And not only that; to a large extent, GitHub is a *social network for developers*, and, on some occasions (say, while searching for a job), you might be judged based on the existence of an account and the quality of the code exposed on the service.

GitHub serves as the remote server for your code. In the cloud, you can push your code there, and pull a new version back, manage branches, and so on. Due to its remoteness, GitHub can serve any machine; for example, you can develop the code on your local machine, and deploy the code from GitHub to your production servers. Furthermore, there is a large ecosystem of tools and services built around GitHub. Some of these will be covered in Chapter 15, *Packaging and Testing with Poetry and PyTest*.

Practical example

If you're following the code for this book, you might have cloned it directly from GitHub. In that case, there should be a hidden (your operating system won't show it by default) .git folder inside—that's where all the old files are stored. You can access this folder at .git, or see it using ls -la command—but you shouldn't change it manually until you're sure you know what you're doing. As we don't want to break this repository, let's create a new project.

First, let's create another, empty folder—you can do that via the standard graphical interface on your machine, or via the Terminal. The following code will create a new folder and add a README file to it:

```
$ cd ../../
$ mkdir MyProject;
$ cd MyProject;
$ echo MyProject > README.md
```

Now, we need to initiate git in the folder, and add the README file via the first commit:

```
$ git init
$ git add .
$ git commit -m "My first commit"
```

Now, we have our first commit, that is, the stored state of the project that we can always revert to.

Now, try adding anything to README.md in the VS Code. As you may notice, the editor highlights new lines with a green line on the left and marks deletions with a red triangle – you can click on either to see how this part of the code appeared before the change. VS Code will only show changes to the last commit. Once you store the new version in a new commit, those lines disappear.

Similarly, VS Code will color files and folders in the Explorer menu to highlight those that you have changed. If you switch to the third tab—Git interface—you can select which files to add to the commit, and which you don't want to—and then commit the change with the message. Now, let's try adding something to README and then committing this new change via the VS Code interface. This interface is quite handy, but not necessary for working with Git. For example, you can see the state of the repository by using git status in the command line. Furthermore, you can go through the history of the commits by using git log with one of multiple options, for example, oneline mode:

```
$ git log —pretty=oneline

6caa0f3ee610f50dc3fb48beec034a7870f7fb9 (HEAD -> master) another commit
5b0c88aa1a99a38d6c4d6db900d63c154c5127bf first commit
```

For you commit caches will be different! Now, let's go to the previous state by using the hash for the first commit:

```
$ git checkout 5b0c88aa1a99a38d6c4d6db900d63c154c5127bf
```

The preceding code will return you to the first version, but it won't allow you to then go back to the last one, or easily at least. Alternatively, you could return to the AND commit and create a new branch based on it:

```
$ git checkout -b old-state
```

Here, the old state is the name of this new branch, and is stored in parallel with the original branch, master. Feel free to work and commit other projects. Once you're bored with this branch, just go back to the master one, using the checkout command:

```
$ git checkout master
```

gitignore

Git is very effective for storing and tracking code, which is usually distributed in relatively small text-based files. It does not, however, behave well with data files, which are large and change frequently. Also, there is no reason to store and track multiple backup files. And, of course, never ever add any credentials to the repository!

A `.gitignore` file defines which file Git will ignore. It will accept wildcards – for example, `data/*.csv` will mask all `csv` files in the data folder directly. Note that this will not remove any files that are already tracked in the repository, as there are plenty of byproduct utility files we don't need to track (such as `__pycache__` and `.ipynb_checkpoints` files). You can create and reuse your own `gitignore` files, or use any one of a few services to generate a default one for you (`https://www.gitignore.io/`).

Git is large and complex, and there is enough material to write many books on Git specifically, but for now, we'll have to move on. Just don't forget to add and commit your code in logical steps—you will thank yourself for this many times in the future!

Conda

Last, but not least, let's talk about Conda. Yes, this is a tool, developed by Anaconda, hence the name. If you installed Python via Anaconda, you have it already. Conda represents two things at the same time – a package manager, and a virtual environment manager. Let's now discuss these two roles in more detail.

First, and foremost, Conda allows you to install Python packages (and other tools). Compared to Python's original `pip` package manager, it is language-agnostic, and can install any type of software; this feature is vital to the data science stack, as many tools are based on code, written in the C, C#, and Fortran languages—Conda just pulls a binary suitable for your operating system, if there is one.

In order to see all the packages already installed, type `conda list` in your terminal, and hit *Enter* – this will print out all the packages Conda installed, with the version specified. You can always install more—just type `conda install my_package_name`—this will take care of the rest, installing the package and all its dependencies from the internet. The packages available (most of them are) are grouped by channels. The default one, the Anaconda channel, represents Anaconda Inc.'s official repository of packages—all packages here are checked and guaranteed to install properly. The downside is the fact that only very popular packages are stored here, and new ones are added slowly. Among many others, representing different communities (such as Bioconda—a channel for biology-related packages), the most prominent is `conda-forge`, an open channel for any kind of package maintained by a group of volunteers. It is relatively easy to get your package on this channel, so here you can find most of them. The downside is that some packages could be abandoned, won't install properly, or – in theory – may even be malicious. It is a good idea to specify the channel you want to install from (many of them overlap) by using the `-c` flag:

```
conda install -c conda-forge tqdm
```

By default, it will try to install the most recent version of the package that is available for your system. You can, however, request a specific version explicitly, or even require a version to be above the specific one:

```
# specific version of the package
conda install -c conda-forge tqdm=4.31.1

# most recent package available, with version larger
# or equal to specified
# if conda can't get the version recent enough -
# it will not install it, and raise an Exception
conda install -c conda-forge tqdm>= 4.30
```

Now, let's discuss another use for Conda—as a virtual environment manager.

Conda for virtual environments

In many cases, it is beneficial to be able to switch between different versions of Python – for testing purposes, or if some specific package or tool does not support the version you normally use. Moreover, in some cases, it might be nice to switch between different sets of installed packages (or different versions of the same ones), again for the purpose of testing, or if they somehow conflict with one another. You can easily do both things using Conda environments.

Compared to virtual machines, environments do not allocate resources, memory or CPU, but merely substitute paths to specific tools – in our case, Python, and install packages, temporarily, tricking a machine into running different versions as if they were just swapped. In fact, you were using one Conda environment – root – all this time! Even if you're not going to run tests, it is a very good idea to create a separate environment for your work. Sooner or later, you will accidentally break your environment by either installing something bad or in another way. If this is a secondary environment, you can simply remove it, and then recreate it within 5 minutes. As a bonus, we can declare all the packages required for the specific project in a text file and share it with others, so that they can create an identical environment for their work.

In order to create a new environment, just type the following:

```
conda create -n myenv python=3.7 jupyter scikit-learn
```

In this code, `myenv` is the name of your new environment, and everything after this is the base packages you want to install there – don't worry, those are optional, and the list doesn't need to be complete.

Now, in order to start working in the environment, type `conda activate myenv` – you'll notice that the start of the line will change. Now, anything that you install using Conda, or PIP (Python's original package manager) will be installed in that environment – and every Python operation will use the corresponding Python version. You can always exit the environment by typing `conda deactivate`.

Now, by way of example, let's install pandas via `conda install pandas` and pretend that the resulting environment is the final version we want to store, in order to recreate it later, ourselves, or share it with colleagues. It's simple! Just type the following:

```
conda env export > environment.yml
```

This will generate and store specifications for the currently active Conda environment as a YAML file. You can edit this file, by adding and removing packages, store it in Git, share it with anyone, and so on. Once you want to use it, write the following:

```
conda env create -f environment.yml
```

You can further specify the preferred name of the environment, overriding the naming from the file itself.

Conda and Jupyter

There is one non-obvious caveat to using Conda environments: it is easy to run Jupyter in the wrong environment so that it won't see the packages you have installed, or the version of Python will differ. In fact, while you can run Jupyter from a specific environment, this method is not recommended: as Jupyter moved from a Python-specific workflow to the concept of an abstract notebook-kernel protocol, it is recommended you execute it from the base operating system, giving it access to all environments and kernels at once.

There are two ways to register a specific environment in Jupyter. First, you can use the dedicated registration command of `ipykernel` from the environment:

```
conda activate myenv
python -m ipykernel install --user --name myenv --display-name "my new
environment"
```

Another way (it is just a semi-automated wrap around the preceding method, but is better in our opinion) is to install the `nb_conda` package in your root environment:

```
conda deactivate
conda install nb_conda
```

This package, developed and supported by Anaconda, will scan all the Conda environments available, and register all of them with Jupyter. Now, you can run Jupyter from the root environment. Within the Jupyter launcher, you'll see new buttons for Python in each new environment. You will be able to switch kernels (environments) from within each notebook as well.

Make

GNU Make, or simply Make, is a utility tool designed initially to help to compile code from its source. It is provided as part of any Unix system, so chances are you have it on your Mac or Linux. On Windows, the NMake tool (https://docs.microsoft.com/en-us/cpp/build/reference/nmake-reference?view=vs-2019) can be used as a replacement.

In a nutshell, Make can run one of a few recipes from a Makefile – a tiny text file that is very easy to write. While we obviously don't need to compile Python, Make's interface is so simple, it is quite popular as a common interface for utility scripts or operations. Inside, it has nothing but shell commands. The following is an example Makefile, containing two recipes – test and upload. Both instructions are declared PHONY—this means that they don't result in a file; if we don't declare that, Make will assume that the recipe will produce a file of the same name, and if that file exists, Make will consider the recipe as already having been done and won't run it:

```
.PHONY: test upload

test:
  echo 'testing!'

upload:
  aws s3 cp ./ s3://mybucket/wikiwwii --recursive --dryrun
```

To run instructions, all you need is to get to the folder and type the following:

```
$ make test
echo 'testing!'
testing!
```

It is that simple. Makefiles are especially neat if you have to type a long command with many parameters, for example, uploading files using an AWS client somewhere or running PyTest with some flags.

Make requires every line after the instruction name to begin with a tab – and not whitespaces! If you're getting a `Makefile:1: *** missing separator. Stop` error, you most likely have some whitespaces in place of tabs. You can replace those in VS Code using a special command, or via the terminal (for example, using nano)

In order to be used by Make, the file needs to be named `Makefile`. If you really need to keep multiple Makefiles in the same folder, you can assign them a meaningful name, and then specify the file, using the `-f` flag. If needed, Makefiles could become quite complex! You can use recipes in other recipes. Documentation relating to Makefiles can be found at `https://www.gnu.org/software/make/manual/html_node/Introduction.html`. You are also free to use environmental variables there, so Makefiles could be quite dynamic.

One byproduct of writing Makefiles is that they work as some sort of documentation for your fellow developers – and yourself in the future. So do yourself a favor, and add these whenever you anticipate repeating any shell command more than once. And, by the way, our next tool, Cookiecutter, frequently includes Makefiles in its templates – do check them out!

Cookiecutter

Another tool we find useful is Cookiecutter. In a nutshell, this is a templating engine for projects. There are two main scenarios where Cookiecutter can be useful.

First, if you are usually working on multiple projects of a similar structure or purpose, you may save some time and emotion by creating a single template of the project. That includes the folder structure, its name, the default files or templates to include, Makefiles (`https://krzysztofzuraw.com/blog/2016/makefiles-in-python-projects.html`), proper `gitignore` settings, and anything else you want. Specific variables can be injected into any text-based files, depending on your selection and configurations. As an illustration, in our practice, we adopted our own templates for our routine data analysis requests.

Second (and specific to programming), building a web app, package, library, or anything based on a certain framework or stack, or with some specific focus will benefit from reusing a single, thoroughly designed structure, and there are dozens of pre-designed ones available for you to use (`http://cookiecutter-templates.sebastianruml.name/`). In fact, many framework/tool developers prepare such a template themselves—for their own benefit, and to facilitate integration for new users.

The best part is the fact that Cookiecutter is itself language-agnostic (hence, there are plenty of templates for projects in GO, Kotlin, and other languages), but is written in Python, so it is easy to modify and add to it.

Now, let's execute a basic example. First, let's set up our configuration file. The default location package is ~/.cookiecutterrc. You can redirect the tool to another location by passing a COOKIECUTTER_CONFIG environmental variable, but for now, let's stick with the default one. The following is a simple template for the configuration file:

```
default_context:
        author_name: "Philipp Kats"
        email: "myemail@emailservice.com"
        github_username: "casyfill"
```

You can pass any value you want to this config file. These values will be used as default ones if a particular template has a corresponding variable in place.

Once a config file is in place, let's create a new project from a template. As has already been mentioned, there are a vast number of templates for different cases; most of them are stored as repositories – the tool can use both public and private repositories. One that is particularly popular among the data community is *Cookiecutter Data Science* (https://drivendata.github.io/cookiecutter-data-science/) – a template for a general-purpose data science project. Let's give it a try.

First, we need to move in our terminal to the folder where our project should be placed. Next, type the following code and hit *Enter*:

```
cookiecutter https://github.com/drivendata/cookiecutter-data-science
```

At this point, the program will start hammering you with questions. Note that it will recognize your name from the configuration. In the future, you can add any other settings, such as the S3 bucket name, to the config file. Once you're done with questions, it will generate the path. Now, open the new folder in VS Code, using code <project_name>, and explore it!

As you can see, there are many files already. These include a README file, with the full project's tree and injected description – one you had to type in the questionnaire phase. Your name is in place in setup.py. The Makefile, a convenient interface for frequent command-line operations, knows the bucket you typed in and can upload all the data there. There are a few other pre-generated features as well.

Now, this template is large, and perhaps too complex for some projects. In fact, an entire web page (`https://drivendata.github.io/cookiecutter-data-science/`) is devoted to how to use it. But that does not mean that you have to adapt to it. Instead, you could clone their template and tailor it to your needs, or even build one of your own, from scratch. For example, we will discuss another excellent tool, DVC, in `Chapter 14`, *Improving Your Model – Pipelines and Experiments*. It seems reasonable to integrate it into this template.

The benefits of using templates may seem few in number at the start, but the returns are somewhat cumulative – the more you use every template, and the more features you add, the more value you'll get from it.

Summary

In this chapter, we covered three distinct technologies that don't directly connect to Python but are extremely useful for productive and professional development. The shell allows you to work on remote servers, automate simple file management, and stitch many utility tools together, skyrocketing your development pace. Git and Conda both allow you to maintain and reproduce your environment and your code, allowing you to experiment and explore possibilities, without risking the safety and stability of your previous work.

In the next chapter, we will learn about Python for data science.

Questions

1. What is a shell? Why and when is it more advantageous compared with using graphical interfaces?
2. What exactly does *version control* mean? Is it suitable for research projects?
3. What is the difference between Git and GitHub? Is Git owned by GitHub?
4. What are Git branches used for?
5. What are the two roles of the Conda tool?
6. How does Jupyter interact with multiple Conda environments?

Section 2: Hands-On with Data 2

This section introduces us to the world of *scientific* (or data-oriented) Python, including its own IDE—Jupyter—and a suite of packages that assist in working with data. We will perform exploratory data analysis, draw some charts, and train a number of models. All of this will be implemented through our three projects, utilizing the data we collected in the first section.

This section comprises the following chapters:

- Chapter 10, *Python for Data Applications*
- Chapter 11, *Data Cleaning and Manipulation*
- Chapter 12, *Data Exploration and Visualization*
- Chapter 13, *Training a Machine Learning Model*
- Chapter 14, *Improving Your Model – Pipelines and Experiments*

Python for Data Applications

10

We have worked with data already in some of the previous chapters in this book, including data collection and some statistical computations. The samples in all of those cases were quite small, though. To run data analysis and train machine learning models smoothly on datasets of millions of records, researchers built a distinctive ecosystem of Python packages.

In this introductory chapter, we won't code much—instead, we'll overview the foundational packages and tools for the data science ecosystem, which we will be using throughout this part of this book, including the following:

- Introducing Python for data science
- Exploring NumPy
- Understanding pandas
- Trying SciPy and scikit-learn
- Understanding Jupyter

Technical requirements

The code for this chapter makes use of two packages—`numpy` and `pandas`, both of which are included in the default Anaconda distribution. The notebook for this chapter is in the `Chapter10` folder in the repository (`https://github.com/PacktPublishing/Learn-Python-by-Building-Data-Science-Applications`).

Introducing Python for data science

The fundamental task of data analysis is to generalize some trends and shared properties over a dataset of multiple—probably many—data points. Imagine how that would look in a standard Python distribution: you'll have a list of, say, `Person` objects, each with its own values. To run some aggregate statistics, we would have to loop over each object, pull its properties, and calculate the statistics. If we need to get a few measurements, the code will quickly grow large and unmaintainable.

Instead, many computations in data analysis can be vectorized. Here, vectorization is a fancy term for saying the same exact loops will be run in C, rather than Python, which speeds things up by a few orders of magnitude. At the same time, it means that we won't need to explicitly write those loops, making code cleaner and more readable. For example, we could represent our animals from Chapter 8, *Simulation with Classes and Inheritance*, as a numeric 2-dimensional matrix, defining their properties as columns and each particular animal as a row in this matrix. This could significantly simplify the code—for example, to age animals and drop the old ones, we could write just one line:

```
animals['age'] += 1
```

See, no loops! And yet, age will be increased for every animal (row) in the matrix.

Consider the following example:

```
import pandas as pd
animals = pd.DataFrame({'survival_skill':[1,2,3], 'age':[0,0,0]})
max_age = 2

animals['age'] += 1                        # this adds one to age of all
animals
animals = animals[animals.age <= max_age]   # this drops all animals with
age above maximum
```

Here, the `animals` variable is a table of two columns (`age` and `survival_skill`) and three rows, each representing a separate animal. Using that table, we now can run vectorized operations: first, we add 1 to the age of every animal in the table. The next line consists of two vectorized operations: code within the square brackets creates a Boolean vector of three values, one per animal, each answering whether the corresponding animal's age is below or equal to the maximum threshold (all of them do). This mask is then used to filter rows in the table, essentially dropping animals that are too old.

This approach is not only simpler but it's also a faster one. You see, Python has *dynamic typing*—we don't have to strictly define the type of each variable beforehand, as in other languages (C and Java). It makes it faster to write code but has its consequences, as the computer needs to check the type of each value, on every operation—even if we are looping through an `age` property of each of the thousands of animals. As properties of objects are independent of each other (for example, the property of one object could have a different type than one of the others), this means that each variable is treated as an independent value—and is sent and cached on the CPU separately.

Instead, we could define the properties of all objects of the same type (or even all of their properties) as having a specific type, and represent the whole collection of objects (for example, all animals on the island) as one object (matrix), which the computer will then treat as one entity, with no need to check the type each time, and this whole object could be sent and cached on the CPU simultaneously. For that to happen, we have to introduce arrays.

As you can now see, operating large sets of data and performing operations on them quickly is a crucial task for modern data science. Using vectorized code allows us to not only do that but also to write the code for those computations in a clean and expressive fashion. At the core of those fast operations are efficient data structures—first of all, multidimensional data arrays. And when we talk about numeric arrays in pandas, those are likely to be NumPy arrays.

Exploring NumPy

NumPy is a library built around the notion of numeric arrays—multidimensional, index-based (like a list) collection of data, which (unlike a list) guarantees the type of the stored values to stay consistent and predefined—say, a 2-dimensional array of integers or 1-dimensional array of floats. It is based on the C code and allows us to boost computation by a few orders of magnitude, compared to base Python. The gap in performance is staggering even on relatively small datasets and grows exponentially for large datasets and complex algorithms. NumPy is capable of handling a few million rows of data and is primarily bounded by the operational memory—not the CPU.

Let's illustrate this staggering difference in performance with an example. Imagine that we need to summarize three lists of values, pairwise. In pure Python, the code will be similar to this one:

```
>>> A, B, C = [1,2,3,4,5]*1000, [2,3,4,5,6]*1000, [10,9,8,7,6]*1000

>>> %timeit result = [sum(row) for row in zip(A,B,C)]
635 µs ± 14.3 µs per loop (mean ± std. dev. of 7 runs, 1000 loops each)
```

Now, let's do the same, using NumPy, as follows:

1. First, we convert all three lists into NumPy arrays using the `np.array` function (it takes any iterable as input). Here is the code:

   ```
   import numpy as np

   Anp = np.array(A)
   Bnp = np.array(B)
   Cnp = np.array(C)
   ```

2. Now, we summarize them:

   ```
   >>> %timeit result2 = Anp + Bnp + Cnp
   4.67 µs ± 22.4 ns per loop (mean ± std. dev. of 7 runs, 100000
   loops each)

   >>> 4.67 / 635
   0.00735
   ```

It takes less than 1% of the time it took normal Python! Now, imagine what we'll gain on more complex operations, where the number of operations grows exponentially with the number of data points!

In the preceding example, we performed vectorized addition—the + symbol, in this case, represented matrix summation. For more complex operations—for example, the `if` switch—we have to use multiple functions and methods built into NumPy, such as the `numpy.where` function for vectorized `if`/`else` operations. Even so, it is still possible to run custom Python functions on each cell, row, or column of the matrices but, most often, this code will be drastically slower than one using NumPy's native operations.

This vectorized code requires a somewhat different way of thinking, as your code will be running most often either on rows or columns of the matrices and not on single values. Therefore, to achieve good performance, it is usually not recommended to write your own, pure Python code, and, of course, loops are generally a no-go. Instead, most problems usually can be redefined using typical operations—ones already made available and efficient.

With the rise of neural networks and other computation-heavy algorithms, scientists and developers are pushing the boundaries of performance; recently, a new package was announced—CuPy—that aims to be a plugin replacement for NumPy, based on leveraging graphical boards instead of the CPU. Given that your computer has a good modern graphical card, it can achieve even more impressive performance, with little to no changes in the code over NumPy.

In this section, we've got to know NumPy, a foundational package for the Python data science ecosystem. NumPy is built around the notion of multidimensional arrays of the same data type. With this, most mathematical operations and matrix transformations can be executed in vectorized form. This vectorized way of data processing is great for any type of data operation, but NumPy can only support numeric operations. To work on a broader set of data types and have an easier, more humane interface for matrices, we'll go to `pandas`.

Beginning with pandas

Of course, not all data—and data analysis—is numeric. To address that gap, and inspired by the R language's dataframe objects, another package—`pandas`—was created by Wes McKinney in 2008. While it heavily relies on NumPy for numeric computations, its core interface objects are dataframes (2-dimensional multitype tables) and series (1-dimensional arrays). Dataframes, in comparison to NumPy matrices, don't require all data to be of the same type. On the contrary, they allow you to mix numeric values with Boolean, strings, `DateTimes`, and any other arbitrary Python objects. It does require (and enforce), however, the data type to be uniform vertically—within the same columns. Compared to NumPy, it also allows dataframe columns and rows to have arbitrary numeric or string names—or even hierarchical, multilevel indices.

Also, `pandas` allows simple grouping and aggregation of data, merging tables à la SQL, time-based transformations, plotting, and many, many other tools. It also makes reading and writing to dozens of different formats—from CSV file to SQL database, to JSON and HDFS/Arrow binaries—a breeze. As a result, it is extremely powerful for data analysis and remains the de facto standard for most data analysis, period.

Let's showcase `pandas` with a simple example:

1. Here, we'll read a CSV file with geocoded cities we created in Chapter 6, *First Script – Geocoding with Web API*:

```
>>> import pandas as pd

>>> df = pd.read_csv('../Chapter06/geocoded.csv')
>>> len(df)  # number of rows in the table
10
```

2. Next, we'll filter data to only the cities in the Eastern Hemisphere (positive longitude):

```
>>> eastern = df[df.lon > 0 ] # those with non-negative longitude
(easter hemisphere)
>>> len(eastern)
8
```

3. Now, we calculate how many cities there are and what their median population is for each country:

```
>>> result = eastern.groupby('country').agg({'population':'mean',
'icon':'count'})
>>> result.rename(columns={'icon':'cities'}, inplace=True)
>>> result
```

```
                    population cities
country
China               22.6825    2
India               25.2725    2
Indonesia           32.2700    1
Japan               38.0500    1
Philippines         24.6500    1
South Korea         24.2100    1
```

4. We'll finally store our results as a new CSV file:

```
result.to_csv('aggregation.csv')
```

That's it! Note that `pandas` also plays well with Jupyter—all tables are nicely rendered HTML tables!

Working with `pandas` requires the same type of thinking as with NumPy—you should try to avoid loops at all costs. Most of the time, there are predefined ways to do what you want, written by others. The resulting code may be somewhat less readable and expressive than pure Python—but will be way faster.

One of the most popular spin-offs from `pandas` is the `geopandas` package, which offers a `pandas`-like interface for geospatial visualization and analysis. It represents collections of geospatial objects (points, lines, or polygons) as a special kind of dataframe. We'll work with `geopandas` in `Chapter 12`, *Data Exploration and Visualization*.

So far, we've reviewed two fundamental packages—NumPy and pandas. Both of them provide serious power in reading, processing, and operating on data—be it numeric arrays or tables of different data types. On top of those complex and fast data structures, yet another layer of packages allows the running of complex algorithms—packages such as **SciPy**, **SimPy**, and `scikit-learn`. You can think of them as a bunch of textboxes on core mathematical, physical, and general-purpose scientific equations and models, all brought to life as a set of Python packages.

Trying SciPy and scikit-learn

The SciPy package essentially kicked off the entire era of scientific Python. Created in 2001 by researchers Travis Oliphant, Pearu Peterson, and Eric Jones, it was formed as a collection of basic and universal scientific techniques. Over time, the package grew and now offers generic tooling and popular techniques for scientific analysis. Its submodules cover linear algebra, integration, optimization, interpolation, statistics, and many more.

With the rise of machine learning, the corresponding submodule of SciPy grew more and more complex. At some point, it became so big, the decision was made to reintroduce it as a separate, independent package—`scikit-learn`. As the mark of its origins, the package kept its name, defined earlier as SciPy kit—learn. Due to its simple and unified interface and a large variety of models, `scikit-learn` quickly became the main go-to tool for machine learning in Python, and its interface for the models is essentially an industry standard. Indeed, many other packages, such as `xgboost` and `fbprophet`, replicate `scikit-learn` model interfaces for their models, allowing us to quickly swap and stack different machine learning algorithms.

As a foundational package for machine learning, `scikit-learn` offers this tooling:

- Data preparation—scalers and transformers
- Model selection—cross-validations, hyperparameter optimization, pipelines, and so on
- Multiple metrics and score/loss functions
- Dimensionality reduction
- Clusterization
- Regression and classification with multiple models

`scikit-learn` assumes data to be in 2-dimensional structures similar to NumPy arrays, so both NumPy arrays themselves and pandas dataframes will work. We are going to use `scikit-learn` to build a predictive model in Chapter 13, *Training a Machine Learning Model*, and Chapter 14, *Improving Your Model – Pipelines and Experiments*.

There are hundreds of scientific Python packages for any given domain—economic, social sciences, game theory, physics, metallurgy, genomics, psychology, neuroscience, and history—the list can go on and on. The vast majority of those packages, though, share their origins, in that, they all use NumPy arrays as data structures and functions from SciPy and `scikit-learn` at the core of their operations. But the list of packages essential to the popularity of Python's data science is not complete without mentioning a crucial environment for all of this code—Jupyter.

Understanding Jupyter

Finally, there is Jupyter. We're familiar with this tool already, as it proved invaluable for teaching—and learning Python on simple examples, but it especially shines for data science; given its rich media and visualization capabilities, Jupyter is an excellent environment for data analysis. It allows quick iteration and experimentation, supports markdown documentation and rich media—images, plots, interactive widgets, video, and so on. Of course, Jupyter is 100% open source and free.

Jupyter is also language agnostic. At the moment, there is a handful of languages to use with Jupyter, including Ruby, C, Rust, R, and many more. It also supports third-party plugins, for example, leaflet and Mapbox viewers for GeoJSON files or the Vega data visualization viewer. Another advantage is that Jupyter Notebooks are properly rendered on GitHub, so you can read other people's code from the repository with no need to run your own server.

On top of that, Jupyter can be spawned remotely using JupyterHub, on one server or even on a cluster of machines via Kubernetes or similar orchestration software. Hence, it is a perfect engine for remote work (if, for example, your data is too big to access on one machine or cannot be transferred due to security reasons). It is also a great environment for teaching, as it helps teachers to ensure all students have the same environment and are generally in an equal position. Finally, it is proven to be a good tool for writing code-related books—this way, all code is executable and can be tested.

Recently, notebooks started to get traction as some sort of interactive logs: large data-driven companies, such as Netflix, realized they can parametrize notebooks and ran them via some pipeline scheduler (Apache airflow, for example—more on pipelines in Chapter 17, *Let's Build a Dashboard*). Once the pipeline is executed (or failed), a notebook can be stored as an artifact —with all of the warnings, printed samples, and plots. Using certain data visualization libraries and techniques allows the storing of snippets of data within the notebook, keeping the resulting plots interactive.

Jupyter is a great environment for research and constantly adds more functionality. Here, we're finishing our exposé—it is now time to get our hands dirty with data!

Summary

In this chapter, we covered the foundation of Python's data science stack—the NumPy, pandas, SciPy, scikit-learn, and Jupyter libraries. By doing so, we were able to gather an understanding of this ecosystem, why and when we need all of these packages, and how they relate to each other. Understanding their relationships helps to navigate and search for a specific functionality or tool to use.

We also touched upon the reasons why NumPy-based computations are so fast, and why this leads to a somewhat different philosophy of data-driven development. We further showcased how pandas complements NumPy arrays by supporting plenty of data formats and types, and SciPy and scikit-learn build upon those data structures, allowing us to quickly train and use machine learning models. Finally, we discussed why Jupyter plays such an important role in this process and what are the current developments and new use cases for Jupyter Notebooks.

In the following chapters, starting right with the next one, we'll use all of the packages and tools we mentioned and more, to process data and build data-driven projects. In the next chapter specifically, we'll explore and process the data on WWII battles we collected in Chapter 7, *Scraping Data from the Web with Beautiful Soup 4*, so that it will be ready for data analysis and visualization.

Questions

1. Why should we use a special stack of packages for data analysis?
2. Why are NumPy computations so fast compared to normal Python?
3. What is the use case and benefit of using Pandas over NumPy?
4. What does `sklearn` stand for?

11
Data Cleaning and Manipulation

Before we dive into data analysis, data needs to be properly prepared and structured. Some datasets, for example, structured computer logs, are ready to go from the start, but, most of the time, the majority of the time is spent preparing data properly. This process inevitably requires certain decisions that depend on the specifics of the task.

In this chapter, we will learn how to prepare the data with `pandas`, using the dataset we collected from Wikipedia in `Chapter 7`, *Scraping Data from the Web with Beautiful Soup 4*, as an example.

We will cover the following topics in the chapter:

- Quick start with `pandas`
- Working with real data
- Regular expressions
- Using custom functions with `pandas` dataframes
- Writing the file

Technical requirements

The code for this chapter makes use of two packages: `pandas`, which is included in the default Anaconda distribution, and `missingo`, which we included in the `environment.yml` file. If you skipped the step of `conda` environment creation, just install `missingo` using the `pip` or `conda` package managers. As always, all the notebooks are stored in the repository, in the `Chapter11` folder (`https://github.com/PacktPublishing/Learn-Python-by-Building-Data-Science-Applications`).

Getting started with pandas

Pandas is *the tool* for data manipulation in Python—it combines speed and convenience, allowing the rapid processing and manipulation of data. Let's first overview a number of basic operations: `pandas` is simple and intuitive to use, but it is still a learning curve.

`pandas` does have two main data structures:

1. `Series` is a one-dimensional array of one data type that also has an index. The index could be numeric, categorical, a string, or datetime.
2. `DataFrame` is a two-dimensional table consisting of a set of columns—each of one single data type. `Dataframe` has two indexes—index and columns. Columns of `Dataframe` can be thought of as `Series`. Rows can be retrieved as `Series` but, in this case, data in the cells will likely be converted to one shared data type *object* (more on that later).

Most of the time, we get our data from external sources: a database, a link, or a file. To do that in `pandas`, just use one of the many `pd.read_...` functions, including, but not limited to, the following:

*   `pd.read_csv` and `pd.read_excel` for CSV and Excel formats. There is also `pd.read_html` to read tables for a given HTML page.
*   `pd.read_sql` and `pd.read_sql_table` for SQL databases (the first expects a query as an argument, while the second will try to collect the whole table).
*   `pd.read_pickle`, `pd.read_feather`, `pd.read_hdfs`, `pd.read_parque` and so on for different binary formats.

Be aware that most of those functions support (where applicable) not only local paths, but also web URLs. In addition, many of them can detect and unarchive archived files—for example, the ./data.csv.gz file will be unzipped and read in memory, seamlessly.

All of the preceding functions have plenty of arguments. For example, for read_excel, you can specify which sheet to use, and, for read_csv , which row to treat as column names (if any), and how many rows to skip at the beginning and drop at the end of the file. You can also specify which columns to parse as a date or time values and whether those should be stitched together; for example, if one column defines the date, and the other the time.

Writing data to a file or database is as easy as reading. pandas support all the same formats for data write—available via multiple df.to_csv, df.to_excel, and many more. As with reading, you can add an archive extension to the end of the path, and pandas will automatically detect those and use the corresponding archiving algorithm.

We now know how to read and write data using pandas. Let's now talk about how to select and edit values.

Selection – by columns, indices, or both

Now, let's learn how to access and edit specific values in pandas data structures. We'll start with a toy example—here, I will generate a dataframe from a dictionary of lists:

```
import pandas as pd

data = {'x':[1,2,3], 'y':['a', 'b', 'c'], 'z': [False, True, False]}
df = pd.DataFrame(data)
```

Now, we can take a look at the data we just stored:

```
>>> df
   x  y  z
0  1  a  False
1  2  b  True
2  3  c  False
```

As you can see, this frame has three rows and two columns. Let's see how it works:

1. First, let's start selecting columns. Any column can be selected using indexing via square brackets with the column name. As we're asking for one column, it will be returned as a `pandas Series` object:

```
>>> df['x']
 1
 2
 3
Name: x, dtype: int
```

2. Now, a similar approach can be taken to select multiple columns—to do this, we just pass a list of column names instead of one name:

```
>>> df[['x', 'y']]
    x   y
0   1   a
1   2   b
2   3   c
```

In this case, a dataframe will be returned. Even if we have only one column name in the list, df[['x']], it will return a dataframe.

If we need to get a specific row or rows, we need to use the `loc` method. You can use `loc` in a similar way to columns: `df.loc[0]` will select one row as a `pandas Series`. In order to select multiple rows, pass a list of indices—`df.loc[[0,2]]`. In both cases, numbers represent indices of the rows, which have to be neither ordered, nor numeric, nor unique.

In fact, `.loc` can be used to select both rows and columns; in other words, any arbitrary subset of a dataframe. To do so, just pass any definition of rows first, and then the definition of columns as a second argument:

```
>>> df.loc[[0,1], 'z']  # first two rows, column z
    False
    True
Name: z, dtype: bool
```

If one index and one column name are passed, `loc` will return a **raw** value, not a series!

Selection can be used for both reading and writing data—or even creating new columns provided there are none with the same name:

```
>>> df['new_column'] = -1
>>> df['new_column']
0    -1
1    -1
2    -1
Name:new_column, dtype: int
```

You can pass either a collection of the same length (same number of rows) or a scalar (single) value. You can also write to a specific cell or a specific subset of cells. If needed, you can even pass multiple columns at once as a dataframe.

In some cases, you might need to select according to the order of columns or rows, for example, the first five rows, no matter what their indices say. For that, there is another method—.iloc. .iloc works similar to list slicing; it supports negative indices and much more besides:

```
>>> df.iloc[-2:, 1:]
    y    z       new_column
1   b    True            -1
2   c    False           -1
```

Also, if you just want to get first, last, or random *N* rows, you can use the .head, .tail, or .sample functions, respectively. Each takes an integer as an argument, defining how many rows to return.

Masking

Now, both loc and simple square brackets accept masks. Mask can be represented by a Series, a NumPy array, or a simple list of Boolean values of the same length as the number of rows in the dataframe. If given, this collection will be interpreted as a **mask**—essentially, an explanation of which rows to return. For example, we can use our third column, z, as a mask to filter on. Because we only have a True value in the first row, a dataframe of one row will be returned:

```
>>> df[df['z']]
    x    y    z       new_column
1   2    b    True            -1
```

This is a very important technique, which we'll be using all the time! Such a mask can be generated using any logic operations, for example, an equality operator. Take a look: here, we are creating a mask by checking whether the values in column x are equal to 2:

```
>>> mask = df['x'] == 2
>>> mask
0 False
1 True
2 False
Name:x, dtype:bool
```

This mask can now be used to filter rows in our dataframe or any other one with the same indices. Only the second row will be retrieved—as only the second value in the masking series is true:

```
>>> df.loc[mask, 'y']
1 b
Name: y, dtype: object
```

Data types and data conversion

As you may notice, when we print out a `Series` object, its data type will be declared in the last line. An alternative way is to call `dtype` for each `Series`, or `.dtypes` for the entire dataframe (it will return a `Series` object). Those data types are defined in C, and not Python. The majority of them largely match Python ones; for example, integers, floats, and Booleans. There are, however, a few caveats to be aware of regarding the data types:

- First, there is no existing data type for strings. As you may notice in the last code block, all strings are defined as *objects*, that is, an arbitrary Python object. This type is the last resort, the type that suits any Python value but does not give any computation benefits.
- Next, `None`. This is an **NaN** (**Not a Number**, `numpy.nan`) data type—but it is a subclass of `float`. Most of the time, it does not bother you, but there are two cases where it does: since NaN isn't `None`, neither an equality operation (`df['col'] == None`) nor an `is` statement will work. The only way is to check using `pd.isnull()` and `pd.notnull()` (or their NumPy analogs). Both functions will work on scalars and collections of values. As NaN is a subclass of `float`, and values have to be of the same type in the `Series` or NumPy arrays, any column of integers, once an NaN is added, will be converted to floats.

Finally, some data types—specifically, strings and `DateTime` types, have corresponding special commands in `pandas`, accessible via `column.str` and `column.dt`, respectively. These include `split`, `replace`, `slicing`, and case changes for strings and retrieving a specific number of minutes/hours/days/months/years, and weekdays (we will get to that later in this chapter). Strings can also be added similar to vanilla Python. Datetimes can be subtracted, resulting in time delta objects.

 The situation with the data types may change in the near future for two reasons. First, NumPy defined a standard API for arrays and vectorized functions, allowing other parties to add data types to the ecosystem. Second, Pandas 2.0 will be published soon, based on the `arrow` dataframe representation, instead of NumPy. Arrow promises to support NaN for integers.

Math

Of course, mathematical operations are well present in `pandas`, which actively leverages NumPy's functionality and supports an extra-wide specter of math and statistical functionality. To get a sum, mean, median, max/min, or percentile of a numerical column, just call it as a column's method:

```
>>> N = pd.Series([1,2,3,10])

>>> N.mean()
4.0

>>> N.median()
2.5

>>> N.sum()
16

>>> N.max()
10
```

It also supports operations such as correlation (just call it on another numeric column of the same length), and many more. Most of the time, you can run the very same functions on the dataframes—in this case, axis (direction of operation) will be used as an argument. The default, all operations are run vertically—for example, for `df.sum()` you will get a series of sums, one for each column in the original dataframe. The very same operations with `axis=1` will summarize every row, so you will get `Series` with a cell for each row in the dataframe.

Merging

On occasion, we need to join multiple dataframes together. There could be different ways to do that—let's take a look.

First and foremost, if you have multiple dataframes with the same columns, and you want to join them—never do that iteratively—try to do that once, by passing a list of all of them to the `pd.concat` function with the `axis=0` and `sort=False` arguments (unless you need to sort them):

```
>>> df.shape
(3, 4)

>>> double = pd.concat([df, df], axis=0, sort=False)
>>> double.shape
(6, 4)
```

Similarly, `pd.concat` can merge multiple dataframes horizontally if `axis=1`:

```
>>> pd.concat([df, df], axis=1)
  x y z      new_column x y z      new_column
0 1 a False  -1          1 a False -1
1 2 b True   -1          2 b True  -1
2 3 c False  -1          3 c False -1
```

In this example, we group two copies of the same dataframe, so they, by definition have the same columns and indices. If, however, columns or indices do not match entirely—or at all, an *outer* join will be performed—the new dataframe will have *all* indices or columns—filled with `null` for dataframes that didn't have those indices/columns.

Another way to pull dataframes together is provided by `merge`. If column names overlap, `merge` will use a suffix. Most importantly, `merge` has the following two features:

- It can join dataframes on an index or any other column or group of columns.
- If the values in columns we're merging are not unique, the merge will behave depending on the mode—one of `left`, `right`, `inner`, and `outer`, similar to SQL join modes.

For example, if the mode is `left`, and the left dataframe has multiple occurrences of the same value in the column we're merging by, corresponding rows from the right dataframe will be pulled multiple times. In the same situation, with `right` mode, only the first occurrence of the value in the left merge column—and a corresponding row—will be merged.

In the following, we are merging the dataframe with its own first 2 rows:

```
>>> df.merge(df.head(2), on='y', how='left')
   x_x y z_x    new_column_x x_y z_y   new_column_y
0 1    a False  -1           1.0 False -1.0
1 2    b True   -1           2.0 True  -1.0
2 3    c False  -1           NaN NaN   NaN
```

As the second dataframe only has 2 rows, the third one is filled with NaN values.

> An interesting trick is to merge two dataframes on a column, which has the same values for all rows, both in the right and left dataframes. In this case, `pandas` will return a permutation of all combinations of rows on the left and right sides.

Now that we know some basics of working with pandas, let's get our hands dirty with real data processing.

Working with real data

Let's now try using `pandas` on real data. In Chapter 7, *Scraping Data from the Web with Beautiful Soup 4*, we collected a huge dataset of WWII battles and operations—including casualties, armies, dates, and locations. We never explored what is inside the dataset, though, and usually, this kind of data requires intensive processing. Now, let's see what we'll be able to do with this data.

As you may recall, we stored the dataset as a nested `.json` file. `pandas` can read from JSON files of different structures, but it won't understand nested data points. At this point, the task for us is straightforward (you may think of writing a recursive function, for example), so we won't discuss this much. If you want, you can check the `0_json_to_table.ipynb` notebook in this chapter's folder on GitHub at the following link: `https://github.com/PacktPublishing/Learn-Python-by-Building-Data-Science-Applications/tree/master/Chapter11`. The only new operation there is the `pandas.io.json.json_normalize` function, which expects an array of dictionaries, representing rows, and flattens their nested properties, concatenating keys (in our case, nested belligerents, casualties, strengths, and leader elements). We stored the resulting data as a set of CSVs, representing different theaters of war (see `Chapter11/data/...csv` in the repository). Note that no additional processing, with the exception of unnesting, was undertaken.

With this done, we can now look closer at the data we collected. Let's dive into one of the CSV files and see what we're working with:

```
df = pd.read_csv('./data/Eastern Front.csv')
```

This will read the report and present the data.

Initial exploration

Before anything else, we need to take a look at the data itself, as well as its columns and rows. It's reasonable to start data exploration by understanding the following:

1. How do specific values look like, for example, using `df.head(N)`, `df.tail(N)`, or `df.sample(N)` to retrieve (and print) the first N, last N, or random N rows from the dataset? As regards heads and tails, by default, N = 5. For our sample, it is 1 (one row). Alternatively, the sample method can take a `frac` argument, which will return a fraction of records—for example, `df.sample(frac=0.25)` will return 25% of the initial dataset. Note that printing will omit some columns in the middle if there are too many of them.

2. The overall shape of the dataset—the number of rows and columns. To do this, we can use the `df.shape` attribute, which returns a tuple of two numbers: the first stands for the number of rows, and the second the number of columns. Alternatively, `len(df)` will return the number of rows. For a width dataframe with many columns, it is often useful to print all the column names by converting the index to a list: `list(df.columns)`. Without being converted, columns will hide those names in the middle (this hiding behavior—both for `Series` and rows in dataframe—can be changed via the `pandas` settings, if needed).

3. Learning data types for each column by using the `df.dtypes` attribute on the dataframe, or the `df[col].dtype` attribute of a particular column. The first one will return (so we can print) a series of strings representing the data types for each column. The latter will return one string.

In our case, all but one column in this dataset are objects, which usually means strings. Furthermore, many are vaguely structured, and clearly not ready for quantitative analysis—before we run the numbers, we first need to extract them. From the output of `df.head()`, it is clear that most columns require cleaning in order to be useful. So that's what we'll do next.

Defining the scope of work to be done

Before we dive into the process of data cleaning, which might be very time-consuming, it is always useful to define the scope of work—which columns and rows we actually need to clean. For this chapter, let's restrict the scope to the lowest level of the hierarchy—specific battles (level=100—pages for events with no children). We can use the equality operator to generate a Boolean mask, and then use this mask to filter the dataset:

```
>>> battles = data[data.level == 100]
>>> battles.shape
(147, 23)
```

There are many columns in the dataset—enough for pandas to omit the middle part when printing. As we'll be mostly focused on time, geolocation, names, and casualties of each side, let's define those columns of interest in a list and investigate them more closely:

```
columns = ['Location', 'name', 'Date', 'Result', 'Belligerents.allies',
'Belligerents.axis']
battles[columns].head(3)
```

As a result of this code, we'll get the following table:

	Location	Name	Date	Results	Belligerents.allies	Belligerents.axis	Casualties and losses.allies	Casualties and losses.axis
0	Westerplatte, harbor of Free City of Danzig54°..	Battle of Westerplatte	1–7 September 1939	German victory	Poland	Germany Danzig	15 dead at least 40 wounded Remainder captured	50 dead at least 150 wounded
1	Mokra, Kielce Voivodeship, Poland	Battle of Mokra	September 1, 1939	Polish victory	Germany	Poland	800 killed, missing, captured, or wounded 50 tanks	500 killed, missing or wounded 300 horses sever a...
2	Near Mława, Warsaw Voivodeship, Poland	Battle of Mlawa	1–3 September 1939	German victory	Germany	Poland	1,800 killed 3,000 wounded 1,000 missing 72 tanks..	1,200 killed 1,500 wounded
3	Near Tuchola Forest, Pomeranian Voivodeship, P...	Battle of Tuchola Forest	1–5 September 1939	German victory	Germany	Poland	506 killed \n\n743 wounded	1600 killed 750 wounded Unknown number cap...
4	Jordanów, Kraków Voivodeship, Poland	Battle of Jordanów	1–3 September 1939	Pyrrhic German victory	Poland	Germany	3+ tanks	70+ tanks and AFVs

Now, let's investigate the missing values in the data if the particular column is mostly empty. It makes no sense to spend time cleaning and processing it. The best way to explore the missing values is to make a plot. With the help of the `missingno` library, it is an easy task. Take a look at the code:

```
import missingno as msno
msno.matrix(battles, labels=True, sparkline=False)
```

As a result, the following chart will be plotted:

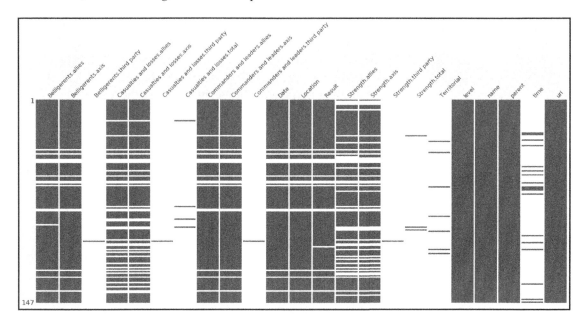

Here, the black rectangles represent non-empty values. As you can see, a few auto-generated columns (level, name, parent, and URL) don't have any misses. Some others, on the other hand, do have just a few non-empty ones (for example, all the columns related to the *third party*). What is even more important is the fact that there is a clear correlation between the missing values on some of the columns—it seems that rows with missing data in `Belligerents` also lack values for `Date` and `Location`. Let's first investigate those columns:

```
>>> mask = battles[['Date', 'Location']].isnull().all(1)
>>> battles.loc[mask, ['name', 'url']]
                                 name
url
39    Pripyat swamps (punitive operation)
https://en.wikipedia.org/wiki/Pripyat_swamps_(...
42    Bombing of Tallinn in World War II
```

```
https://en.wikipedia.org/wiki/Bombing_of_Talli...
46                      Operation Wotan
https://en.wikipedia.org/w/index.php?title=Ope...
47                      Nevsky Pyatachok
https://en.wikipedia.org/wiki/Nevsky_Pyatachok
48            Operation Nordlicht (1942)
https://en.wikipedia.org/wiki/Operation_Nordli...
61                      Operation Büffel
https://en.wikipedia.org/wiki/Operation_B%C3%B...
67                      Operation Kremlin
https://en.wikipedia.org/wiki/Operation_Kremlin
68               Operation Braunschweig
https://en.wikipedia.org/wiki/Operation_Brauns...
70                      Malaya Zemlya
https://en.wikipedia.org/wiki/Malaya_Zemlya
96                      Concert (operation)
https://en.wikipedia.org/wiki/Concert_(operation)
97           Zhitomir–Berdichev Offensive
https://en.wikipedia.org/wiki/Zhitomir%E2%80%9...
152       Operation Nordlicht (1944–1945)
https://en.wikipedia.org/wiki/Operation_Nordli...
157                     Operation Konrad
https://en.wikipedia.org/wiki/Operation_Konrad
175                  Operation Margarethe
https://en.wikipedia.org/wiki/Operation_Margar...
```

From the outcome, it seems that the web pages actually lack this kind of information. Moreover, many of them are not exactly standard battle pages, so perhaps we'd be better off without them—let's throw them out for good:

```
battles=battles.dropna(subset=['Date', 'Location'])
```

Now that we're done with missing values, let's get back to the table we printed. As you can see, there are a few serious issues, including an incorrectly stated axis and `allies` belligerents (refer to rows 3 and 4 of the preceding example), and `Date`, `Location`, and `Casualties` (among others) values stored in an unstructured way. Those issues have to be taken care of before we can move on to analysis. In other words, we need to correct the sides, parse dates, convert locations into coordinates, and parse multiple types of casualties as numbers. Unfortunately, there is no one silver bullet here. To process all those records accurately would require a lot of time. Usually, our time is limited, so we'll have to find some sort of compromise, depending on our end goals.

In this section, we explored the dataset in general, which allowed us to throw away what we won't use, and identify issues with the data that we'll have to fix in the next sections.

But first, how do we even approach data cleaning and parsing? The former is simple – just use masks, filters, and/or imputation strategies. The latter, however, will require us to use yet another technological trick—regular expressions.

Getting to know regular expressions

Strings that store data usually have certain patterns, which can be leveraged to retrieve actual data values in a unified fashion. For example, some location cells have distinctive coordinates, and numbers and symbols of degrees, minutes, and seconds. To extract those values, we could write a custom Python code, but this will be verbose and time-consuming.

This problem – extracting values from text by defining a pattern – sounds like something quite general and useful in many situations. When a problem can be stated as something universal, it usually means that it is, and someone has a solution! This is, by the way, a good approach for programming in general.

Indeed, there is a universal solution, called **regular expressions,** or **regex**. Regex is a special mini-language that defines patterns in a text to look for. It is language-agnostic, and there are implementations for most languages. Python, for example, has a built-in `re` library but, in this case, we don't even need to invoke it explicitly, as `pandas` has the corresponding built-in functions.

In order to use regex, we first need to define our pattern as a string, using its language. This language is relatively easy to write (at least for simple queries), but notoriously hard to read. Here is an example of a regex that detects emails in text:

```
(^[a-zA-Z0-9_.+-]+@[a-zA-Z0-9-]+\.[a-zA-Z0-9-.]+$)
```

Don't worry—it will start making sense soon (also, we won't write the regex in such a complex manner). Here are the basics:

Rule	Example text	Example pattern	Result
Any character except the special ones (., ?, !, /, *, +, |, (), [], {}) represents themselves (have to be exact in the string). This includes white spaces as well.	Hello!	llo	llo
The plus sign (+) means that the character before it can be repetitive (appears one or more times consecutively).	Hello!	l+o	llo
Similarly, the asterisk (*) means that the previous character can be repeated any number of times, or not exist at all.	Hello!	r*o	o
Figure brackets with one or two numbers in them will specify a permissible range of repetition for the character before them.	Hello!	l{2}o	llo

Square brackets ([]) define a choice. Within the brackets, a pipe symbol (|) means or (as in Python), so you can define an option of sub-patterns. Another symbol, ^, within brackets mean anything apart from the following characters.	many or menu	`m[a|e]n[^y]`	`menu`
Square brackets also support a number or alphabet ranges: A-Z, a-z, and 0-9 will fit any digit or character.	Hello!	`[a-z]+`	`ello`
There is a handful of special characters, such as \d for any digit, \D for any non-digit, \s for any type of white space (including tabs and newline characters), \S for any type of non-white space, \w for any alpha-numeric, and \W for any non-alphanumeric, and many more. A slash before special symbols (for example, an exclamation mark) will escape them, so regex will treat them as an actual, literal character.	Hello!	`\w\!`	`Hello!`
The period (.) represents any character. It can be combined with a plus sign, asterisk, or square brackets.	Hello!	`.+`	`Hello!`
A parenthesis defines a **capture group**—which substrings (there could be more than one) to retrieve. Groups can be named in pandas; this will return a dataframe with columns named after group names.	name: Huckleberry Finn	`(\w+\s+\w+)`	Huckleberry Finn
^ and $ match the beginning and end of the string, respectively.	Hello!	`He$`	`no match`

Those are just a few main rules and symbols, but that should suffice for our goals. Combined, those rules can form formidable, complex patterns that are perhaps hard to read (as someone said, regex is meant to write but not to read), but extremely powerful. To learn more about regular expressions, take a look at this documentation (https://www.regular-expressions.info/). There are also quite a few free online editors that help to test your patterns. As regex has a number of minor differences between implementations, we recommend using editors with Python-flavored regex, like this one (http://pythex.org/). There are even regex games (https://alf.nu/RegexGolf)!

Now, let's try using it on the data we collected!

Parsing locations

Let's start with the location column. As you remember, data in this column is supposed to represent the location where the battle took place. In many cases, the value was stored as Wikipedia GeoMarker, which includes latitude/longitude coordinates. Here is what the *raw* value of this marker looks like:

```
>>> battles['Location'].iloc[10]
'Warsaw, Poland52°13'48"N 21°00'39"E\ufeff / \ufeff52.23000°N 21.01083°E\ufeff
/ 52.23000; 21.01083Coordinates: 52°13'48"N 21°00'39"E\ufeff /
\ufeff52.23000°N 21.01083°E\ufeff / 52.23000; 21.01083'
```

Note that this geotag has both a *nice* latitude/longitude pair (with minutes and seconds), as well as its float representation, which is easier to use. In fact, the very same coordinates are repeated at the very end in their most simple form—and that's what we'll extract.

Let's write our first pattern. Usually, it is easiest to write a draft pattern, which will match our example string, and then work from there—adopting, relaxing, and tightening the pattern, where needed. Here is our attempt—a slash, and then two groups, each containing either numeric characters or a period (which we have to escape with a slash):

```
pattern = r'/ ([\d|\.]+); ([\d|\.]+)'
```

It is usually easier to tailor the pattern in an interactive way. Our favorite tool for the job is Pythex (`https://pythex.org/`), an online console for interactive regex testing, tailored specifically for Python-flavored regex (yes, there are some differences).

Let's test this pattern:

```
battles.head(10).Location.str.extract(pattern)
```

It works! You may want to go over addresses and check that ones with no numbers extracted indeed do not have it. We can store the results in two new columns:

```
battles[['Latitude', 'Longitude']] = battles.Location.str.extract(pattern)
```

Note that both columns are still strings, but now they can be converted into floats:

```
for col in  'Latitude', 'Longitude':
    battles[col] =  battles[col].astype(float)
```

Still, many locations did not have coordinates to start with. But how many? Let's check the percentage of empty cells in `Latitude`:

```
>>> 100 * (battles['Lattitude'].isnull().sum() / len(battles))
78.2312925170068
```

That is, 78% of our locations are empty—too many! Other cells don't have any coordinates, but most of them do have an address as a string. Let's try to geocode them using the `nominatim_geocode` function that we wrote in earlier in this book.

Geocoding

As you should recall, geocoding is the process of converting address as a text into latitude and longitude coordinates. As the task is quite complex and requires large datasets, it is usually handled by web-based services, using their API. in Chapter 6, *First Script – Geocoding with Web API*, we wrote a Python function that communicates with such an API, allowing us to send addresses and get latitude/longitude pairs back.

To use it, let's first import the function (we copied the file to the local folder). We will also use tqdm to see how the process goes—it has a solution for pandas—a progress bar will appear on any progress_apply method execution once we register tqdm with pandas:

```
from geocode import nominatim_geocode
from tqdm import tqdm
tqdm().pandas()
```

Now, the function returns many values, but we only want a few. We can deal with that later, but it is easier to define a local wrapper function, instead. In the following code block, we define such a wrapper, which returns only four attributes and only for the first resulting address:

```
def vectorized_geocode(x):
    result = nominatim_geocode(x)
    if len(result) == 0:
        return dict()
    return {k:result[0][k] for k in ('lat', 'lon', 'importance',
'display_name')}
```

Now, let's take a look at those locations that are lacking any coordinates:

```
>>> geo_mask = battles['Lattitude'].isnull()
>>> battles.loc[geo_mask, 'Location'].sample(15, random_state=2019)

46                                                     NaN
49      Southern shore of Lake Ladoga, near present-da...
54                     Kharkov, Ukrainian SSR, Soviet Union
99      175 km sector of the front between Uman and Ki...
27      Brest, Belarusian SSR, Soviet Union (nominally...
133                            near Radzymin, Poland
160               Poznań and nearby area, Poland
25                                   Petsamo, Finland
132                     Western Ukraine/Eastern Poland
148     West Estonian archipelago (Moonsund archipelag...
126               Eastern Poland/Western Belarus
56          Crimean Peninsula, Russian SFSR, Soviet Union
154                   Budapest, Kingdom of Hungary
```

```
7                              Piotrków Trybunalski, Poland
105         Leningrad region, Soviet Union; Narva, Estonia
Name: Location, dtype: object
```

One potential issue here is the word **near**, so let's get rid of it! Also, the Soviet Union no longer exists, and neither does Ukrainian SSR, and so on.

 By the way, this is a great idea for a new service—support time-specific geocoding so that you can identify which country a given location belonged to, at a specific moment in history, or geocode an address for a specific period—for example, knowing what city was called **Constantinople**.

In order to get all the locations right, we need to process all the addresses carefully. For now, let's make a short errata array of values and correct the addresses accordingly:

```
location = battles['Location'].str.lower().str.replace('near ', '')

replacements = {
 'Ukrainian SSR, Soviet Union': 'Ukraine',
 'Russian SFSR, Soviet Union': 'Russia',
 'Russian SFSR': 'Russia',
 'Belorussian SSR': 'Belorus',
 'Soviet Union': '',
 'USSR': '',
 ', Poland (now Ukraine)': 'Ukraine',
 'east prussia (now kaliningrad oblast)': 'Kaliningrad Oblast, Russia',
 ', czechoslovakia': ', czech republic',
 'königsberg, germany (now: kaliningrad, russia)': 'Kaliningrad Oblast,
Russia',
 'lwów, lwów voivodeship, poland': 'Lvov, Ukraine',
 'leningrad region, ; narva, estonia': 'Narva, Estonia',
 'Kingdom of Hungary': 'Hungary'
}

for k, v in replacements.items():
    location = location.str.replace(k.lower(), v.lower(), regex=False)
```

In the future, we can add more addresses to this dictionary, but now let's move on to the geocoding:

```
response = location[geo_mask].progress_apply(vectorized_geocode)
```

The resulting series has a dictionary in each cell. It is easier to convert it to list and build `DataFrame` out of it:

```
geo_df = pd.DataFrame(response.tolist(), index = response.index)
geo_df.rename(columns={'lat': 'Lattitude', 'lon': ' Longitude'},
inplace=True)
```

Now, let's see how many locations we're still missing:

```
>>> rmask = geo_df['importance'].isnull()
>>> rmask.sum() / len(battles)
0.2585034013605442
```

26% is still a lot, but we can definitely go through the list and clean it better or, if needed, add locations to the dataset manually, via, for example, a CSV table. Let's now save the latitude/longitude pairs back into battles. As `geo_df` has the same index as the original `battles` dataframe, we can write values there directly:

```
battles[['Lattitude', 'Longitude']] = geo_df[['lat', 'lon']]
```

It is also a good habit to add a flag, noting that those latitude/longitude pairs are from OSM. Precision, in this case, can vary significantly, and it will be easier to debug and find the root of a problem in the future:

```
battles['geocoded'] = geo_df['lat'].notnull()
battles['geocoded'].fillna('False')
```

We're done with the locations, at least for now. Let's now move on to the next column to parse the time column.

Time

Another column is time. Now, `pandas` has a built-in `DateTime` parser and a very good one! Just use `pd.to_datetime()` on your scalar value or a collection. In this case, however, it won't work, and neither will any external packages that usually help (`dateparser` is our favorite). And all that because cells describe a time range, and not just one specific date.

Again, let's (at least, for now) see whether we can make our life simpler. Indeed, we probably don't care about specific dates—all we need is the month and year. Luckily, all months are properly stated and uniform—and `pd.to_datetime` can parse them. So, all we need is to correctly extract two month-year pairs from each.

Now, it seems hard to define one regular expression that will work here. Instead, we can try to get all years (we know all of them are four-digit numbers, starting with 19) and all months (there are just 12 variants). Then, we can combine them, using the year twice if there is only one value.

Let's try it out! First, we define the patterns:

```
d = ('January', 'February', 'March', 'April', 'May',
     'June', "July",' August', 'September', 'October', 'November',
'December')

month_pattern = r'(' + "|".join(d) + ')'
year_pattern = r'(19\d\d)'
```

Now, instead of `str.extract`, we will use the `str.extractall` method—it will try to retrieve *ALL* occurrences of the pattern in the string. As a result, it will create `multiindex`—an index with multiple levels. In this case, the first level will be the original one, taken from the argument. The second one will represent the number of occurrences within the string. Here, we should use the `.unstack()` function, which will rotate `Series` into `DataFrame`, so that the first level will be its index, and the second its columns.

 As you may have guessed, there is an opposite function, `stack()`, which converts a dataframe into a series with a multilevel index.

In the following code, we run a regex to extract two values—the start and end of the column:

```
year_extracted = battles['Date'].str.extractall(year_pattern).unstack()
```

Notice that there are four, not two, columns here. Those are empty for most of the columns, but its mere existence means that there is at least one row where this last column is not empty. In the following code block, we mask our dataframe to show only records where the last column is not null:

```
>>> year_extracted[year_extracted.iloc[:, -1].notnull()]
                   0
match 0    1    2    3
94    1943 1943 1943 1943
```

It seems that only one record has a value in there. Let's take a look at the corresponding raw value:

```
>>> battles.loc[94, 'Date']
'3 November 1943 - 13 November 1943(Offensive operation) 13 November 1943 -
22 December 1943(Defensive operation)'
```

The corresponding record indeed has four-year values, but all of them are the same. Another row has three values, but again, all of them are the same—so there is no harm in dropping all but the first two columns:

```
year_extracted = year_extracted.iloc[:, :2]
```

We can also fill empty cells of the second row with values from the first one, using the fillna() function. This function can fill empty cells in a series with a given scalar value, or corresponding values from another series of the same length (our case), or even from the series itself, using one of a few methods (for example, using the value in the previous cell). The following code does precisely that in that it fills the empty second column with the corresponding values from the first one:

```
year_extracted.iloc[:, 1].fillna(year_extracted.iloc[:, 0], inplace=True)
```

Now, let's do the same with Months except that this time, we'll use the fillna from left to right, and use the first and the last columns (as we require the beginning and end of the event):

```
month_extracted = battles['Date'].str.extractall(month_pattern).unstack()

for i in range(2, month_extracted.shape[1]+1):
    month_extracted.iloc[:, -1].fillna(month_extracted.iloc[:, -i],
inplace=True)

month_extracted = month_extracted.iloc[:, [0, -1]]
```

Finally, we need to combine the two. Let's rename the columns so that we can use .loc, and then just loop over them:

```
year_extracted.columns = month_extracted.columns = ['start', 'end']
I = battles.index

for col in 'start', 'end':
    combined = month_extracted.loc[I, col] + ' ' + year_extracted.loc[I, i]
    battles[col] = pd.to_datetime(combined)
```

Yay! We're done with our second column – time. It wasn't easy, but we were able to convert the text into datetime values so that we can analyze them in the future. Next in line is belligerents.

Belligerents

Lastly, as we noticed, in some rows, the `axis` and `allies` parties are swapped. It is slightly confusing for this specific dataset. For example, in this dual model, we'll have to mark `Soviets` as `axis` when they attacked Poland during the initial stages of the war. Let's take a look at all the possible combinations:

```
battles['Belligerents.allies'].value_counts()
```

Here, `value_counts()` calculates a number of occurrences of each value. Hence, the index of those series represents unique values. There is a more intuitive alternative – the `unique()` function (which is also faster). However, this is a NumPy function and it returns a NumPy array, which Jupyter prints badly—that's the only reason we prefer to use `value_counts`.

From the examination, we can observe that all the incorrect values contain either one of `'Germany'`, `'Italy'`, or `'Estonian conscripts'`. We can use these to run our swap operation:

```
words = ['Germany', 'Italy', 'Estonian conscripts']
for word in words:
    mask = battles['Belligerents.allies'].fillna('').str.contains(word)

    axis_party = battles.loc[mask, 'Belligerents.allies']
    battles.loc[mask, 'Belligerents.allies'] = battles.loc[mask,
'Belligerents.axis']
    battles.loc[mask, 'Belligerents.axis'] = axis_party
```

Note that we had to use `fillna()`, as pandas won't run `string` operations if any values in the column are not strings.

OK, that was relatively easy. Finally, we've reached our final column to parse—casualties. This is the most complex task we're doing so far in this chapter!

Understanding casualties

Casualties are probably the most verbose and non-structured columns of the dataset. It will be extremely hard to make use of all the nuances of information here, so again—perhaps we can simplify the task, getting only the things we really want to use. Perhaps we can use code words to extract any digit preceding them; for example, `([\d|,]+)\s*dead` should extract any consecutive digits or commas before the word `'dead'`. We can define similar patterns for all types of casualties and loop over all of them, testing the patterns. There are, unfortunately, many keywords that mean the same thing (`'captured'`, `'prisoners'`, and many more), so we have to make them optional, similar to the preceding month expression:

```
digit_pattern = '([\d|\,]+)(?:\[\d+\])?\s*(?:{words})'

keywords = { 'killed': ['dead', 'killed', 'men'],
             'wounded': ['wounded', 'sick'],
             'captured': ['captured', 'prisoners'],
             'tanks': ['tanks'],
             'airplane': ['airplane'],
             'guns': ['artillery', 'gun'],
             'ships': ['warships', 'boats'],
             'submarines': ['submarines']
}
```

Now, for each keyword, we can generate a custom regular expression and extract all their cells with multiple occurrences (casualties from the different countries involved). In this case, however, we can preemptively convert them into numbers and summarize. By itself this is easy—but before we do that, we need to remove commas, filter empty cells, and convert strings to integers. There is probably a way to do some of that using regex, but it seems easier in this particular case to write a custom pure-Python function (note—it may or may not be the slowest part of the timeline):

```
def _shy_convert_numeric(v):
    if pd.isnull(v) or v == ',':
        return 0
    return int(v.replace(',', ''))
```

This function can be applied to every cell via `applymap`. After that, we can finally summarize every row. The result can be viewed as follows:

```
results = {
    'allies' : pd.DataFrame(index=battles.index), # empty dataframes with
the same index
    'axis' : pd.DataFrame(index=battles.index)
}
```

```
for name, edf in results.items():
    column = battles[f'Casualties and losses.{name}']

    for tp, keys in keywords.items():
        pattern = digit_pattern.format(words="|".join(keys))
        extracted = column.str.extractall(pattern).unstack()
        edf[tp] = extracted.applymap(_shy_convert_numeric).sum(1)
    results[name] = edf.fillna(0).astype(int)
```

Let's now see the result of `results['axis'].head(5)`:

	killed	wounded	captured	tanks	airplane	guns	ships	submarines
0	50	150	0	0	0	0	0	0
1	500	0	0	1	0	0	0	0
2	1200	1500	0	0	0	0	0	0
3	1600	750	0	0	0	0	0	0
4	0	0	0	0	0	0	0	0

Note, that there is a caveat to our casualties parsing approach that we'll have to keep in mind—due to the pattern we use, in all cases where a range of casualties is stated, we take the last number mentioned. It will be the maximum digit in the range (for example, the *100-150 killed* pattern will return `150`) and the minimum in other cases (for example, the *10+ tanks* pattern will return `10`).

Finally, let's reconnect both of those new dataframes to the original one. This time, let's create a multilevel column structure of our own so that we can select casualties for `axis/allies` without the need for the long column name. We're going to use the `pd.concat` function, which can join dataframes both vertically or horizontally. Our `allies/axis` casualties data is already in the proper dictionary format; we just need to add the rest of the data to the dictionary and then join the datasets together:

```
results['old_metrics'] = battles
new_dataset = pd.concat(results, axis=1)
```

As a result, we now have a clean, numeric dataframe of casualties for both sides in the conflict, divided by the type of casualty—be it a warship, plane, tank, or soldiers.

Multilevel slicing

The good part is that given a dictionary of dataframes, `pd.concat` will create a multilevel column index, which will come in handy in a bit. This means, however, that it's not enough now to pass the column name as a string; we need to use multilevel slicing. Let's use an alias:

```
idx = pd.IndexSlice
```

Now, if we want to get a specific column in this dataframe, we have to use `.loc` with this indexing object for columns. The `IndexSlice` interface is very similar to `loc`. For one column, we'll use it like this:

```
df.loc[:, idx['old_metrics', 'url']]
```

Note that because we defined a specific value on all the levels, the result will be `pandas Series`. We can, however, relax our query, by using colons: for example, `df.loc[:, idx[:, 'killed']]` will return a dataframe of two columns—killed for `axis` and for `allies`.

This multilevel index can be quite handy if we compare multiple attributes of multiple sources or entities—exactly our case. This is the final cleaning operation we're doing. Our dataset is finally ready to be used and analyzed. Before we move on to analysis, though, it is a good and often critical practice to check the quality of the result.

Quality assurance

I know we have spent a lot of time cleaning the data, but there is still one last task we need to perform – quality assurance. Proper quality assurance is a very important practice. In a nutshell, you need to define certain assumptions about the dataset (for example, minimum and maximum values, the acceptable number of missing values, standard deviation, medians, the number of unique values, and many more). The key is to start with something that is somewhat reasonable, and then run tests to check whether the data fits your assumptions. If not, investigate specific data points to check whether your assumptions were incorrect (and update them), or whether there are still some issues with the data. It just gets a little more tricky for the multilevel columns. Consider the following code:

```
assumptions = {
  'killed': [0, 1_500_000],
  'wounded': [0, 1_000_000],
  'tanks': [0, 1_000],
  'airplane': [0, 1_000],
```

```
    'guns': [0, 10_000],
    ('start', 'end'): [pd.to_datetime(el) for el in ('1939-01-01',
'1945-12-31')]
}

def _check_assumptions(data, assumptions):
    for k, (min_, max_) in assumptions.items():
        df = data.loc[:, idx[:, k]]
        for i in range(df.shape[1]):
            assert df.iloc[:, i].between(min_, max_).all(), (df.iloc[:,
i].name, df.iloc[:, i].describe())


_check_assumptions(data, assumptions)
```

Here, we use a dictionary to describe our assumptions—a key representing the column, and a value being minimum and maximum values. Using multilevel slicing, we can treat the key as the lowest column name—hence, testing both `allies` and `axis` casualties in the same pass. The `describe()` method returns a series of descriptive statistics for the column (in this case) or the entire dataframe—minimum and maximum values, most frequent value, and many more.

Note that the preceding assumptions will not hold. Feel free to run them and investigate which battles go beyond your expectations and whether their values are correct. The QA checkup process usually does require some back-and-forth on the first try, as you usually have to relax your requirements somewhat. This is a valuable process on its own—even here, you're usually learning some new information about your data.

Finally, let's write our resulting clean dataset so that we can use it in our next section.

Writing the file

Finally, we have all the data we wanted, in a more-or-less good condition. Let's store it in CSV format. We can always use other formats instead. For example, the pickle format, by definition, preserves all the data types and properties of the dataframe (we won't need to convert dates from strings again), but can't be read manually (it also has a number of security risks). CSV, on the other hand, can be opened manually or with something like Excel, edited, and then stored again if you observed that there are factual errors in the data or something that is easier to correct manually.

In the following code block, we export our CSV file into a dataframe just to specify a relative path to the file we want it to be. The `index=None` argument is optional—this ensures that the index (a generic range of numbers in our case) won't be written:

```
new_dataset.to_csv('./data/EF_battles.csv', index=None)
```

With that, our data is processed, converted, checked, and stored as a new CSV file. We're now ready to move on and (finally) analyze the data we obtained.

 Given the sensitivity of the subject, we went ahead and cross-checked the main values, row by row, manually, and indeed, had to correct a few values. This work cannot be completely automated. The corrected version is stored as `EF_battles_corrected.csv` and will be used in all further chapters referring to the WWII dataset.

Summary

In this chapter, we spent time cleaning the data we acquired in Chapter 6, *First Script – Geocoding with Web APIs*. Unless data was carefully prepared for the exact purpose of analysis, the chances are that cleaning will take a lot of time and effort. Here, we learned the basics of pandas, and how to filter and mask the data. We discussed how to investigate missing values, saw how to use regular expressions to extract specific values from non-structured text, creating data of a proper structure and type, and learned how to apply custom functions to each cell in the entire `Series` or `DataFrame` and then used that information to geocode locations where we lacked coordinates.

Finally, we stored all the data we processed, along with the original values, in another CSV file, ready to be explored in our next chapter.

Questions

1. Why, if there is an empty cell in the Pandas column, are integer values in this column converted into floats?
2. What is the benefit of plotting missing values?
3. What is `regex`? Is it a separate language?
4. How can we use `regex` in Python?

5. How is a `regex` pattern defined? How can we combine and modify patterns dynamically within the code?

6. Is it a good idea to run ordinary Python functions on dataframe cells? What are the pros and cons of that approach? Should we use loops for that?

Further reading

- *Pandas Cookbook,* by Packt (`https://www.packtpub.com/big-data-and-business-intelligence/pandas-cookbook`)
- *Python Regular Expressions,* by Packt (`https://www.packtpub.com/application-development/mastering-python-regular-expressions`)
- *2018 Python Regular Expressions – Real-World Projects,* by Packt (`https://www.packtpub.com/big-data-and-business-intelligence/2018-python-regular-expressions real-world-projects-video`)

12
Data Exploration and Visualization

In the previous chapter, we went deep into data cleaning and preparation. But what is inside this dataset? What story does it tell about the war, and how can we make those stories clear? Knowing how to dissect data, understand it, and extract insights is one of the crucial skills for data analysis and is a mandatory step before building anything driven by this data. In this chapter, we'll learn how to explore a dataset, compute aggregate statistics, and understand outliers and general trends through data visualization. The skills we'll learn are essential to any data analysis and are used throughout the industry and academia.

In particular, the following topics will be covered in this chapter:

- Descriptive statistics
- Aggregation and resampling
- The ecosystem of modern visualizations using `matplotlib` with `pandas`, `altair`, and `datashader`
- Basic data visualization with `pandas` and `matplotlib`
- Interactive charts with `altair`
- Visualizing millions of records with `datashader`

Technical requirements

In this chapter, we'll make use of three additional visualization libraries: geopandas, altair, and datashader. All of them can be installed via Anaconda or PIP and are included in our environment.yaml file. As always, if you followed the instructions in Chapter 1, *Preparing the Workspace*, you're all set. If not, you can install them using conda.

Exploring the dataset

For this chapter, we'll use the dataset on WWII battles we collected earlier in Chapter 7, *Scraping Data from the Web with Beautiful Soup 4*. As you may remember, the dataset includes dates, results, sides, leaders, and the number of troops and casualties of those battles. But what questions can we answer with this information? Let's start with something simple: which battles took the most casualties on both sides? Where were most of the tanks destroyed? How was the number of casualties distributed over time and geography?

 In the previous chapter, we cleaned and processed most of the data; however, given the sensitivity of the subject, we went ahead and cross-checked main values row-by-row, manually, and, indeed, had to correct a few values. This work cannot be completely automated. In this and further chapters, we'll work with the corrected version, stored in this chapter's folder.

Before we start answering those questions, we have to import the libraries and load our data. As we know that the start and end columns contain properly structured DateTime values, we can tell pandas to parse those while reading. The library has a certain capacity to deduce dates, but it is better—and slightly faster—to explicitly state them (we can always convert them later, as well). To let pandas know of the DateTime columns, we pass a parse_dates argument. In the following code, we import pandas and load the data:

```
import pandas as pd
raw_data = pd.read_csv('./data/battles_corrected.csv',
parse_dates=['start', 'end'])
```

We didn't drop any columns from the original dataset, but we're unlikely to use many of them. Let's now, within the Notebook and without touching the underlying data, specify the columns we're interested in and their order:

```
cols = ['name',
        'allies killed', 'axis killed',
        'allies tanks', 'axis tanks',
        'allies  airplane', 'axis airplane',
        'Lattitude', 'Longitude', 'start', 'end', 'Location', 'url',
  'parent']

data = raw_data[cols].set_index('name')
```

Finally, we may want to look at a small sample of data— for example, with `df.head`—and the data type for each column, with `data.dtype`, to assure everything parsed fine. Let's print the first three rows of the dataset and take a closer look.

Let's print the first three rows of the table, first:

```
data.head(3)
```

As a result of this code, this table will be shown:

Name	Allies killed	Axis killed	Allies tanks	Axis tanks	Allies planes	Axis planes	Latitude	Longitude	Start	End	Location	URL	Parent
Battle of Westerplatte	21	400	0	0	0	0	54.4075	18.67139	1939-09-01	1939-09-01	Westerplatte, harbor of Free City of Danzig54°...	https://en.wikipedia.org/wiki/Battle_of_Wester...	German Invasion of Poland
Battle of Mokra	500	800	1	50	0	0	NaN	NaN	1939-09-01	1939-09-01	Mokra, Kielce Voivodeship, Poland	https://en.wikipedia.org/wiki/Battle_of_Mokra	German Invasion of Poland
Battle of Mlawa	1,200	1,800	0	72	0	0	NaN	NaN	1939-09-01	1939-09-01	Near Mlawa, Warsaw Voivodeship, Poland	https://en.wikipedia.org/wiki/Battle_of_Mlawa	German Invasion of Poland

From the table, we can get a general understanding of the features. This small sample, however, does not give us any understanding of the overall shape of the data—a range of the values, averages, and so on. For that, we need to calculate some descriptive statistics.

Descriptive statistics

Now, having a dataframe in place, let's answer some simple questions; for example, which battles took the most lives on both sides? To answer that, we need to add two columns, sort the dataframe by the result, from larger to smaller, and print out first *N* records. Let's do it:

```
>>> kill_cols = ['allies killed', 'axis killed']
>>> data['killed total'] = data[kill_cols].sum(1)
>>> data['killed total'].sort_values(ascending=False).head(3)

>>> name
Battle of Stalingrad      1997993.0
Battle of Moscow          1203428.0
Battle of Kiev (1941)      661958.0
Name: killed total, dtype: float64
```

The next question might be on the typical number of casualties for each battle. Before we calculate the statistics, we have to filter rows with unknown (NaN) or zero values—in both cases, records shouldn't be included. Here, we'll use the pipe operator, |, as a vectorized equivalent to *or* in ordinary Python.

Consider the following code. We're assigning a mask as a logic OR of two Boolean arrays (hence the pipe). The first array checks whether any of the values in the `kill_cols` columns we assigned previously is `null`. As there are multiple columns, the result will be in the form of a 2-dimensional array. To convert it into a 1-dimensional array, we further use the `any` method, passing 1 to identify horizontal (axis=1) direction of the operation—in other words, the result will tell us, for each row, whether any value in this row is `True`.

The second operation (after the pipe) works similarly, but, instead, we check whether the value is zero. As a result, the mask variable will be a 1-dimensional array with a Boolean value for each row in the original dataset. Those values tell whether, in this row, values in any of kill columns is null or equal to zero:

```
mask = data[kill_cols].isnull().any(1) | (data[kill_cols] == 0).any(1)
```

Next, we need to drop rows for which `mask` is true and keep the rest. For that, we need to invert our mask, using the tilde symbol; similar to the pipe, the tilde ~ works as a vectorized *not* (or exclamation mark). In the following, we're filtering data, keeping only rows with the proper "kill" columns, and computing the median only for them. Here is an example: we use ~mask as NOT; for example, the row does not have zero nor null values.

Using this inverted mask, we filter the dataset and compute the median of the `killed total` values:

```
>>> data.loc[~mask, 'killed total'].median()
37316.0
```

This mask can now be used on many occasions. As a final example, let's compute the main statistics for the `tanks` columns for both sides, using the `describe` method (here, we use `mask` as a proxy for good records with meaningful results). Many battles have casualties, but no tanks lost or reported to be lost, and this seems fine:

```
>>> data.loc[~mask, ['allies tanks', 'axis tanks']].describe()
       allies tanks axis tanks
count  79.000000    79.000000
mean   352.683544   65.911392
std    897.692848   235.066831
min    0.000000     0.000000
25%    0.000000     0.000000
50%    0.000000     0.000000
75%    254.000000   18.000000
max    4799.000000  1500.000000
```

The values are interesting—as you can see, most battles don't have tank losses on either side. On average, though, the allies lost six times more tanks than the axis. Furthermore, in `75%` of battles, the axis lost `18` or fewer tanks—but the allies lost `254`—an even larger ratio!

Our analysis is getting more complex. It is getting hard to manually read and understand more than 10 numbers at once. To make sense of larger sets, we need to start visualizing our dataset on the charts.

Data visualization with matplotlib (and its pandas interface)

We had experience working with `matplotlib` already—first, in Chapter 3, *Functions*, and later, in Chapter 8, *Simulation with Classes and Inheritance*. Luckily, `pandas` has a built-in interface for working with `matplotlib`, making visualization very easy and intuitive. But first, we need to prepare the Notebook to display charts:

```
%matplotlib inline
import pylab as plt
plt.style.use('fivethirtyeight')
```

Now, let's plot the histogram of total casualties. It's possible to do that with the `matplotlib` itself—but `pandas` has a simple interface built-in. For better or worse, we still have to set labels and titles via a standard `matplotlib` interface—in this case, as follows:

```
data.loc[~mask, 'killed total'].hist(bins=20, figsize=(10,10))

plt.suptitle('Histogram, overall casualties per battle')
plt.xlabel("killed")
plt.ylabel("frequency")
plt.tight_layout();
```

We will get the following result:

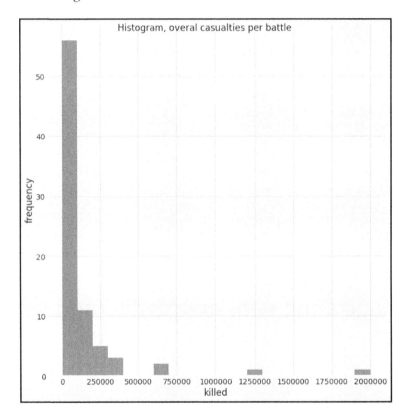

We were able to gather a general understanding of the data, but some pieces are still missing. To drill down and understand the properties of significant subsets—for example, several events in a period of time or average casualties for specific fronts and operations—we need to aggregate our data.

Aggregating the data to calculate summary statistics

To aggregate values over some grouping, `pandas` has the `groupby` operation—one of the library's killer features. This function creates a `GroupBy` object, which can behave as an iterable of (`name`, `group`) tuples, or similar to a dataframe, you can select one or many columns the same way you'd do for a dataframe.

Most importantly, those objects have two special methods:

- `agg`, which will perform the given aggregation function (say, calculate averages) for each group, and return them as a dataframe with one row per each group.
- `transform` does all of the same—except that it will return the corresponding group's aggregate values for each row in the original dataframe.

The great part of both of those functions is their flexibility—they both accept a handful of options as their arguments, including the following:

- Strings with operation names (`count`, `median`, and more).
- Custom functions.
- A dictionary with specific operations (either strings or functions) for specific column names; we can even pass a dictionary with a list of multiple operations for one column.

For example, let's see how the casualties statistics change for each operation, which we store in the `parent` column:

```
aggregate = data[~mask].groupby('parent').agg({'axis killed': ['sum',
'median', 'count'],
                              'allies killed': ['sum', 'median'],
                              'killed total': ['sum',
'median']}).astype(int)
```

Here are the first three rows of the outcome:

	Axis killed			Allies killed		Killed total	
Parent	Sum	Median	Count	Sum	Median	Sum	Median
Axis invasion of the Soviet Union	440,560	20,364	12	2,811,366	103,166	3,251,926	111,681
Battle for Narva Bridgehead	200	200	1	3,000	3,000	3,200	3,200
Battle of Berlin	60,000	60,000	1	20,000	20,000	80,000	80,000

Note how the result has multilevel columns, the first level being the original column names and the second, the specific operations we performed. In many ways, this multilevel index is useful but can also make things more complex. In particular, now we can't select a column by name—instead, we need to use so-called pandas.IndexSlice. For example, to get a column, 'axis killed', 'sum', we need to use this code:

```
>>> idx = pd.IndexSlice
>>> aggr[idx['axis killed', 'sum']].head(3)

parent
Axis invasion of the Soviet Union 440560
Battle for Narva Bridgehead 200
Battle of Berlin 60000
Name: (axis killed, sum), dtype: int6
```

The nice part is that IndexSlice, similar to normal pandas slicing, supports semicolons and non-specified levels. For example, we can pull 'sum' values for both sides like this (for some reason, it requires a loc method):

```
>>> aggr.loc[:, idx[:, 'sum']].head(3)
                                axis killed    allies killed    killed total
                                        sum              sum             sum
parent
Axis invasion of the Soviet Union 440560          2811366         3251926
Battle for Narva Bridgehead          200             3000            3200
Battle of Berlin                   60000            20000           80000
```

Now, in continuation of our visualization spree, let's plot all given operations as a scatterplot, using casualties for both sides as x and y coordinates. For that, pandas has a dedicated interface, as well. Consider the following example:

```
idx = pd.IndexSlice

aggr.plot(kind='scatter',
          x=idx['allies killed', 'sum'],
          y=idx['axis killed', 'sum'],
          figsize=(7,7),
          title='Deaths on both sides')

plt.axis('equal');
plt.tight_layout();
```

Here, all we need is to execute the `plot` command, specifying the kind of a plot, the columns to be used for the x and y coordinates, and a few other parameters. Here, we also have to use `IndexSlice` to specify columns. The `plt.axis('equal')` method ensures that the x and y coordinates preserve the same scale for comparison. The following is the resulting image, showing the trend of axis/allies casualties by battle. Note that, in this case, we didn't have to specify axis labels—they were generated automatically from the column names:

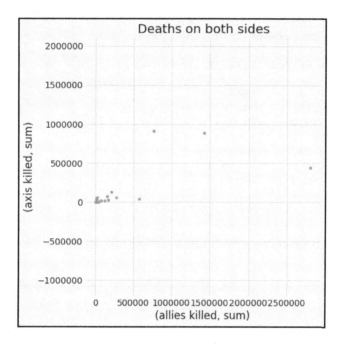

The scatterplot we made definitely tells a lot, but we have to guess which battle is represented by which point. Don't worry—we'll get to interactive charts very soon.

Let's now finish with aggregation methods by covering another technique: time-based resampling.

Resampling

A separate form of aggregation is time-based resampling. You can think of this practice as grouping by time period—except that statistics will be filled for missed time periods, too.

For example, let's count casualties for each month of the war, assuming the end of each battle as a time point. For that, we'll have to set `DateTime` as an index, first. For the sake of simplicity, let's create a copy of the dataframe to perform on:

```
ts = data[['axis killed', 'allies killed', 'end']].copy()
ts = ts.set_index('end').sort_index()
```

Now, all we need to do is define the frequency and aggregation method, and we're good to go:

```
>>> timeline = ts.resample('1Y').agg('sum')
>>> timeline
            axis killed allies killed
end
1939-12-31 23727.0       166092.0
1940-12-31 36682.0       2741.0
1941-12-31 226230.0      1644334.0
1942-12-31 346949.0      2300836.0
1943-12-31 1110704.0     1456498.0
1944-12-31 640690.0      770208.0
1945-12-31 684689.0      622996.0
```

Moreover, for all of the dataframes and series with the `DateTime` index, `pandas` will plot the line charts automatically, one per column. Running `timeline.plot()` will get us to the following diagram. Here, we can estimate the number of casualties on both sides every year:

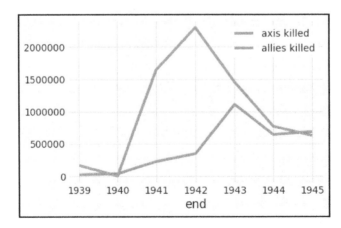

Starting with version 0.25.0, `pandas` offers a unified specification for visualizations. This means that any visualization library that supports certain methods can be registered and used instead of `matplotlib`. This is a brand-new feature and, as far as we know, there are no alternatives to `matplotlib` just yet. That being said, later in this chapter, we'll work with `altair`, another library for visualization. It won't surprise me if it will soon be possible to register `altair` as a renderer and get `altair` charts instead of `matplotlib`, preserving the same interface for the preceding clients we used!

The resulting time series is remarkable! It also reminds us that, aside from time, we have location coordinates for most of the battles. Can we use those to create maps? You bet!

Mapping

In `Chapter 11`, *Data Cleaning and Manipulation*, we spent a considerable amount of time geocoding battles. Let's use the coordinates to pin battles on the map—perhaps this will give us some better understanding of the data.

For that, we'll use a special (and spatial) library: `geopandas`. As you can guess, `geopandas` is based on pandas and provides multiple geospatial methods. In essence, `geopandas` allows us to read geospatial data and work with it as a pandas dataframe, providing geospatial methods (adjacency, spatial inclusion, Boolean operations, and more) and plotting capabilities.

Before we start plotting, it would be nice to have some sort of a base map for our data, as a context. Here, we used an open dataset of modern country boundaries, based on the *Natural Earth* dataset (`https://www.naturalearthdata.com/`). We don't even need to download it—the data is small enough for us to read it from the web on every run. As the boundary file is naive—there is no specific projection; we'll add the MERCATOR reference system manually—this is optional but will help us to remap to a different projection:

```
import geopandas as gp
url = 'https://unpkg.com/world-atlas@1/world/50m.json'
MERCATOR = {'init': 'epsg:4326', 'no_defs': True}

borders = gp.read_file(url)
borders.crs = MERCATOR
```

Now, let's see what the borders look like overall:

```
borders.plot(figsize=(10, 5))
```

This code will result in the following screenshot:

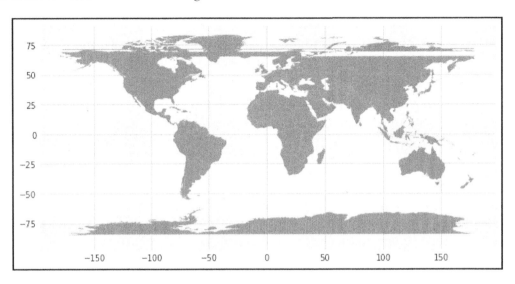

Okay, we see that the borders cover the whole planet (there is a glitch with Russia as its territory stretches over 180 degree longitude, into negative degrees—luckily, we won't have this issue once we zoom in).

As we'll be plotting Europe, let's use an appropriate projection, ETRS-LAEA. Its EPSG number can be found on `https://spatialreference.org/`.

To convert into other projections, just use the `to_crs` method:

```
borders = borders.to_crs(epsg=3035)
```

Next, we need to convert our existing dataframe into `GeoDataFrame` with points. Luckily, `geopandas` has a built-in helper function for that. We'll convert them into the same projection, as well:

```
gdf = gp.GeoDataFrame(
  data, geometry=gp.points_from_xy(data['Longitude'],
data['Latitude'])).to_crs(borders2.crs)
```

Now, we can combine the two, encoding the total casualties for the marker size:

```
ax=borders2.plot(color='lightgrey', edgecolor='white', figsize=(12,12))

gdf.plot(ax=ax, color='red', markersize=(data['killed
total']/1000).clip(lower=1), alpha=.2);


ax.margins(x=-.4, y=-0.4) # Values in (-0.5, 0.0) zooms in to center
ax.set_axis_off()
```

Note how we use the output of the first plot and store it in `ax` variable, which we then path to the second chart—this way, both will plot on the same canvas in the order they execute as margins essentially "zooming in" on Europe while `set_axis_off` removes axes for the chart.

Here is the outcome:

The circles represent battles, with the size matching the number of total casualties. As you can see, the Stalingrad siege is quite an outlier—both spatially and by the number of casualties.

 Please refer the graphic bundle of the book for all images of the book

Great! We were able to plot our graphics on the map, and indeed it gives us a better understanding of the data we're working on. One limitation with this map and all of the other charts we made so far is that they are static. matplotlib has some interaction capacity; for example, you can set your chart to be pannable and zoomable, but it won't provide tooltip, selection, or any other advanced interaction. Luckily, we have other visualization libraries that can do that, for example, altair.

Declarative visualization with vega and altair

Until now, we have used the matplotlib library, via the built-in pandas interface. matplotlib is powerful and essential to Python's data visualization ecosystem. It is not, however, the only visualization library we can use. In fact, there are a plethora of visualization tools, different in their format, focus, or even philosophy. In this section, we'll introduce you to a different tool—and different concept of data visualization—and that is altair, which is a Python library based around the Vega engine. What makes it so different? A couple of things, in fact.

First of all, its core philosophy is based on the declarative approach, which can be boiled down to the following principle: the core idea is to write each chart in code as a declaration—basically, a recipe. This declaration would define what to do with the data but doesn't have to include data, implementation, or aesthetical features—colors, fonts, and more. There are a few outcomes of that approach:

- First, the declaration itself is a plain JSON file that can be written either manually or in any language. Hence, Vega is language-agnostic in its nature. In our case, Altair is a Python-side declaration generator; the declaration is then passed to the Vega engine, so that we don't need to work (or even know) JavaScript, per se. Also, because of the way the declaration works as an intermediate, the resulting visualization can be easily published as a standalone chart.

- Second, the default engine of Vega is based on JavaScript (D3) and supports `svg` and `canvas` (raster). However, as Vega's interface is defined as a mini-language, decoupled of the specific implementation, there can be other engines. In fact, there are a few alternative engines already.
- Because both style and data can be stored independently of the declaration, Vega is perfect for branded visualizations—as a user, you won't need to even think of the style guides, and designers can iterate over designs independently. Similarly, as data can be stored separately, one visualization can be re-used for other datasets or can even be used to show live data—you just need to update the linked dataset.
- Vega also supports advanced interactions, allowing the developer to build complex systems without going into specifics. This interaction can be very useful for exploration analysis!

Let's test Altair out by replicating the charts we just built. We always start by creating an Altair `Chart` object:

```
import altair as alt

chart = alt.Chart(data)
```

Next, we define the type of marks—for example, to build a scatterplot, we use circle marks. Here, we can provide the properties of the mark, which are not dependent on the data:

```
chart = chart.mark_circle(size=60)
```

Finally, we add encodings, defining which column in the data should be encoded as x coordinates and which features to show in the tooltip. If we want the model to be interactive, all we need to do is call an `interactive()` method at the end. By default, this will add zoom and pan capabilities. We'll also pass the `result` property, representing the winner of a particular battle, to be encoded as shapes. Here is the code:

```
chart.encode(
    x='allies killed',
    y='axis killed',
    shape='result',
    tooltip=['name', 'allies killed', 'axis killed', 'start']
).interactive()
```

And here is the outcome! This diagram is similar to the one we made in `matplotlib`—but this time, we can zoom, pan, and hover over specific points, allowing us to better explore the data:

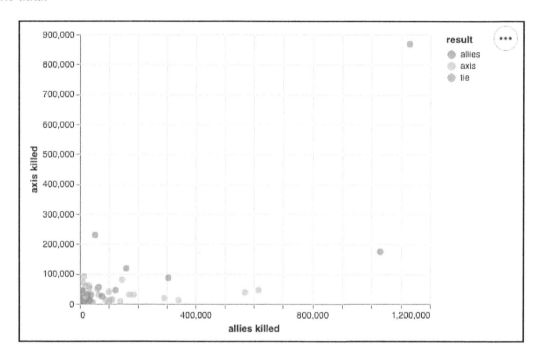

In the making of this chart, we had to overwrite the `chart` object multiple times; usually, most of the settings are done in one piece, like this:

```
chart = alt.Chart(data).mark_circle(size=60).encode(
    x='allies killed',
    y='axis killed',
    color=alt.Color('parent', legend=None),
    tooltip=['name', 'allies killed', 'axis killed', 'start']
).interactive()
```

The great feature of Altair's design is that all of the properties can be overwritten—and the `chart` object will always return the resulting object; hence, we can create the templates, swapping only what we need for a particular visualization.

 Note the triple-dot button in the upper-right corner of the chart—this menu (which, by the way, can be removed) offers to export the chart into a vector or raster, open it in the online editor, or store the specification.

What else can we visualize with Altair? A lot! For a fair comparison, let's draw another map of the battles.

Drawing maps with Altair

Now, let's reproduce the map. It is actually pretty straightforward. First, we need to specify the source for the boundaries dataset and the properties of the projection:

```
url = 'https://unpkg.com/world-atlas@1/world/50m.json'

data_geo = alt.topo_feature(url, feature='countries')
proj = {'center':[10, 52], 'type':'conicEquidistant', 'scale':800}
```

As you can see, Altair can be linked to the data source and will pull the data from the web during runtime. It is a nice feature, as we can similarly link it to the dataset we'll be constantly updating, hence getting a real-time data snapshot. We'll use that option in Chapter 17, *Let's Build a Dashboard*, to build a dashboard. Now, we will create another chart object, using projection and the data source—this will be our base map:

```
basemap = alt.Chart(data_geo).mark_geoshape(
    clip=True,
    fill='lightgray',
    stroke='white',
).properties(
    width=700,
    height=700,
).project(**proj)
```

Finally, we need to get the points and create another chart object, encoding coordinates, marker size, and the projection:

```
mask = data[['Latitude', 'Longitude']].notnull().all(1)
points = alt.Chart(data[mask]).mark_circle(clip=True, color='red',
opacity=.5).encode(
    latitude='Lattitude',
    longitude='Longitude',
    size=alt.Size('killed total:Q', scale=alt.Scale(type='linear',
range=[10, 1000], domain=[10, 1_500_000]), title='Casualties'),
    color=alt.value('red'),
    tooltip=['name', 'killed total'],
    href = 'url'
).project(**proj)
```

Finally, we need to overlay the two charts into one. In Altair, it is very easy—all we need is to add them together (note, however, that, in this case, the order of charts is important—whichever is last in the operation will be on top of the other). Similarly, the pipe and division symbols put charts on a side or below one another:

```
map = basemap + points;
map
```

Here is the resulting map. Note that we have tooltips with the values we defined, and, thanks to the `href` argument, a Wiki page will be opened on a click for each object:

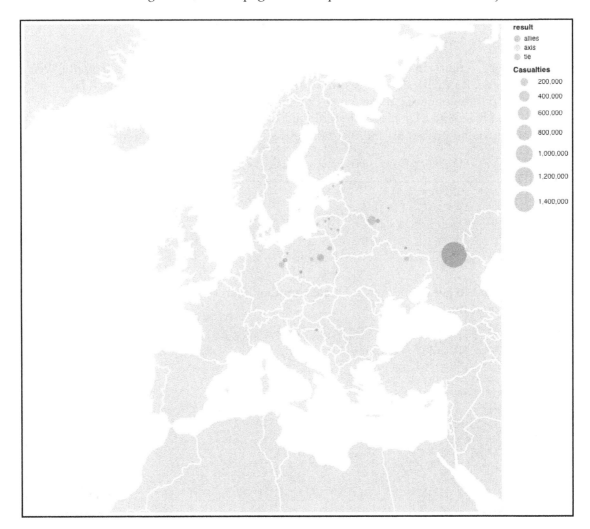

Unfortunately, due to various reasons, Vega—and, therefore, Altair—does not support pan/zoom for maps, for now. If you need to zoom into your map, the Folium library (a Python wrapper around the famous `leaflet.js` library) might be a better choice. Folium supports both `geopandas` dataframes and Altair specifications.

Now, Altair charts can be useful inside your Notebooks—but how to export them as a static image or—better yet—a standalone interactive application?

Storing the Altair chart

One simple way to export your chart as a raster or vector image is via the triple-dot button. But you can also do this programmatically if you need to. First, we need to store the composite chart as an object. Next, we just execute the save; the method-specific type of export will be inferred from the file type:

```
chart = basemap + points
chart.save('chart.png') # or 'chart.svg' for vector
```

Programmatic export for both `png` and `svg` requires the Selenium package and either Google Chrome or Mozilla Firefox browser, plus a corresponding driver to be installed—check the documentation via https://altair-viz.github.io/user_guide/saving_charts.html#png-and-svg-format.

An alternative to this is to store a raw specification. For that, just change the path to `chart.vl.json`. This specification can be later used by another instance of a Vega-Lite application. JupyterLab will render this specification automatically, and there is a plugin for VS Code that will do the same.

Finally, the simplest way to publish your chart on the web is to export it as an HTML application (in fact, it just stores exactly the same HTML app every time, just with a different JSON specification):

```
chart.to_html('chart.html')
```

Go ahead and open this HTML in your browser—it should show up and behave (including all of the interactions) exactly the same way it did in the Notebook! Now, the only thing left to do is to move this file somewhere online, for example, onto an Amazon S3 bucket or similar service.

In this section, we just scratched the surface of what is possible with `altair`, but no worries! We'll go for a deeper round in `Chapter 17`, *Let's Build a Dashboard*, when we'll build an interactive data dashboard.

Big data visualization with datashader

Big data also needs to be visualized! Big data visualizations are somewhat rare; in part because they are hard to do, but also because they are hard to interpret and communicate insights. A big data visualization is usually either a network, a map, or a mapping (similarity-based, computed 2- or 3-dimensional distributions). They are usually astonishing and complex! In fact, a few early inventors of big data visualizations, such as Eric Fisher, became famous for their work with big data.

As we mentioned, big data visualizations are generally hard due to the mere size of the dataset. Standard tools won't work— for `matplotlib`, even with a raster engine, it will take hours to plot millions of points, and Altair won't do it at all. For a long time, there wasn't an easy solution to this problem. This changed with the announcement of yet another Python library: `datashader`. `datashader` leverages a few modern techniques and packages for fast computation (specifically Numba, another package for fast computation that leverages just-in-time compilation, which we'll discuss in `Chapter 20`, *Best Practices and Python Performance*), and a smart approach to the visualization itself—it bins data to a grid of pixels, computing the aggregate for this grid under the hood. Indeed, binning can save a lot of time on visualization, and using a pixel grid resolves all of the drawbacks of larger bins—you can't see anything within a pixel, anyway. On top of that, once `datashader` computes a matrix of pixel values, we can change the appearance of the picture without the need to re-aggregate values.

Let's try `datashader` on one example. None of the datasets we've worked with so far are large enough, so we'll use a new one—an open dataset of 311 complaints for New York City for the whole year of 2018. We briefly mentioned this data, and shared code to collect it, in `Chapter 6`, *First Script – Geocoding with Web API*. Just in case, the code we used to collect this data is also stored in this chapter's folder, as an `_pull_311.py` script. To get the data, just run this script from the Terminal: `python _pull_311.py`. The code for visualization is stored in the `3_big_data_viz_311.ipynb` notebook.

311 is a municipal public service that is meant to process citizens' input regarding non-urgent issues; in other words, it is something similar to 911, but for non-threatening, non-urgent issues such as noise, litter, fallen trees, graffiti, and more. Complaints can be filed via a phone call, text message, email, application, or web form. The city of New York shares anonymized records of such complaints daily, including the time of the complaint, coordinates, type of complaint, relevant city department or institution, and time of complaint closing and some other information.

The data we collected is stored in 12 CSV files, one for each month of 2018, and includes 2,747,985 records. This is not big data per se—at least it can fit in memory on modern machines, but it is hard to work with and definitely already non-trivial to visualize.

Let's try to load the data, first. Because we're dealing with multiple CSVs, let's use `glob`, a built-in Python function for getting multiple files from a pattern:

```
import pandas as pd
from glob import glob
```

Now, we need to specify a pattern, and run `glob` on it:

```
>>> paths = './data/311/*.csv'
>>> files = glob(paths)
>>> files
['./data/311/2018-06.csv',
 './data/311/2018-12.csv',
 './data/311/2018-07.csv',
 './data/311/2018-11.csv',
 './data/311/2018-05.csv',
 './data/311/2018-04.csv',
 './data/311/2018-10.csv',
 './data/311/2018-01.csv',
 './data/311/2018-03.csv',
 './data/311/2018-02.csv',
 './data/311/2018-09.csv',
 './data/311/2018-08.csv']
```

And finally, we can now traverse over those files, load them one by one, and concatenate into a single dataframe:

```
data = pd.concat([pd.read_csv(p, low_memory=False, index_col=0) for p in
glob(paths)])
```

Here, we used the `low_memory=False` flag, which helps `pandas` to correctly match the data type of each column.

If your machine has a small memory size, you might want to load fewer months. Alternatively, and only for some maps, data can be read by month, aggregated with `datashader` separately within the generator, and then summarized all together. `datashader` stores `canvas` matrices as simple 2-dimensional numeric `numpy` matrices, so it is easy to do.

Now, we can plot a simple density distribution of complaints. First, let's load `datashader`:

```
import datashader as ds
import datashader.transfer_functions as tf
from datashader.colors import inferno
```

Now, we'll create a canvas (essentially, a 2-dimensional matrix of pixels). Next, we'll use this canvas to aggregate our data. The last argument, `ds.count()`, is an aggregation function, in this case, counting the number of records (complaints) for each pixel:

```
cvs = ds.Canvas(plot_width=1000, plot_height=1000)
agg = cvs.points(data, 'x_coordinate_state_plane',
'y_coordinate_state_plane', ds.count())
```

Once this is done, we can move to the actual visualization with a single command:

```
tf.shade(agg, cmap=inferno, how='eq_hist')
```

Here, we essentially just colorize the `agg` matrix, converting values into colors. Notice the last argument: it describes how to distribute values along the color map. A `linear` strategy will map values to color without any distortion— maximum values will get edge colors, and all values in between will get color proportionally. However, often data is not distributed evenly—there are spikes and long tails with relatively small values—leading to small blurbs of distinct colors, and everything else in the same color. To fight that, other strategies can be used, for example, `log` and `cube` will colorize the logarithm and cubic root of the values, respectfully. A *weapon of last resort*, `eq_hist` will, essentially, colorize the rank of the value—this way, there will be about the same number of pixels of each tone. A choice of strategy depends on the specifics of a dataset.

Because of the high density of elements on the plot, and the nature of visualization itself, we couldn't use anything but color; not all colors are properly represented on B/W images, so we recommend checking those visualizations in the repository (`https://github.com/PacktPublishing/Learn-Python-by-Building-Data-Science-Applications/blob/master/Chapter12/3_big_data_viz-311.ipynb`).

Here is the resulting chart. The map is gorgeous—and very detailed. From the distribution, we can see a distinct shape of two islands, roads, towns, and structures:

Let's look closer at the chart. Here, lighter colors (yellow, originally) represent a higher density of complaints. Darker colors mean a smaller number of complaints.

 Since the colors are not visible here, please refer to the graphics bundle link (https://static.packt-cdn.com/downloads/9781789535365_ ColorImages.pdf) for all images in the book.

As you see, density generally decreases from the center of the city to its edges, and that makes sense. At the same time, we can eyeball areas of a higher or lower number of complaints, compared to the surroundings. Most of them are quite meaningful for the person familiar with the city: for example, why is the Bergen Beach (dark corner in the lower center of the image) so distinctive from the surroundings? Why is the eastern edge of the Central Park (the white rectangular on Manhattan) so dark compared to the surroundings? Why is the density so high on the eastern side of Prospect Park (the right-hand white shape in the middle of Brooklyn) than on the western side? The high level of resolution allows us to drill down to the smallest elements on the map, questioning even small spatial irregularity.

Let's do a similar map, but this time aggregate by the most typical source of complaint, which is stored in the `open_data_channel_type` column. First, let's check all of the possible sources:

```
>>> data['open_data_channel_type'].value_counts()
PHONE    1469034
ONLINE   565348
UNKNOWN  366890
MOBILE   314247
OTHER    32466
Name: open_data_channel_type, dtype: int64
```

As there are only five sources, it seems easier to manually define a color to each:

```
colors = {
 'PHONE':'red',
 'ONLINE':'blue',
 'UNKNOWN':'grey',
 'MOBILE':'green',
 'OTHER': 'brown'
}
```

We also have to convert this column into the `category` data type. The `category` data type is way more compact than strings (it stores an integer number for each category), but is also required by `datashader` for category-based operations—otherwise, `datashader` simply won't work:

```
data['open_data_channel_type'] =
data['open_data_channel_type'].astype('category')
```

Now, let's aggregate by most typical cause:

```
agg_cat = cvs.points(data, 'x_coordinate_state_plane',
'y_coordinate_state_plane',
                    ds.count_cat('open_data_channel_type'))
```

With color keys, there is no need to specify a coloring method—you just pass colors:

```
tf.shade(agg_cat, color_key=colors)
```

Here is our result. Here, we're looking at exactly the same dataset, just colored by the most frequent source for each pixel:

As with the previous map, this one contains multiple interesting patterns—we can eyeball it for hours! For example, we could notice chains of pixels on Staten Island (lower-left corner)—perhaps those are highways. Through the city, we can notice clusters of blue (online) and green (mobile)—those, most likely, can be attributed to offices and transit areas.

At our final step, let's see how the average time it takes to close the complaint is distributed across the city. Before mapping, we need to compute this time as a number—for example, subtract two timestamps, and convert the `timedelta` object into a number of minutes as an integer:

```
data['created_date'] = pd.to_datetime(data['created_date'])
data['closed_date'] = pd.to_datetime(data['closed_date'])
data['time_to_close'] = (data['closed_date'] -
data['created_date']).dt.seconds
```

Now, we can calculate the average of `time_to_close` for each pixel:

```
agg_time = cvs.points(data, 'x_coordinate_state_plane',
'y_coordinate_state_plane', ds.mean('time_to_close'))

tf.shade(agg_time, cmap=inferno, how='eq_hist')
```

And here is the outcome:

Again, there is plenty of interesting stuff here (most likely, a large difference in time to close is a result of the different nature of complaints). Even more interesting is to compare different maps—some areas share similar properties in one context, but drastically different in the others. The best part is that we, relatively easily, created a bunch of insanely detailed maps that communicate both the overall picture of the dataset and all of the intricacies of specific locations. Indeed, big data visualizations often introduce us to unexpected patterns that are hard to catch in any other way.

Summary

In this chapter, we discussed how to derive insights from the raw data—compute descriptive statistics and aggregates and draw basic plots of relationships—and use special tools for big data visualization. As a result, we've learned how to start working with the dataset, investigate its overall properties, and drill down to specific details. We also learned how to visualize data, a vital skill for both personal data exploration and sharing the insights with a broad audience. These skills are fundamental for data analysis—knowing what to ask and how to answer your question with the data and noticing patterns and anomalies in the data and being able to interpret them and speculate on their origins.

In our next chapter, we'll go a step further in that direction, leveraging statistical and machine learning models to guide our interpretation.

Questions

1. How can we understand some general properties of dataset in `pandas`?
2. What does the `resample` function do in `pandas`? How is it different from aggregation?
3. How does visualization work in `pandas`?
4. What are the benefits of declarative data visualization (for example, with Altair)?
5. In which cases can big data visualization be useful?

Further reading

- *Data Visualization with Python*, by Mario Döbler, Tim Großmann, et al., published by Packt (https://www.packtpub.com/in/big-data-and-business-intelligence/data-visualisation-python)
- *Learning Python Data Visualization*, by Benjamin Walter Keller), published by Packt (https://www.packtpub.com/big-data-and-business-intelligence/learning-python-data-visualization-video-0)

13
Training a Machine Learning Model

As we have learned in the last chapter, data always contains valuable insights. Exploring with statistics, filters, and charts is a great tool for this. However, data has another internal value—its predictive power; it can be used to fit an algorithm (machine learning model) that will then be able to predict the values of interest and explain its judgment.

Machine learning (ML) is a large and complex topic that is clearly out of the scope of this book. Indeed, building an advanced and complex model requires deep theoretical knowledge of the specific domain and a lot of time and exploration. However, some ML models are very simple and easy to comprehend, and the basic underlying principles are all the same. Many ML models don't provide a good interpretation—but here, we'll use the ones that do.

In this chapter, we'll discuss the basics of ML and train a few basic ML models on our WWII dataset. We'll further interpret their behavior and caveats and how to mitigate some of the issues. In particular, we'll cover the following:

- Basics of ML
- Unsupervised learning (clustering) using the k-means algorithm
- Supervised learning with k-nearest neighbors and linear models

Technical requirements

The code for this chapter requires two packages—`scikit-learn` and `pydotplus`. As usual, you can find all of the code in the repository, in the `Chapter13` folder.

Understanding the basics of ML

As it's implied in its name, **Machine Learning** (**ML**) is the science of building machines (algorithms) that can learn from data. In other words, this class of algorithms generates certain outcomes (predictions) based on the relations they infer from the training data—not from the hardcoded, predetermined rules. Usually, ML is described as having two main branches—supervised and unsupervised ML.

Unsupervised models attempt to find structure in the data itself, without any given *supervision* or *target* to focus on. The usual task is to find clusters of similar records (for example, users) to understand the underlying **latent** logic (for example, using target audiences and the corresponding use cases for the service).

Supervised learning is all about *training* the model by feeding it pairs of *independent features* and the correct values of the target variable of interest as a training set. For example, supervised ML is used to detect fraudulent activity, given a user's actions or to get an estimate of a certain value (for example, the price of a house)—all by inferring the result from the training dataset, which includes the target variable.

Many models use complex math and require huge computation power, but that is not always the case—some of them are very simple to use and easy to comprehend. Most importantly, ML runs solely on mathematics; although it might be incredibly useful and it can empower and enable, it can never replace common sense and critical thinking.

Let's now go around and see how different supervised and unsupervised models can be trained and used to analyze our WWII dataset.

Exploring unsupervised learning

First, let's try *clustering* our data. Clustering is a type of unsupervised learning with the goal of grouping records based solely on their features. It is often used to get a better understanding of the data before building a supervised model or as part of the exploratory analysis. It also could be used on its own. One common task is defining the target audience for the service or product. In our case, this should reveal the similarities between the battles across the dataset.

This task may seem to be simple for a 1- or 2-dimensional (one- or two-column) datasets—indeed, our eyes and brains are splendid at finding clusters visually. It is, however, a near-impossible task for a human when the number of dimensions grows beyond three. To automate that process, we will use a **k-means clustering algorithm**—simple, performant, and easy to interpret and debug.

k-means is one of the most popular algorithms for the task, mainly due to its fast performance and the small set of **hyperparameters**—external parameters of the model, which have to be chosen outside of the training process itself. The main drawbacks of this method are the inability to catch complex shapes (k-means only supports convex and isotropic shapes) and the number of clusters that have to be predefined. This necessity to specify the number of clusters can be both a curse and a blessing. There are methods to find *the best* number of clusters (for example, the **elbow** method), or there can be an obvious, business-driven need for a specific number of clusters.

Before we run the model, we'll need to load and prepare the dataset:

1. First of all, let's think about which features can and should be used here. For our first attempt, let's use the raw number of soldiers, tanks, and guns on each side:

   ```
   cols = [
       'allies_infantry', 'axis_infantry',
       'allies_tanks', 'axis_tanks',
       'allies_guns', 'axis_guns'
   ]
   ```

   This choice is arbitrary but will have a direct impact on the outcome, as we'll soon see.

    We didn't use any time-specific or belligerent-specific values as these values will just group records together based on their place in history, which is what we know already.

2. As with most ML models, k-means does not itself support empty cells and can only run on numeric values. There are multiple ways to resolve both issues—depending on the specifics of the goal and other considerations. All of the features we picked are numeric already, but we'll have to take care of the missing values. For now, we'll take only records with existing infantry numbers and fill empty cells in other columns:

   ```
   mask = data[['allies_infantry', 'axis_infantry']].notnull().all(1)
   data_kmeans = data.loc[mask, cols].fillna(0)
   ```

3. Finally, we can run the clustering on this dataset.

4. Let's split our data into five groups. It is, again, an arbitrary number. There are some methods to define the *best* number of clusters in terms of particular metrics (for example, inertia), but we won't do that in our case for the sake of simplicity. We also set a `random_state` seed for reproducibility—k-means is robust, but not deterministic and can randomly swap cluster numbers:

```
from sklearn.cluster import KMeans
model = KMeans(n_clusters=5, random_state=2019)
```

5. After this, the algorithm is ready to spit out the labels. The following code does exactly that by running a standard `predict` method on our data. Labels are just integers representing each group, starting with zero. For visualization purposes (so that there won't be **Cluster O**), we add 1 to each:

```
>>> labels = model.fit_predict(data_kmeans) + 1

>>> print(labels)
[1 1 1 1 4 1 1 1 1 1 1 1 1 1 1 1 1 1 1 1 4 4 4 1 1 4 4 1 4 1 4 1 1 1
 4 5 1 3 5 4 2 3 1 1 1 1 3 4 3 1 1 3 3 1 1 1 1 1 1 1 1 1 1 1 2 1 1 1 1
 1 1 4 3 1 1 1 1 1 1 3 3 4 1 1 2 1]
```

6. Let's now take a look at the result by visualizing the dataset with the new column:

```
data_kmeans['label'] = ('Cluster ' +
    pd.Series((labels+1)).astype(str)).values
data_kmeans[['name', 'result', 'start']] = data.loc[mask, ['name',
'result', 'start']]

c = alt.Chart(data_kmeans).mark_point().encode(
    color=alt.Color('label:N', legend=alt.Legend(title='Cluster')),
    x='allies_infantry', y='axis_infantry', shape='result',
    tooltip=data_kmeans.columns.tolist()).interactive()

c
```

7. And here is the outcome. As you can see, there is a somewhat distinctive pattern—clusters tend to be grouped together, both by *x* and *y* coordinate axes as if only those two properties were used:

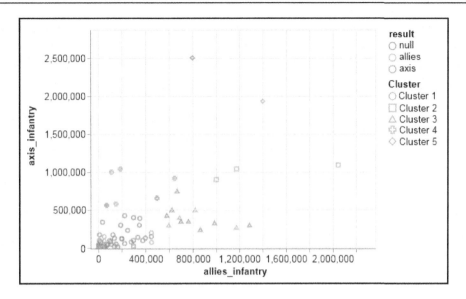

Why is that so? To answer this question, let's talk about how the algorithm works, first. There are a few simple steps:

1. *k* centroids are generated randomly in the features space (in other words, we generate k random rows with the same features and within the same range as the dataset).
2. For each of those centroids, a Euclidean distance to all of the data points of the dataset is calculated (theoretically, k-means can use other distances as well, but that is quite rare).
3. All data points are then assigned to the closest center point. For each group, a centroid is calculated, and the center point is moved there.
4. From that, the cycle is repeated—points are re-assigned, centroids are recalculated, and center points are moved. This happens over and over again until center points stop moving.

As a subsequence of that approach, the model is always in Euclidean space—that is, all units for all of the features are viewed as *equal*. At the same time, we obviously have thousands of soldiers but only dozens of tanks and airplanes in our dataset. Therefore, infantry features are treated as way more important by definition.

One way to make the model to pay more attention to tanks, airplanes, or any other feature, is to standardize them—for each feature, we will subtract its mean and divide the result by the standard error—that way, they will all be spread equally around zero. In fact, `sklearn` has built-in functionality for that task.

In the following code, we're using the `sklearn` function, `scale`, to scale multiple columns at once. The function may give you a warning if some of the columns are integers —it will convert them into floats as part of the scaling process. It also returns a `numpy` array, not a dataframe, but that's okay in this case:

```
from sklearn.preprocessing import scale
data_to_scale = data_kmeans.drop(['label', 'name', 'start', 'result'],
axis=1)
data_scaled = scale(data_to_scale)

labels_scaled = model.fit_predict(data_scaled) + 1
data_kmeans['label 2'] = ('Cluster ' +
    pd.Series((labels_scaled)).astype(str)).values
```

But does the scaling affect labels? Let's see! We will re-run the model again, as follows:

```
c.data = data_kmeans
c.encode(color=alt.Color('label 2:N',
        legend=alt.Legend(title='Cluster')))
```

This time, shapes are mixed—clearly, infantry numbers are not the only features in play. Here is what the new clustering looks like:

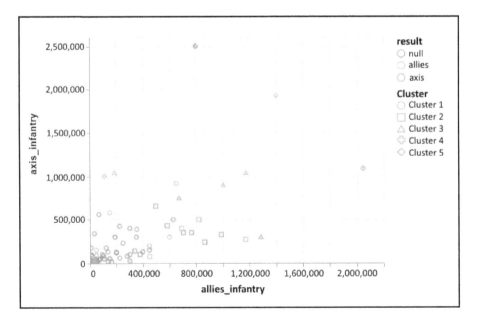

But does it offer any insights? We'd argue that it does. Combined with the interactivity given by Altair, clusters help us to highlight some internal similarities. For example, **Cluster 1** clearly represents battles with small numbers on both sides. **Cluster 2** represents battles with a considerably larger number of infantry for allies. **Cluster 3** groups together battles where allies have a lot of tanks and/or guns. **Cluster 4** represents battles with a small to none number of vehicles—including a battle for Voronezh and Prague offensive—in both cases, it is clear that the number of tanks wasn't reported due to the mere scale of the operations. Finally, **Cluster 5** seems to represent battles with a large number of axis tanks.

Moving on to supervised learning

Now, let's try supervised learning. As we discussed earlier, supervised models are designed to predict, or estimate, target variables—either a continuous value (**regression problem**) or a specific category (**classification problem**). Other types of problems (tagging, semantic segmentation, and many more)—can then be defined as one of those two. Let's glance over a suite of relatively simple models now.

One simple yet often pretty performant model is the **k-nearest neighbors** (**KNN**) **algorithm.** It is quite similar to k-means, as it also performs in Euclidean space.

k-nearest neighbors

KNN is both interpretable and fast and for small and medium datasets (for large ones, there is a scalable modification—approximate KNN). It also has an important property—similar to k-means, it works on distances, and therefore sees the *interaction* between the features, which many other algorithms can't do.

The logic behind KNN is very simple—for each record it predicts, it finds *k* nearest records (neighbors—hence the name) most similar (close in the feature space) to the given one in the training set and infers data from them. The algorithm can be used both for classification (in this case, a most frequent class for the *neighbors* will be taken) or regression (calculated as a weighted average of the neighbors' values). The following sections explain these in detail.

Of course, KNN has its drawbacks as well:

- It can't extrapolate beyond the training set—similar to k-means, it depends on the unit scales.
- It also has to store all data in the object itself, so it won't be a great choice (at least, in its basic version) to run on big datasets.

- This algorithm cannot ignore features or treat them as less important. Adding bad features to the dataset may lead to a decrease in performance.
- KNN has also a somewhat limited value for interpretation—it can spill out the neighbors but won't reveal any meaningful trends, nor estimate the relationship between the target value and particular features.

Let's try to use KNN to predict the outcome of each battle, using the same scaled dataset we used for the clustering problem. Let's see how it is done:

1. Before we run the model, we first need to convert the `result` variable into a numeric feature, as well. As some battles have no clear victory, we'll have three outcomes—negative for an `axis` victory, positive for an `allies` victory, and zero for a tie as shown here in the code. The following code will replace `axis` with `-1`, `allies` with `1`, and fill all null values with `0`. For debugging purposes, we then count the number of all unique values in the column:

```
>>> data['result_num'] = data['result'].map({'axis':-1,
'allies':1}).fillna(0)   # 0 for tie
>>> data['result_num'].value_counts()

-1.0 93
 1.0 34
 0.0 6
Name: result_num, dtype: int64
```

2. Next, we need to split the data into two parts: training and testing, as we'll need to measure the quality of the outcome. Luckily, there is a `sklearn helper` function for that, as well. All we need is to specify a test size (as a fraction) and `random_state`—to be sure the change in the metrics is not attributed to change in the data splits:

```
from sklearn.model_selection import train_test_split

mask = data[cols].isnull().any(1)
X = data.loc[~mask, cols]
y = data.loc[~mask, 'result_num']

Xtrain, Xtest, ytrain, ytest = train_test_split(X, y,
 test_size=0.2, random_state=2019)
```

3. To scale the data or not depends on the case. Scaling ensures that all given features are equally contributing to the clustering—this may be important for the performance, but will undermine the interpretability of the model and, especially for KNN, may decrease the accuracy—KNN cannot *ignore* features. In this specific case, accuracy for the unscaled dataset is better—perhaps as points are further away from each other.

4. The `fit` method, in this case, essentially internalizes the training dataset. The following code initializes the model, fits it to the training set, and predicts values for the test set:

```
from sklearn.neighbors import KNeighborsClassifier
model = KNeighborsClassifier(n_neighbors=5) # again, arbitrary
number
model.fit(Xtrain, ytrain)
y_pred = model.predict(Xtest)
```

But how to measure the performance of the model? For the classification model, it seems logical to start with accuracy—a ratio of correct predictions to the total number of them. This metric—and many others—is also built into `sklearn`. Let's use it to measure our model's performance. The following code does exactly that:

```
>>> from sklearn.metrics import accuracy_score
>>> accuracy_score(y_test, y_pred)
0.5
```

The result is, of course, not very impressive—we didn't perform better than a coin flip. The round number, however, can give us hints—as we dropped any data points with missing values, our testing sample is very small. With this sample size, metrics are very volatile and hard to interpret. Still, this model can be used to further explore our dataset, as KNN can spill out the neighboring records in addition to the estimate.

In the following table, we're getting the five neighbors for the first record in the test dataset, using the model's `kneighbors` method:

```
>>> Xtest.head(1)
     allies_infantry axis_infantry allies_tanks axis_tanks allies_guns
axis_guns
106          378000.0      100000.0       1000.0      350.0      3241.0
2000.0

>>> Xtrain.iloc[model.kneighbors(Xtest.head(1))[1][0]]

     allies_infantry  axis_infantry  allies_tanks  axis_tanks  allies_guns
axis_guns
55          1173500.0      1040000.0         894.0       950.0      13451.0
```

3000.0					
66	1286000.0	300700.0	2409.0	625.0	26379.0
5500.0					
98	1002200.0	900000.0	1979.0	900.0	11265.0
6300.0					
126	1171800.0	270000.0	1600.0	772.0	5425.0
434.0					
73	822000.0	500000.0	550.0	146.0	4600.0
2389.0					

The preceding table shows the records for the data points in the metrics. Here, the first row with index `106` represents the Battle of the Dukla Pass in the Carpathian mountains. Its five most similar neighbors are Operation Uranus, Operation Kutuzov, the Lvov–Sandomierz Offensive, the Vienna Offensive, and the Leningrad–Novgorod Offensive, all solely in terms of the number of troops. It seems that they all share advantages in the number of troops for the allies and that they were all fought in the second half of the war by the Soviets—the model didn't know all that, but it is hidden behind the values. In other words, only Soviets on that front had armies of that scale, and only in the second part of the war—it's not really hard to guess, but still useful for understanding the data.

Linear regression

Finally, let's review yet another model—arguably, the most established and popular around the world. Linear regression is actually a statistical model with a long history. The idea behind linear regression is as follows.

Assuming that variables have linear relationships, independent variables are not correlated, and there is a certain variance in the features, we can estimate the linear relationship between independent and target variables. As a result, our model will be present as a set of coefficients, one per each feature (independent variable), plus one for bias:

$$y_i = \beta_0 + \beta_1 x_{i1} + \cdots + \beta_p x_{ip} + \varepsilon_i \qquad i = 1, \ldots, n$$

Here, i stands for the record index and p for the index of the feature. Epsilon represents an error that the model couldn't explain. This way, to calculate our estimate of y for the record (row) i, we simply need to multiply each feature in the row by the corresponding coefficient and add them up together with the bias (beta zero). All coefficients are universal and calculated beforehand, during the model training. Take a look at the following diagram:

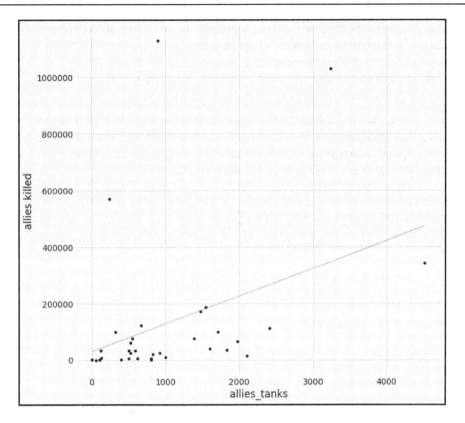

The preceding is a scatterplot of the allies' casualties, plotted against the number of tanks the allies had in each battle. The (red) line here represents a linear model—it is defined by a bias (its *Y* coordinate at *X=0*) and the slope—coefficient for our feature—represents the number of tanks. As you can see, the direct correlation here is positive; the trend is set upward, which is not surprising—more tanks means larger armies on both sides, hence larger casualties overall. Note the three outlier records beyond all others—they significantly impact the model.

Linear models have distinctive properties, in particular:

- Linear models are easy to interpret. Essentially, they define an interpretable coefficient of impact for each feature. Say we predict the price of the apartments: it will attach a price tag, in dollars, for every square foot that would be the price of that square foot, on average.
- They don't require scaling.

- Assuming non-collinearity (that features are not correlated between themselves), those coefficients are independent of other features—for example, the price of a square foot will be estimated on average, independently of the location.
- Linear models are easy to train and very easy to infer (even manually), as it boils down to simple multiplication of a few numbers.
- In contrast to KNN, linear regression generalizes to the absolute—all you get is a set of coefficients, one per feature (plus **bias** constant), each answering what is the impact, on average, of this feature on a target variable. It is useful and easy to digest—but there is no way to go deeper than that.

At the same time, due to its linear nature, this algorithm can't account for complex nuances in the data and usually performs badly as a prediction model. It is also not robust to outliers—if there are outliers in the dataset, it is a good idea to drop them before training the model.

Let's try building a linear model on our dataset. Here, we need to predict a continuous value, so let's try to predict the number of casualties for the allies:

1. First, let's prepare the dataset:

```
cols = [
    'allies_infantry', 'axis_infantry',
    'allies_tanks', 'axis_tanks',
    'allies_guns', 'axis_guns',
    'start_num'
]

mask = data[cols + ['allies killed']].isnull().any(1)
```

2. Now, we can split the features and prepare training and testing sets:

```
y = data.loc[~mask, 'allies killed']
X = data.loc[~mask, cols]

Xtrain, Xtest, ytrain, ytest = train_test_split(X,
                                                y,
                                                test_size=0.3,
                                                random_state=2019)
```

3. Finally, we can train the data and see how it performs.

4. In the following code, we initiate the linear regression model and train it. Lastly, we predict values for the test and store them in the `ypred` variable:

```
from sklearn.linear_model import LinearRegression
from sklearn.metrics import median_absolute_error

model = LinearRegression()
model.fit(Xtrain, ytrain)

ypred = model.predict(Xtest)
```

But how should we measure the performance of the model? The model itself usually uses the mean of the squared errors, but for interpretation, we can use the median (or mean) absolute error as it will preserve units—in our case, the number of casualties. Indeed, our model does not perform extremely well—it has a median error of `42584` people, as shown here:

```
>>> median_absolute_error(ytest, ypred)
42584.419274116095
```

As the test dataset is very small, we can print the errors and check them manually.

Here, we're calculating the errors, as follows:

```
>>> (ypred - ytest)

111     4.934710e+04
27     -3.582174e+04
42      2.148667e+04
106    -1.191980e+03
54     -1.007381e+06
49     -9.226890e+05
Name: allies killed, dtype: float64Summary
```

You can see the difference between correct and predicted values of *y*. As you can see, all but two cases underestimate the real number of casualties. Well, we didn't expect it to be perfect; despite the large errors, this linear model can give us a *bird's-eye view* of the trends—something easy to digest and discuss. Let's take a look at the coefficients representing the impact of each feature on casualties:

```
>>> pd.Series(model.coef_, index=X.columns)

allies_infantry    0.024922
axis_infantry      0.079912
allies_tanks     -25.215543
```

```
axis_tanks        -19.178557
allies_guns         3.797002
axis_guns           0.387496
start_num         -50.093280
dtype: float64
```

In this table, each coefficient represents the number of deaths associated with one unit for each feature, on average. For example, we see that each tank for the allies decreases casualties by `-25`. If that was a causal relationship, this digit would be an actionable point for generals and government to consider. However, correlation is not causation! If you look underneath, each axis tank decreases the number of casualties as well. Isn't it supposed to be the other way around? It is unclear, but perhaps we know the answer: larger tank armies could mean battles outside of the cities and we can imagine that those usually have way less infantry involved—hence, fewer casualties. One trend that is worth discussing is that the number of casualties decreases over time.

Decision trees

Finally, we arrive at our last model in this chapter: decision trees. Similar to linear models, decision trees are spread out and good—although not as easy to digest—for interpretation. The core idea behind trees is very different from linear models but is easy to comprehend. To estimate the outcome, the model generates a binary tree—a tree-like diagram—where each note (intersection) represents a single question, based on the known features, with a yes/no answer. Usually, it is something like the *number of casualties is smaller than 1,000*. At the end of each branch, a corresponding estimate is attached. The tree is generated so that the average accuracy of predictions is maximized.

As the depth of the tree can vary, decision trees can, in theory, predict 100% accuracy on the training set—simply by asking questions until there is only one record on each end. This will, however, decrease the accuracy of any external data. This phenomenon is called **overfitting**. We will talk about how to mitigate it in the next chapter.

Another weak spot of decision trees is that they work on each feature separately—no more of the interactions we enjoyed with KNN. Hence, it is way harder for them to detect any interaction between multiple features. Creating a smart set of features, for example, a ratio of axis troops to allied troops, might lead to a significant gain in performance. For the same reasons, decision trees do not care about scaling, as they don't compare features to each other in any way.

Let's try building a decision tree on our dataset—the same data we ran for the KNN:

```
>>> from sklearn.tree import DecisionTreeClassifier
>>> tree_model = DecisionTreeClassifier(random_state=2019)
>>> tree_model.fit(Xtrain, ytrain)
>>> accuracy_score(ytest, tree_model.predict(Xtest))
0.5
```

In this case, the decision tree performed at the same level the KNN did—perhaps we need to work on our features. But how can we diagnose the model? The sklearn algorithm for decision trees can generate a diagram, defined in the *dot* language of the Graphviz software. This definition can then be rendered, in our case, straight in the notebook.

Following is the code for the diagram generation:

1. First, we need to import a corresponding function from sklearn export_grapvis, together with the pydotplus package for rendering, StringIO for in-memory, file-like objects, and IPython's Image object for visualization within the notebook:

   ```
   from sklearn.tree import export_graphviz
   from io import StringIO
   from IPython.display import Image
   import pydotplus
   ```

2. Now, we need to create a file-like object (we can write like a real file to the disk, instead, if we want).

3. After that, we run the export_graphviz command, passing the tree to be written to the file as a diagram:

   ```
   dot_data = StringIO()

   export_graphviz(tree_model, out_file=dot_data,
                   filled=True, rounded=True,
                   special_characters=True, feature_names=cols)
   ```

4. Finally, we ask pydotplus to render the chart from our pseudo-file and use Image to show the resulting image within the notebook:

   ```
   graph = pydotplus.graph_from_dot_data(dot_data.getvalue())
   Image(graph.create_png())
   ```

5. Here is the outcome:

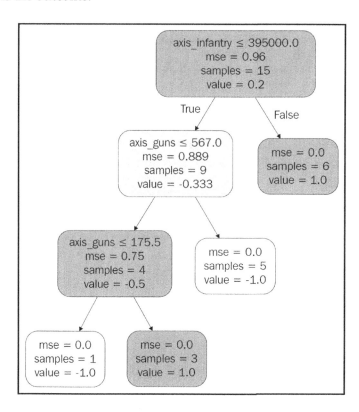

As you can see, according to the model (and our training set), of all features available, the axis infantry is the most significant predictor, followed by the number of guns on the axis side.

In this section, we reviewed unsupervised and supervised machine learning models, which help us to understand the data, their internal relationships, and attempts at predicting values. The models can also be useful beyond prediction itself as, in doing so, they allow the highlighting of relationships within the dataset, quirks in the data, and the role of different properties of each record.

Summary

In this chapter, we learned about two branches of machine learning—the supervised and unsupervised learning—and practiced building four machine learning models, each with its pros and cons. Each of those models can be used directly to create an estimate or analyzed to understand the most important features or trends. In many instances, the latter is more important and useful than the estimate itself. While these models are not as hot and complex as others (ahem, neural networks), they are widely adopted and used everywhere—in healthcare, military, engineering, city planning, policy analysis, logistics, and operational management—chances are one of them is running in some form on the device you have in your pocket or the computer that's sitting on your desk, right now.

The particular models we trained in this chapter had the default settings and used raw features we collected from Wikipedia.

In the next chapter, we'll learn how to improve the models—by engineering a better set of features, optimizing the hyperparameters, or switching to a more complex model. Using this process as a starting point, we will also learn to run computational experiments, keeping track of both code and data and ensuring reproducible outcomes.

Questions

1. What is machine learning?
2. What is the difference between supervised and unsupervised learning?
3. What are the drawbacks of k-means clustering? Why do we need to use a scaler?
4. How does the KNN model work? What are the benefits and limitations of such a model?
5. Why does linear regression give more interpretations? Do we need to scale data in this case?
6. How do decision trees work compared to other models we described?

Further reading

For further information, you can visit the following link: `https://www.packtpub.com/tech/machine-learning`.

14
Improving Your Model – Pipelines and Experiments

In the previous chapter, we trained a basic **machine learning (ML)** model. However, most real-world scenarios require models to be accurate, and that means the model and features need to be improved and fine-tuned for a specific task. This process is usually long, iterative, and based on trial and error.

So, in this chapter, we will see how we can improve and validate model quality and keep track of all of the experiments along the way. As a result, we will improve the quality of the model and learn how to track our experiments and log metrics and parameters. In particular, we'll learn the following:

- Understanding cross-validation and overfitting
- Adding features in order to improve models
- Wrapping models and transformations into pipelines
- Version control of our datasets and metrics using the dvc package

Technical requirements

In this chapter, we will introduce you to the `dvc` package. If you don't use the environment for this book, you can install it with `pip install dvc`. The last part, visualization of the tree, will also require the `pydotplus` package.

As usual, all of the code is shared via a notebook, stored in the repository under `Chapter14` (`https://github.com/PacktPublishing/Learn-Python-by-Building-Data-Science-Applications`).

Understanding cross-validation

In the previous chapter, we built a model with certain assumptions and settings, measuring its performance with accuracy metrics (the overall ratio of correctly classified labels). To do this, we split our data randomly into training and testing sets. While that approach is fundamental, it has its problems. Most importantly, this way, we may fine-tune our model to gain better performance on the test dataset but at the expense of other data (in other words, we might make the model worse while getting a better metric on the specific dataset). This phenomenon is called overfitting.

To combat this issue, we'll use a slightly more complex approach: cross-validation. In its basic form, cross-validation creates multiple so-called folds or data subsections. Usually, each fold has approximately the same size and can be further balanced by target variable representation or any other criteria. Additionally, cross-validation generates all combinations of folds, so that there is one combination with each fold being the test set, and everything else is the train set. It further trains the same model on training data from each combination and measures performance on the corresponding test set. Once it is done, we estimate the average value for each metric across all splits.

Before we start improving our model, let's recreate our model from Chapter 13, *Training a Machine Learning Model*:

```
model1 = DecisionTreeClassifier(random_state=2019, max_depth=10)

cols = [
    'allies_infantry', 'axis_infantry', 'allies_tanks', 'axis_tanks',
    'allies_planes', 'axis_planes', 'duration'
]

y = data['result_num']
```

It is easier not to create the X variable, but to get a subset of columns instead, as we'll be adding more features throughout this chapter.

We don't need to split the data into training and testing sets—cross-validation will do that for us. Let's import the function and run it. We will split the data into 4, as we only have 4 tie cases:

```
from sklearn.model_selection import cross_validate

cv = cross_validate(model1,
                    data[cols], y,
                    cv=4)
```

Now, let's convert cv from a dictionary into a dataframe:

```
>>> cv = pd.DataFrame(cv)
>>> cv
    fit_time  score_time  test_score
0   0.003015  0.001030    0.500000
1   0.003033  0.000937    0.571429
2   0.002311  0.000868    0.428571
3   0.001939  0.001125    0.250000

>>> cv['test_score'].mean()
0.4375
```

This function, cross_validate, is the basic, core function. In the next sections, we'll use cross_val_score—a simple wrapper around cross_validate, that returns only scores. As you can see here, on average, our performance is pretty sad—45% accuracy. This is our starting point; let's now improve it. For that, let's first understand how feature engineering works!

Exploring feature engineering

Now that we made a system to fairly compare models with no fear of overfitting, let's think about how we can improve our model. One way would be to create new features that might add more context. One way to go about this is to create features of our own, for example, calculate a proportion of armies on different sides or the absolute difference in the number of soldiers—we can't say in advance which would work better. Let's try it out with the help of the following code:

1. First, we'll create a ratio of soldiers on either side:

```
data['infantry_ratio'] = data['allies_infantry'] /
data['axis_infantry']
cols.append('infantry_ratio')
```

2. Now, we won't do that for tanks, planes, and so on, as the numbers here are very small and we'll have to deal with division by zero. Instead, we'll compute the difference in absolute numbers:

```
for tp in 'infantry', 'planes', 'tanks', 'guns':
    data[f'{tp}_diff'] = data[f'allies_{tp}'] - data[f'axis_{tp}']
    cols.append(f'{tp}_diff')
```

3. Now that we have created those five new features, let's run our model over again:

```
scores = cross_val_scores(model,
                          data[cols],
                          data['result_num'],
                          cv=4)
```

4. Now, let's print the resultant score (fingers crossed):

```
>>> pd.np.mean(scores)
0.5141774891774892
```

Accuracy is now at 51.4%—almost 8% improvement over the previous 43.7%!

Let's see what else we can add to the mix. One feature we haven't used quite yet is the `leaders` columns—each containing a few names. Let's count how frequent each name is in the dataset and create a binary (one-hot) feature for the most frequently mentioned leaders. For that, we can use the `Counter` object we learned about in `Section 1`, *Getting Started with Python*, of this book!

Consider the following code:

```
from collections import Counter

def _generate_binary_most_common(col, N=2):
    mask = col.notnull()
    lead_list = [ el.strip() for _, cell in col[mask].iteritems() for el in
cell if el != '']
    c = Counter(lead_list)
    mc = c.most_common(N)
    df = pd.DataFrame(index=col.index, columns=[name[0] for name in mc])
    for name in df.columns:
        df.loc[mask, name] = col[mask].apply(lambda x: name in
x).astype(int)
    return df.fillna(0)
```

The `_generate_binary_most_common` function, as follows, generates a dataframe with the top most frequent names as columns and the original data index. All values are binary, indicating whether each name is present in the original column.

With that, we can add our new features to the dataset. Consider the following code:

```
axis_pop =
_generate_binary_most_common(data['axis_leaders'].str.split(','), N=2)
allies_pop =
_generate_binary_most_common(data['allies_leaders'].str.split(','), N=2)
```

Here, we run the function we just created on the leaders columns for each side, with *N=2*. This results in a dataframe of two columns, filled with binary (0 and 1) values. These values represent whatever specific leader (one of the two most common) took part in each particular battle.

Now, all we need is to add those dataframes to our features and run cross-validation one more time:

```
data2 = pd.concat([data, axis_pop, allies_pop], axis=1)
cols2 = cols + axis_pop.columns.tolist() + allies_pop.columns.tolist()

scores = cross_val_score(model1,
                         data2[cols2],
                         data2['result_num'],
                         cv=4)
pd.np.mean(scores)
>>> 0.5369047619047619
```

This added 2% to our performance on average. N=2 was found by manual iteration—it seems that both an increase and a decrease of the value from here leads to a drop in performance.

Failed attempts

The example-based narrative of this book may mislead you into thinking that each hypothesis or idea improves accuracy. In fact, in order to write this chapter, we had to try and test a handful of other features and methods that didn't work out. For example, one idea we tried was to use the dates of each battle as a feature; you would think that allies lost more battles in the first half of the war and won more in the second. In reality, it actually lowered our performance on the testing dataset.

We also tried filling the missing values. At the very beginning of this chapter, we filled empty cells for planes, tanks, and guns with zeroes. In reality, the authors of Wikipedia had different sources; some of them had detailed data on the number of guns/planes/tanks, and some didn't. Most of the time, though (at least for a large number of soldiers), there were at least some values—but not others. It seems natural to inject at least an approximate number—for example, an average—into each empty cell. However, this didn't help the case either—filling with averages also lowered the score for the model.

Improving the model is a constant process of iterations, trial, and error. It can be an exhausting and frustrating experience and, generally, the performance gains get smaller on each iteration. So, brace yourself, think strategically, and be ready to work hard, with no guarantee of a result at all.

Feature engineering is the king, but there is a second way to improve your performance, parallel to the features selecting the model and model parameters and that is parameter selection. Let's talk about parameter selection in the next section.

Optimizing the hyperparameters

There are probably a lot of other features to add, but let's now shift our attention to the model itself. For now, we assumed the default, static parameters of the model, restricting its `max_depth` parameter to an arbitrary number. Now, let's try to fine-tune those parameters. If done properly, this process could add a few additional percentage points to the model accuracy, and sometimes, even a small gain in performance metrics can be a game-changer.

To do this, we'll use `RandomizedSearchCV`—another wrapper around the concept of cross-validation, but this time, one that iterates over parameters of the model, trying to find the optimal ones. A simpler approach, called `GridSearchCV`, takes a finite number of parameters, creates all of the permutations, and runs them all iteratively using, essentially, a brute-force approach.

Randomized search, on the other hand, takes parameter distributions and gets random samples. It has two advantages over the grid search:

- Randomized search can find the parameters you didn't explicitly offer (some very specific ratio value).
- It usually converges faster than grid search.

Let's take a look at how it works:

1. First, we need to import a `randint` method and `RandomizedSearchCV`:

   ```
   from sklearn.model_selection import RandomizedSearchCV
   from scipy.stats import randint as sp_randint
   ```

2. Now, we'll declare a feature space to search for a better combination. Here, each key represents a model parameter, and the value, the options to search in. The `randint` function allows us to specify range boundaries for a random value search:

   ```
   param_dist = {"max_depth": sp_randint(5, 20),
                 "max_features": sp_randint(1, len(cols2)),
                 "min_samples_split": sp_randint(2, 11),
                 "criterion": ["gini", "entropy"]}
   ```

3. Finally, having this feature space, we can run our randomized search:

```
rs = RandomizedSearchCV(
    model1,
    param_distributions=param_dist,
    cv=4, iid=False,
    random_state=2019,
    n_iter=50
)
```

In lieu of the general philosophy of `scikit-learn`, `RandomSearchCV` behaves as if it was a model—it has `fit` and `predict` methods. Under the hood, it iterates over parameters, averaging parameters over folds. As a result, it can return both the best score and the best corresponding estimator—the one that got the highest score on average. Consider the following code:

```
>>> rs.fit(data2[cols2], data2['result_num'])
>>> rs.bestscore
0.5613636363636363

>>> rs.best_estimator_
DecisionTreeClassifier(class_weight=None, criterion='entropy', max_depth=5,
            max_features=3, max_leaf_nodes=None,
            min_impurity_decrease=0.0, min_impurity_split=None,
            min_samples_leaf=1, min_samples_split=8,
            min_weight_fraction_leaf=0.0, presort=False,
            random_state=2019, splitter='best')
```

As you can see, the process was indeed able to tweak the parameters, finding the most generally performant model configuration, and it improved our accuracy by ~2%. Let's generate a diagram for the resultant model:

```
dot_data = StringIO()

export_graphviz(rs.best_estimator_, out_file=dot_data,
                filled=True, rounded=True,
                special_characters=True, feature_names=cols2)

graph = pydotplus.graph_from_dot_data(dot_data.getvalue())
Image(graph.create_png())
```

Here, the code is similar to the one we ran in the previous chapter—we emulate a file with an in-memory object, generate a diagram, render it with `pydotplus`, and inject it into the notebook.

And here is the resultant diagram:

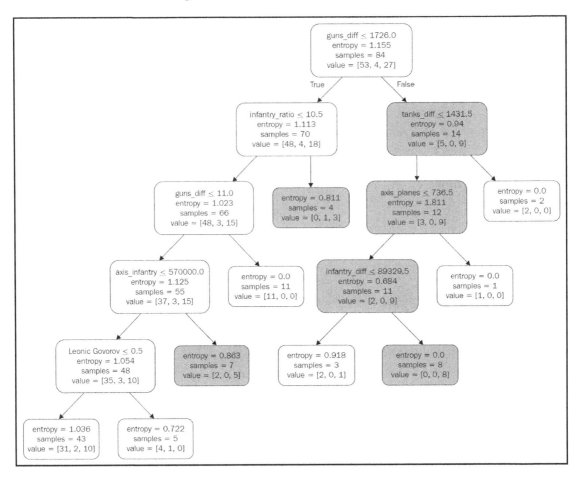

As you can see, the difference in guns, the infantry ratio, and a difference in tanks pop up all over the diagram—those are the main features the model makes use of.

Did it use our `leaders` features? Only one! The only commander who got into the model is Leonid Govorov—which is quite interesting. As we mentioned in the previous chapter, correlation is not causation, especially given the causal relationship between the events and imperfect data—but it is still a useful insight to spur a discussion or direct further research. What context are we completely missing? Is it true that artillery (guns) on average is more important than tanks or planes? Do those features play as important a role in the different theaters of war?

The visual representation of the decision tree allowed us to understand the logic of the model and better navigate the data. The model, in this case, works as an objective analytical tool. As a result, we are able to generate quite a few questions and hypotheses on the nature of data and the underlying historical events.

So far, we have been working with simple models, which are easy to interpret. However, these models are usually not as good at predictions, so why don't we try something more complex and performant, now that we know our dataset pretty well?

Using a random forest model

Decision trees, introduced in `Chapter 13`, *Training a Machine Learning Model*, and which we have been using so far, are fast and easy to interpret. Their weak point, however, is **overfitting**—many features might seem to be a great predictor on the training dataset, but turn out to mislead the models on the external data. In other words, they don't represent the general population. The problem is that decision trees (another algorithm) don't have any internal mechanics to detect and ignore those features.

A suite of more sophisticated models was developed on top of decision models to fight overfitting. These models are usually called tree ensembles, as all of them train multiple decision trees and aggregate their predictions. There are a few models in this family, namely, **Adaptive Boosting**, **Extra-Trees**, and **random forest**. The last one is, arguably, the simplest one to understand of them all—random forest is essentially a flat collection of decision trees, each of which was trained on the subset of the records and a subset of the features of given training data. The result is then aggregated as a majority vote (for classification) or weighted average (for regression). Because each tree gets its own subset of features and records, all trees are trained differently. The mere number and diversity of the trees results in the overall model's robustness and tolerance to overfitting and enables it to capture more nuanced dependencies, at the same time.

Let's see if we'll be able to squeeze more performance from our WWII data using the random forest model! Luckily, all `sklearn` models share the same interface, so we won't need to change much in the code. Let's run a model with the default properties, first:

1. In the following code, we initiate the model with the default values and a specific random state and run cross-validation on this model:

```
from sklearn.ensemble import RandomForestClassifier
rf = RandomForestClassifier(random_state=2019, n_estimators=10)

scores = cross_val_score(rf,
                         data2[cols2],
```

```
                            data2['result_num'],
                            cv=4)
```

```
>>> pd.np.mean(scores)
0.5346861471861473
```

As you can see, it didn't outperform the decision tree just yet.

2. Let's now tune the parameters. As all of the parameters are the same, except for the number of estimators, we can reuse our old parameter distribution, as follows:

```
param_dist['n_estimators'] = sp_randint(50, 2000)

rs2 = RandomizedSearchCV(
    rf,
    param_distributions=param_dist,
    cv=4, iid=False,
    random_state=2019,
    n_iter=50
)
```

3. Now, let's run the search and check the results:

```
rs2.fit(data2[cols2], data2['result_num'])
```

```
>>> rs2.bestscore
0.5812229437229437
```

Indeed, now the model outperformed decision trees by ~2%. Great!

In this section, we were able to replace the decision tree model we were using before with another, more complex algorithm—random forest. As a result, just this swap allowed us to boost the accuracy of the prediction by 2%, and we didn't even run any hyperparameter optimization. Random forest is prone to overfitting, can learn more complex dependencies, and generally performs better than decision trees. There is no free lunch, though; the random forest is too complex to be directly interpretable (although there are tools such as SHAP (https://github.com/slundberg/shap) that can help with that) and takes longer to run.

As you can now see, there are plenty of directions to try and experiment. With all of this feature engineering, different models, hyperparameter optimization, and whatnot, it is easy to lose track of your work. While Git and GitHub are great for using code, they are not as useful for experimentation—you can't store your data, features, models, and metrics there. To help to track your progress and control different versions of your data and models, let's introduce DVC.

Tracking your data and metrics with version control

As with all ML projects, there is always room for improvement—especially if we converge on the actual use case scenario. But let's switch gears and talk about the technical side of the question.

As you probably noticed, in this chapter, we had to constantly iterate, adding and removing features from the data or settings to the model. And again, as we mentioned, only one-third of the initial experiments went into this book. This is probably fine for this toy dataset and this third of the code but eventually, we might be swamped in different versions and iterations of the model.

In Chapter 9, *Shell, Git, Conda, and More – at Your Command*, of this book, we learned about git—a system that stores versions of code, so you can safely switch to the previous version or even keep work on different versions of the code in parallel. This definitely will work for the code behind the model, especially if we carefully explain the differences in the commit messages.

However, in a real-world situation, ML pipelines won't be enough. We need to track metrics and store data and models for each version of the code, especially if the models take hours or even days to train, which is quite often. There is a need for reproducibility when storing not only code but also data, and by data, we mean not only the datasets but also any derivatives, models, and metrics so you can compare different iterations (experiments) and reproduce every one of them, on demand. It may be tentative to use git itself and, for the small datasets, it will work. It won't work for even a medium-size dataset, however, let alone the large ones.

There are a few systems and technologies that help to track experiments, but the field is very young and dynamic. The most popular solutions seem to be sacred, mlflow, and dvc. While all three products generally address similar goals—experimentation and reproducibility—each operates under a certain set of predefined conditions and opinions. For example, sacred is a Python library that helps to store the outcomes and settings of experiments and visualize them later on a dashboard, while mlflow is a powerful framework that prefers to have a separate server for tracking and supports a few languages.

The last one, dvc, is focused on data version control (**DVC** literally stands for **Data Version Control**), is small and language-agnostic, and does not require any servers—everything is communicated via the flat files. It also does not require any changes nor additions to the code itself, which is good. dvc tries to keep its interfaces very similar to git and relies on git itself for many of its features. It supports multiple cloud providers but can be used without a remote as well (similar to git). Let's now try to use DVC on our small pipeline.

Starting with data

It is very easy to incorporate dvc into your workflow. First, we need to install it with pip install dvc. After that, we gradually set it up. You should always start by adding the raw data to dvc. Let's assume data is collected outside of the workflow; we'll just store the files. To do so, perform the following steps:

1. First, open the Terminal (in VS Code, for example), make sure you're in the right folder—the same place where git was initialized (and therefore the .git folder is located)—and type this:

   ```
   dvc init
   ```

2. If you succeed, DVC will print out a few links to documentation and offer to commit changes to git. If you type git status, you'll notice a new folder generated, .dvc, with two files in it: .gitignore and config. So, let's commit this change to git:

   ```
   git add .
   git commit -m "dvc initialized"
   git push # optionally
   ```

3. Now, let's register our data file in DVC:

   ```
   dvc add Chapter14/data/EF_battles_corrected.csv
   ```

If you check the git status, you'll notice a new file was generated—EF_battles_corrected.csv.dvc. Feel free to open it in the text editor. The most important element here is the string of gibberish—the unique MD5 hash. This string is generated using a special deterministic algorithm and represents your data. If the data changes, the new hash won't match the one stored in the .dvc file, so DVC will understand that it is changed and store a new version.

This is the same reason it is used as the path to the file in the `.dvc` folder and on the remote server. By committing this file to `git`, you essentially entwine this specific version of the code with a specific version of data: anyone who pulls the code and the `.dvc` file will be able (given access to a server, of course) to pull a specific version of the dataset. Given that `git` tracks all versions of this file, we'll always be able to align the version of code with the corresponding version of data.

Let's commit it to `git`:

```
git add .; git commit -m "adding the first dataset to dvc"
```

It should be noted that the data itself will not be uploaded—DVC explicitly adds it to `gitignore`; given there is no remote storage for DVC, it will be kept locally. For now, we won't use remote storage for DVC—but if you have an S3 bucket, FTP server, or Azure or Google Cloud account, feel free to use them with `dvc remote`. Once the remote is set up, just run `dvc push` every time data is updated (this can also be set to run automatically on every `git` commit). Others can then clone the `git` repository and pull the data, using the `.dvc` file with the hash.

Adding code to the equation

Now, let's say that we want to keep track of the metrics for each consecutive iteration of the code, using a specific dataset. There is no simple way to do that with a Jupyter Notebook (this could be done using a `papermill` package: `https://github.com/nteract/papermill`), so we copied the code from the notebook and stored it in the script, `predict_result.py`. This takes data and writes down accuracy and model settings to the `metrics.json` file.

> One nice feature of VS Code is that it can convert Jupyter Notebooks into code and back. Just type `import jupyter` in the command palette and select the notebook. It will still require some tweaks but saves a sufficient amount of time anyway.

With that (and the script itself is very simple—just some basic structuring), we can run the code under DVC with the `dvc run` command (this time, we can do that from the chapter folder):

```
dvc run -f Dvcfile -d ./predict_result.py -d
./data/EF_battles_corrected.csv -m ./data/metrics.json python
./predict_result.py
```

Here, the `dvc run` part tells DVC that we're running something, with dependencies (the `-d` flag) and a metric output (the `-m` flag). Once it's done, all information will be stored to `Dvcfile` (it is the same `.dvc` file we generated for data, just for the outcome metrics). Open the file—it will describe both the script and the data as its dependencies and store a hash function for both.

Let's commit to `git` one more time:

```
git commit -am "first ran of a script"
```

This time, we entwined the whole sequence—dataset, code, and resultant metrics. Try running `dvc repro` (by default, it will use `Dvcfile`—that's why we named it that way); it won't run the script because the hash functions are the same.

Metrics

Now, let's play with the metrics functionality, as follows:

1. First, we'll tag our current version to name it, so we can navigate and understand what is inside each commit (metrics are always tracked, but the command-line interface will show them for either tagged commits or branches):

   ```
   git tag -m leaders -a "basic-features-and-leaders"
   ```

2. Now, for the sake of testing, let's test our model without the `leaders` feature; just temporarily remove the corresponding feature from the list of features to use, which we defined in the code. Now, let's reproduce the model:

   ```
   dvc repro
   ```

3. Once the new model is done, we commit changes and tag a new commit:

   ```
   git commit -m "same model with no leader features";
   git tag -m no-leaders -a "basic-features"
   ```

4. Feel free to push all changes to the remote to pass tags; we need to push with the `--tags` flag, but none of that is required for DVC.

5. Finally, let's check in the code with the `random forest` model. Add the `random forest` model to the script and run DVC again, as follows:

```
dvc repro;
git commit -am "random forest";
git tag -m rf -a "random-forest"
```

Now that metrics for the two models are cached, we can use DVC to show the changes (here, a draft is our current branch and last commit).

6. The following code will ask DVC to show metrics (for example, the file we specified as `metric`) across all tagged commits:

```
dvc metrics show -T -x accuracy
>>>
working tree:
        data/metrics.json: [0.5965367965367965]
basic-features:
        data/metrics.json: [0.5488095238095239]
basic-features-and-leaders:
        data/metrics.json: [0.5959415584415585]
random-forest:
        data/metrics.json: [0.5965367965367965]
```

As you can see, this command allows us to check changes in accuracy across all of the tagged commits. Using a combination of `git` and DVC, we can always switch to any of those commits and have a correct version of both the code and data pulled.

According to this list, the `leaders` feature added substantial performance gain to the model. Switching to the random forest model adds a little more gain too. The best part is that we can continue working on our model, keeping track of metrics for the next iterations as well. All of the data, code, and metrics are properly stored and easy to get back to.

It is hard to overestimate the importance of proper tracking and version control for experimentation and reproducibility—both in academic environments and in the industry. This level of transparency allows you to showcase your improvements and communicate and collaborate in a breeze. Now, let's review what we learned in this chapter.

Summary

Over the course of this chapter, we worked iteratively on improving the machine learning model we built in Chapter 13, *Training a Machine Learning Model*—adding features and tuning it to achieve maximum performance. As the code and iterations get more complex and multiple trial-and-error attempts are required, it is important to keep track of your research. Therefore, we further discussed how to keep track of not only the code but also data and metrics, making sure we can always switch back and reproduce any of the previous versions.

In the next chapter, we'll take another stab at our Wikipedia scraping code, building it into an independent Python library you could share with your friends and colleagues. Throughout the rest of this book, we will focus on different ways of delivering our code as a product to the client—as a standalone package, scheduled data pipeline, online dashboard, or API endpoint.

Questions

1. What is overfitting?
2. Why should we use cross-validation?
3. Why can it be bad if our metrics are improving on the test set? Which features are useful for improving model performance on cross-validation?
4. Why do some features decrease the performance of a decision tree on test data or in cross-validation?
5. What is the difference between the random search and grid search algorithms for parameter optimization?
6. Why is Git not sufficient for data version control?
7. What are the alternatives to DVC for data version control and experimentation logging?

Further reading

You can refer to this book for further information: Data Science Projects with Python (https://www.packtpub.com/big-data-and-business-intelligence/data-science-projects-python).

Section 3: Moving to Production 3

In this final part, we'll discuss how to prepare your code to be used in a production environment, as a package, as a scheduled process, or through an API. We will use the three projects to implement these different approaches.

This section comprises the following chapters:

- Chapter 15, *Packaging and Testing with Poetry and PyTest*
- Chapter 16, *Data Pipelines with Luigi*
- Chapter 17, *Let's Build a Dashboard*
- Chapter 18, *Serving Models with a RESTful API*
- Chapter 19, *Serverless API Using Chalice*
- Chapter 20, *Best Practices and Python Performance*

15
Packaging and Testing with Poetry and PyTest

Until now, all our code has lived in either notebooks or Python files. While that is totally fine, with the growth in volume and complexity of our code, it is increasingly becoming a good idea to form one or more go-to sources for the code we use most frequently, as well as sources for the complex code that we don't want to risk adding mistakes to.

In this chapter, we will learn how to build our own packages for use in multiple projects or to be easily shared with others, using the poetry package. A package can work as a deliverable—something you can pass to or share with your client! Building and testing packages is a vital skill that increases your productivity and allows you to save time and reduce stress by enabling you to reuse the same properly tested body of code again and again.

Building packages also likely to improve your overall coding skills, as packages require code to be abstract and flexible and allow you to spend time on efficient implementation.

The following topics will be covered in this chapter:

- The benefits of having a custom package
- A few ways to develop a package
- Defining dependencies and resources with Poetry
- Workflow with the editable package installation
- Testing your code with PyTest
- Documentation with sphinx
- Testing with CI

Technical requirements

For this chapter, we will need the following packages (as always, they are included in our base environment):

- `poetry`
- `pytest`
- `sphinx`

As we're creating an independent package, all the code is stored on GitHub at `https://github.com/PacktPublishing/Learn-Python-by-Building-Data-Science-Applications`.

Building a package

So far in this book, we have been either using third-party packages, such as `requests` and `pandas`, or writing raw code as `.py` scripts or notebooks. While using Python files directly is absolutely fine for certain projects, it makes it hard for code to be reused and built upon; it is not sustainable for complex algorithms and tools that can be used over and over again. Such code is also hard to share as it has no overall structure, tends to decay over time, and doesn't have a robust dependency system; the code may not work on other systems with other packages (or other versions of packages) installed. Last but not least, this kind of practice affects the quality of our code, as we tend to write and use the code as a one-time solution. The best way to mitigate all those issues at once is to form your code into a package.

But what is a package? In Python, packages are defined as specific bodies of code that are registered in the system (via a system path) and thus can be imported and used in any specific code base. Packages are stored on the dedicated system paths and are not meant to be changed or deployed manually. Instead, it is preferable to use dedicated tools, such as the built-in `setuptool` package or package managers (for example, `pip` or `conda`). We'll learn about these in detail in the coming sections.

Bringing your own package

Most of the packages that we've taken a look at so far are very generic—for instance, `requests` works with HTTP on the client side, while `pandas` is focused on data analysis. Why should you write your own package with a very specific task in mind that's not necessarily useful or applicable to another person's use case? Simply put, because you'll be the first to benefit!

The main goal that packages solve is to create a deliverable; any new user on a new machine will be able to install the package, as well as all the packages it requires to work properly, at once. As a byproduct, packages remain isolated from the code you write every day. This isolation is a good thing—it makes you, as a package designer, build your packages in a structured and more abstract and extendable fashion. Finally, packages are explicitly versioned. Using version control, you will always be able to run any specific version you need at any moment, without worrying about new features or interfaces breaking your code.

In other words, if the code you've made might be used on more than one project, you definitely should consider converting it into a package. The good news is, it is actually a pretty easy task to do.

Using a package manager – pip and conda

All the packages we've introduced so far are publicly accessible for everyone via one of two package managers—`pip` and `conda`. The role of the package manager is to provide a unified interface to securely install, upgrade, and uninstall packages in a system. As most packages depend on other packages (usually specific versions), it is also the job of the package manager to resolve those dependencies—that is, to install packages that fit the version criteria for all installed packages that will depend on them.

`pip` and `conda` are by far the two most popular package managers for Python. The first one is officially supported by the Python Software Foundation. It is the main Python package management, period.

Why do we use `conda` at all, then? Historically, `pip` and PyPI (a corresponding online service) did not support binaries as part of packages. Binaries have to be compiled for each OS separately, and they are (obviously) written in languages other than Python itself. Thus, providing support for binaries was considered too demanding.

It turned out, however, that this is exactly what is required for fast numeric operations—as we've mentioned before, `numpy`, `pandas`, and `sklearn` all run C and even Fortran under the hood. For a long time, the lack of support meant that everyone had to compile binaries locally every time they installed those new packages. As such, the Python leadership offered to build a package manager that would support binaries—and `conda` was born. As an additional bonus, `conda` can also create separate virtual environments, so you can safely replicate a full Python environment from a shared `.yaml` file or have multiple versions of Python and packages at the same time.

Unfortunately, `conda` requires a bit more effort to work with, compared to `pip`. Most critically for us, it does not support the installation of packages from a Git repository (even a private one), while `pip` does. Another feature of `pip` is that it allows the installation of packages in editable mode—that is, with the code stored on a non-system path and ready to be edited. In this chapter, we will build a package targeted at `pip`.

Creating a package scaffolding

So, how do we start? First of all, we need to create a scaffolding—a default package structure with all the necessary folders, files with metadata and configs, and so on. Our code will be stored on GitHub, so let's start by creating a new repository:

1. This step is easy. Go to `https://github.com/`, log in, hit the **New** button, and fill in all the information. In our case, we'll name the repository the same as the package—`wikiwwii`. We'll also add a standard Python `.gitignore` file and a `README.MD` file. You can also add a license of your choice for your repositories.
2. Next, we create the repository and copy the path to the clipboard. With that, we can open a terminal, go to the proper location on the hard drive, and write this, replacing `<repo>` with the path you copied from GitHub:

   ```
   git clone <repo>
   ```

With that, a copy of the repository will be downloaded, with a link to the remote version being stored. Try adding notes to `README.MD`. Now commit the change by typing `git -am commit "adding to README"`, and then use `git push`. This will send our first commit to the master branch on GitHub.

Now let's see how we can build a package.

A few ways to build your package

The structure of a Python package is defined by a few specifications (`https://packaging.python.org/specifications/`) and **PEPs** (short for **Python Enhancement Proposals**, such as PEP517—`https://www.python.org/dev/peps/pep-0517/`, PEP518—`https://www.python.org/dev/peps/pep-0518/`, and PEP427—`https://www.python.org/dev/peps/pep-0427/`), and the overall definition comes from the **Python Packaging Authority (PyPA)**. In essence, a package is required to have, in addition to the actual code, a special file with metadata, including the package name, the description version, the tags, Python version support details, the authors, and the dependencies. This file could be a Python `setup.py` file—which was the standard solution for a long time—or a `pyproject.toml` file. The latter is a new, safer approach, but does not have as well-designed a specification.

It is entirely possible to build a package manually. All it takes is a little structure and a file with the metadata. It is, however, a tedious task, so there are quite a few packages designed to help with packaging. A standard bundle is `distutuls`. There is also `setuptools`. Both of them expect a `setup.py` file.

One of the challenges with package building is managing dependencies between packages. One package may depend on another, which may depend on several more—so don't be surprised if your package requires the installation of dozens of other packages. There is even a fair chance that some of those packages will depend upon different versions of the same package, so *someone* will have to figure out a way to install versions that suit all the requirements or somehow install two versions of the same package. This is a challenge that the previous generation of package builders didn't fully solve.

Recently, a few new tools arrived—namely, `flit` and `poetry`—and both of them support `pyptoject.toml` files and work well to resolve dependencies. In this chapter, we will use `poetry` to build our package. This package has a slick and expressive interface and supports `.toml` format. It also builds a dedicated virtual environment for developers and has two levels of dependency description: a flexible list of packages required for the user, and one explicit and precise package, for developers, which contains a list of exact versions of all dependency packages installed on the developer's machine. It also has tools for dependency diagnostics and package publishing.

Trying out code with Poetry

Poetry, like `flit`, is one of the most recent packages aimed at helping with package development in Python. Among its features are the ability to write a `pyproject.toml` file, which is more secure and easy than the older approach with `setup.py`, and the ability to create a dedicated virtual environment for a project, with all dependencies pinned. Even more importantly, it has a thorough dependency resolution engine that makes sure all dependency versions fit with each other, and an interface to monitor and bump your dependency tree.

But first, we will start by creating a project template. First, type this:

```
poetry new --name=wikiwwii my-package
```

This will generate a new folder, `my-package`, with default files and folders within. Copy and paste everything from this folder into our existing repository folder; delete the `README.rst` file (we already have `README.md`). The most important thing we've got from `poetry`, for now, is the `pyproject.toml` dummy file—this specification will be used to generate a `setup.py` file upon installation.

Let's check the structure of our repository:

```
>>> tree wikiwwii
├───── README.md
├───── pyproject.toml
├───── tests
│   ├───── __init__.py
│   └───── test_wikiwwii.py
└───── wikiwwii
    └───── __init__.py
```

If everything looks fine, feel free to commit the changes to GitHub (generally, you should commit after each and every logical step—we can always squash commits into one later, for readability purposes).

Adding actual code

Now that the package structure is in place, we can start adding the actual code. For starters, we copy and paste the code from Chapter 7, *Scraping Data from the Web with Beautiful Soup 4*, for the `wiki.py` package. As we want to have code for both collecting and cleaning in the same package, it sounds smart to create two sub-folders—`collect` and `parse`. The code from Chapter 7, *Scraping Data from the Web with Beautiful Soup 4*, will go to the latter one. For now, we will create two files—`battles.py` and `fronts.py`—in the `parse` folder. In Python, upon import, they will be mapped to a path such as `wikiwwii.parse.battles`, enabling access to all the functions and variables in them.

Next, we add the code for cleaning in a similar fashion. However, most of the cleaning code here is stored in the `1_data_cleaning.ipynb` notebook. Of course, we could run a Jupyter server and copy and paste all the files into **Visual Studio** (**VS**) Code, but there is an even better option. Instead, open the command palette (*Shift* + command/*Ctrl* + *P* by default), select **Python: Import Jupyter Notebook**, and pick our notebook. As you'll see, VS Code will convert the file into a normal script, marking cells with the comments.

VS Code actually even allows the running of converted cells interactively, step by step. Moreover, it supports converting this file back into a notebook. This is useful when you need to tweak something in a notebook from within VS Code.

Here is the folder tree after we moved the actual code:

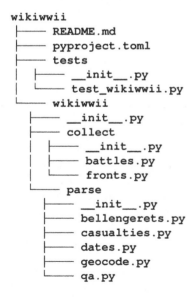

```
wikiwwii
├──── README.md
├──── pyproject.toml
├──── tests
│     ├──── __init__.py
│     └──── test_wikiwwii.py
└──── wikiwwii
      ├──── __init__.py
      ├──── collect
      │     ├──── __init__.py
      │     ├──── battles.py
      │     └──── fronts.py
      └──── parse
            ├──── __init__.py
            ├──── bellengerets.py
            ├──── casualties.py
            ├──── dates.py
            ├──── geocode.py
            └──── qa.py
```

The code in packages is not generally meant to be run directly on import; thus, it (usually) consists only of functions, variables, and objects. Until it is clearly needed, consider it a bad practice to actually execute code directly in a package—it will then be executed every time someone import from this file. Similarly, where possible, try not to import packages you don't need, or generate big structures, until you actually need them. It is a good practice to import dependency packages only where they are necessary so that even if the package is missing, some code will still be executable.

Defining dependencies

Now, as you may have noticed, our code from Chapter 7, *Scraping Data from the Web with Beautiful Soup 4*, relies on two libraries—requests and BeautifulSoup4—to work. Parsing requires another package, pandas. For our imaginary user, it would be preferable to install those packages and, even better, make sure that we install versions we think will support what we need. This is where poetry thrives. In your Terminal, type the following:

```
poetry add requests beautifulsoup4 pandas
```

Poetry will scan our current environment, detect the version of those packages we use, and add their characteristics to both pyproject.tamp and a new file, poetry.lock. The former is a (recently added) standard specification—it will be used, upon publication, by PyPI or pip. Note that it specifies only direct dependencies and you don't have to define a specific version of them. The poetry.lock file is specific to the poetry package; it will ensure a precise version match on installation, as it defines the versions of all dependencies recursively.

Once every package is added, you may check the list of dependencies in the .toml file and, perhaps, tweak the versions as required:

```
[tool.poetry.dependencies]
python = "^3.6"
requests = "^2.22"
beautifulsoup4 = "^4.7"
pandas = "^0.24.2"
```

Here, ^ means any versions that are the same or later as the one specified. It might be safer to replace it with a tilde, ~, which represents any version that is equal or above but only within minor updates. So, ^3,6 will fit any version that is numerically larger or equal to 3.6; ~3.6 will fit any version within the range (3.6, 4.0). By general semantic versioning convention, major numbers represent breaking changes, while minor numbers (numbers after the dot) do not. Alternatively, a wildcard, *, can be used instead. In our Python example, 3.* will fit any value within the (3.0, 4.0) range.

Non-code resources

If your package needs to include something besides the Python files—for example, a small dataset or a query template—you'll need to add it explicitly as part of the package in pyproject.toml, as here:

```
[tool.poetry]
include = ["*.sql"]
```

In some cases, you may not want to include some Python scripts in the actual package (for example, some support scripts). For that, you need to add a similar exclude line in the same section:

```
[tool.poetry]
include = ["*.sql"]
exclude = ["wikiwwii/uploader.py"]
```

We don't have any files to add or exclude in the package we're building—at least right now—so we won't have this section in the .toml file.

Publishing the package

Now, assuming everything looks good, we can try installing dependencies with poetry install. This won't (despite the somewhat misleading name) install that package in your current environment—instead, poetry creates its own virtual environment for testing purposes.

Once that's done, we can build and publish our package to PyPI (using poetry build and poetry publish) so that it will be available for everyone. Let's not hurry—our package is in its infancy and is not yet tested and secured.

Instead, let's use GitHub as a sharing platform. Once your current version is pushed to the repository, the package can be installed straight from GitHub itself—`pip` supports that as well:

```
pip install git+https://github.com/Casyfill/wikiwwii.git
```

If needed, `pip` can install from the specific branch or tag. This way, we can keep our packages private for, say, commercial use, using private repositories. At the same time, your friends and colleagues can install and reuse your package, raise issues, or even contribute to the project.

Development workflow

Now, with great power comes great responsibility. For now, we are committing to the master branch, which is the default one for installation, so we probably don't want to add some unreliable code there. So, let's adhere to the following, rather simple, practice—we should never push code directly to the master branch. Instead, we should work on a separate development branch, push it to GitHub, and then—once we're satisfied with results—merge the branch into the master. For that, GitHub even supports code review and discussions. Let's switch to a development branch now:

```
git checkout -b tests
```

As you may notice, VS Code will mark the current branch in the lower-left corner of the window. In fact, you can click on it and switch to a different branch or even create a new one manually. Next comes testing the code and checking how it works.

Testing the code so far

How would we know whether the code is good, anyway? The only good way is to rigorously test your code. While it may sound like a lot of somewhat unnecessary work, it is a practice that will repay you many times over in the future—once you're sure your code behaves as intended, it is much easier to add new features and be sure that they didn't break any of the existing ones. Furthermore, you can upgrade dependencies or compare different implementations, all being sure that your code behaves as intended.

As for many other things, Python has a standard library for testing—unittest. In contrast to most of the standard libraries, however, unittest is fairly unpopular. Instead, another library, pytest, is considered the de facto industry standard for Python testing, as it provides a clean and reusable pattern of code and has support for plugins—indeed, there are a lot of plugins available to support.

When poetry generated a scaffolding for our package, it generated a tests folder. That is where our tests will live; this way, they live separately from the package and won't be installed with it. Now let's dive in and write our first test.

Testing with PyTest

In fact, poetry even generates a test function for us, though it doesn't test our code; instead, it checks the version. Take a look at the code here:

```
from wikiwwii import __version__

def test_version():
    assert __version__ == '0.1.0'
```

Here, two things are worth discussing. First, as you can see, the test is just a function with the word "test" in its name. Having this word is necessary—this is the way pytest finds all the tests. Second, each test results in one or a few assert statements. To pass the test, assert should not raise any issues. That's all the basics of test development.

Now let's run this existing test; generally speaking, all we need is to type pytest tests on the command line. With poetry, however, we have a hidden virtual environment intended for development, so that's where we should run our tests; for that, type poetry run pytest tests. If everything is okay, pytest should print out a small report with the version of Python, pytest, the package, and a description of the tests, as follows:

```
>>> poetry run pytest tests
========================== test session starts
========================================
platform darwin -- Python 3.7.1, pytest-3.10.1, py-1.8.0, pluggy-0.12.0
rootdir: /Users/philippk/Dropbox/personal_projects/wikiwwii, inifile:
collected 1 item

tests/test_wikiwwii.py .
[100%]

=========================== 1 passed in 0.02 seconds
========================================
```

Yay! This test has passed.

Writing our own tests

But seriously, let's write a test of our own now. First, let's start with something relatively basic, such as finding out how our functions extract data from a given page and its elements.

There is not much value in testing the ability of the requests library to collect pages from the web—it is safe to assume it does, and it has its own tests. Because of that, we moved all the parsing code from the parse_battle_page function into a private _parse_page function. This way, we can focus on testing the parsing, not the internet.

First, we'll store an HTML page of a few battles in the tests/data/pages folder. Now we will create a file called test_collect_battles.py—here we'll store all our tests for this particular module. Inside, we use import pytest and create a test function:

```
import pytest
from pathlib import Path
data_folder = Path(__file__).parent / 'data' / 'pages'

def test_parse_page(dom, answer):
    from wikiwwii.collect.battles import _parse_page
    result = _parse_page(dom)
    assert result == answer
```

To feed this test with specific dom and answer instances, we write a utility script that pre-generates answers from data and stores them in the same location. The code of this script is trivial enough not to discuss here but it is stored as a part of both repositories.

 Note that as a result, we store some HTML and JSON as part of the repository. None of those files are too big to worry about, but generally speaking, it might be a good case to use with DVC tool we discussed in Chapter 9, *Shell, Git, Conda, and More – at Your Command.*

Now let's load the resulting file and create a helper function that loads an HTML file and converts it to a DOM object, all in the same file as our test:

```
with (data_folder / 'answers.json').open('r') as f:
    answers = json.load(f)

def _load_dom(path):
    from bs4 import BeautifulSoup
```

```
    with path.open('r') as f:
        return BeautifulSoup(f.read(), 'html.parser')
```

With that, we could loop through the names and answers and assert each of them from within our test itself. But there is an even better way for that, that is already built into `pytest`. Using a `pytest` decorator, we can externalize the loop, generating multiple actual tests from our code. The benefit of that, aside from the proper counting, is that `pytest` will outline the specific inputs if any case fails. In order to use it, just add a special decorator to the function:

```
@pytest.mark.parametrize("name, answer", answers.items())
def test_parse_page(dom, answer):
    from wikiwwii.collect.battles import _parse_page
    result = _parse_page(dom)
    assert result == answer
```

Here, the decorator maps our `answers` dictionary to the `name` and `answer` parameters, running the test suite for each pair.

Let's try our tests now. They should work and show all five tests (one pre-existing test, and four tests for each of the four web pages we downloaded).

Now comes the most important part: we have to manually look over the `answers` file and ensure we agree with all the content there. Right now, those tests are not helpful, but they will raise an issue any time we'll change the parsing functions, making it safe to add functionality and work on the code - as long as tests are passing and they are extensive, we'll be sure we won't break anything. And a good practice would be to add a new example or test for every new issue, edge case or problematic page we'll encounter.

Let's now shift focus to our other submodule—parse. For example, let's test the most complex function, `_parse_casualties`. For that, we'll create another file, `test_parse.py`. As the function works on a series of text elements, we could create one test with all the caveats; here, we will create our own cases, rather than use the real ones. Because we won't iterate over it, it should be marked as `fixture`:

```
import pytest
import pandas as pd

@pytest.fixture()
def case():
    return {
        'col': pd.Series([
            '10,000',
            '37,000 dead, 7,000 POW (Soviet est)',
            '29 aircraft destroyed (ground)',
```

```
                '20 men, 4 tanks, 20 guns',
                ''
        ]),

        'answer': pd.DataFrame({
            'killed':[10_000, 37_000, 0, 20, 0],
            'airplane': [0, 0, 29, 0, 0],
            'guns': [0, 0, 0, 20, 0],
            'tanks': [0, 0, 0, 4, 0]
        })
    }

def test_parse_casualties(case):
    from wikiwwii.parse.casualties import _parse_casualties

    parsed = _parse_casualties(case['col'])

    for col in case['answer'].columns:
        mask = parsed[col] == case['answer'][col]
        comp = pd.DataFrame({'col': case['col'],
                             'result': parsed[col]})

        assert mask.all(), (col, comp[~mask].to_string())
```

The two tests we wrote are just a start. Ideally, we need to cover all lines of our code with our tests. In fact, the amount of lines covered by tests is a standard metric called **coverage**, and it's used to track test coverage over time. Let's compute our coverage using a plugin for pytest—pytest-cov. To compute the coverage, first we need to add pytest-cov to the poetry environment, as we would for other packages:

```
poetry add pytest-cov
```

Now, poetry automatically adds all dependencies to the .toml file. But this package is not a dependency per se—it is required for testing, but not for the functioning of the package itself. Thus, we have to move this dependency under a separate header—[tool.poetry.dev-dependencies].

Now we can run our tests as before, just pointing out that we need to compute the coverage for our package:

```
poetry run pytest --cov wikiwwii tests
```

Once all the test information is printed, another report will be generated:

```
---------- coverage: platform darwin, python 3.7.1-final-0 ----------
Name                              Stmts Miss Cover
---------------------------------------------------------
wikiwwii/__init__.py                  1    0  100%
wikiwwii/collect/fronts.py           34   34    0%
wikiwwii/collect/battles.py          55   15   73%
wikiwwii/parse/__init__.py            4    0  100%
wikiwwii/parse/bellengerets.py       12   10   17%
wikiwwii/parse/casualties.py         19    0  100%
wikiwwii/parse/dates.py              15   10   33%
wikiwwii/parse/geocode.py            41   30   27%
wikiwwii/parse/qa.py                  8    8    0%
---------------------------------------------------------
TOTAL                               189  107   43%
```

Now, the computed metric is 43%. Generally, your coverage should be at least at 70%-75%, so we have quite a lot of room for improvement. This metric is useful to motivate the team and prevent coverage from degrading (for example, it may call for tests to be required for every new feature of a project). At the same time, this metric alone does not ensure that the tests are meaningful and will protect your code from mistakes and errors—this is a challenge for us to work on. In general, the following strategy is most useful:

1. Write tests for all new code. In fact, it may be a good idea to write tests first, as a way to think of the different use cases for the new functionality.
2. For existing code, start with large tests that cover the main, most important functions; this will, at least, make sure that any new code or changes you introduce won't break your existing code.
3. Spend time learning about `pytest` and testing in general. There are many tools and features that help you to keep tests lean and structured and to reuse existing code. Another great package to use is `hypothesis`, as it generates edge cases for your tests automatically, depending on the argument types. We will talk more about the hypothesis in `Chapter 20`, *Best Practices and Python Performance*.

If all our tests do pass, it is a great moment to commit our code one more time. At this point, we have a suite of tests that we can run or ask our collaborators to run, before committing the code. Over time, this test suite may grow, making testing a time-consuming process. Furthermore, while we can test our code for different Python versions, it is hard to test it for different OSes locally. Lastly, the process is a little opaque—there is no easy way to share testing results with team members. To mitigate all those complications, an external service can be used; simply put, all your tests could run externally, in the cloud, and shared with the team via GitHub as part of the development process. Let's learn how to do that!

Automating the process with CI services

Now, as you may recall, we are working on a `tests` branch of our repository. If you go to GitHub, it may offer to create a pull request—a procedure meant to merge your branch into the master branch or any other branch, as in the yellow section of the following screenshot. Even if the interface does not offer this (it won't if there was already a pull request a few minutes before), you can create a pull request yourself, via the **New pull request** button. See the following screenshot:

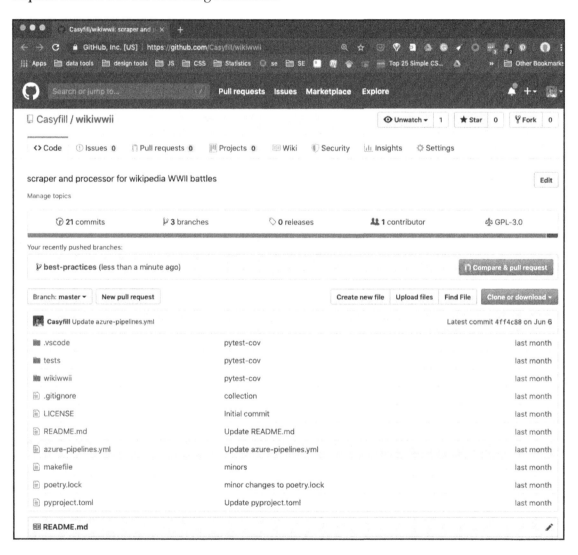

Using GitHub, you can request other people to review your changes, comment on them, and more; GitHub will also confirm whether merging is possible or whether you'll need to resolve conflicts first.

While, in our case, we did run our tests locally and we know it is safe to merge, there is no way for others to check that easily. In order to make life simpler for everyone, and save some time for you (for large projects, proper testing might take a while), **continuous integration (CI)** services are used. Most of the time, all CI services do is trigger on a new commit, pull code to a virtual machine, run your tests, then report back whatever the tests succeeded in determining. Because of CI services' automatic nature, it is easy to run even multiple machines with different environments—say, one service could test your code on Python 3 and one on Python 2.

 Note that CI services can do more than this. For example, they can automatically re-generate documentation from a repository and publish it, push your package to the registry, and upload any other artifact objects somewhere else. Explore these options!

Generally speaking, CI services do cost money. Most of them, though, have free tiers for open source projects. As our package is open source and open to anyone, let's leverage the free tier of a CI service. There are plenty of great services around, and all of them are more or less the same. We will use Azure pipelines, but you can pick something else if you want.

To get started, we need to go through a few simple steps:

1. First, we need to go to the Azure DevOps website (`https://azure.microsoft.com/en-us/services/devops/`) and register. We'll give it access to our GitHub account and create a build pipeline for the `wikiwwii` repository. In a moment, Azure will offer you a few scenarios, starting with Python—this is what we need.

2. Next, it will show a simple pipeline as a YAML file. It will, by default, offer to run multiple instances with different Python versions. We can drop all but 3.7.

3. As we are using `poetry`, we can replace the `pip install` line with the command for `poetry` installation as per Poetry's installation guide. On the next line, the `pytest-azurepipelines` package is installed. We can't use that, because we need to install it via `poetry`, so we'll have to add it into the `poetry` development dependency list. At the same time, there is no sense in having this package locally, so we can mark it as an extra:

```
poetry add --dev --extras azure pytest-azurepipelines
```

4. Here is the first step of our pipeline:

```
script: |
            curl -sSL
https://raw.githubusercontent.com/sdispater/poetry/master/get-poetr
y.py | python
            source $HOME/.poetry/env
            poetry --version
            poetry install -E azure
            displayName: 'Install dependencies'
```

5. Now, the second step is simple—just run `pytest` from within Poetry:

```
- script: |
            poetry run pytest --cov=wikiwwii tests
            displayName: 'pytest'
```

6. Last but not least, the default pipeline works on any activity on the master branch. Instead, let's trigger it on a pull request to the master. To do that, just replace the trigger with `pr` in the YAML:

```
pr:
- master
```

And we're done! Now allow Azure to submit that code to the master branch; don't forget to commit the new version of the package with `pytest-azurepipelines` added. Let's try a pull request.

If everything worked as it is supposed to, GitHub will show a small yellow circle near the last commit in a list in the pull request section. If you hover on it, it will show the current CI status as either queued or running. Once the pipeline runs, the circle will turn either green or red, depending on the results. The following screenshot shows this:

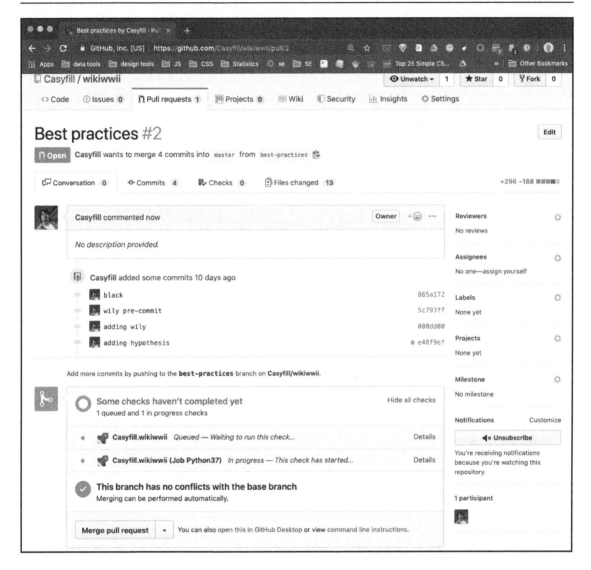

And now we're done with CI. All other CI systems are very similar; most of them use YAML as a declaration of processes, so it is easy to switch between different CI systems if needed.

Up next, let's generate some documentation for our pet project.

Generating documentation generation with sphinx

Documentation is king when it comes to supporting consumers of your code and convincing newcomers that it actually makes sense to buy in and use your package. For most people, a documentation website is the first place they go to learn about the package. It is, by definition, assumed to be the single source of truth on the code in its current version.

The role of documentation is usually threefold:

- Explain how to install your package and what the general requirements are (for example, which Python versions are supported)
- Show how to use the package (preferably with a quick example showing its immediate value)
- Express the general idea and philosophy of the package

A documentation website does benefit from having tutorials, example cases, and a roadmap. With that being said, the core of any documentation website is, obviously, documentation—lists of all functions, classes, and modules, for instance, with explanations of what they do, how to use them, and which variables to pass.

Now, it may sound like a large task on its own (and it generally is), but there are tools to make this bearable—especially the code documentation part. Remember how we tasked you with writing docstrings in Chapter 3, *Functions*? Now is the payday—those docstrings can (and will, in a minute!) be used to form documentation. Cool, huh? In order to generate a static website with documentation, we'll use sphinx—a Python package and a tool that is designed to build documentation.

Let's give it a try. First, go to your package's root directory in a terminal. Assuming sphinx is installed, run the following command:

```
sphinx-quickstart ./docs --ext-autodoc --ext-coverage
```

Here, we pass a docs folder as a place to store everything related to documentation (there will be a lot of files, so you'd better separate them from the package itself). The two parameters that we've passed will tell sphinx to use two built-in plugins for our project—autodoc and coverage. The first is the piece of code that will utilize your docstrings. The other calculates the overall documentation coverage (for example, the percentage of functions/modules/classes that have docstrings) in your code—don't confuse this with test coverage.

Next, this script will ask you a series of questions. The default values are pretty good, so there's no need to change them. Besides, everything can be changed later, or you can always delete the `docs` folder and re-run the script, if you want.

Once that's all done, the script will generate all the settings necessary for the tool to run. Now you can run the tool manually, like this (replacing directories as you wish):

```
$ sphinx-build -b html <sourcedir> <builddir>
```

If you agreed to create a makefile, this will help `sphinx` add the directories you picked to it automatically. Here is how to run it:

```
$ cd docs;
$ make html
```

It should be noted that in the `wikiwwi` package, we copied and pasted part of the code from the `docs`/makefile to the `Makefile` in the root, to avoid going in and out of the folder.

 We're focusing on web page documentation (HTML), but Sphinx can also generate documentation in other formats, including PDF, JSON, and LaTeX.

If everything goes as expected, a (mostly empty) documentation package will be generated under `docs/build/html`. You can open the files in the browser, or spin a simple server (we use VS Code's Live Server plugin). The index (root) file is generated from a corresponding file, `docs/source/index.rst`. In order to add more content, just edit this file. For example, let's add a small introduction, which will then be shown at the beginning of the web page:

```
`wikiwwii` is a package aiming at collecting and processing the data on
WWII battle from the Wikipedia. The list of all battles is taken from
Battles_.
```

The underscore in `Battles_` is an `rst`-specific symbol, adding a reference to the link. At the bottom of the page, we'll use it to link to Wikipedia:

```
.. _Battles: https://en.wikipedia.org/wiki/List_of_World_War_II_battles
```

Once the file is stored, we re-generate the page and the text should appear.

By default, sphinx is using **reStructuredText** (**rst**) format. If you prefer Markdown (which is a similar but simpler and more limited format), follow these instructions: https://www.sphinx-doc.org/en/master/usage/markdown.html.

Now, let's focus on our main task—showing our Python documentation on this site. To do that, we first need to do a few more tweaks:

1. First, open the conf.py file and uncomment the code after -- Path setup --. This path needs to point at the root directory of your repository, where your Python package lives. Here is how it will look in our case:

```
import os
import sys
sys.path.insert(0, os.path.abspath('../..'))
```

2. Next, go to the extensions section and add one more extension—sphinx.ext.napoleon. It only does one thing: it can parse non-rst docstrings. It is a subjective choice, but we're not fans of it. Here is how the section will look afterward:

```
extensions = [
    'sphinx.ext.autodoc',
    'sphinx.ext.coverage',
    'sphinx.ext.napoleon'
]
```

3. Finally, let's add an autodoc directive to our web pages. Here is the one for the geocoding file (yes, we'll need to add one per file, but it actually makes sense; you wouldn't want to get everything on the same page):

```
.. automodule:: wikiwwii.parse.geocode
   :members:
```

Upon building, this should result in a list of functions from that file, such as `geocode_location` and `extract_latlon`. Before we move on, there are a few things worth mentioning regarding the docstrings and the code itself:

1. First of all, while `sphinx` won't fail on bad docstring formatting, it won't be able to format them nicely either. Please check your docstrings and format them to one of the standards that Napoleon supports, such as NumPy or Google style.

2. As you might have noticed, there is no documentation for some functions, such as `_get_dom` from the `collect.fronts` module, even though we do have a small docstring for that function! That's because its name starts with an underscore, which, according to a widespread convention, means that the function is private (not meant to be used directly by module consumers) and `sphinx` respects that. It is a great feature, allowing you to declutter your documentation. Use it wisely!

3. In the original version of the code for `wikiwwii`, we passed a few dictionaries as default arguments for some functions. While code-wise this is okay, `sphinx` tries to print their values in the documentation and the result is hard to read. The choice to do this is completely subjective and optional, but to keep documentation little cleaner, you can (and this is what we did for this package) pass a different default value, such as `none` or `default`, and if the argument is equal to that, then replace it with the true default value—just make sure to make that clear in the documentation. A side benefit of that solution is that Git won't see any difference in documentation files if you change those defaults.

As our package is twofold, we created a separate file for each subpackage and added all the corresponding docstrings there. Then we linked the root page to both submodule ones via `toctree` (see the following code):

```
.. toctree::
   :maxdepth: 2
   :caption: Contents:

   collect
   parse
```

And that, essentially, is it! The re-built documentation is now actually useful. Of course, it is missing the installation part, tutorials, and examples, but the first step has been taken. Here is a screenshot of our version 1.0 documentation web page:

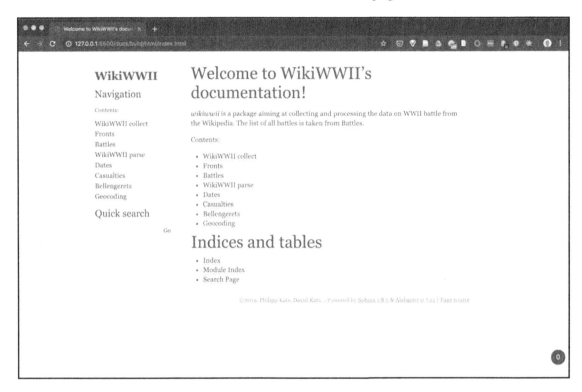

In a few lines, we have deployed a simple web page with auto-generated documentation, including a place on the web page for the basic information working search and index functionalities. You can add more text, a logo, charts, and more to the documentation in the same way. You can even change the look of the site by swapping one of many themes (https://sphinx-themes.org/). You can always customize the templates to your taste, as well.

Any time you add new features to the package, you can regenerate the documentation—with one script! Once built, this documentation can be copied (for example, using the same CI process that we followed before) to any host (such as an AWS S3 bucket) or readthedocs.org—a service that hosts public documentation for free (and monetizes by injecting ads).

Now that a documentation page has been set up, let's move on to the last topic we'll cover in this chapter—the useful trick of working with packages in editable mode.

Installing a package in editable mode

As we have mentioned, you can install a package from GitHub and it will behave the same as any other installed package—it can be upgraded or uninstalled.

Often, however, you will want to use a package while developing it. It would be hard to do both in the normal installation routine; you'd have to either update or re-install the package every time you made any developmental changes, just to reflect those changes. To get around this, there is a great feature that keeps the advantages of both worlds—your code is treated as a package but can be easily modified in place. This feature is called editable mode. Essentially, it means the folder on your filesystem is registered as a package, and so the imported package will always reflect all the changes that you've made.

In order to reap these benefits, you have to have a repository of the package in question on your local machine. We obviously have our package, but it is also easy to pull the raw code via `git clone my/package/url`. Next, you open the terminal, and while being one step above the `package` folder, you type the following:

```
pip install -e wikiwwii
```

Boom! You have an editable package. You can test it in your Jupyter Notebook:

```
>>> import wikiwwii
```

See? It behaves as if it is a properly installed package but you can make changes to your code and they will be immediately applied upon your next import.

 At the time of writing this book, editable mode is not supported for the TOML-based packages. This should change soon.

This section helped you to install a package in editable mode, so now we should be good to try out some new code files!

Summary

In this chapter, we went over all the processes of packaging code. In particular, we created a GitHub repository, generated a template via `poetry`, and added all the dependencies, meaning everyone can now install the package from GitHub using `pip`. We then went further, adding a few tests to make sure our package works as expected throughout future development. To simplify the process and make it transparent, we integrated a CI service, Azure pipelines, to run tests on each pull request in order to prevent us from merging failing code into production.

In the next chapter, we will review another case, building a robust, secure, production-ready data pipeline using `luigi`.

Questions

1. What are the benefits of packaging code?
2. What is the main difference between `conda` and `pip` as package managers?
3. What is dependency resolution, and why is it hard?
4. What are the benefits of `poetry` over standard `setuptools`?
5. Why do we need tests?
6. What is the purpose of CI?

Further reading

- *Getting Started with Python Packages* (`https://hub.packtpub.com/getting-started-python-packages/`)
- *Writing a Package in Python* (`https://hub.packtpub.com/writing-package-python/`)
- *Testing Tools and Techniques in Python* (`https://hub.packtpub.com/testing-tools-and-techniques-python/`)

16
Data Pipelines with Luigi

Until now, we have been writing code as separate notebooks and scripts. In the previous chapter, we learned how to group those scripts into a package so that it can be distributed and tested properly. In many cases, however, we need to execute certain tasks on a strict schedule. Often, it is needed to process certain data—pull off analytics, collect information from external sources, or re-train an ML model. All of this is prone to errors: tasks may depend on other tasks, and some tasks shouldn't run before others. It is important that tasks should be easy to orchestrate, monitor, and re-run for ease of use.

In this chapter, we will learn to build and orchestrate our own data pipelines. Building good pipelines is an important skill that can save tons of time and stress for anyone who masters it.

In particular, we will cover the following topics:

- Introducing the ETL pipeline
- Building the first task in Luigi
- Scheduling with cron
- Time-based task scheduling
- Structuring with Luigi

Technical requirements

For this chapter, we'll use a package called `luigi`. Last few tasks will require two more packages—`boto3` and `sqlalchemy`. We will also use the `wikiwwii` package we built in Chapter 15, *Packaging and Testing with Poetry and PyTest*. You can build it yourself by following the chapter or install it by running this:

```
pip install git+https://github.com/Casyfill/wikiwwii.git
```

All of the code is in the repository, in the `Chapter16` folder (https://github.com/PacktPublishing/Learn-Python-by-Building-Data-Science-Applications).

Introducing the ETL pipeline

Data pipelines are important and ubiquitous. Even organizations with a small online presence run their own jobs: thousands of research facilities, meteorological centers, observatories, hospitals, military bases, and banks all run their internal data processing.

Another name for the data pipelines is **ETL**, which stands for **Extract**, **Transform**, and **Load**—three conceptual pieces of each pipeline. At first glance, the task may sound trivial. Most of our notebooks are, in a way, ETL jobs—we load some data, work with it, and then store it somewhere. However, building and maintaining a good pipeline requires a thorough and consistent approach. Processes should be reliable, easy to re-run, and reusable. Particular tasks shouldn't run more than once or if their dependencies are not satisfied (say, other tasks haven't finished yet).

It is not, however, something new—a market for ETL and the corresponding programmatic solutions is well established. There are quite a few frameworks on the market, both enterprise and open source. To name a few, there is Airflow, Pinball, Azkaban, Bubbles, and a dozen others. There is also a new kid on the block, Prefect. Airflow is arguably the most popular at the moment. Developed by Airbnb, Airflow allows the running of tasks on a cluster using arbitrary tasks (not necessarily written in Python) and orchestrating them from a web-dashboard—the user does not need to have anything installed in their machine. Airflow is a great tool but requires significantly more hassle to deploy and maintain, which makes it a hard choice for this book or any *one-off*, simple pipeline, in general.

In this chapter, we'll use `luigi`, a relatively lightweight and flexible framework that allows the running of pipelines locally, with no remote server required, and with a comparatively small overhead. Because of that, `luigi` is easy to play and experiment with and might be very useful for structuring any, even a small, process—for example, training a machine learning model.

Let's start our introduction from a conceptual overview. `luigi` is based on a few core principles:

- Every project should be represented as a **Directed Acyclic Graph** (**DAG**), where each node represents one logical step in the process, usually called **tasks**. Edges define the sequence and dependency of each task. Some tasks will depend on the completion of one or a few other tasks.

- Tasks can be parameterized (say, run for a specific date) and can send information (including those parameters) to each other.
- For every task, there is a simple and unambiguous way to check whether the task is complete. The scheduler will not run the same task twice.

In `luigi`, DAGs are not predefined—you operate on the tasks, specifying for each its outcomes (say the file or table it will store its data to) and dependencies and which tasks are required to be running before this one. The following is a basic form of a `luigi` task. As you can see, it inherits from a template class and has one parameter, `date`, and two methods, `output` and `run`:

```
class MyTask(luigi.Task):
    date = luigi.DateParameter(default='2019-06-01')

    def output(self):
        return luigi.LocalTarget(f'./data/data/{self.date:%Y/%m-
        %d}.csv')
    def run(self):
        # do stuff
        # ...
        data.to_csv(self.output().path)
```

Luigi is meant to be used via class inheritance. On execution, `luigi` will do the following:

1. Check whether `MyTask` is complete, using its `complete` method, built into `luigi.Task`. By default, it returns true if the output file exists.
2. If not, `luigi` will check whether `MyTask` has any dependencies, defined in the `requires` method. As we didn't override the method, `luigi` uses the one from the template, which returns no dependencies. If a task does have dependencies, and they are not complete (as shown in the preceding code), the scheduler will look at them first (go to the start of this list). Once they are executed successfully, the scheduler will eventually switch back to this task.
3. As `MyTask` doesn't have any dependencies, it will be executed immediately, by running the `run` function.
4. The parameter (`date`) will be encoded in the output path.

For each and every task we add, the key is to define (override) the `run`, `requires`, `output`, and, if necessary, `complete` functions (for example, if the task produces more than one file, and you want to check completeness by the existence of a particular one).

Redesigning your code as a pipeline

But how can you define a pipeline? What are the best steps to split your code to keep it both cost-efficient and low-maintenance? From our experience, it mainly depends on a combination of two factors:

- How reliable is the data source?
- How critical is this information, or will the data be available to re-pull after a while?

As a rule of thumb, if the dataset is external and hence unreliable (for example, a Wikipedia page or Open Data Portal), we'd recommend splitting your injection pipeline into distinctive steps. In the first step, you'll collect all of the data the way it is provided—say, store the whole HTML page. For data, use JSON or CSV—something with no strict schema. After raw data is stored, you can extract the clean data. Even if something goes wrong, you keep an original on hand.

If the source is reliable (for example, specific internal data with a defined schema) or the dataset can be re-pulled at any time, you can probably wrap your code into a single task. You may still want to keep one task per logical step—so that tasks could be used for other purposes or as part of a different pipeline.

Enough talk! Let's build a task of our own!

Building our first task in Luigi

Luckily, `luigi` allows us to start small. We'll start by building a task that pulls all of the links on the battles, using the code from our `wikiwwii` package. First, we will import all we need in a separate file, `luigi_fronts.py`:

```
# luigi_fronts.py
from pathlib import Path
import json

import luigi
from wikiwwii.collect.battles import collect_fronts
URL = 'https://en.wikipedia.org/wiki/List_of_World_War_II_battles'
folder = Path(__file__).parents[1] / 'data'
```

Here, we declared a link for the battles, imported our `collect_fronts` function, and specified a relative folder to store the data in. Now, let's write the task itself. In the following, we'll create a task class, define the URL as a `luigi` parameter with a default value (more on that later), and add (or, rather, override) two methods—`output`, which returns a local target with the `path` data, and `run`, which describes the actual code to run—it collects the data and writes it to the file, defined in `output`. Indeed, the actual business logic here is in one line—thanks to the `wikiwwii` package we made in the previous chapter:

```
class ScrapeFronts(luigi.Task):
    url = luigi.Parameter(default=URL, description='page url')

    def output(self):
        name = self.link.split('/')[-1]
        path = str(folder / f'{name}.json')
        return luigi.LocalTarget(path)

    def run(self):
        data = collect_fronts(self.url)
        with open(self,output().path, 'w') as f:
            json.dump(data, f)
```

Let's run it! Luigi provides a convenient command-line interface for that:

```
$ python -m luigi --module luigi_fronts ScrapeFronts --local-scheduler
```

Here, we specify the file to use `luigi_fronts` and a specific task, `ScrapeFronts`. As a result, you should get the following summary:

```
===== Luigi Execution Summary =====

Scheduled 1 tasks of which:
* 1 ran successfully:
    - 1
ScrapeFronts(url=https://en.wikipedia.org/wiki/List_of_World_War_II_battles
)

This progress looks :) because there were no failed tasks or missing
dependencies

===== Luigi Execution Summary =====
```

The most important indicator here is the smiley face—which means that everything ran smoothly—and, as you can check, the data file was created. For the sake of experiment, try running it one more time. It will result in the following:

```
===== Luigi Execution Summary =====

Scheduled 1 tasks of which:
* 1 complete ones were encountered:
    - 1
ScrapeFronts(url=https://en.wikipedia.org/wiki/List_of_World_War_II_battles
)

Did not run any tasks
This progress looks :) because there were no failed tasks or missing
dependencies

===== Luigi Execution Summary =====
```

This means *I checked and the result file is already there*. If we need to re-run the task anyway, we'll have to delete or rename the file.

Connecting the dots

So far, we've created just one task. Even on its own, it has some value, as it formalizes the work and the output. Now, let's add tasks to collect data for battle. It will look very similar to the previous one—we create a task, inheriting from the `Task` class:

```python
# luigi_battles.py
from misc import _parse_in_depth
from luigi_fronts import ParseFronts


class ParseFront(luigi.Task):
    front = luigi.Parameter()

    def requires(self):
        return ScrapeFronts()
    def output(self):
        path = str(folder / 'fronts' / (self.front + '.json'))
        return luigi.LocalTarget(path)

    def run(self):
        with open(self.input().path, 'r') as f:
            fronts = json.load(f)
```

```
front = fronts[self.front]
result = {}

for cp_name, campaign in front.items():
    result[cp_name] = _parse_in_depth(campaign, cp_name)

with self.output().open('w') as f:
    json.dump(result, f)
```

We also introduced a few additional elements:

- First, we use the `requires` method, which, as we mentioned earlier, defines the prerequisite task.
- Next, we use the `input` method, which is tied to prerequisites and represents access to the corresponding data, similar to `output()`.
- Finally, we added a parameter—this is how the `luigi` task can be parameterized.
- Note that output and input objects (targets, really) do have an `open` method. It is a good idea to use it—you'll see why soon.

> Use Luigi parameters! It is essentially *free* command-line interface and could be of tremendous value. There are quite a few parameter options, allowing you to pass dates, Booleans, and time periods; specify a range or list of possible values and so on. Luigi will even parse data types according to the expected parameter type. For more information on parameters, check the documentation.
>
> For example, we can add a Boolean flag for *production* mode so that everything will be written to the staging path by default or the production path, on request. In one line, we get away to safely run tasks without affecting our *production*. Another example—with date parameters, Luigi can run multiple tasks by pre-generating multiple dates within the given range—and running the task for each of those days.

Given that, we now can collect data for a specific front:

```
$ python -m luigi --module luigi_battles ParseFront --front "Eastern Front"
--local-scheduler
```

Finally, let's collect data for all of the fronts, at once:

```
class ParseAll(luigi.Task):
    fronts = ["African Front", "Mediterranean Front",
            "Western Front", "Atlantic Ocean", "Eastern Front",
```

```
                   "Indian Ocean","Pacific Theater", "China
                   Front","Southeast Asia Front"]

    def requires(self):
        return [ParseFront(front=f) for f in self.fronts]
```

As you can see, this task has neither `run` nor `output` methods overwritten, as we don't need them. At the same time, we return not one task but many as the outcome of the `requires` method. Luckily, Luigi supports both lists, generators, and even dictionaries, as the outcome of the `requires` and `output` functions.

Here is how this process looks like a graph. Here, each box represents one task, and arrow—task dependency. We always run the *last* task in the graph if we want to run all of them. The system then checks whether its dependencies are resolved. If they are not, it then checks their dependencies, and many more, until it finds tasks that are ready to run. All other tasks then run, one by one:

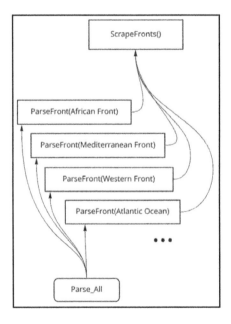

Now, as there will be a few tasks running in parallel, and all of them are heavy on I/O, it may be beneficial to run them in parallel, which is very easy to do with Luigi, you just need to specify the number of workers, as follows:

```
$ python -m luigi --module luigi_battles ParseAll --workers 2 --local-
scheduler
```

And voilà! We just collected all of the battle information in a robust, production-ready manner. At any step, we can change the code, delete the output file, and re-run `luigi`. The system will understand which tasks it needs to run and which ones are done already.

We were able to pull data from Wikipedia as a one-time job, but how would we use `luigi` with scheduled processes? Let's talk about that in the next section.

Understanding time-based tasks

Pipelines are especially useful to schedule data collection, for example, downloading new data every night.

Say we want to collect new data on 311 calls in NYC for the previous day, every morning. First, let's write the pulling function itself. The code is fairly trivial. You can take a look at the **Socrata** (the data-sharing platform New York uses) API documentation via this link, https://dev.socrata.com/consumers/getting-started.html. The only tricky part is that the dataset can be large—but Socrata won't give us more than 50,000 rows at once. Hence, if the length of the input is equal to 50,000, most likely, the data was capped, and we'll need to make another pull with the offset, over and over until the number of rows is smaller. `resource` in the arguments represents a unique ID of the dataset—you can obtain it from the dataset's web page:

```
def _get_data(resource, time_col, date, offset=0):
    Q = f"where=created_date between '{date}' AND '{date}T23:59:59.000'"
    url = f'https://data.cityofnewyork.us/resource/{resource}.json?$limit=50000&$offset={offset}&${Q}'

    r = rq.get(url, headers=headers)
    r.raise_for_status()

    data = r.json()
    if len(data) == 50_000:
        data2 = _get_data(resource, time_col, date, offset=(offset +
                50000)
        data.extend(data2)

    return data
```

Now, let's write the task itself. It is actually fairly short—all we do is define a resource, `time_column` (on which we'll query the API), and the date to pull for:

```
class Collect311(luigi.Task):
    time_col = 'Created Date'
    date = luigi.DateParameter()
    resource = 'fhrw-4uyv'

    def output(self):
        path = f'{folder}/311/{self.date:%Y/%m/%d}.csv'
        return luigi.LocalTarget(path)

    def run(self):
        data = _get_data(self.resource, self.time_col, self.date,
            offset=0)
        df = pd.DataFrame(data)
        self.output().makedirs()
        df.to_csv(self.output().path)
```

The task can essentially be used on any dataset Socrata provides—all you need is to specify `resource` and the column on which to query. The data parameter also defines the outcome path to the file. Now, we can run the task from the command line:

```
$ python -m luigi --module luigi_311 Collect311 --date 2019-06-07 --local-
scheduler
```

We can now run this task even in batches, using the `DateRange` feature:

```
$ python -m luigi --module luigi_311 RangeDaily --of Collect311 --start
2019-06-01 --days-back 10  --local-scheduler
```

The preceding code will generate up to 10 tasks, one for each of the 10 days—today and 10 days back, but no further than June 1, 2019. This trick is especially nice for scheduling—even if something will prevent the task from running on the date, it will re-run the next day or the day after that, and so on.

Scheduling with cron

We have mentioned scheduling multiple times already—but how do we do it? For better or worse, this is not something Luigi is capable of on its own. But fear not—this is a proper task for your operating system. On Windows, it can be done using the `Schtasks` utility. On macOS and Linux, scheduling is managed by the `cron` tool, via so-called `crontabs`.

Crontab has its own mini-language for scheduling: every command starts with five symbols, representing the specific minute, hour, day, month, and day of the week (an asterisk can be used when we have no specific value). For example, if we want to run a task every day at 05:00, we'll use the following command:

```
0 5 * * * <our command>
```

Crontab supports multiple values, as well. For example, if we need a task to run on the first day of every quarter, we can just specify 4 months:

```
0 5 1 1,4,7,10 * <our command>
```

We want to run our task every day, so we'll use the first example:

```
$ python -m luigi --module luigi_311 RangeDaily --of Collect311 --start
2019-06-01 --days-back 10  --local-scheduler
```

This will run your task every day, at 05:00. If you're running on a local machine, keep in mind that it won't run if your computer is turned off at the time it is supposed to run. The safest solution would be to deploy the code on a dedicated server. Alternatively, you can use the anacron utility, which will run the skipped tasks once the computer is turned on.

In any scenario, another level of security is that Luigi can automatically try to back-fill tasks on each run: this way, if some previous task didn't run (or failed), it will be re-executed.

Next, let's talk about how to use luigi to store data remotely and in different data formats.

Exploring the different output formats

In the code of the *Scheduling with cron* section, we used local targets, writing to the filesystem of our computer. In a real-world scenario, that will rarely suffice—you'll be probably writing either to a database or file stored in the cloud. In fact, we highly encourage you to write tasks to the cloud (for example, S3 buckets) from the get-go, if there is no reason not to. Luigi supports FTP, S3, Azure Blobs, Google Cloud, Spark, MongoDB, SQL databases, and many more. The only question is to create those resources and set up credentials to access them. The best part for many of them is that the interface is very similar, so it is easy to swap *targets* for existing tasks, by changing only a few lines of code.

Writing to an S3 bucket

S3 buckets and similar blob storage services have proven to be a great tool. Given the small price and ease of use, they are arguably the best solution for shared data exchange in the cloud. Here, we won't go in depth on S3 and **Amazon Web Services** (**AWS**) in general. Instead, we'll show how to modify your existing pipelines to redirect them to S3. Aside from data being in the cloud, this has the benefit of a shared state—if another computer or user tries to run the pipeline, they will find that the data is there already.

Let's assume you have registered as an AWS customer and have an S3 bucket. To work with buckets, luigi uses the boto3 package, an official library for AWS-related operations, built by Amazon. This means that luigi will accept any forms of authorization that work with boto3—via the AWS configuration file or credentials as environmental variables. Alternatively, you can specify credentials in luigi configs, under the s3 header:

```
[s3]
aws_access_key_id = <your-key-id>
aws_secret_access_key = <your-secret-access-key>
```

Now, our access to the S3 service should be ready. Let's rewrite our luigi_battles.py file, to throw all of the information to S3. First, let's import all we need in the code and specify the bucket name:

```
# luigi_battles_s3.py
from luigi.contrib.s3 import S3Target, S3Client
bucket = 'your_bucket_name'
```

Next, we need to add client as a task attribute and swap the LocalTarget object with S3Target:

```
class ParseFront(luigi.Task):
    front = luigi.Parameter()
    client = S3Client() # <<< client if needed, you can add credentials
here, as well

def requires(self):
    return ScrapeFronts()

    def output(self):
        path = f's3://{bucket}/wikiwii/fronts/{front}.json'
        return S3Target(path=path, client=self.client) # <<< swapped local
target with s3

    def run(self):
        with open(self.input().path, 'r') as f:
            fronts = json.load(f)
```

```
front = fronts[self.front]
result = {}

for cp_name, campaign in front.items():
    result[cp_name] = _parse_in_depth(campaign, cp_name)

with self.output().open('w') as f:
    json.dump(result, f)
```

Note that we didn't have to change anything to write here, as both `LocalTarget` and `S3Target` support the `open` method. Another nice part is that we don't need to change anything else in the pipeline. Even if you read the data in the next package, you can keep the same code, assuming you also use the `open` method of the target. Let's run the code and check whether the files are there:

```
$ python -m luigi --module luigi_battles_s3 ParseAll --local-scheduler
```

Seems that everything is now stored in the bucket.

Writing to SQL

In many cases, it is preferable or more convenient to write to a database rather than a flat-file. Let's illustrate this case with our 311 data pipeline.

Writing data to a database is quite similar and we won't need to change much. One major difference is task completion detection—for an obvious reason, there is no *file* to check for existence. As a workaround, `luigi` creates a utility table that stores unique records of the complete tasks. This process is integral to the framework, so most of the time, there is no reason for us to think about it. With that being said, SQL-based pipelines have two, pretty strong, caveats:

- As the task does not result in an isolated task, there is no simple way to pull data from this specific task. A new task or your external code will need to query for the right slice of data.
- For the same reason, if something goes wrong, you will need to remove both a specific subset of data (as mentioned previously) and a marker record in the utility database.

On the flip side, Luigi has a couple of helper tasks to make use of. For example, we can use a `CopyToTable` task object instead of the default one. As the name suggests, this task has everything predesigned to upload certain data to a certain SQL table. To make it run, we need to add just a few bits of information.

For our example, we will use an SQLite database, for the sake of simplicity. Luigi has a set of solutions, tailored for PostgreSQL, MySQL, MSSQL, Hive, and others. It doesn't have a specific code for the SQLite, so we'll have to fall back to the universal SQLAlchemy solution. Here is how it works:

1. We inherit from the `luigi.contrib.sqla.CopyToTable` task.
2. The task has to contain certain attributes, including `table` (the table to write to), `connection_string` for the SQLAlchemy connection, and the `columns` iterable, which contains the `sqlalchemy` data types for each column.
3. Finally, we don't need to override the `run` function, which contains an implementation of data inset. Instead, we will override the `rows` method. This method should return tuples of values, one for each row of data, and is compatible with the columns we mentioned.

Let's see the following example. First, we have to define a table schema. Both for simplicity and security, we decided to keep everything as a string, except `unique_key`, which we will use as a primary key. A few columns with rather long values we defined them as a `Text` data type:

```
from sqlalchemy import String, Integer, Text

COLUMNS_RAW = [
    (["address_type", String(64)], {}),
    (["agency", String(64)], {}),
    (["bbl", String(64)], {}),
    (["borough", String(64)], {}),
    ...
    (["y_coordinate_state_plane", String(64)], {}),
    (["resolution_action_updated_date", Text()], {}),
    (["resolution_description", Text()], {}),
    (["location", Text()], {}),
    (["unique_key", String(64)], {"primary_key": True})
]
```

Note that, alternatively, we can create the database separately and then pull the data types from the table itself on each run—`sqlalchemy` supports that. Let's rewrite our task now. All we need is to add a few attributes, rename `run` as `rows`, and make it yield rows. It seems that the simplest way to do that is via `df.values.tolist()`. Consider the following code:

```
class Collect311_SQLITE(sqla.CopyToTable):
    time_col = "Created Date"
    date = luigi.DateParameter(default=date.today())
    resource = "fhrw-4uyv"
```

```
    columns = COLUMNS_RAW
    connection_string = SQLITE_STRING
    table = "raw"

    def rows(self):
        data = _get_data(self.resource, self.time_col, self.date,
        offset=0)
        df = pd.DataFrame(data).astype(str)
        df['unique_key'] = df['unique_key'].astype(int)

        for row in df.values.tolist():
            yield row
```

As you can see, our task has barely changed—that's the power of luigi!

Expanding Luigi with custom template classes

In the previous section, we used the CopyToTable class as the template instead of luigi.Task. In fact, this is a good pattern to use! If there is any custom configuration or code you can use from one task to another, feel free to create a custom task class of your own. For example, in our practice, we use a custom S3Task class, similar to the one that follows:

```
from luigi.contrib.s3 import S3Client, S3Target
import pandas as pd
from io import StringIO, BytesIO

class S3Task(luigi.Task):
    client = S3Client()

    def _upload_csv(df, path):
        content = df.to_csv(float_format="%.3f", index=None)
        self.client.put_string(
            content=content, destination_s3_path=path,
            ContentType="text/csv"
        )

    def _upload_binary(self, df):
        format_ = path.split(".")[-1]
        funcs = {"msg": "to_msgpack", "fth": "to_feather", "pkl":
                "to_pickle"}
```

```
        if format_ not in funcs:
            raise ValueError(
                f"format {format_} is not supported yet, should be one
                of {funcs.keys()}"
            )

        buffer = BytesIO()
        getattr(df, funcs[format_])(buffer, **kwargs)
        buffer.seek(0)

        bucket, key = self.client._path_to_bucket_and_key(path)
        self.client.s3.meta.client.upload_fileobj(
            Fileobj=buffer,
            Bucket=bucket,
            Key=key,
            ExtraArgs={"ContentType": "application/octet-stream"},
        )
```

This class has an S3 client by default and can easily write both CSV and binary formats to the cloud, given the dataframe. You might want to expand customization even further. For example, for a special type of task, make sure the data lands on a proper path and the need for a task-specific code is minimal:

```
class NYCOD(S3Task):
    resource:str = None # resource to pull
    timecol:str = 'CreationDate'
    project:str = 'Undefined'
    date = luigi.DateParameter(default=date.today())
    s3_path:str = 's3://mybucket/{project}/{date:%Y/%m/%d}.csv'

    def output(self):
        path = self.s3_path.format(project=self.project,
                date=self.date)
        return S3Target(path, client=self.client)

    def run(self):
        data = _get_data(self.resource, self.time_col, self.date,
                offset=0)
        df = pd.DataFrame(data)
        self._upload_csv(df, self.output().path)
```

Let's say you have a few tasks collecting data from the NYC OpenData portal. All of them are scheduled and you want to store a CSV file for each day and for each project. Then, we can wrap more shared code in a class on top of our S3Task.

With that template, our 311 complaint collection task will be quite short:

```
class Collect311(NYCOD):
    time_col = "Created Date"
    resource = "fhrw-4uyv"
    project = '311'
```

And, even better, we can create tasks for other datasets from the portal with the same four lines! For example, here is a task that will collect and properly store building permits:

```
class CollectBuildingPermits(NYCOD):
    time_col = "Issued Date"
    resource = "rbx6-tga4"
    project = 'building_permits'
```

As you can see, these tasks are now ridiculously short and simple to write, all thanks to the thorough layers of class inheritance. It's not only the concise form—the unification of tasks allows us to concentrate solutions in one place. It makes it easy to test and maintain the code, make it *DRY*, and change the behavior of all of the corresponding pipelines, at once.

Ease of customization is one of the advantages of Luigi. A thorough *arsenal* of custom tasks will significantly boost your development pace. All in all, adopting luigi will solidify your processes and make you work on the new stuff, not plumbing the same leaking data pipes—making it true to its name.

Summary

In this chapter, we learned how to form our code into production-level data pipelines that can be scheduled and re-run on demand. Building good pipelines is an important skill, as it enables you to have the data up to date and work on your business logic (for example, parsing the information), rather than running and re-running pipeline scripts or building your own *bicycle* solution. This reliable and robust solution is a good way to deploy and schedule your code as a deliverable. In the later part of this chapter, we learned about the different output formats and custom templates in luigi.

In the next chapter, we'll build on top of the pipeline we set up. We will use the data we collected to build a couple of interactive dashboards, allowing us to monitor the process and analyze ongoing trends in the data.

Questions

1. What are the benefits of writing tasks rather than using simple scripts?
2. What is the base element of Luigi jobs?
3. How are DAGs defined in Luigi? What are the benefits of that architecture?
4. How can we parametrize a task?
5. What is the best way to run time-based tasks in bulk?
6. How can we schedule a job with Luigi?

Further reading

Data Pipelines (`https://hub.packtpub.com/data-pipelines/`).

17
Let's Build a Dashboard

In the previous chapter, we learned how to create robust pipelines and schedule them so that we have metrics updated every day. With that, our valuable data product is automated! What should we do? Perhaps it is a good moment to discuss dashboards. Dashboards are essentially the entry point for you to monitor the behavior of the system (your service, markets, users, or anything else) via a set of data visualizations. Dashboards help teams and companies to ensure the business is running smoothly or to detect—and adjust to—changes or anomalies. So, to help us understand them better, let's see how they work.

The following topics will be covered in this chapter:

- Different ways to build a dashboard
- Building a static dashboard
- Building and serving a dynamic dashboard
- Pros and cons of different approaches
- Debugging Altair

Technical requirements

The following packages are required for the code in this chapter to run:

- `matplotlib`
- The `altair` visualization package, version 3 or above
- `panel`

As usual, all of the code for this chapter is in the GitHub repository, in the `Chapter17` folder: `https://github.com/PacktPublishing/Learn-Python-by-Building-Data-Science-Applications`.

Building a dashboard – three types of dashboard

In `Chapter 12`, *Data Exploration and Visualization*, we explored a dataset by visualizing different features, using two packages—`matplotlib` and `altair`. The differences between those visualizations and a dashboard are twofold:

- The audience for the dashboard is meant to be wide, so it should be easily accessible via an internet browser. Visualizations are often made for self-consumption.
- Dashboards are meant to be frequently updated and, to some extent, interactive. Visualizations are often done on-the-spot, are static, and show only specific aspects of the data.

To a large extent, dashboards are full-blown projects requiring regular improvement and maintenance! However, as the demand for this kind of product is large, and the task is easily generalizable, there are plenty of solutions, tools, and services at our disposal. We can group them into three main categories:

- Third-party services, such as Tableau (there is still a running server behind it—it's just not yours to manage)
- Static—those without an active server behind them and all interactions happen on the client's machine
- Dynamic—those with an active server (or servers) behind them

Throughout this book, we focus on building stuff with code, rather than consuming, so we won't review services, of which there are dozens, now. If you're willing to build and support your own dashboards, it is totally possible! Let's study these in the upcoming sections.

Static dashboards

Despite the name, static dashboards are not static per se—they are not just still images. Here, static refers to the fact that the dashboard is served as a flat HTML file; all of the interaction happens in the client's browser. As a result, the dashboard can be uploaded anywhere on the web (say, an S3 bucket or similar service) and stay there almost for free, with little maintenance required. It is also easy to update the dashboard or data, with essentially no downtime. And of course, this approach means you won't need to think about the scalability and performance of the dashboard.

Obviously, that approach has its downsides, as well. First of all, it is limited to a specific amount of data it can use, and the dataset will be basically available for everyone, directly. If your dashboard requires complex queries and real-time aggregation, this approach will not work. It would be hard to create authentication or to customize the dashboard for a specific user. In a nutshell, this type of dashboard is perfect for the following:

- Serving a wide audience.
- It uses a relatively small dataset that is fine to share with everyone.
- This data is updated occasionally—definitely not in real-time (the computation may take a lot of resources).

One obstacle in going down that path for many backend developers and data scientists is JavaScript itself. This is virtually the only option with which to write interactive web applications. At the same time, most data scientists and Python developers don't know JavaScript well enough to use it in production, and, often, don't even want to write JavaScript. There are a few ways to dodge that, for example, compiling your code to WebAssembly (which browsers can also run), but that, at least for now, is a hard task in its own right and is a huge overkill.

Another, arguably better, alternative is to use one of the existing Python tools and packages that will generate both HTML and JavaScript code for us. Earlier, we mentioned the difference between visualizing in the notebook and on the dashboard, but this kind of tool can generate charts for both cases.

In the previous chapter, we built a pipeline that collects data on 311 calls every day and then generates a report. Now, let's built a static dashboard of this data, using the altair library we used to plot interactive visualizations in the notebook. We will start in the same way: in the Notebook then store it as HTML; finally, we will redirect the visualization to use an external dataset—the one we're scheduled to update.

Let's start preparing our notebook and loading the dataset:

```
import pandas as pd
import altair as alt

alt.data_transformers.disable_max_rows()

data = pd.read_csv('./data/top5.csv', parse_dates=['date',]).fillna(0)
```

Now, what would we want to have on a dashboard? Usually, a primary goal is to highlight any temporal abnormalities—say, a day that was skipped in data collection or whether the number of complaints deviated significantly. One way to do that is to show a line chart of the total number of complaints—say, split by boroughs:

```
timeline = alt.Chart(data, width=800).mark_line().encode(
    x='date',
    y='value',
    color='boro'
).transform_filter(
    (alt.datum.metric == 'complaints')
)
```

The code results in this diagram:

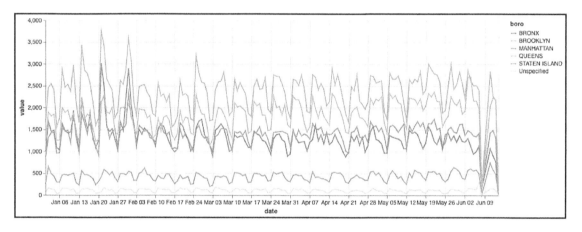

And already, we see some interesting stuff: missing values for June 7 and some peaks in January and February. This is a good example of the type of insight quick graphical overviews can give. We can also see different levels of complaints for different boroughs—Brooklyn has, for some reason, more than the others.

Now, it would be great to see what this is all about—which types of complaint are the most popular within a given interval of time. Let's first build a bar chart of the top five complaint types for the entire period:

```
barchart = alt.Chart(data, width=800).mark_bar().encode(
    x='svalue:Q',
    y=alt.Y(
        'metric:N',
        sort=alt.EncodingSortField(
            field="svalue", # The field to use for the sort
            order="descending" # The order to sort in
```

```
        )
    ),
    color=alt.value('purple'),
    tooltip=['metric', 'svalue:Q']).transform_filter(
    "datum.metric != 'complaints'").transform_filter(
    "datum.boro == 'NYC'").transform_aggregate(
    svalue='sum(value)',
    groupby=["metric" ]).transform_window(
    rank='rank(svalue)',
    sort=[alt.SortField('svalue', order='descending')])
    .transform_filter('datum.rank <= 10')
```

Here, we have to filter for NYC (to avoid counting metrics twice) and for the complaints metric, for the same reason. As we want to drop the long tail, we have to generate a rank for each row and then filter by its value. The following is the result:

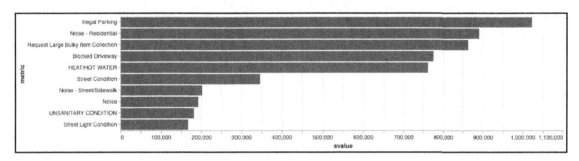

Finally, we want to combine the two: selecting the time period and seeing a distribution of complaint types for that period. It is just a combination of the two, with a `brush` element added:

```
brush = alt.selection_interval(encodings=['x'], empty='all')

T = timeline.add_selection(brush)

B = barchart.transform_filter(brush)

dash = alt.vconcat(A, B, data=data)
```

Here, the `dash` variable represents a combined chart that knows how to filter bars based on the interval on the timeline. Feel free to play around and see how top complaints change over time! Of course, there are plenty of features to add (for example, see different complaint types for a particular time of the day), but those features and transformations will quickly grow too exponentially complex for rapid design—that's the downside of using a Vega stack and computing everything in the browser, in general.

On the following diagram, you can see a screenshot of the resulting dashboard:

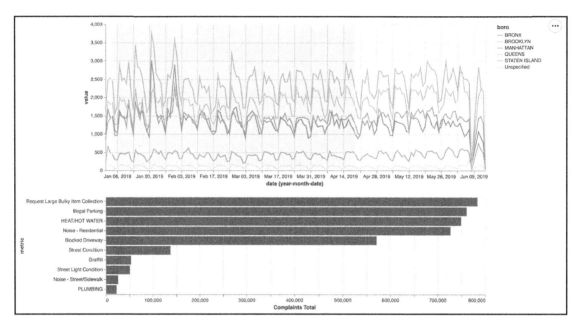

The gray area on the timeline represents the selected range. The bar chart then shows the overall number of complaints for the top 10 complaint types within the period. This interactivity allows us to dive deeper into the data, exploring more nuanced trends of a particular time period.

 We could imagine linking our dashboard to an API as an alternative to serving flat files. This way, the dashboard will show the data upto the current moment; it is also possible to connect Altair/Vega to a data stream, so that the dashboard will be updating in real time.

Working with Altair is great, as it is easy to create a beautiful visualization with advanced interaction—except for the cases when it won't work. In the next section, let's talk about the ways we can debug your plots and understand what is going wrong.

Debugging Altair

The preceding example works, but in the real world, any development is a process of trial and error. Debugging might be daunting with the Vega stack due to the layered nature of the product (Altair converts charts into Vega-Lite, Vega-Lite converts them into Vega, and the Vega engine works in JavaScript) and because we're working in this non-Pythonic world.

As with all code in general, the process is to isolate different parts and layers of the application to identify the root of the problem. Identification will give you ideas on how to solve the problem and work around it. Unfortunately, we can't just split parts of the specification. So, what can we do if your chart does not work as intended?

Despite all of the issues, the stack has one advantage in that regard: everything lives upto the specifications, which are human-readable and, generally speaking, human-writable. The simplest way to debug is to open a chart in the **Vega editor** (for example, via the triple-dot button) and start tinkering around. Here is a screenshot of the same dashboard in the editor:

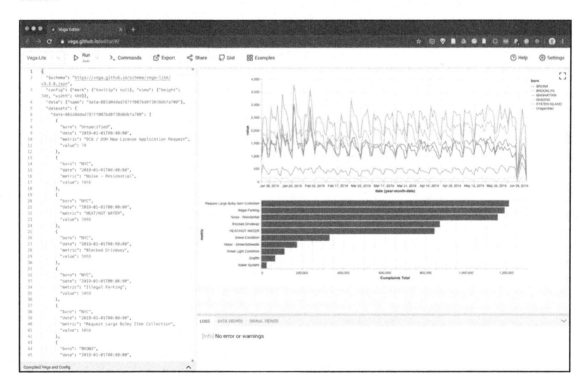

Sometimes, what you want is not available via the Vega-Lite specifications—then, in the same editor, you can convert them into Vega and continue editing there. Once the issue is resolved, you have two options: one is to adjust your Altair code accordingly— often, it is easy. Alternatively, you can store the specifications separately and just use them via Altair or the Vega app.

There are some other options, too. For example, the **Voyager** tool, also free and hosted on the web, tries to help you to pick the right visualization for specific data, while **Lira** (also hosted and free) is meant as drag-n-drop software, based on Vega. Both could help you at the start of your project, and you can always juggle your specifications between the tools, according to your current needs. All of the afore mentioned tools—and then some—can be found on Vega's official web page: `https://vega.github.io/`.

Connecting your app to the Luigi pipeline

Once the dashboard is working and looks good, we can discuss its deployment details. For now, all of the data is internalized in the dashboard itself, which makes the specification large and a little hard to update. Let's link the chart to the external CSV file we generated with Luigi and stored on the S3 bucket. We could use the URL (path to the file) from the beginning; it's just easier to be able to open and investigate the dataset. Copy the URL to the dataset and override the attribute:

```
url = 'https:/path/to/your/dataset.csv'
dash.data = url
```

Make sure it is still working! Now, we can write the dashboard to the HTML, as follows:

```
dash.save('chart.html')
```

As we discussed in `Chapter 12`, *Data Exploration and Visualization*, this will store a standalone HTML page with a working dashboard. The last step is to publish the chart itself (for example, on the same S3 bucket). Published, the chart will reflect the changes whenever we update the CSV. We can further automate that update by scheduling a Luigi pipeline to run every day: with this, we'll get a "live" dashboard for monitoring 311 situations in the city.

This dashboard costs virtually no money (only whatever we spend on S3 buckets) and requires no time to maintain. It could be easily customized and developed as an Altair object, a Vega-Lite/Vega application, or a standard HTML/JS-based app. Lastly, this dashboard can be easily styled and restyled according to your design guidelines. Being cheap and simple, this approach has its limitations: as with most client-based visualization solutions, Vega is limited in the amounts of data it can reflect, and the whole dataset needs to be publicly exposed, which is not always an option.

All of that makes Altair a great solution for public-facing charts and dashboards. Often, though, we need an internal dashboard, with access to large amounts of data and the ability to drill-down to specific records. For that, a different type of dashboard should be used: dynamic, server-dependent dashboards. Let's discuss them in the next section.

Understanding dynamic dashboards

An alternative approach to building a dashboard of your own is to make an actual web application, with a live server running Python on a backend; this will, upon request, show you a dashboard. This approach is, essentially, the exact opposite of a static dashboard in terms of pros and cons: it requires maintenance, needs to be scaled if the traffic is heavy, and could be slower. It also allows you to configure access, customize dashboards for any user or group of users, and compute the results live, even for a comparatively large dataset, without the need to share this dataset as a whole with the audience.

Of course, we could build an entire web application, controlling each and every feature (we won't do that), or use one of the specialized dashboard packages, such as uperset (essentially, a full-blown platform that requires database access) or Dash, a dashboarding tool based on the `plotly` Python library (very similar to Altair/Vega, but not as flexible). On the other side of the spectrum (further from static pages) are hybrid solutions, namely, `panel` and Voila. The latter is extremely new at the moment, so let's try building a dashboard using the `panel` package.

First try with panel

The idea behind `panel` (and Voila) is very simple and appealing: given that we essentially build web pages with our code and charts—the notebooks—we simply convert them into dashboards. The best part of that is that all of the code and every visualization library that can be used in Jupyter can be used in the dashboards; we could even use our existing Altair charts if we wanted. Let's try building something from the same dataset! As with Altair, we'll start with a Jupyter Notebook:

```
import sqlite3

import param
import panel as pn
import datetime as dt
pn.extension()
```

Now, the `panel` package is designed to make it extremely easy to build interactive widgets as part of your exploration process. To build an interaction, you just need a function with default values—`panel` will use them to understand the value types and generate input widgets accordingly. Here is an extremely naive example:

```
def interact_example(a=2, b=3):
    plot = plt.figure()
    ax = plot.add_subplot(111)
    pd.Series({'a':a, 'b':b}).plot(kind='bar',ax=ax)

    plt.tight_layout()
    plt.close(plot)
    return plot

pn.interact(interact_example)
```

The following screenshot is a result of the preceding code. The bar chart is interactive and responds to changes in input:

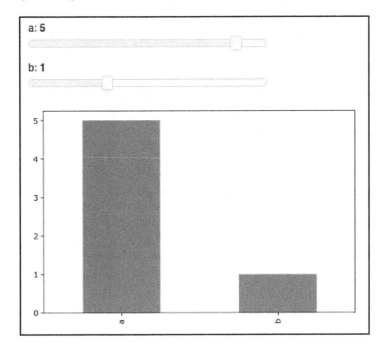

Here, we use `matplotlib` as a base visualization tool. Let's now try it on with a more complex task—showing the aggregate statistics on the 311 data we collected in `Chapter 16`, *Data Pipelines with Luigi*, live.

Reading data from the database

Before we dive into the nitty-gritty of visualization, let's get our data. Here, we will use the database connection to the SQLite file created. First, we'll create a connection to the file:

```
import sqlite
con = sqlite3.connect('../Chapter16/data/311.db')
```

Next, we will define a simple query to aggregate raw records into statistics:

```
Q = '''
SELECT date(created_date) as date, lower(borough) as boro, complaint_type,
COUNT(*) as complaints
FROM raw WHERE borough != 'Unspecified' GROUP BY 1,2,3;
'''
```

Finally, we will pull the data using the `pandas` SQL command. As we're dealing with SQLite, we'll have to re-parse date-times in Python:

```
DATA = pd.read_sql_query(Q, con)
DATA['date'] = pd.to_datetime(DATA['date'])
```

Alternatively, we could create `VIEW` with that query in the same file. That would allow us to pull data directly for this and other tasks.

For the timeline part of the chart, we could further aggregate our dataset:

```
>>> boro_total = DATA.groupby(['date',
'boro'])['complaints'].sum().unstack()

>>> boro_total.head(5)
      boro bronx brooklyn manhattan queens staten island
date
2019-01-01 995   1657     859       1237   249
2019-01-02 1675  2444     1307      1880   649
2019-01-03 1450  2532     1420      1799   484
2019-01-04 1472  2407     1417      1835   425
2019-01-05 1085  1551     954       1250   292
```

Now, our data is ready to be visualized! Let's get to it.

Creating an interactive dashboard in Jupyter

The functional approach we used in the previous section is convenient for exploration within the notebook. For a complex dashboard, however, it is better to use a somewhat declarative approach for more complex dashboards. In order to do that, we need to inherit from the Panel's `param.Parameterized` object and declare the parameters as it's attributed. For each view, we will create a separate method, using the `@param.depends('param1', 'param2')` decorator to bind the view refresh with the corresponding parameter updates. Let's give it a try:

1. First, we'll define the `DateRange` parameter, using a simple tuple of date-time values:

   ```
   bounds = (dt.datetime(2019,1,1),dt.datetime(2019,5,30))
   dr = param.DateRange(bounds=bounds, default=bounds)
   ```

2. Another parameter we want to use is boroughs. As we want to be able to select multiple boroughs at the same time, we'll have to explicitly pass them:

   ```
   boros_list = ['Manhattan', 'Bronx', 'Brooklyn', 'Queens', 'Staten
   Island']
   boros = param.ListSelector(default=boros_list, objects=boros_list)
   ```

3. Once the parameters are defined, we can create our view object, based on the dummy `param.Parametrized` class, as follows:

   ```
   class Timeline(param.Parameterized):
       dr = dr
       boros = boros
   ```

4. Next, we need to draw visualizations. As everything here runs in Python, all we need is to access the input parameters, filter data by them, and make a chart, returning the plot. The decorator will tell the Panel which parameters we want the chart to be updated on. We'll start with the timeline:

   ```
   # method for Timeline
   @param.depends('dr', 'boros')
   def view_tl(self):
       start, end = pd.to_datetime(self.dr[0]),
                   pd.to_datetime(self.dr[1])
       tl_data = boro_total.loc[(boro_total.index >= start) &
               (boro_total.index <= end),
               [el.lower() for el in self.boros]]
       plot = plt.figure(figsize=(10,5))
       ax = plot.add_subplot(111)
       tl_data.plot(ax=ax, linewidth=1)
   ```

```
ax.legend(loc=4)
plt.tight_layout()
plt.close(plot)
return plot
```

Similarly, we will create a chart for the top five complaint types. It also consists of a decorator, filtering, and visualization parts. Consider the following code:

```
@param.depends('dr', 'boros')
def view_top(self, N=5):
    start, end = pd.to_datetime(self.dr[0]),
                    pd.to_datetime(self.dr[1])
    boro_mask = DATA.boro.isin([el.lower()
                    for el in self.boros])
    time_mask = (DATA.date >= start)
                    & (DATA.date <= end)
    top = DATA[boro_mask & time_mask]
    S = top.groupby(['complaint_type', 'boro'])
        ['complaint_type'].count().unstack()
    topN = S.iloc[S.sum(1).argsort()].tail(N)
    plot = plt.figure()
    ax = plot.add_subplot(111)
    topN.plot(kind='barh',stacked=True, ax=ax)
    plt.tight_layout()
    plt.close(plot)
    return plot
```

This concludes the logic behind the dashboard. Now, we need to define its layout. For that, we will create a simple grid, using Panel's Row and Column objects. For more advanced layouts, panel also has a Grid object, but we will not use it here:

```
panel = pn.Column( '<h1>NYC 311 dashboard</h1>',
                T.view_tl,
                pn.Row(T.param, T.view_top,),
    sizing_mode='stretch_width')
```

Now, all we need is to start serving panel:

```
panel.servable()
```

As a result, we'll get the following dashboard:

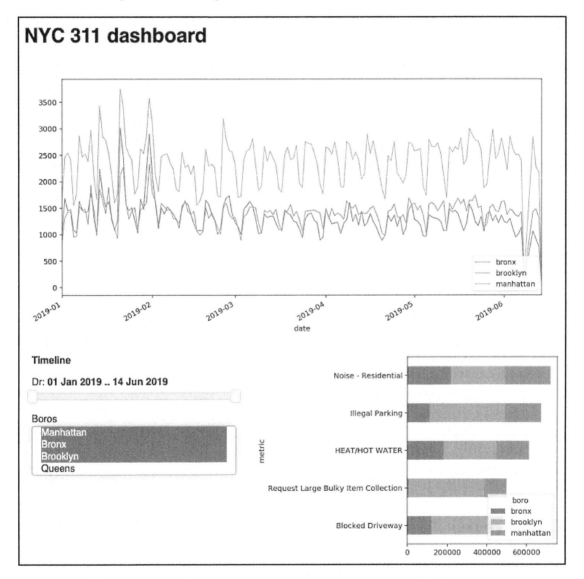

Dashboards can be represented as separate windows, using two object methods of an—either `panel.show()` or `panel.servable()`. Both will result in a new browser tab, serving the dashboard. The difference between them is that, with the second method, we can also run the dashboard with no Jupyter Notebook attached, using a bash command:

```
panel serve --show 2_panel.ipynb
```

Using `panel serve`, we can deploy our dashboard as an independent web application. All we need is to deploy the environment (all of the packages we need and Python itself) on a dedicated machine and make it run this command. In this case, we could swap the SQLite connection with one to the external database, so that the data will be shared between the dashboard and any other applications. The power of dynamic dashboards lies in their large capacity and flexibility. Here, we ignored the intermediary step of computing top complaint types per day and were able to run our analytics on the raw data. If needed, we could always drill-down and check the properties of a specific record, as well.

As everything is running on the server, in Python, we can use any package and are very flexible in designing the dashboard. As we mentioned, Panel supports any visualization that can be rendered in the notebook, so you can even reuse some visualizations you already have, including those we built in Altair.

One limitation to this approach is that we can only control the appearance of the visualizations to the extent that all of the libraries we use allow us to do so; for example, while we can use Altair, there is no way, at least currently, to pull back its parameters and use it to interact with other packages.

Overall, dynamic dashboards allow a wide range of possibilities for exploring and communicating your data. Compared to the static ones, they are easy to write, support any Python package, and can do the heavy lifting of data consumption and aggregation, pulling from raw data. This, of course, requires a dedicated server and may require maintenance and governance, especially if available to the public.

Summary

In this chapter, we learned to build two similar dashboards—a static one, with no server needed and using Altair, and a dynamic one, built from an ordinary Jupyter Notebook with arbitrary code and visualization packages, using the `panel` package. We discussed the pros and cons of each approach and when to select one over the other.

Either way, the dashboard is a great way to communicate your data product to your colleagues and clients. Dashboards allow us to get insights into business processes and spot issues early on. In many cases, that would make a perfect deliverable. In some cases, though, you might need to create a programmatic access point for your code, for example, a machine learning algorithm for an external application (a website, mobile app, or some analyst from their Jupyter Notebook) to use.

In the next chapter, we'll do exactly that, by building our own data-serving RESTful API, similar to the one we ourselves used not too long ago, in Chapter 6, *First Script – Geocoding with Web APIs*, and Chapter 11, *Data Cleaning and Manipulation*. Building an API allows our customers to directly access our application (for example, a predictive model) and use it on their data within their environment.

Questions

1. What are the main differences between visualizing data in a notebook and on a dashboard?
2. Why do we call some dashboards "static"? What are the pros and cons of a static dashboard?
3. What are the benefits of using a dynamic dashboard?
4. What are the features of the panel package?

Further reading

- *Apache Superset Quick Start Guide* by Shashank Shekhar, published by Packt (https://www.packtpub.com/big-data-and-business-intelligence/apache-superset-quick-start-guide)
- *Visualization Dashboard Design* (https://hub.packtpub.com/visualization-dashboard-design/)

Serving Models with a RESTful API

18

In the previous chapter, we discussed how to create dashboards. While one approach we took was to build a static, serverless web page, another required a server and the client parts of the application. In this chapter, we'll discuss the next logical step: providing programmatic access to your data and/or algorithms, via a RESTful API—similar to the ones we used in `Chapter 9`, *Shell, Git, Conda, and More – at Your Command*. An API is arguably the most ubiquitous and convenient way of delivering your service; it has few requirements for the consumer (essentially, an internet connection), is easy to publish and distribute, and can be constantly improved upon. Knowing how to build your own API is an essential skill for a developer.

The following topics will be covered in this chapter:

- What is a RESTful API?
- Building a basic API service
- Building a web page
- Speeding up with asynchronous calls
- Deploying and testing your API service loads with the Locust package

Technical requirements

In this chapter, we'll use the following libraries:

- FastAPI
- pydantic
- uvicorn
- locust

Make sure to install them, if you haven't done so already. To test our API, we'll use the `curl` command-line tool. On Windows, you can install `curl` or use the built-in `Invoke-Webrequest` tool, aliased to `wget`.

Alternatively, you can use Postman, `https://www.getpostman.com`, a standalone and free application for testing and exploring web APIs with a nice graphical interface. To install Postman, go to the website and hit **Get Started**, then select **Download**. Postman has versions for Windows and Linux. Its interface is quite clean and easy to learn, so we won't cover it here.

All of the code is available in the GitHub repository, in the `Chapter18` folder (`https://github.com/PacktPublishing/Learn-Python-by-Building-Data-Science-Applications`).

What is a RESTful API?

We worked with APIs before, in `Chapter 9`, *Shell, Git, Conda, and More – at Your Command*, as clients. So, it would be safe enough to assume we have some idea about an API: it is just an interface that allows us to exchange data with the service. Technically, APIs can use any protocol or means of communication, and there are plenty of applications with all types of interfaces. However, these days, when people say API, they likely mean RESTful API. Here, the **REST** part stands for **Representational State Transfer**. REST is based on six guiding architectural principles, but what is more important for us is that it is based around HTTP requests, similar to the ones our browsers execute when we type in a URL.

Behind each RESTful API is a server—or, most likely, a group of servers—ready to execute the command; this command could serve the entire, rich HTML page, or—in the case of an API—some information, either as a binary or some other kind of data structure—the most popular ones are XML and JSON.

The servers behind each API run a corresponding application. Python is a great language to create such an application! As usual, there is a handful of packages designed to help with the making of APIs. Due to the complexity of the task, these tools tend to be more proactive and involved in the process than your average library, so they are usually called **frameworks**. Indeed, as it is often said, libraries are what you use in your code and frameworks are what you stick your code into. Let's take a look at the assortment of Python web frameworks we can use in the next section.

Python web frameworks

Web frameworks play an important role as the backbone of the web application and an intermediary between the web server and your custom code. Thanks to the web framework, you can write just a handful of functions and classes, and make them accessible for your clients via URLs and web interfaces; all of the internals of routing, protocols, error handling, and security precautions are taken care of by the frameworks.

Python has a variety of web frameworks for any taste and scale. The most popular are Pyramid, Django, and Flask. Both Pyramid and Django are great options for large and complex applications and incorporate many useful features, including CMS, authentication mechanisms, and many other features, out of the box. In contrast, Flask is a smaller and simpler one and is often used for standalone APIs; it doesn't have many built-in features; hence, it's smaller and simpler to learn, but you will have to integrate those features yourself later on if you need them. All three are mostly focused on serving HTML web pages but could be used to serve RESTful APIs, if needed. In this chapter, we'll use a framework called FastAPI: it is very new, focuses 100% on APIs, and incorporates a handful of nice features for building them.

In particular, FastAPI has the following features:

- Lightweight
- Performant
- Can work in asynchronous mode (we'll talk about it later in this chapter)
- Leverages Python typing for schema/validation
- Supports data validation with OpenAPI (previously known as Swagger) and JSON Schema off the shelf

The selection of a framework will have long-standing consequences, as you might have to maintain and expand it for a long time. As FastAPI is small and simple, it is easy to learn and to make your own opinion—and to switch it with something else, if needed. But how does it all work in practice? Let's have a look.

Building a basic API service

A good practice is to start with something simple, where we don't risk having issues in our code—so we can test the framework, first. Let's start with a simple *hello world* application.

Let's dive in and start with a simple hello world-style application that will return the predefined values, with no computations at all:

1. First, we will need to import the library and initialize the main application object:

```
from fastapi import FastAPI
app = FastAPI()
```

2. Next, let's define our toy database:

```
db = {'noise': 24,
      'broken hydrant': 2}
```

3. We now define the function that will be executed for each URL request and return the value:

```
def complaints(complaint_type: str, hour:int) -> dict:
    return {"complaint_type": complaint_type, "hour": hour, "q":
db.get(complaint_type, None)}
```

Note that we use type annotations for the arguments. With FastAPI, this is important—those type hints are used for validation and in the autogenerated documentation.

4. Lastly, we need to register our function as an endpoint for the application, using a decorator:

```
@app.get("/complaints/{complaint_type}")
def complaints(complaint_type: str, hour:int) -> dict:
    return {"complaint_type": complaint_type, "hour": hour, "q":
db.get(complaint_type, None)}
```

Note that we specify the type of the request via the `app.get` method (similar to the methods of the requests library) and encode one variable, `complaint_type`, as part of the URL, like an f-string. The framework will take care of the rest.

5. Now, we can run the server locally:

```
uvicorn hello_world:app --reload
```

By doing so, we trigger `uvicorn` and `ASGI server` to run, serving `app` from the `hello_world.py` file, locally.

6. Once the application is ready, `uvicorn` will print a line pointing to the correct IP address, similar to this one:

```
INFO: Uvicorn running on http://127.0.0.1:8000 (Press CTRL+C to
quit)
```

Now, this link itself won't do anything—there is no app served on the root directly.

7. To test our application, we need to specify a resource, add the path we used in our decorator, and specify the complaint type, as in the following example:

```
http://127.0.0.1:8000/complaints/noise?hour=12
>>> {"complaint_type":"noise","hour":12, "q":24}
```

8. Let's check that the application is indeed live—write something clearly wrong as a complaint type, don't pass a value, and see what happens:

```
http://127.0.0.1:8000/complaints/wrong
>>> {"detail":[{"loc":["query","hour"],"msg":"field
required","type":"value_error.missing"}]}

http://127.0.0.1:8000/complaints/wrong?hour=2
>>> {"complaint_type":"wrong","hour":2,"q":null}
```

Let's now discuss what happens under the hood. In our function, we declared two arguments: `complaint_type` and `hour`, each with a specified typing. The former is defined within the route we provide; the latter is not specified there knowing that, FastAPI assumes it will be provided as a parameter. Furthermore, everything in the URL is a string; as FastAPI knows what to expect from the type annotation, it will attempt to parse our values appropriately—note that, in the response, an hour is an integer, and it is not wrapped in quotes.

When we pass an incorrect URL, the first thing that triggered is that there is no hour parameter; therefore, FastAPI raises a scheme validation issue; once an hour is passed, the request is considered successful (except there is no value, of course), as FastAPI does not know which values are acceptable for `complaint_type` (and `hour`, for that matter). So, what happens next?

Exploring service with OpenAPI

Now, don't stop the server just yet; append `/docs` to the given IP address, and you'll open an OpenAPI service:

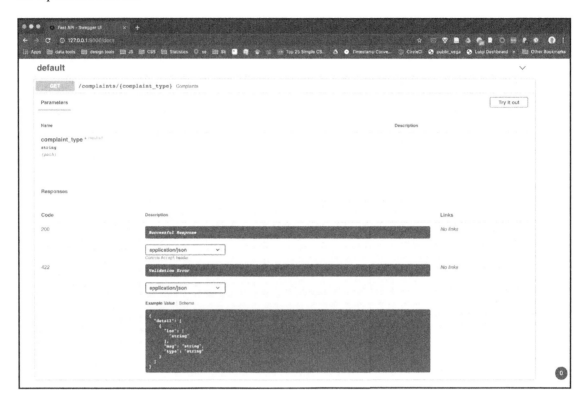

As you can see, it shows the one (and only) API endpoint we have. This page is interactive—you can open the endpoint's tab, write your own parameters (for example, `broken hydrant`), execute the request, and check out the results. As if that isn't enough, there is alternative documentation—to access it, just replace `/docs` with `/redoc`.

Once this is done, let's move on to finalizing the first iteration.

Finalizing our naive first iteration

Let's imagine we're building a service for the 311 call center. The goal is to estimate the expected time it will take to close the complaint. We will start with a terribly naive model—one that returns a median value for a given type of complaint. As such, it is essentially a pre-computed lookup, similar to the one we used earlier; computing the median is trivial, so we won't cover it. If needed, the code is stored in the repository. As a result, we have a JSON file with a simple key-value structure; for each type of complaint, it stores the median time.

Now, let's modify our existing API to use this data:

1. First of all, copy the file and call it `311v1.py`. Now, let's create a simple class that resembles a `scikit-learn` model, using lookup data:

```python
class naive_model:
    data = None

    def __init__(self, path='./data/model.json'):

        with open(path, 'r') as f:
            self.data = json.load(f)
    def predict(self, type_):
        return self.data.get(type_, None)
```

Why do we make it similar to the `scikit-learn` models? Because that way, it would be easier to swap it with the real one in the future!

2. Now, we only need to initialize the model on load and replace the hardcoded `hour` value with `expected_time`, predicted by the model:

```python
app = FastAPI()
model = naive_model()

@app.get("/complaints/time/{complaint_type}")
def complaints(complaint_type: str):
    return {"complaint_type": complaint_type,
            "expected_time": model.predict(complaint_type)}
```

3. Again, run it via Uvicorn:

```
uvicorn 311v1:app --reload
```

4. Specify the type of complaint, as in the following example:

```
$ http://127.0.0.1:8000/complaints/time/noise
{"complaint_type":"water quality","expected_time":19.29}
```

Next, let's see how to validate this data.

Data validation

There is one nasty problem with our current implementation: it is easy to misspell a complaint type—and the API won't let us know of any issue; instead, it will pass it to the model, which will return a null value because it couldn't find a corresponding complaint type.

To make behavior more transparent and easy to work with and to not spend any computations on the invalid requests, we'll need to validate all inputs. In order to do that, let's pre-define the complaint types we have, using the Enum library; mixing with str allows FastAPI to incorporate it into the schema, as follows:

```
class ComplaintType(str, Enum):
    other = "other"
    commercial = "commercial"
    park = "park"
    residential = "residential"
    street = "street"
    vehicle = "vehicle"
    worship = "worship"
    truck = "truck"
```

Now, we modify our app request function by adding ComplaintType as our type hint. We added a simple formatting logic; in a real app, it would make sense to simplify the complaint type in the data so that the app logic will be cleaner (and a tiny bit faster):

```
@app.get('/complaints/noise/{complaint_type}/time')
def complaints(complaint_type: ComplaintType):
    if complaint_type == ComplaintType.other:
        ct = "noise"
    else:
        ct = f"noise - {complaint_type.value}"

    return {
```

```
        "complaint_type": complaint_type,
        "ct": ct,
        "expected_time": model.predict(ct),
    }
```

We didn't really change much in our code, but the class allows FastAPI to know which values are valid and which ones are not; now, instead of returning null, our application will raise a validation error, notifying us that our complaint type is invalid. Here is how it looks in practice:

```
>>> curl -X GET http://127.0.0.1:8000/complaints/noise/wrong/time -H
"accept: application/json"

{"detail":[{"loc":["path","complaint_type"],"msg":"value is not a valid
enumeration member","type":"type_error.enum"}]}
```

And the best part is that this expectation is reflected in the documentation! Our OpenAPI page now has a drop-down menu with all of the types our endpoint supports:

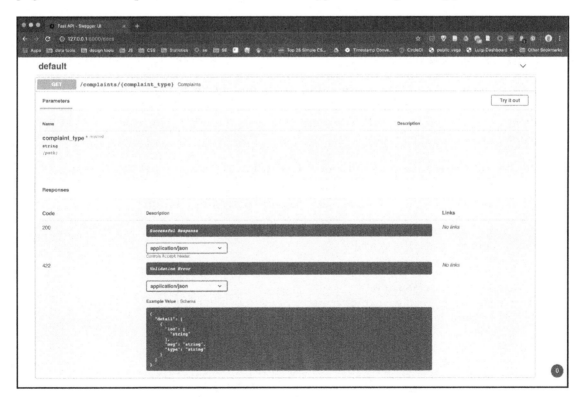

So, this is how our API finally looks. Next, let's move on to sending data with POST.

Sending data in with POST requests

All of this time, we used the @app.get method, which represents the expected HTTP GET request. As its name implies, this command is supposed to retrieve information and therefore is designed to store small snippets of data in itself. This data could be passed as resource—part of the URL, like complaint_type in the preceding example—or appended as a parameter, like hour in our first example.

However, there are cases when you need to pass a significant data structure as part of your request. For that, there is another command: POST. You see, every request, technically, has three means of passing information:

- URL, which can contain resources and parameters
- BODY, which can store arbitrary data
- HEADERS, a small section for metadata, which describes desired server behavior, and should not be used for API behavior

On top of that, the HTTP specification recommends not to use a body part for GET requests, as it goes against the semantics. The bottom line is this: if you need to pass a rich data structure to an API, use the POST method and keep this data structure in its body.

Let's imagine that, for some reason, our application now needs to handle the input of new complaints. Every complaint stores multiple pieces of information: location, time, type of complaint, some description, and so on. And of course, there are some rules on what values are acceptable for each data type.

To deal with data structures and validation, FastAPI uses another package: pydantic. Let's describe the structure we're expecting as a pydantic object. As we'll have to specify the complaint type, we'll reuse the Enum object from the preceding example:

```python
from pydantic import BaseModel
from datetime import datetime


class Complaint(BaseModel):
    complaint_type:ComplaintType
    timestamp:datetime = datetime.now()
    lat:float
    lon:float
    description:str

@app.post("/input/")
def enter_complaint(body: Complaint):
    return body.dict() # for the sake of simplicity just returns value back
```

Here, we declare a `Complaint` object, which includes the complaint type as `Enum`, and four other parameters. As we wrap our function with a `post` method, a variable not defined in the path is assumed to be the body. We define this parameter to be `Complaint` object, by definition.

Adding features to our service

At this point, our API has two `GET` calls and one `POST` call. The `GET` call estimates the time it will take for each type of complaint to be closed, based on the historic median for each type of call. However, this approach is obviously very naive—it takes into account neither location, time, nor a number of similar complaints in the queue for the same area. To improve our estimate, let's use an ML model, trained to predict a given complaint type, location, and time. You can find all of the details on model training in the `311model.ipynb` notebook. What is important is that the trained model is stored as a Pickle file and expects four features (we collected earlier): type of complaint, latitude, longitude, and time complaint was filled.

Let's now modify our code so that it will take those features and run a model:

1. First, we need to load a model from `pickle` in our code (we use `joblib`, which is a little more efficient for `scikit-learn` models, or any objects containing NumPy arrays, for that matter):

   ```
   clf = joblib.load('model.joblib')
   ```

2. Now, because we use a custom transformer for time features, we need to import it into the file:

   ```
   from ml import TimeTransformer  # this line should be at the top
   ```

   One inconvenient property of `pickle` (and `joblib`) objects is that they don't store all of the dependencies internally; to make it all more complicated, they reference those dependencies, expecting them to be at the same location, relative to the object. In other words, you have to import everything exactly as it was done when the object was stored.

3. And finally, we can implement the method as follows:

```
@app.get('/predict/{complaint_type}', tags=['predict'])
def predict_time(complaint_type:ComplaintType, latitude:float,
longitude:float, created_date:datetime):

    obj = pd.DataFrame([{'complaint_type':complaint_type.value,
                         'latitude':latitude,
'longitude':longitude,
                         'created_date':created_date},])
    obj = obj[['complaint_type', 'latitude','longitude',
'created_date']]


    predicted = clf.predict(obj)
    logger.info(predicted)
    return {'estimated_time': predicted[0]}
```

4. Once the application is reloaded, go to the docs, and try to execute the method:

```
>>> curl -X GET
"http://127.0.0.1:8000/predict/vehicle?latitude=40.701258&longitude
=-73.935493&created_date=2019-06-08%2018%3A00%3A10" -H "accept:
application/json"

{
  "estimated_time": 0.59
}
```

5. Voilà! Our first ML model is up and running. Here is what it looks like via the OpenAPI page:

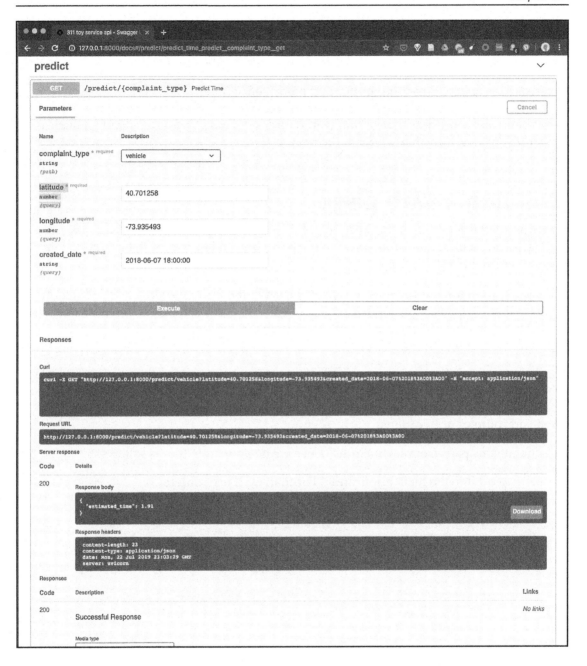

We were able to build a working API application, serving predictions of our pre-trained model. This application may be used by the government or concerned citizens, eager to know how long it is likely to take 311 to review and close the application.

RESTful APIs are the bread and butter of data-driven software and services. Their technical look, however, may intimidate and confuse the inexperienced person. As an alternative, we could build and serve a web page that would be easy to read and understand for such an audience. Let's see how that works in the next section.

Building a web page

While FastAPI is focused on the APIs, it is still entirely possible to serve HTML pages as well. The code will be almost identical to the preceding code—except that our functions need to return this HTML code.

The most common approach to generate HTML in Python is to use the Jinja2 templating engine—that way, you write the template as an HTML code with some injections of Python and later render them by feeding it with the variables; Jinja will execute and hide the injections, returning the resultant page.

For the sake of building a simple example, however, we will use another package: VDOM, which allows us to generate **VDOMs** (short for **Virtual Document Object Models**) in Python and then convert them into HTML. Flask is great for smaller projects, but not for large and complex applications.

To separate this page from the main API, let's create a separate file, as follows:

1. Add it to the main application. For that, we'll use routers:

```
# webpage.py
from fastapi import APIRouter
router = APIRouter()
```

2. Now, we can create a new endpoint, using a router as if it is an app object:

```
@router.get('/dashboard', tags=["dashboard"])
def get_dashboard():
    pass
```

3. Now, let's generate a very simple VDOM object. To make it a little bit more interesting, let's use some pre-generated images:

```
image_url =
"https://pbs.twimg.com/profile_images/775676979655929856/jn13Vq3D.j
pg"
barplot_url =
"https://github.com/PacktPublishing/Learn-Python-by-Building-Data-S
cience-Applications/blob/master/Chapter18/barchart-01.png"
from vdom.helpers import b, div, h1, img, p, span

def dashboard():
    return div(
        span(img(src=image_url, style=dict(width='100',
                                           heigth='100')),
            h1('Smart 311 Dashboard')),
        img(width='400', src=barplot_url),
        p('Written in Python, 100%')
    )
```

Here, we use multiple `vdom.helpers` objects. All of them represent corresponding HTML tags and accept class, ID, and all other corresponding attributes, such as `source` for image object, as well as a `style` argument, which expects to receive a dictionary with both keys and values as strings. For now, this object is still a Python object. In a Jupyter Notebook, it can be rendered using the `IPython.display.display` method. For FastAPI, we can convert it into raw HTML, using the `to_html` method.

Now, one obstacle is that, by default, FastAPI converts all returning values into JSON, using the built-in JSON response method of `starlette`, the underlying server FastAPI is built upon. To prevent it from doing that, we can explicitly use another response, one built for serving HTML.

Let's tweak the method we wrote earlier to return the dashboard, wrapped into HTML. Consider the following code for it:

```
from starlette.responses import HTMLResponse

@router.get('/dashboard', tags=["dashboard"])
def get_dashboard():
    content = dashboard().to_html()
    return HTMLResponse(content=content)
```

Lastly, we need to connect our `router` entity back to the main application, so that they can coexist; adding routers is the proper way to add more endpoints to the application without storing them in the same file. Open `311v2.py` and add these two lines:

```
import webpage # here, webpage is the file with the router
app.include_router(webpage.router, prefix='/dashboard')
```

Now, you can check whether the dashboard is loading:

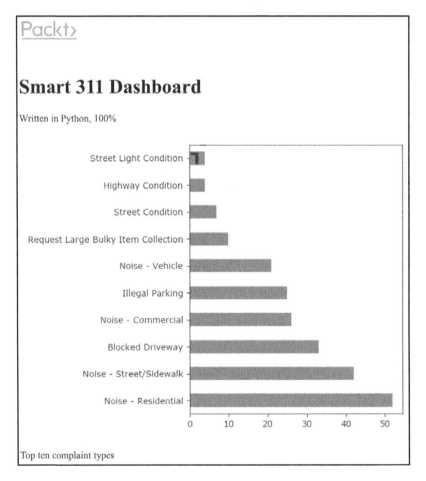

Excellent! As we mentioned, FastAPI is focused on APIs and hence has little to offer in the context of web pages, but it still can be used that way. For example, it makes sense to use the same service to support both APIs and some sort of dashboard, if both are required.

Let's now address one more interesting feature FastAPI supports: asynchronous execution.

Speeding up with asynchronous calls

Now, let's turn to the question of performance. Once in a while, our application will need to be constantly monitored and, if needed, scaled and optimized. There are a few ways to speed things up incrementally, for example, by installing the `ujson` package, which works exactly like built-in `json` but is more performant (because it is written in C). In that case, FastAPI will automatically switch to using this library instead.

Potentially, more significant improvement in performance is built into FastAPI, Uvicorn, and based on the new features of Python 3.4 and later versions, *asynchronous calls*. We did spend some time discussing this feature in `Chapter 3`, *Functions*. In a nutshell, all of the code we generally write in Python is executed sequentially—once one line is executed, Python will go to the next, and so on. It means that, when the operation requires some data to be acquired from the web or the database, or if the operation is computation-heavy but runs on a single CPU, we could run some other tasks in the meantime. This is the promise of an asynchronous computation.

As we said, FastAPI and Uvicorn both support asynchronous calls. What it means practically is that every endpoint function, if it relies on something (library, database connection, and so on) that supports asynchronous calls, or does not rely on anything at all, could be asynchronous. To make it asynchronous, just add `async` before `def`. If it indeed relies on some asynchronous call, you need to state that with `await`. Given that, Uvicorn will automatically run those methods as asynchronous—this won't speed up each individual call, but will allow the server to execute some other requests, when applicable, scaling its overall performance. For example, here is our prediction model, made asynchronously (we also changed the name to keep both methods in place):

```
@app.get('/predict_async/{complaint_type}', tags=['predict'])
async def predict_time_async(complaint_type:ComplaintType, latitude:float,
longitude:float, created_date:datetime):

    obj = pd.DataFrame([{'complaint_type':complaint_type.value,
                        'latitude':latitude, 'longitude':longitude,
                        'created_date':created_date},])
    obj = obj[['complaint_type', 'latitude','longitude',
            'created_date']]
```

```
predicted = clf.predict(obj)
logger.info(predicted)
return {'estimated_time': predicted[0]}
```

You can test that this endpoint runs as good as the non-asynchronous one.

We don't recommend trying to use asynchronous calls from the get-go, especially if you don't have much experience. However, if you're on the lookout for better API performance, asynchronous calls can be a good option. On many occasions, asynchronous calls can make a drastic difference in performance, compared to traditional, synchronous execution. For some features and entire products, the difference could be critical. But how do we measure performance and how do we determine whether it is okay to publish an endpoint? For that, let's go to the next section.

Deploying and testing your API loads with Locust

Once the application is deployed, but before it is publicly announced or used, it is a good idea to estimate how many requests it can handle. Usually, you can roughly predict the requirements for the service by estimating the number of requests it needs to execute at peak periods, how long those periods are, how fast it should respond, and so on. Once you're clear on the requirements, you'll need to test-load your application.

Test-loads should be performed on the actual, deployed server, not your localhost. Here, we skip over the whole topic of deploying your model. We also didn't use ngnix or any similar gateway servers, which would cache requests, boosting the performance of the API significantly. Deployment of the application deserves a separate book and can be achieved in many ways, depending on your existing infrastructure and resources and the importance of the application. One popular way is to generate a Docker container that can then be pulled and deployed by any cloud infrastructure platform. We will touch on containers in Chapter 20, *Best Practices and Python Performance*.

To run a test-load, Locust requires a simple Python script, which they call a locustfile. Let's see how to use it:

1. The following code is the file we wrote for our 311 API:

    ```python
    from locust import HttpLocust, TaskSet, task

    class WebsiteTasks(TaskSet):
        @task
        def preduct(self):
    self.client.get("/predict/residential?latitude=40.675719430504&long
    itude=-73.860535138411&created_date=2019-06-14T00%3A02%3A11.000")
        @task
        def preduct_async(self):
    self.client.get("/predict_async/residential?latitude=40.67571943050
    4&longitude=-73.860535138411&created_date=2019-06-14T00%3A02%3A11.0
    00")
        @task
        def dashboard(self):
            self.client.get("/dashboard/dashboard")

    class WebsiteUser(HttpLocust):
        task_set = WebsiteTasks
        min_wait = 5000
        max_wait = 15000
    ```

    Here, we target two prediction endpoints and a dashboard, keeping all of the parameters the same.

2. For more rigorous testing, it would be a good idea to generate random request parameters each time, but for now, let's keep it simple. Having the file, let's fire up `locust`:

    locust --host=http://127.0.0.1:8000

3. Now, head to `http://127.0.0.1:8089`.

4. In the Locust initial form, specify the desired number of users and growth (other parameters could be set in `locustfile.py`) to simulate and hit **Run**. For the following screenshot, we set 5,000 users maximum, with a growth of 10 per second.

5. Once the simulation is started, you can monitor the resultant performance, as well as failures and thrown exceptions, in real time, via the Locust dashboard:

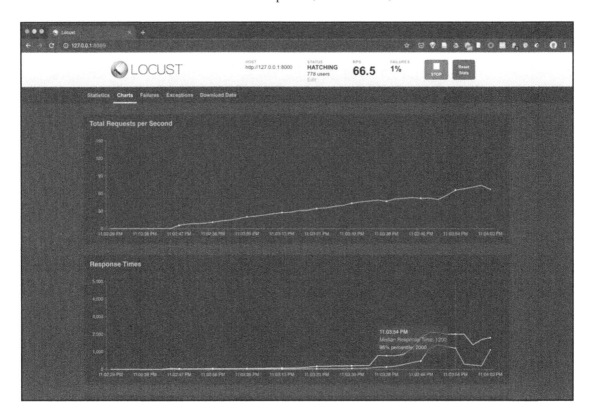

Upon running, Locust will offer you a plan of attack: how many users and at which rate of growth to emulate. Once values are defined, it will start loading the traffic and will show you the results in real time. It's now up to you to monitor and analyze the result, and give a final verdict: did your application pass the test?

Building a web endpoint is an exciting phase of the work. Indeed, you're making your work available for the world to use. Do not rush, skipping the testing part! Making sure your application is written effectively and is fast and up to the traffic loads may save you a lot of time—and nerves—down the road.

Summary

In this chapter, we built our own API and deployed an ML model to send predictions as an endpoint. Using FastAPI's built-in features, we were able to generate interactive documentation and define a schema to validate both inputs and outputs. We further created a simple HTML dashboard, generating charts upon request, and we learned how to tune the performance of the API, leveraging asynchronous functionality. Lastly, we modeled a traffic load on our system, using an open source tool, Locust.

By doing so, we made a fast run over the full cycle of API development: choosing a framework, adding your business logic, and testing. The skills we learned along the way are useful if you want to get the flexibility, scalability, and richness of providing your service via an API.

Building your own web service is a great option—definitely the best if the API is popular and needs to withstand constant and intensive loads of requests.

In the next chapter, we'll look at a different approach: running the same prediction model as a serverless application, which allows us to keep the API cheaper and more scalable, if we don't need to serve many requests or if the loads are sporadic.

Questions

1. What is a RESTful API?
2. What Python packages can be used to build a RESTful API?
3. What are the key features of the FastAPI framework?
4. Why OpenAPI (Swagger)?
5. Why do we need Uvicorn or Gunicorn servers?
6. What metrics does the Locust package measure?

Further reading

- *Building REST APIs with Python* by Wayne Merry, published by Packt (https://www.packtpub.com/web-development/building-rest-apis-python-video)
- *Building RESTful Python Web Services* by Gaston C. Hillar, published by Packt (https://www.packtpub.com/application-development/building-restful-python-web-services)

Serverless API Using Chalice

In the previous chapter, we created a REST API that served our prediction model forecasts by managing our own server and application. While that approach is by far the most popular, there is another that is also very useful for specific tasks—using serverless applications.

In this chapter, we will use the Chalice Python package to build an API that's similar to the one we built in Chapter 18, *Serving Models with a RESTful API*, but it will run in the cloud as a serverless application. Along the way, we will discuss along the way all the pros and cons of this approach.

In this chapter, we will learn about the following:

- What a serverless application is
- How to build a simple application using the Chalice package
- How to mitigate Chalice's limitations
- Scheduling a serverless process
- Deploying a larger-than-limit application with Zappa

Technical requirements

The code for this chapter requires the `chalice` package, version 1.9.1. We recommend installing Chalice from `conda-forge` and use this specific version for reproductivity: `conda install -c conda-forge chalice=1.9.1`.

As usual, the code for this chapter is in the GitHub repository, under the `Chapter19` folder (`https://github.com/PacktPublishing/Learn-Python-by-Building-Data-Science-Applications`).

Understanding serverless

The word "serverless" might be somewhat misleading—serverless applications still do run on servers. There is a major difference is responsibility zones, though. With serverless, we don't rent computers and deploy our own APIs; instead, we send Python (or JavaScript, or Go, or whatever else) functions, along with our requirements, to a provider (which could be **Amazon Web Services** (**AWS**), Google Cloud Platform, or something else), and they execute those functions on their servers when triggered to do so. We don't need to think about configuring servers, turning them on and off, or scaling—the functions we trigger will work when needed on the scale that is needed (the providers will add computers, if required, behind the scenes). The best part? We'll only pay for the fact of execution—if a function wasn't triggered, we'll pay nothing.

Because of that, serverless applications can be a great alternative to running your own servers in the following cases:

- If requests are infrequent and you would otherwise have to pay for a server with little to no payload. Providers such as AWS provide solutions to trigger serverless applications automatically on specific events, such as a new file being uploaded to an S3 bucket. A serverless application could also serve as an API endpoint, running when you request it to.
- If the requests rate is hard to predict or very sporadic, so it would be hard to scale and adjust the number of workers yourself.
- If the function in question itself is relatively simple and fast.
- If you only need a few simple and stateless endpoints (serverless functions can invoke other services and serve their outcomes, such as serving the frontend for a large and complex **machine learning** (**ML**) model).

Of course, serverless has its own limitations and caveats as well:

- Code needs to be pre-packaged in a specific way.
- There is a cap of 50 MB on the memory required to upload your code and assets, including all the dependencies, except a few default ones.
- The problem of cold starts: if an endpoint has not been used for a certain time, the virtual server will be stopped and resumed on the next request. This means that the first few requests after that period of having been stopped may take longer to execute. If that is critical, we could ping the endpoint once in a while so that the server won't stop—but that would mean some additional costs.

Building a serverless application manually requires some time and can be a tedious process. Everything should be isolated and zipped, and the archive should meet certain criteria. Luckily, there are a few Python packages that help to prepare and deploy code as a serverless application.

To summarize, serverless applications are services that allow you to focus on the code for your specific task; running the code, server configuration, scheduling, scaling, and so on are taken care of by the service provider. You only pay for the fact of execution. The code for the application needs to be prepackaged and has some requirements to meet. Luckily, there are frameworks that help us to simplify the workflow.

Now that we know what serverless is, in the next section, we'll build our own serverless application using Chalice.

Getting started with Chalice

Let's try replicating the API endpoint we did for 311 in the previous chapter as a serverless application. For that, we'll use a framework called **Chalice**.

Chalice is a Python package for serverless applications on AWS, and is itself developed by Amazon. It can take care of an application, from its template all the way to deployment. It's also great for testing, as it emulates deployment with no fee, authentication, or even internet connection required.

Before we start working on our serverless application, let's ask Chalice to generate a template. In your terminal, type this:

```
chalice new-project
```

After this, type the name of the project: `311estimate`. This will generate a new folder with a few files:

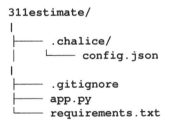

```
311estimate/
|
├─── .chalice/
|    └─── config.json
|
├─── .gitignore
├─── app.py
└─── requirements.txt
```

Those files are all you need to write and deploy an endpoint; first, take a look at app.py. Inside, chalice invokes an app object—very similar to what FastAPI does (and other web frameworks). To continue the pattern of similarity with FastAPI, Chalice uses a decorator around the function with the GET method, defining the routing for the endpoint. The dummy function returns a dictionary, which will be converted to JSON under the hood—exactly like FastAPI would do.

Before we start adding our own code, let's try running this application locally:

```
$ chalice local
Serving on 127.0.0.1:8000
```

Now, we can pass a request in our browser or by using curl in the Terminal:

```
$ curl -X GET http://localhost:8000/
{"hello": "world"}
```

Clearly, Chalice is working—we're serving a dummy API as a serverless application. In the next section, let's override the code to make it serve actual models!

Setting up a simple model

Similar to how we built a REST API in Chapter 18, *Serving Models with a RESTful API*, let's start by serving median values from a JSON file. This will help us to set the model for working with Chalice:

1. First of all, we need to load the JSON object:

   ```python
   import json

   with open('./model.json', 'r') as f:
       model = json.load(f)
   ```

2. Now we will rename the route and define the last resource to map to the complaint type (in the same way we would for FastAPI, again!). We will also have to import a Response object:

   ```python
   from chalice import Response

   @app.route('/predict/{complaint_type}', methods=['GET'])
   def predict(complaint_type:str) -> Response:
   ```

3. Finally, finalize the function by adding simple lookup logic; here, we decided to be nice and let our user know if they pass a wrong complaint type:

```
@app.route('/predict/{complaint_type}', methods=['GET'])
def predict(complaint_type:str) -> Response:
    if complaint_type in model:
        return Response(status_code=200,
                        headers={'Content-Type':
                                    'application/json'},
                        body={'status': 'success',
                                'complaint_type': complaint_type,
                                'estimated_time':
                                        model[complaint_type]})
    else:
        return Response(status_code=400,
                        headers={'Content-Type':
                                    'application/json'},
                        body={'status': 'failure',
                                'problem': 'Complaint type is
                                        not in database',
                                'complaint_type': complaint_type})
```

4. Then, we deploy it locally, as we did before:

```
$ chalice local
Serving on 127.0.0.1:8000
```

5. Now let's try it out from another terminal:

```
$ curl -X GET http://localhost:8000/predict/appliance
{"status":"success","complaint_type":"appliance","estimated_time":6
3.53}
```

6. Let's see what happens if we ask for a wrong complaint type:

```
$ curl -X GET http://localhost:8000/predict/wrongtype
{"status":"failure","problem":"Complaint type is not in
database","complaint_type":"wrongtype"}
```

As you can see, it will return an error, with the message we passed. Let's now refactor our code so that the data will be stored outside of the Python script.

Externalizing medians

This was quite a simple script so far, but you probably would want to update the JSON constantly—without needing to re-deploy the function every time. Let's do exactly that. We'll move the JSON to some public bucket (or not a *public* bucket—just make sure to use credentials with the rights to access it), and let a function download it upon request or upon deployment. We'll use the built-in `urllib` package, not `requests`, as we don't want to spend our 50 MB memory on one more dependency package. Delete the local JSON to keep the code slim, and add this code:

```
import json, urllib.request
url =
'https://raw.githubusercontent.com/PacktPublishing/Python-Programming-Proje
cts-Learn-Python-3.7-by-building-
applications/master/Chapter18/data/model.json'

obj = urllib.request.urlopen(url).read()
model = json.loads(obj)
```

Here, we have a choice: we could load `json` outside the function, which means it will be pre-loaded on spawn and update ever so often. Alternatively, we could load the measurements within the `request` function, meaning values will be updated via the API the second we override the file on S3. This would, however, affect the execution time of the function, so it's up to you to decide.

If everything works locally, let's deploy it! For that, just type this:

```
chalice deploy
```

It may take a few seconds to prepare the package, and does require AWS credentials to be set up. Once done, Chalice will print out the name of the function and the URL to hit. Once deployed, our function is publicly available for everyone! See here:

```
$ curl -X GET
https://<unique_aws_id>.execute-api.us-east-1.amazonaws.com/api/predict/app
liance
{"status":"success","complaint_type":"appliance","estimated_time":63.53}
```

In this section, we were able to deploy a basic prediction model API endpoint that reads values from a JSON file stored on GitHub but is accessible for everyone on the web. Now let's go one step further and set up an actual ML model.

Building a serverless API for an ML model

Getting public access to data in 10 lines of code is useful. But let's now do something more complex than that—say, serving an actual ML model.

Let's create one more app—311predictions. As before, we would need to call chalice new-project and type our new project's name.

Now, for the previous application, we didn't need any dependencies; in order to serve the ML model we used in the previous chapter, we need to have pandas and sklearn. The problem is that both of them cannot fit into the 50 MB limitation. In fact, until recently, there was no easy way to fit either of them there—normal pip install requires all the source code to be downloaded and compiled on the machine. Luckily, now a pre-compiled version can be installed, and chalice will explicitly look for a pre-compiled binary, generated for a Linux machine we'll be running.

Still, we have to decide how to shrink our memory usage. In this particular case, there are not many options. We definitely can't serve the model without sklearn, so we'll have to get rid of pandas. Let's add sklearn to the requirements (note that it has a different name in pip):

```
scikit-learn==0.21.2
```

Now let's recreate the API, using only sklearn and NumPy (which is a dependency of sklearn, anyway). First, let's load our model from S3:

```
import boto3

BUCKET, KEY = 'philipp-packt', 'model.pkl'

def _load_pickle(bucket, key):
    S3 = boto3.client('s3', region_name='us-east-1')
    response = S3.get_object(Bucket=bucket, Key=key)
    body = response['Body'].read()
    return pickle.loads(body)

model = _load_pickle(BUCKET, KEY)
```

Note that this model will be preloaded on each deployment, not for each request. To shave even more time off the request itself, let's predefine a NumPy singleton object (a one-row matrix that will be populated with data from the request:

```
singleton = np.empty(shape=(1, 4), dtype='object')
```

Unlike FastAPI, there is no built-in parsing mechanism, so we'll have to parse values on our own. Let's predefine a parsing mechanism for each parameter, except `complaint_type`, which does not need to be parsed:

```
dtypes = {
    'lon': float,
    'lat': float,
    'date': np.datetime64
}
```

Now we can start writing the endpoint itself. In the following code, we use the `app.current_request.query_params` dictionary, which stores all the parameters in the URL. There is a similar dictionary for the body of the request.

Another useful command is `app.log.debug`. If lambda is running in debug mode, this will spill the values out to the logs:

```
@app.route('/predict/{complaint_type}', methods=['GET'])
def index(complaint_type:str):
    try:
        app.log.debug(app.current_request.query_params)
        singleton[0, 0] = complaint_type

        for i, col in enumerate(dtypes.keys(), 1):
            singleton[0, i] =
dtypes[col](app.current_request.query_params.get(col, np.nan))

        app.log.debug(singleton.astype(str).tolist())
```

Finally, we can add the prediction itself and define the responses—both for failure and success cases. This part looks pretty similar to the FastAPI version. Here is the whole function:

```
@app.route('/predict/{complaint_type}', methods=['GET'])
def index(complaint_type:str):
    try:
        app.log.debug(app.current_request.query_params)
        singleton[0, 0] = complaint_type

        for i, col in enumerate(dtypes.keys(), 1):
            singleton[0, i] =
dtypes[col](app.current_request.query_params.get(col, np.nan))

        app.log.debug(singleton.astype(str).tolist())
        prediction = model.predict(singleton)[0]
        app.log.debug(prediction)
```

```
        return Response(status_code=200,
                        headers={'Content-Type': 'application/json'},
                        body={'status': 'success',
                              'estimated_time': prediction})
    except Exception as e:
        return Response(status_code=400,
                        headers={'Content-Type': 'application/json'},
                        body={'status': 'failure',
                              'error message': str(e)})
```

This is all the code we need. If you try running it, however, it will throw an error—there are still two issues we need to figure out.

First, the pickled model stores the objects, but not its dependencies (such as external libraries). To make it even worse, it expects to find them exactly where they were imported at the time of serialization, relative to the loaded pickle. For example, it expects `TimeTransformer` to be not only available but available as part of the `ml` namespace. Theoretically, we could hack the namespace, but it seems easier to copy the `ml.py` file and import the object. Indeed, this is a better option—except that `chalice` won't push any Python files from the folder, except `app.py`. To push our `ml` file, we need to create a folder called `vendor`, then create another folder called `ml` and treat it as a package, moving the code there. As we need to match the exact `ml.TimeTransformer`, we'll create an `__init__.py` file—in fact, to keep it simple, we can just move `ml.py` there and rename it.

The second issue is within `TimeTransformer` itself: it uses `pandas`, which we can't ship—it's just too large. How can we drop `pandas` from the dependencies?

As you may remember, this object transforms any given array of dates into an array of three numeric features: the time of the day, the day of the year, and the day of the week. The first part of the question is how to execute that logic with NumPy. Luckily, every `DateTime` object is just a large integer of seconds that have passed since midnight January 1, 1970, UTC. Therefore, all those operations can be viewed as a combination of subtraction, division, and getting a reminder. We can use a hack of converting `DateTime` values to different units and back. Consider the following code:

```
def day_of_week_num(dts):
    return (dts.astype('datetime64[D]').view('int64') - 4) % 7

def day_of_year_num(dts):
    return (dts.astype('datetime64[D]').view('int64') -
dts.astype('datetime64[Y]').astype('datetime64[D]').view('int64'))

def time_of_day_num(dts):
```

```
            return dts.astype('datetime64[s]').view('int64') -
    dts.astype('datetime64[D]').astype('datetime64[s]').view('int64')
```

Similar to `pandas` implementations, all three functions will return the corresponding values as numbers.

Great! But the `TimeTransformer` object still relies on `pandas`. One solution would be to get rid of it completely—just use the preceding functions both in the application and in the model training; after all, those operations are independent of the training set. This solution is totally fine.

Alternatively, you might notice that `TimeTransformer` needs `pandas` to find `DateTime` columns and operate on them. This means that we can store indices of the columns in the same way we store column names and then use them if we get a NumPy array instead of a DataFrame. Indeed, this is totally doable (see the repository for the full code). The best part? We don't even need to retrain our model again—while our pipeline uses the `TimeTransform` object under the hood, it does not require it to be identical to the one used for training, as long as it has the same name and behaves similarly.

Finally, our ML model is ready to be served! Let's deploy the model and test it live, using a URL like this:

```
<deployment_url>/predict/commercial?lat=40.636626&lon=-73.951694&date=2019-
06-08 00:00:09
```

We get a timeout. It seems that inference requires more operation memory. We could change that via the AWS web console (there are tons of other options, too, such as the use of environmental variables), or we could add a corresponding `config` for `lambda_memory_size` to `.chalice/config.json`:

```
# .chalice/config.json

{
  "version": "2.0",
  "app_name": "311predictions-v2",
  "stages": {
    "dev": {
      "api_gateway_stage": "api",
      "lambda_memory_size": 520
    },
  ""
  }
}
```

Redeploy it one more time. Now it works! See here:

```
$
<deployment_url>/predict/commercial?lat=40.636626&lon=-73.951694&date=2019-
06-08 00:00:09
{
    "status": "success",
    "estimated_time": 1.36
}
```

When we're still out of memory

We were able to shrink the size to just under the memory limit. However, it is not always possible or desirable to do this. If our dependencies are complex and our files are large, we have two more options:

- First, the lambda can be just an entry point—it could invoke a Docker image (an isolated virtual environment running somewhere else in the cloud), pass the parameters there, and communicate the results back.
- Alternatively—and this is a bit of a hack—we could download all the dependencies in the same way that we downloaded our model: during runtime. This data will be lost once the server is down, which will happen if a serverless function is not triggered by anything. Redeployment can take a significant amount of time, so it might make sense to try keeping the server running. All this is an additional hassle, but luckily, it can be taken care of by another package—Zappa (`http://github.com/Miserlou/Zappa`).

We won't do any of that in this book, but both of those options are available.

Let's now take a stab at using serverless for scheduled data pipelines.

Building a serverless function as a data pipeline

So far, we have only used serverless functions as API endpoints, but they can serve in many other ways as well. For example, they can be triggered to run for each new file uploaded to a specific folder on S3, or scheduled to run at a specific time.

Let's create one more application for data collection. We can specify that we need the `requests` library in `requirements.txt`. We can also copy and paste the `_get_data` function from Chapter 15, *Packaging and Testing with Poetry and PyTest*, along with the resource and time columns. One part of the code that we are still missing is that for uploading data to S3. Here is the code:

```
def _upload_json(obj, filename, bucket, key):
    S3 = boto3.client('s3', region_name='us-east-1')
    key += ('/' + filename)

    S3.Object(Bucket=bucket, Key=key).put(Body=json.dumps(obj))
```

Having all the necessary pieces, let's pull them together as one function. Here is the code:

```
from datetime import date, timedelta

def get_data(event):
    yesterday = date.today() - timedelta(days=1)

    data = _get_data(resource, time_col, yesterday, offset=0)
    _upload_json(data, f'{yesterday:%Y-%m-%d}.json', bucket=BUCKET,
key=KEY)
```

Finally, all we need now is to add a `chalice` decorator, `@app.schedule('rate(1 day)')`. Here, instead of the `app.route` decorator, we use `app.schedule` and define a corresponding frequency. Here is how it will look as a whole:

```
import json
from datetime import date, timedelta
BUCKET, FOLDER = 'philipp-packt', '311/raw_data'
resource = 'fhrw-4uyv'
time_col = 'Created Date'
app = Chalice(app_name='collect-311')

def _upload_json(obj, filename, bucket, key):
    S3 = boto3.client('s3', region_name='us-east-1')
    key += ('/' + filename)

    S3.Object(Bucket=bucket, Key=key).put(Body=json.dumps(obj))


def _get_data(resource, time_col, date, offset=0):
    '''collect data from NYC open data
    '''
    Q = f"where=created_date between '{date:%Y-%m-%d}' AND '{date:%Y-%m-
%d}T23:59:59.000'"
    url =
```

```
f'https://data.cityofnewyork.us/resource/{resource}.json?$limit=50000&$offs
et={offset}&${Q}'
    r = rq.get(url)
    r.raise_for_status()

    data = r.json()
    if len(data) == 50_000:
        offset2 = offset + 50000
        data2 = _get_data(resource, time_col, date, offset=offset2)
        data.extend(data2)

    return data

@app.schedule('rate(1 day)')
def get_data(event):
    yesterday = date.today() - timedelta(days=1)
    data = _get_data(resource, time_col, yesterday, offset=0)
    _upload_json(data, f'{yesterday:%Y-%m-%d}.json', bucket=BUCKET,
key=FOLDER)
```

Once deployed, this function will run every day, collecting data for the previous date and storing it as JSON in our S3 bucket. But can we go further and prepare medians for our prediction model, automatically? Let's find out in the next section.

S3-triggered events

So far, we have written a lambda function that's driven by API requests or is scheduled to be triggered. Now let's complete our application's data cycle by adding an S3-triggered task that will compute the medians for each category every time a new dataset is collected—in other words, once the scheduled task is finished.

In order to do so, we'll add one more operation to the same data collection application that we've been working on:

1. First, let's redefine the median computation. The original code also used pandas, so we have two options: use NumPy as we just did for the ML part, or use vanilla Python. As our raw data collection doesn't need NumPy, let's stick with the second option. Here is the no-dependency code for the medians:

   ```
   from statistics import median
   from datetime import datetime
   parsestr = '%Y-%m-%d %H:%M:%S'

   def _calc_medians(data):
       results = {}
   ```

```
      for record in data:
          ct = record["complaint_type"]
          if ct not in results:
              results[ct] = []
          spent = datetime.strptime(record['closed_date'], parsestr)
  - datetime.strptime(record['created_date'], parsestr)
          spent = spent.seconds / 3600 # hours
          results[ct].append(spent)
      return {k : median(v) for k, v in results.items()}
```

2. Now we'll add two more functions:
   - One will check whether a new object fits the pattern for the data we're interested in (the trigger will be executed on *any* file creation event in the bucket).
   - The second one will pull the data using the `requests` library.

   In both cases, the code is fairly trivial:

```
def _is_dataset(key):
    '''check if triggered by data we're interested in '''
    return ('311data' in key) and key.endswith('.json')

def _get_raw_data(bucket, key):
    r = rq.get(f'https://{bucket}.s3.amazonaws.com/{key}')
    r.raise_for_status()
    return r.json()
```

3. Finally, we can now pull all three functions together under one overarching function. For data upload, we'll reuse the _upload_json function that we wrote for the scheduled data collection:

```
MEDIANS_FOLDER = '311/'

def compute_medians(event):
    if _is_dataset(event.key):
        data = _get_raw_data(bucket=event.bucket, key=event.key)
        medians = _calc_medians(data)
        _upload_json(medians, 'medians.json', bucket=BUCKET,
key=MEDIANS_FOLDER)
```

4. Lastly, we need to add a decorator, setting the trigger. Here is how the code will look as a whole:

```python
def _is_dataset(key):
    '''check if triggered by data we're interested in '''
    return ('311data' in key) and key.endswith('.json')


def _calc_medians(data):

    results = {}
    for record in data:
        ct = record["complaint_type"]
        if ct not in results:
            results[ct] = []
        spent = datetime.strptime(record['closed_date'],
                                  '%Y-%m-%d %H:%M:%S')
                - datetime.strptime(record['created_date'],
                                    '%Y-%m-%d %H:%M:%S')
        spent = spent.seconds // 3600 # hours
        results[ct].append(spent)
    return {k : median(v) for k, v in results.items()}



def _get_raw_data(bucket, key):
    r = rq.get(f'https://{bucket}.s3.amazonaws.com/{key}')
    r.raise_for_status()
    return r.json()



@app.on_s3_event(bucket=BUCKET,
                 events=['s3:ObjectCreated:*'])
def compute_medians(event):
    if _is_dataset(event.key):
        data = _get_raw_data(bucket=event.bucket, key=event.key)
        medians = _calc_medians(data)
        _upload_json(medians, 'medians.json', bucket=BUCKET,
                     key=MEDIANS_FOLDER)
```

Chalice is capable of defining other events that would trigger your actions. Alternatively, you can specify an event via the AWS web console, as it has more options. For example, you can trigger your lambda by talking to Alexa—in fact, any conversation with Alexa that you've had was running as a Lambda function!

Just a quick reminder—if you deployed your versions of API, especially the scheduler pipeline, don't forget to stop them or you will start getting invoices in a few years.

Summary

In this chapter, we introduced you to serverless functions—a different approach to APIs and computation in general. Serverless functions don't need maintenance, scale automatically, are secure, and are simple to write. They may be a great option for operations that don't need a huge amount of requests, or for when demand spikes unpredictably. In addition to serving as APIs, lambdas can be scheduled with one line of code or triggered by an external event, such as a new file landing in an S3 bucket. The downside of serverless applications is that they have strict memory limitations that could be a serious barrier for certain tasks. The response time could also be longer for the first time after a long break—but there are ways to solve that issue to some extent.

As a practice exercise, we were able to recreate our 311 API endpoints as serverless applications. In addition, we wrote two more functions for scheduled data collection and the computation of medians. In other words, we used lambdas to recreate the functionality we achieved in Chapter 17, *Let's Build a Dashboard*, and Chapter 18, *Serving Models with a RESTful API*, together—all with serverless applications.

In the next chapter, we will learn about some best practices for using Python, a few issues with using Python, and the performance of Python.

Questions

1. What does a serverless application mean?
2. What are the limitations of the serverless approach?
3. What are the benefits of serverless APIs?
4. What role does Chalice play in the development of a serverless application?

Further reading

Serverless Architectures with AWS by Mohit Gupta, published by Packt Publishing (https://www.packtpub.com/networking-and-servers/serverless-architectures-aws).

20
Best Practices and Python Performance

After going through the preceding chapters and learning various things about Python, we have come to the last chapter. Here, we want to discuss some general strategies that you can implement and how to write code that works faster, is cleaner, and is easier to maintain. These approaches can be used for data-oriented code—or any other type of code, for that matter.

This chapter is split into three parts. The first section will discuss how you can analyze and speed up your code, the second section will cover best practices for maintaining your code so that you'll code faster and cleaner, and in the third and final section, we'll go through a brief overview of the non-Python technologies that you might find useful for your projects.

The following topics will be covered in this chapter:

- Ways to monitor performance and identify bottlenecks
    - Efficient computations with NumPy
    - Using specialized algorithms
    - Computing on many cores—or multiple machines—with Dask
    - Speeding up code by using LLVM with Numba
- Adopting best practices for coding
    - Setting and following formatting standards with `black`
    - Measuring code quality with Wily
    - Advanced testing with Hypothesis
- Tools and technologies beyond this book
    - Other flavors of Python
    - Docker
    - Kubernetes

Technical requirements

The code for this chapter can be found in this book's GitHub repository (`https://github.com/PacktPublishing/Learn-Python-by-Building-Data-Science-Applications`), which is stored in the `Chapter20` folder. The code requires an array of packages to be installed, including the following:

- `numpy`
- `scipy`
- `numba`
- `dask`
- `black`
- `wily`
- `hypothesis`
- `line_profiler`
- `python-graphviz` and `graphviz`

Speeding up your Python code

In the previous chapter, we talked about different best practices, approaches, and ways to boost code performance. As a toy example for performance, we'll build our own KNN model, which we used in `Chapter 13`, *Training a Machine Learning Model*. As a reminder, KNN is a simple ML model that predicts the target variable by identifying *K* closest records in the training set, then taking a mode (for classification) or weighted average (for regression) of the target variable. Obviously, there are quite a few implementations of KNN already, and so we will use one as an example.

For starters, let's write a naive implementation; it has already been fairly optimized through the use of NumPy commands. First, let's import all the Euclidean distance measuring functions and define a function to get the *N*-closest records. Take a look at the following code:

```
from sklearn.metrics.pairwise import euclidean_distances

def _closest_N(X1, X2, N=1):
    matrix = euclidean_distances(X1, X2)
    args = np.argsort(matrix, axis=1)[:, :N]
    return args
```

Here, we pass two datasets with the same number of features and pass the *N* argument. First, a matrix of distances between the two datasets is computed. From that, for each row (the data point in the first dataset) we sort the columns (the data points in the second dataset), by their distance, take the *N* closest ones, and return their IDs. This function is the main engine of an algorithm.

Now, we can write an estimator class, which will store X, y, and N arguments, and will execute the preceding function on the `predict` method, `sklearn`-style. Here is the code:

```
class NearestNeighbor:
    X = None
    y = None
    N = None
    def __init__(self, N=3):
        self.N=N
    def fit(self, X, y):
        self.X = X
        self.y = y
    def predict(self, X):
        closest = _closest_N(X, self.X, N=self.N)
        result = pd.Series(np.mean(np.take(ytrain.values, closest)
                                  , axis=1))
        result.index = X.index
        return result
```

Note that even this naive model is vectorized (since we use `pandas`) and uses a specialized function, `euclidean_distances`, from `sklearn`. Let's see how it performs. For this, we'll use a sample of 2,500 records from the 311 complaints dataset we used previously. Here is the measurement:

```
>>> %%timeit
>>> naiveKNN.predict(Xtest)
1.43 s ± 78.8 ms per loop (mean ± std. dev. of 7 runs, 1 loop each)
```

It predicts `1.43` s on average, which is quite a lot!

Premature optimization is the root of all evil—it usually results in bad, fragile code. In order to avoid that, we need to understand what part of the code we should tinker with. It is a bad idea to optimize before you know which specific part of your code is slow. If we run `lprun` for the predict method, it is clear that 99.9% of the time is taken up by the `_closest_one` function. Therefore, we should focus on this function alone.

Now, if we run the same `lprun` again for the `_closest_one` function, we'll get the following:

```
>>> %lprun -f _closest_one naiveKNN.predict(Xtest)

Timer unit: 1e-06 s

Total time: 1.44122 s
File: <ipython-input-124-90edea23066c>
Function: _closest_N at line 4

Line #      Hits         Time  Per Hit   % Time  Line Contents
==============================================================
     4                                            def _closest_N(X1, X2,
N=1):
     5         1     196149.0 196149.0     13.6       matrix =
euclidean_distances(X1, X2)
     6         1    1245072.0 1245072.0    86.4       args =
np.argsort(matrix, axis=1)[:, :N]
     7         1          1.0      1.0      0.0       return args
```

As you can see, approximately 86% of the time is taken up by sorting, while the remaining 14% is taken up by Euclidean distance computations.

Rewriting the code with NumPy

NumPy is a library that's used for fast numeric computation and serves as a foundation for Python's scientific ecosystem. It's also the backbone for SciPy and Pandas. Since we have slow, numeric code, NumPy is a great place to start with your optimization attempts.

The algorithm is mostly written in NumPy already—we couldn't perform a true closest-N search in pandas since it doesn't support multidimensional indexing. However, there is one low-hanging fruit: our naive model uses `argsort` to pick the N closest records, which does sort the whole dataset. We don't need sorting, even for those N closest ones—let alone any other element. Here, we can swap the `np.argsort` method with `np.argpartition`. This function does exactly what we want—it puts the N smallest distances first (no matter the order) and keeps all the rest to the right:

```
def _closest_N2(X1, X2, N=1):
    matrix = euclidean_distances(X1, X2)
    return np.argpartition(matrix, kth=N, axis=1)[:, :N]
```

To ensure that the functions are interchangeable, let's write a simple test function:

```
def _test_closest(f):
    x1 = pd.DataFrame({'a':[1,2], 'b':[20,10]})
    x2 = pd.DataFrame({'a':[2,1, 0], 'b':[10,20, 25]})

    answer = np.array([[1,0, 0]]).T
    assert np.all(f(x2, x1, N=1) == answer)

_test_closest(_closest_N2)
```

Feel free to add more test cases (this is where you can leverage PyTest suites)!

Now, we can create a new version of the KNN by using this new function:

```
class numpyNearestNeighbour(NearestNeighbor):
    def predict(self, X):
            closest = _closest_N2(X, self.X, N=self.N)
            return np.mean(np.take(ytrain.values, closest), axis=1)
```

Note that we also got rid of `pd.Series`. This will speed up the algorithm, but you'll probably have to wrap values to the series outside. Let's get our customers to decide on that.

Now, let's see how that version performs on the same dataset:

```
>>> numpyKNN = numpyNearestNeighbour(N=5)
>>> numpyKNN.fit(Xtrain.values, ytrain.values)

>>> %%timeit
>>> _ = numpyKNN.predict(Xtv)

448 ms ± 14.3 ms per loop (mean ± std. dev. of 7 runs, 1 loop each)
```

We went from 1.43 seconds to 448 ms—that's a boost of 69%! Let's look at the distribution by line:

```
>>> %lprun -f _closest_N2 numpyKNN.predict(Xtv)

Timer unit: 1e-06 s

Total time: 0.440021 s
File: <ipython-input-134-29fa1851d880>
Function: _closest_N2 at line 1

Line #  Hits  Time          Per Hit   % Time    Line Contents
==============================================================
     1                                          def _closest_N2(X1, X2, N=1):
```

```
     2 1      212103.0    212103.0  48.2          matrix =
euclidean_distances(X1, X2)
     3 1      227918.0    227918.0  51.8          return
np.argpartition(matrix, kth=N, axis=1)[:, :N]
```

This time, it seems that the matrix and partition take approximately the same time (this will change for larger datasets, though). To summarize, vectorizing the code with NumPy allowed us to boost our computations by 68%—all while making our code cleaner and more expressive. For most tasks, NumPy remains the first solution to try out—and often, the result is good enough already.

 NumPy is essentially a foundation and industry standard for Python numeric computations. Many libraries are based on NumPy or interact with it. In fact, modern NumPy does a great deal of work defining the interface, allowing other libraries to plug in the actual computations and be interchangeable. One example of that is CuPy—a GPU-based alternative for NumPy with a near-identical interface.

If you want to dive deeper into NumPy-based computations, take a look at these resources:

- *The "NumPy" Approach*, by James Powell: `https://www.youtube.com/watch?v=8jixaYxo6kA`
- *NumPy Essentials*, by Leo (Liang-Huan) Chin and Tanmay Dutta: `https://www.packtpub.com/big-data-and-business-intelligence/numpy-essentials`

Specialized data structures and algorithms

Another (arguably the best one, in general) way to make things more performant is to make use of the right data structures and algorithms—in other words, we need to design our code better and use the right tools for the job in the first place. In our case, any spatial query, especially for a large dataset, will gain from the use of a spatial index. Essentially, this creates a hierarchical index, based on the spatial distribution itself. It allows it to measure the distances within a small subset of records. Let's try to make use of it in our model:

```
from scipy.spatial import cKDTree

class kdNearestNeighbor:
    _kd = None
    y = None
    def __init__(self, N=3):
        self.N=N
    def fit(self, X, y):
```

```
        self._kd = cKDTree(X, leafsize=2*self.N)
        self.y = y

    def predict(self, X):
        d, closest = self._kd.query(X, k=self.N)
        return np.mean(np.take(ytrain.values, closest), axis=1)
```

As you can see, now, the code is even simpler—cKDTree takes care of most of the actual logic, behind the scenes. Note that it also has a fair amount of parameters, which we could tune for additional performance gain on a specific dataset. But how does it perform? Let's take a look at the following code:

```
>>> kdKNN = kdNearestNeighbor(N=5)
>>> kdKNN.fit(Xtrain.values, ytrain.values)

>>> %%timeit
>>> _ = kdKNN.predict(Xtv)
11.3 ms ± 237 µs per loop (mean ± std. dev. of 7 runs, 100 loops each)
```

`11.3 ms` is less than one percent of our initial performance! Of course, there is a small trick to this: `cKDTree` creates an index during the fit. Due to this, the `fit` method will be considerably longer to run, but most of the time, this is a trade-off we're happy to make.

Here are a couple of resources on spatial indexes and other algorithms and data structures in Python:

- *Spatial Range Queries Using Python In-Memory Indices*, by Alexander Müller: https://www.youtube.com/watch?v=_95bSEqMzUA
- *Python Data Structures and Algorithms*, by Benjamin Baka: https://www.packtpub.com/application-development/python-data-structures-and-algorithms

Dask

So far, everything we've run was run on one CPU, sequentially—with the exception of some ML models and transformations, which support the number of jobs (parallel executors); for example, `cKDTree` supports multiprocessing, if needed.

The caveat here is the overhead—in order to run a multicore process, a lot of additional memory needs to be allocated and data needs to be copied; it is essentially a fixed cost. Because of that, most of the tasks we ran wouldn't benefit from multiple cores, except for cases where data is very large and computations are fairly parallelized. On the flip side, once we run a task on multiple cores, spreading it across multiple machines is simple.

While the most typical task for Dask to deal with is heavy computation on multiple cores or machines, it also allows you to run computations nicely on data that wouldn't fit in a computer's memory (by loading and operating chunks of data, one per core, at a time). Thus, in theory, it can be used to run some analysis on small IoT devices—especially given that it also supports streaming.

Most of the time, using multiple cores—or multiple machines—will not boost the computations you're able to run on the local machine, loading all the data in memory. However, if your data is big enough, you have to use chunks, and computation will take hours to run. Due to this, using distributed computation could be your only choice (obviously, assuming the bottleneck is not bad code).

For that, we need to introduce Dask—a system that allows you to run heavy computations with big datasets on multiple cores of one machine, or on a cluster of machines. The best part (for us) of Dask is that it emulates the behavior of Pandas or NumPy on the surface. In many cases, Dask's dataframe can be used as if it was a Pandas dataframe—except that it is spread across cores and machines. One big difference in using Dask is that no computation is executed until you ask it to compute.

Let's try pulling the same data we were using for 311 predictions. Since Dask is meant to be used with large datasets and multiple files, it can handle path patterns—we don't need to glob explicitly (also, it can glob on the S3 bucket and read from there). To do so, we'll import the `dask` dataframe, specify a path, `pattern`, using an asterisk (wildcard) to identify parts of the path that vary. Finally, we will use the `read_csv` method to read those, just like we'd do with `pandas` (we do this because Dask runs Pandas' `read_csv` method under the hood here). Setting `blocksize` to `None` here explicitly makes Dask use one worker (core) per file. We also explicitly set Dask to use processes (multicore) scheduler. Here's what this looks like in code:

```
from dask import dataframe as dd
import dask
dask.config.set(scheduler='processes')
```

As you will notice, the code won't take long to execute—this is because it didn't actually run anything. For now, `df` is just a schedule object that will execute once we call a `compute()` method. Let's continue coding as if it was a dataframe:

```
df = df[df.complaint_type.str.lower().str.contains('noise')]
cols = ['x_coordinate_state_plane', 'y_coordinate_state_plane',
'created_date', 'closed_date', 'complaint_type', 'open_data_channel_type']

df = dg.dropna(subset=cols)
```

```
X = df[['x_coordinate_state_plane', 'y_coordinate_state_plane']]
X['dow'] = df['created_date'].dt.dayofweek
X['hour'] = df['created_date'].dt.dayofweek
X['doy'] = df['created_date'].dt.dayofyear
```

Like before, the code didn't take long to execute—for the same reason. The tasks are combining, though, and are forming a directed graph. We can cross-check that graph as follows:

```
X.visualize(filename='chart.png')
```

This is what we'll get:

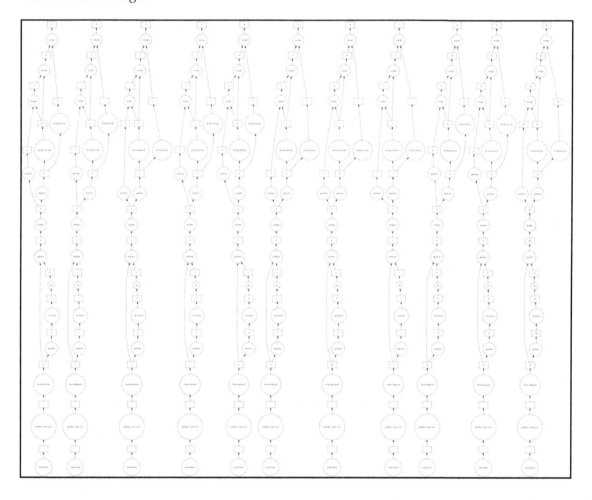

Here, each separate graph represents a chunk that could live on a separate CPU, while each node represents an operation. It is very useful to cross-check those graphs, especially for complex operations (think `groupby` and `similar`). Once you're ready, hit `compute`:

```
data = X.compute()
```

The best part is that while the preceding code will execute on the local machine, it is easy to deploy a cluster of machines on the cloud. Once that is done, Dask can be configured to spread your computation to those machines, with no changes needing to be made to the code on Dask's side (obviously, it will benefit from having data stored in storage that's accessible to all the machines in the cluster).

> Dask is a Python-based framework for big data computation. Its more famous alternative is Spark, and the PySpark package for Python. Spark is a great tool and can scale easily. At the same time, the core code of this technology is written in Java, and so you'll have to be prepared to debug Java code. Dask, on the other hand, is 100% Python and has familiar APIs, so you won't need to change that much code.

For more information on Dask, take a look at *Scalable Data Analysis with Dask*, by Mohammed Kashif: `https://www.packtpub.com/web-development/scalable-data-analysis-python-dask-video`

Dask-ML

Dask is not necessarily a good way to scale up your model training—most models require interaction, and therefore should stay within one machine. At the same time, most `sklearn` models can work on multiple CPUs on their own, and so Dask isn't required.

With that being said, there are plenty of cases when using Dask could be beneficial. For that, there is an additional layer over Dask—Dask-ML. Dask-ML helps connect Dask to `sklearn` and other ML libraries (for example, XGBoost and TensorFlow), thereby allowing you to run some parallelizable models (linear models, for example, or some clustering algorithms), execute hyperparameter searches with different hyperparameters being executed on different servers, or connect distributed datasets to large modules, such as XGBoost.

Numba

In this final subsection, we want to talk about Numba. It is probably one of the hottest ways to speed up your Python code with almost no changes. Numba compiles Python code—vanilla Python or NumPy-based—into C code using LLVM. By doing so—and by leveraging a suite of optimizations along the way—it drastically increases the speed of the code, especially if you use a lot of loops and NumPy arrays.

The great thing about Numba is that, in the best-case scenario, it will improve your code by adding a simple decorator over your function or class—that is, if you're lucky. If you're not, you'll have to work through the documentation and somewhat obscure error messages and experiment with datatype annotations. In some cases, Numba could be more performant than NumPy! As if that isn't enough, Numba can also compile your code for CUDA, leveraging the heavy performance of GPUs—which are often an order of magnitude faster than CPUs!

Here is a simple example. The `compute_distances` function resembles the behavior of `euclidean_distances` and performs fairly well:

```
def distance(p1, p2):
    distance = 0
    for c1, c2, in zip(p1,p2):
        distance += (c2-c1)**2
    return np.sqrt(distance)

def compute_distances(points1, points2):
    A = np.zeros(shape=(len(points1), len(points2)))
    for i, p1 in enumerate(points1):
        for j, p2 in enumerate(points2):
            A[i, j] = distance(p1, p2)
    return A

%timeit compute_distances([(0, 0)]*100, [(1,1)]*200)
```

The performance (output) of the preceding code snippet is as follows:

```
>>> 43.8 ms ± 1.46 ms per loop (mean ± std. dev. of 7 runs, 10 loops each)
```

However, once we add a decorator to each function, performance increases more than tenfold:

```
@jit()
def distance(p1, p2):
    distance = 0
    for c1, c2, in zip(p1,p2):
        distance += (c2-c1)**2
```

```
        return np.sqrt(distance)


@jit()
def compute_distances(points1, points2):
    A = np.zeros(shape=(len(points1), len(points2)))
    for i, p1 in enumerate(points1):
        for j, p2 in enumerate(points2):
                A[i, j] = distance(p1, p2)
    return A

%timeit compute_distances([(0, 0)]*100, [(1,1)]*200)
```

The performance (output) of the preceding code snippet is as follows:

```
>>> 3.02 ms ± 101 µs per loop (mean ± std. dev. of 7 runs, 1 loop each)
```

On that run Numba shows a deprecation warning—future versions will require to specify a list type; in the current version it works as it is.

In our experience, Numba is great for non-trivial, multi-nested computations, where it is easier to write in pure Python (and optimize with Numba) than in NumPy. At the same time, it isn't very mature code (as NumPy is), and different changes occurring in the API happen fairly often.

In this section, we covered a few ways to improve the performance of Python code. Starting from a naive, slow, but easy algorithm implementation, we took on different angles in order to make it faster, such as using vectorized C-based loops, specific data structures that are efficient for the task, running operations on multiple cores or multiple machines, and using modern compilers. Some of those solutions can and should be combined. All of them have their own benefits, limitations, and requirements—larger memory, more CPUs and computers, specific knowledge, and so on. Don't rush to implement any optimization before you're sure you need it. Once you are sure, though, a wide range of possibilities is available.

 Numba is not the only way to compile Python into a more performant C version. In fact, there are quite a few other ways to do this. Among the most popular ones is Cython. The idea behind this package is somewhat similar to Numba, but there is no LLVM involved, and code is compiled to C directly—by doing this, you can store and use the compiled code. In addition, Numba can be compiled to CUDA and run on a GPU!

For more information on Numba, check out the following resources:

- *Numba—Tell Those C++ Bullies to Get Lost, SciPy 2017 Tutorial, Gil Forsyth and Lorena Barba*: `https://www.youtube.com/watch?v=1AwG0T4gaO0`
- *Accelerating Python with the Numba JIT Compiler, SciPy 2015, Stanley Seibert*: `https://www.youtube.com/watch?v=eYIPEDnp5C4`

Now, let's talk about an important topic we've ignored so far—concurrency.

Concurrency and parallelism

Concurrency is the simultaneous execution of multiple pieces of code. Theoretically, concurrency can significantly increase the speed of code execution and it is widely used in software. For example, tasks that require some sort of big loop that does exactly the same operation many times with no interaction between those operations (for example, vectorized operations on dataset columns) are often called **embarrassingly parallel** and present a good target for concurrent execution. That being said, it has its limitations and suits some tasks (for example, where a number of tasks are independent of each other) better than others—read about *Amdahl's law* for some theoretical background.

Different types of concurrency

There are various ways to achieve concurrency in Python, including threads, tasks, processes, and so on. First, while we *say* that a concurrent task occurs simultaneously, this is not always the case. In fact, threads and tasks don't really run concurrently—instead, the CPU can switch between different threads really fast so that they seem to be running in parallel, but it always executes one thread at a time. This is ensured by part of the Python interpreter called **Global Interpreter Lock**, or **GIL**. Threading can still boost your code execution, which it does by switching to other threads when the CPU is waiting for data to be loaded from the network—we'll talk about that in a minute.

Even then, there are multiple ways to execute code on one CPU. Python's built-in `threading` library allows the operating system to stop threads and switch between them—the code itself doesn't need to do anything. The problem with threading, in general, is that the OS can stop threads at any moment—even in the middle of writing or computing data—so you should be extremely careful when sharing any data between threads and not use it anywhere until all of the computations are complete. The problem of shared data is often referred to as **thread safety**.

Another built-in library, `asyncio` (one that allows asynchronous functions, which we touched on in `Chapter 18`, *Serving Models with a REST API*), works slightly differently—synchronous tasks declare that they are done or blocked, in which case another task will start (or continue) running. Thus, tasks cannot be switched while the process occurs until you allow that from within the task.

However, you can run parts of your code truly in parallel (this feature is usually called **parallelism***). There are two ways to do this. First, we can leverage other CPUs on your machine—many modern computers have at least two or four CPUs. In order to do that, you can use the built-in `multiprocessing` library, or any code/library built on it (for example, Dask can run on multiple CPUs of one machine). While this approach allows you to actually run in parallel, it has a large overhead of copying data and orchestrating the process. Because of that fixed cost, multiprocessing generally does not make sense, except for computationally heavy operations.

Lastly, yet another option is to run code simultaneously on many machines. This option was rarely feasible for ordinary developers, even a few years ago, but with the modern cloud-based infrastructure that we have and software tools such as Kubernetes (which we'll discuss later) that are quite accessible and relatively cheap, this is possible. There is no built-in library for that, but frameworks such as Dask and PySpark can help. Running on multiple machines has the same issues as multiprocessing, to the power of ten—deploying machines, loading data, orchestrating tasks, then pulling results together is a huge overhead! But, for better or for worse, there is simply no alternative for huge computations with large datasets that wouldn't fit into one machine's memory. The good news is that, once running a cluster, you can easily add more and more machines when needed—there is virtually no limit (except for the price, of course).

Two types of problems

Now, let's get back to the task at hand. There are two general types of problems concurrency can solve—CPU-bound and I/O-bound tasks. As you can guess from their names, CPU-bound tasks require more computing power than one CPU can provide. For obvious reasons, this kind of problem can't be solved by threading or asynchronous execution, and so multiprocessing and cluster computing are our only options.

The second type, I/O-bound, is limited by the input/output (for example, it has to wait for the database or network). Network resources are *usually* way slower than the CPU, so in this case, our computer just waits for data to come. This is where threading and asynchronous execution shines.

Before you start rewriting your code

Don't rush into rewriting your code in a concurrent fashion just yet. There are plenty of reasons *not* to write concurrent code. Let's look at a few reasons here:

- First of all, don't do it if you don't *need* that boost—any type of concurrency adds code complexity and makes debugging exponentially harder.
- Second, the code for many specific computation-demanding tasks is already written. For example, multiple `sklearn` models support multicore execution—you just need to specify the number of CPUs to use. Some solutions, such as Numba, can release the GIL for specific operations, without large code changes being made.
- Some important packages do not support concurrent operations—asynchronous execution in particular—such as `sqlalchemy` and most database access tools in general.

All in all, make sure you really need your code to run concurrently or in parallel before investing your time and effort. As cool as it sounds, concurrent code is notoriously difficult and takes significantly more time to develop, optimize, and maintain.

If you want to get a deeper understanding of concurrency in Python (which is a very wide topic), we can recommend the following resources:

- *Curious Course on Coroutines and Concurrency*, by David Beazley: `https://www.youtube.com/watch?v=Z_OAlIhXziw`
- *Concurrent Execution* (`https://docs.python.org/3/library/concurrency.html`)

 PEP 554 (currently in draft status) proposes to use sub interpreters (isolated instances, controlled by the main interpreter process) to allow better multiprocessing without GIL getting in the way. To learn more about this proposal, read the PEP: `https://www.python.org/dev/peps/pep-0554/#about-subinterpreters`.

Speaking of maintenance, let's talk about the other side of the same performance coin — apart from code performance, there is *coding* performance. On many occasions, the ability to write code faster, add changes quickly, and introduce fewer bugs could be even more valuable than the speed of code itself. Thus, let's talk about best practices when it comes to coding and tools that will help you be a better developer.

Using best practices for coding in your project

In this section, we'll switch to another, although adjacent, topic—best practices for maintaining good quality code. Here, we will define "good" in a broad way—as dry, concise, expressive, easy to read, change, and build upon. To illustrate this topic, we will review the `wikiwwii` package we built in `Chapter 15`, *Packaging and Testing with Poetry and PyTest*.

 All the changes we make to the package throughout this chapter are stored on the `best-practices` branch in this book's GitHub repository.

Code formatting with black

First of all, let's talk about formatting. It may sound like a minor issue—and it generally is—but formatting won't affect your code performance. In a team, however, formatting matters. It improves readability and allows quicker reading through the code; good formatting highlights both typical and non-trivial areas of the code, helping to skim through trivial parts and focus on what's important. At the same time, formatting, if not automated, takes time and can cause arguments within a team, given that PEP8 does not have strict rules on any single aspect, and there are always matters of taste.

Now, there are quite a few tools that help with formatting—and statically finding potential issues in code—including wrong syntax, non-used variables, and so on. These tools are called **linters**. Arguably the most popular linter for Python is **flake8**. Under the hood, it combines three linters:

- PyFlake 8
- `pycodestyle` (formerly PEP8)
- McCabe

Another popular one is `pylama`, which combines seven linters, including the preceding ones, under the hood (it helps with linting docstrings, too!). Among others, there is **Bandit**, **Radon**, and **MyPy**, which specifically check code versus the given type hints. The good news is that many IDEs and code editors support running linters in the background, highlighting potential errors while you code. In order to use one in VS Code, just go to the command palette and type `select linter`—VS Code will offer you a list of supported ones and will install and start running the chosen one all by itself.

You should definitely use linters! However, they were designed to *inform* you, and can be configurable (for example, to ignore specific errors). To automate the process further—and make everyone on the team follow the same set of formatting rules—we will introduce `black`.

`black` is designed to be a deterministic, automated formatter. It is easy to set up as a pre-commit hook (in other words, it will run automatically before every Git commit). Therefore, you don't need to change your personal formatting habits (or lack thereof)—once the code is ready to be committed, `black` will take over and process everything. The best part is that `black` is not configurable, so there is no room for debates in the team regarding which formatting style is the best.

Let's check whether we can improve the readability of our `wikiwwii` package. `black` has a `diff` option and will show which files will be changed without changing them. Let's run this first:

1. In the repository root folder, type the following in the Terminal:

   ```
   black ./wikiwwii --diff
   ```

   Quite a few lines were affected—`black` replaces all the single quotation marks with doubles, makes sure that the comment symbol is separated from the code by two whitespaces, and so on and so forth. Where possible, it keeps elements on the same line—if not, it will keep every argument on the same indentation level.

2. Let's run that without `--diff` to reformat our code. Feel free to revise all the changes via VS Code:

The preceding is a `diff` visualization (available via the **GIT** tab) of the file before and after black formatting (on the left, red lines and characters with a minus sign near the line number were removed/modified, while green ones with the plus sign on the right were added or changed).

I think you'll agree that those changes make sense—some of them are more important than others, but still, it definitely looks better than it did before.

3. Now, how could we set that to run automatically? The easiest way is to leverage another package that deals with GitHub hooks, called `pre-commit`. In order to use it, we'll create a new file in the repository's root and name it `.pre-commit-config.yaml`. Inside, type the following settings:

```
repos:
-   repo: https://github.com/python/black
    rev: stable
    hooks:
    - id: black
      language_version: python3.7
```

With that setting in place, we can run `pre-commit install`, which will "deploy" the preceding settings into a hook.

4. Finally, we can set a few settings that `black` accepts. As per the developers' recommendation, it is better to set that up via the `pyproject.toml` file:

```
[tool.black]
line-length = 88
target-version = ['py37', 'py38']
exclude = '''
/(
    \.eggs
  | \.git
  | \.hg
  | \.mypy_cache
  | \.tox
  | \.venv
  | \.dvc
  | _build
  | buck-out
  | build
  | dist
)/
'''
```

Now, everything should be in place. Let's try committing the changes.

For the first run, the black hook will take a few seconds to download and run. From now on, if the code is not formatted on a Git commit, it will be reformatted, and the commit process will halt (so that you can check the commit results). Once you feel safe to proceed, commit one more time, and you're all good. The best part is that once this code is on GitHub, every collaborator will have to format with those exact settings!

Lastly, we want to add `black` to our development dependencies in the `pyproject.toml` file so that our fellow developers get `black` as part of their development environment automatically:

```
[tool.poetry.dev-dependencies]
pytest = "^3.0"
pytest-cov = "^2.7"
pytest-azurepipelines = "^0.6.0"
black = "^19.3"
```

Don't forget to run `poetry add black` and `poetry update`. For more on `black` (or, rather, the motivation behind it), please check out this video from PyCon 2019 by Łukasz Langa, the creator of `black`: https://www.youtube.com/watch?v=ia19n_yK4Qs.

Good code formatting is important, and settling on one style within the team is even more so. But what are the other dimensions of good code? And, more importantly, how can we measure them? That's what we'll talk about in the next section.

Measuring code quality with Wily

So far, we've figured out how to keep code formatted, but is this the only factor when it comes to code quality? Of course not; in fact, there are plenty of abstract metrics to take into consideration when it comes to the quality of code, such as the following:

- Lines of code (the fewer lines there are, the fewer bugs there will be).
- Cyclomatic complexity, which counts the number of logical branches in the code; for each `if/else` loop, or another indentation block, complexity grows by one.
- Maintainability index—a measurement that mixes cyclomatic complexity, lines of code, and the number of variables.

But how are those metrics useful? Every task is different, and there are problems that require code that's complex and hard to maintain. Therefore, we shouldn't be too serious when it comes to comparing metrics across different code bases. With that being said, it is a great idea to track metrics over the same code base, measuring trends. Often, those metrics can highlight problematic areas—or problematic new code—and spur a conversation, and, perhaps, critical rethinking.

To track our maintainability metrics over time, we'll use a `wily` package. First, we'll have to build a cache of all the previous commits. It will take a couple of seconds for `wikiwwii` to do this, but for larger datasets, it could take longer:

```
wily build wikiwwii
```

Now, we can measure the code's quality via a table, or by drawing a plot:

```
wily report wikiwwii cyclomatic.complexity -n 10
```

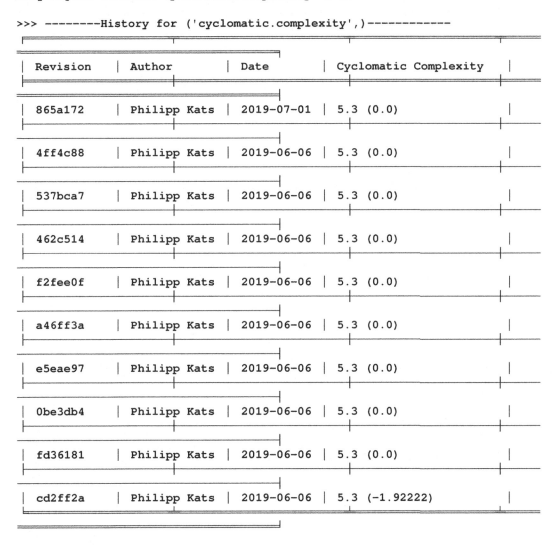

```
>>> --------History for ('cyclomatic.complexity',)------------
```

Revision	Author	Date	Cyclomatic Complexity
865a172	Philipp Kats	2019-07-01	5.3 (0.0)
4ff4c88	Philipp Kats	2019-06-06	5.3 (0.0)
537bca7	Philipp Kats	2019-06-06	5.3 (0.0)
462c514	Philipp Kats	2019-06-06	5.3 (0.0)
f2fee0f	Philipp Kats	2019-06-06	5.3 (0.0)
a46ff3a	Philipp Kats	2019-06-06	5.3 (0.0)
e5eae97	Philipp Kats	2019-06-06	5.3 (0.0)
0be3db4	Philipp Kats	2019-06-06	5.3 (0.0)
fd36181	Philipp Kats	2019-06-06	5.3 (0.0)
cd2ff2a	Philipp Kats	2019-06-06	5.3 (-1.92222)

Since our package is very young, not many changes have to be made. We won't want to check this report every time; instead, we'd rather automate this check and ensure we're not decreasing the code's quality. For that, there are two ways to achieve that:

- First, `wily diff` will show differences between the current version of the code and the previous commit; it is a good idea to check code quality throughout your work.
- Second, we can integrate Wily as a pre-commit hook, similar to how we made it with `black`; we'll start by adding a corresponding `config` to the `.pre-commit-config.yaml` file, just below the `black` settings:

```
- repo: local
  hooks:
  - id: wily
    name: wily
    entry: wily diff
    verbose: true
    language: python
    additional_dependencies: [wily]
```

Now, we will rerun `pre-commit install`. Finally, it is a good idea to add `wily` as a dev-dependency to poetry with `poetry add wily` and check the `pyproject.toml` file:

```
[tool.poetry.dev-dependencies]
pytest = "^3.0"
pytest-cov = "^2.7"
pytest-azurepipelines = "^0.6.0"
black = "^19.3"
wily = "^1.12.2"
```

With that, let's commit our new changes. Now, there are now two pre-commit processes.

Writing tests with hypothesis

Finally, we're going to go back to a topic we've already covered—unit tests. Unit tests are very important; they will give you peace of mind during development—you really don't want to play a whack-a-mole game with your bugs.

Now, testing a data-heavy application is hard. Depending on complex datasets, data structures expose us to dozens of rare, but possible, quirks and edge cases. Often, we don't even need to think of those possibilities, instead focusing on the datasets we have at hand. For example, any function that operates on a dataframe should deal (one way or another) with an empty dataframe, the dataframe of a wrong datatype, a NumPy array, a dataframe of null values, and so on.

One approach to mitigate this problem is to use pre-generated suites of tests that are focused on quirks and possible issues of specific data structures.

To illustrate this idea with an example, let's use `hypothesis`, as follows:

1. Let's play in a sandbox environment of a Jupyter Notebook. We'll start by importing all the necessary pieces:

```
from hypothesis.strategies import integers, randoms, composite
from hypothesis.extra.pandas import series
from hypothesis import given, strategies as st
```

2. Now, we will define a custom strategy (a sample generator). Consider the following code. Here, we are synthetically creating a series of strings that resemble the ones from the Wikipedia entry—they do have numbers and keywords to parse:

```
units = [
    ' men',
    ' guns',
    ' tanks',
    ' airplanes',
    ' captured'
]

def generate_text(values, r):
    r.shuffle(units)
    result = ''
    for i, el in enumerate(values):
        result += str(el)
        result += (units[i] + ' ')
    return (values, result.strip())

StrSintetic = st.builds(generate_text,
                st.lists(st.integers(min_value=1, max_value=2000),
                        min_size=1, max_size=5),
                    st.randoms())

SyntSeries = series(StrSintetic)
```

3. Now, we can pass `SyntSeries` as a sample value for our tests:

```
@given(SyntSeries)
def test_parse_casualties_h(s):
    from wikiwwii.parse.casualties import _parse_casualties

    values = _parse_casualties(s)
    assert ( values.sum(1) > 0).all(), values
```

A new sample will be generated every time. It won't be completely random, however — strategies memorize previous examples—and failed tests—and will start with the values that failed on the previous runs, and new examples if everything prior passed. This particular test has passed.

4. Just to illustrate, let's add an explicit case of an empty string—it will be raised. Parsing the empty strings will result in a zero value sum:

```
@given(SyntSeries)
@example(pd.Series(["", ""]))
def test_parse_casualties_h(s):
    from wikiwwii.parse.casualties import _parse_casualties
    values = _parse_casualties(s)
```

The output on adding an explicit case of an empty string is as follows:

```
> assert (values.sum(1) > 0).all(), values.to_string()
E AssertionError: killed wounded captured tanks airplane guns ships
submarines
E 0 0.0 0 0 0 0 0 0 0
E 1 0.0 0 0 0 0 0 0 0
E assert False
```

As we can see, this failed. Note that if you run the code for a second time, it will fail faster—Hypothesis will run the same failed sample first. Those generators, called strategies, are the main superpower of the package. Due to this, Hypothesis ensures that the code behaves well not only on a few hand-picked cases but also in the wild when fed with synthesized datasets. The test we added may seem not-so-useful (we tested that function before), but it will be quick to catch if we break parsing by mistake—and will start with the failed case on the next run to check whether the code was fixed. It also has a set of smart strategies that have been built for the most popular datatypes.

Hypothesis is a great tool for data-driven testing, as it will automatically generate most of edge cases and make us cover edge cases we haven't even thought about. Because of that, it proves to be a valuable asset for any data-heavy application.

Beyond this book – packages and technologies to look out for

Throughout this book, we've shared a wide range of Python frameworks and libraries for data-driven development. However, there are some tools we couldn't fit in, but that you need to be aware of. We'll discuss some of them here. In particular, we want to cover three somewhat connected topics—Python flavors, Docker containers, and Kubernetes.

Different Python flavors

In the *Numba* section, we showed you how to use Numba to speed Python code up. To do so, Numba uses a modern compilation engine. It does so by exploiting the C nature of Python. Another project, Cython, does the same—it compiles Python code into C using a somewhat different approach.

A third (or, chronologically, the first) option is PYPY (not to be confused with PYPI)—a totally separate interpreter for the Python language. Compared to Numba and Cython, PYPY does not need any changes to be made in the code itself—all the optimization is done under the hood in the interpreter. While this is convenient, the problem is that PYPY requires some work since it needs a proper installation of Numpa, `sklearn`, and basically any other beyond-simple-Python package, so it is rarely used on data-heavy applications.

But there is a whole slew of other options as well! For example, Jython (as you can guess from the name) is a Java-based Python interpreter, which can come in handy if you want to integrate your Python code as part of broader Java code or applications. Another, known as Brython, is a JavaScript-based interpreter that you can use to write both the backend and frontend of your website in Python. In fact, there is a package called `vue.py` (https://stefanhoelzl.github.io/vue.py/), based on the Brython and Vue frontend framework, that attempts to cover both backend and frontend web development at the same time. Of course, we should note that while Numba and Cython try to make Python faster, Brython's goal is to run JavaScript via a Python interface. Due to this, performance is a lot slower.

Something that sits aside from other projects is the PyIodide project. It does not mimic Python in any other language. Instead, it compiles it into WebAssembly format—a special type of binary format that can be executed in a browser, and so anywhere you can open a browser—whether it be a mobile phone, a tablet, or a smart fridge. It can also interact with web pages similar to JavaScript, on any major browser! While being somewhat slower, this approach works and is very promising.

As an example, Pyodide offers a notebook-style application to try out (`https://github.com/iodide-project/pyodide`)—it almost looks like Jupyter—except that this time, there is no Python server—everything (for example, `matplotlib`, `sklearn`, and so on) runs on your machine. Here's what it looks like:

Similarly, the PyIodide package can run other languages—Rust, Go, and more—all in a browser, with no installation required. For more information on PyIodide, check out this video by Michael Droettboom for PyData New York, 2018: `https://www.youtube.com/watch?v=iUqVgykaF-k`.

Another far-fetched but very interesting application for PyIodide (and WebAssembly in general) is as a lingua franca for packaging so that you don't need to worry about adding dependencies, Python, and so on—just download the file and run it. But this is all perspective—for now, we have Docker containers to do that.

Docker containers

Docker containers allow developers to isolate and package certain code and some parts of the surrounding operating system as a binary file. This file can then be run on any other machine with a similar OS, with no changes needed. Because Docker images do not include the whole OS, they are relatively small (a few gigabytes in size) and can be pulled over the internet. At the same time, they are fairly isolated and can be run with little exposure. Multiple containers can run on the same machine at once. Using Docker software, an image can be compiled into a set of layers, similar to how classes inherit from each other. For this compilation, you should use a short text file, commonly called a `Dockerfile`, that's convenient to store in a Git repository.

Compared to, say, Python packages, Docker containers may be a better way to deliver your code to a customer as they won't need to install anything, except the image. In fact, many CI/CD and web services use Docker internally.

For more information on Docker and its application for data-driven applications, please refer to this video by Andy Terrel: `https://www.youtube.com/watch?v=i8vrWFZW2xk`.

In the repository for this book, you will find a `Dockerfile` that was used to generate a corresponding image—one that has Python 3.7, all the Python packages that we used throughout this book, and the code from the repository, installed. Alternatively, you can download this image instead of Python.

Kubernetes

Kubernetes (also known as K8S) is an orchestrating engine that operates over a pool of machines—physical or virtual—and can spawn and wind off containers dynamically. Technically, any container technology can be used, but Docker is by far the most popular one.

For example, it is typical to use Dask on Kubernetes—in this case, Kubernetes will spawn more worker machines when you need them, and can either shut them down or switch to other users, once you're done—all without your intervention. Similarly, it can preserve a composition of containers performing different roles—for example, a load balancer for a web API, which then will redirect requests to different workers, who might operate on one or many database servers—all under the control and orchestration of a Kubernetes server.

This may seem like an approach that's too large and complex for a beginner developer and small services, but it is way easier to operate your services that way: you won't need to log and manually set up specific containers. Many technologies, including load balancers, databases, and so on, have pre-generated images already. In fact, you can even find and reuse predefined instructions on how to start running systems as a whole—including multiple servers—by default.

For more context on this technology, check out this video on *Using Kubernetes for Machine Learning Model Deployment*, by Niels Zeilemaker, PyData Amsterdam, 2017: `https://www.youtube.com/watch?v=f3I0izerPvc`.

Being a developer means constantly learning new things. I can guarantee that, next year, there will be at least a couple of new, cool packages that every developer should learn about. New technologies usually boost productivity and streamline the development process. The secret to productive learning is understanding the scope and requirements of what you actually need—not jumping on a new cool thing just because it is cool.

Summary

In this final chapter, we covered multiple topics on code performance and quality and discussed a few important technologies beyond Python. In particular, we discussed how the combination of efficient code, a better understanding of requirements, and smart usage of appropriate data structures can significantly speed up the performance of code—in our case, a hundred times more performant! Then, we discussed how we can deal with big data by computing in parallel on multiple CPUs—or multiple machines in the cluster.

In the second part of this chapter, we discussed a few ways to keep code quality under control—by running sophisticated non-deterministic test suits, automating code formatting, and tracking code maintainability.

Both code performance and quality are important. Knowing ways to measure and improve both are necessary skills for a professional developer, and will increase your productivity and the complexity of what you can build by orders of magnitude.

Questions

1. How can we measure which line in the code took the most time to complete?
2. Does NumPy run faster than Pandas?
3. When should we use Numba? What are the challenges and benefits of using Numba?
4. When should we use Dask?
5. Does code formatting matter? Why is Black better than linters?
6. How does Hypothesis help you test your code?

Further reading

Architectural Patterns and Best Practices with Python, by Anand Balachandran Pillai: `https://www.packtpub.com/application-development/architectural-patterns-and-best-practices-python-video`

Assessments

Chapter 1

What version of Python do we use?

Throughout this book, we are using the Anaconda distribution, along with Python version 3.7.3.

Will it work on a Windows PC?

Absolutely! Python is a cross-platform language and will run on any Windows, Mac, or Linux device. In fact, it can even run on Raspberry Pi, Lego Mindstorms, and Arduino boards!

Do I need to install any additional packages?

Not if you've installed them in bulk using the `environment.yaml` file from the repository, or using a Docker image. Otherwise, you need to install packages using PIP or Conda.

What is a Jupyter Notebook?

Jupyter Notebook is a special file format, based on JSON, and used by Project Jupyter; in a nutshell, it represents code in an interactive and descriptive manner and can mix code with text, rich media, and interactive widgets.

When and why should we use Jupyter Notebooks?

Jupyter Notebooks are great for research and educational projects as they allow you to tweak and debug your code in an interactive manner, mix code with text and equations, and show the outcome of each code snippet immediately.

When should I switch to VS Code?

Compared to the Jupyter Notebooks, VS Code is a classical text-oriented editor. VS Code has a built-in Git client, debugger, terminal, code analyzers, testing interface, and hundreds of other features, making it very convenient when it comes to writing large amounts of Python code and developing complex apps and packages. We will switch to VS Code to build standalone scripts, packages, and applications.

Can I run the code from this book on my smartphone/tablet?

Yes and no. There is no way to run the code from this book *on* a smartphone/tablet (although the **Pythonista** app on iOS will be able to run some snippets), but you can access the MyBinder service (or, as an alternative, Azure Notebooks or Google Colab), which will deploy a virtual machine with all this book's code on it and everything to run it. This way, you can run the code through any device that has a browser! This has one limitation, though—all of those services have limitations on computations; MyBinder will discard the virtual machine after a 2-hour session, dropping any new code and changes you make.

Chapter 2

Why do we need to use variables in code?

Variables work as aliases or symbols in mathematic equations. With variables, we can write business logic, or *how*, without knowing specific values, or *what*, beforehand – we don't have to repeat doing so over and over again.

What is the recommended way of naming variables? Why does it matter?

There are a few simple requirements when it comes to naming variables that are mandatory—they can't start with a number, contain whitespaces, or special characters. Finally, none of the keywords that are reserved by Python can be used.

That being said, there is some guidance on to better naming; first of all – PEP8. According to PEP, it is recommended to name variables meaningfully and consistently so that they are easy to understand. It is also suggested to use "snakecase" (lowercase whitespace represented by an underscore) for functions and variables and "camelCase" (words joined together, with second and further words beginning with an uppercase letter). None of this execution, but it will help you navigate the code.

What do data types mean and why do they matter for computation?

Data types define core properties of values—how much memory to allocate for them, what the corresponding methods are, and how other objects interact with them.

What are the four most popular data types in Python?

The most popular (common) data types are string, integer, float, and Boolean.

What does the @ operator stand for? Why doesn't it work?

Starting with Python 3.5, it is reserved for matrix multiplication, but it is not implemented (neither are matrices) in core Python.

What are the two operators that will work with strings?

Addition (+) will concatenate two strings together; for example:

```
>>> 'Good ' + 'Morning'
'Good Morning'
```

Multiplication by an integer (*) will repeat a string a corresponding number of times; for example:

```
>>> 'Repeat'*3
'RepeatRepeatRepeat'
```

How would you combine the results of two tests if we need to return a True value, but only when both of them return True? What about when at least one returns True? What about if only one (but not both) returns True?

This can be done using the AND, OR, and XOR operators. Take a look:

```
>>> (1 > 0) and (0 > -1)
True
>>> (1 > 0) or (0 > 1)
True
>>> (1 > 0) ^ (0 > -1)
False
```

Simple!

Chapter 3

What are functions, and when should we use them?

In programming, a function is the named section of the code that encapsulates a specific task and can be used relatively independently from the surrounding code.

How can data be provided to functions?

Conceptually, code in a function can access data from outside. The best way to pass the data, however, is via arguments—special temporary variables used exactly for that.

What does indentation mean? Is it required?

Yes; in Python, indentation is required and defines the grouping of code.

What should be covered in the docstring function? How can I read the docstring function?

Ideally, every module, function, and class should have a docstring. In all those cases, a docstring can be shown using the `help` function, or accessed programmatically via the `__doc__` attribute.

When could it be useful to use type annotations?

Type annotations do not affect computation, per se (at least when it comes to standard Python), but could be helpful to identify incorrect usage of the code, or as a way to validate incoming data in different frameworks, such as the FastAPI framework.

How can a function be designed if I don't know the exact number of arguments or their names beforehand?

For that, we can use `*args` and `**kwargs` as arguments – both allow us to pass an arbitrary number of values, represented within the function as a list or dictionary, respectively.

What does "anonymous function" mean? When should they be used?

Anonymous functions are different types of functions—smaller in size and shorter in definition, they are great to be used, for example, as a one-time function to be passed as argument (as a key argument for sort function). You shouldn't use anonymous functions for something non-trivial as they are somewhat harder to debug.

Chapter 4

How do we retrieve one element from a list? How do we retrieve the last element of the list without computing its length explicitly?

To retrieve any element from a list, we can pass its index (order, starting with zero) in square brackets: `mylist[0]` will get the first element. Similarly, negative indices will return elements in reverse order—`mylist[-1]` will get the last element, no matter how many of them are stored.

How do we get all the elements of a list – except the first one and the last one – in reverse order?

For that, we can use *slicing*. In a slice, the first number represents the start, the second number represents the end, and the third one represents the step. A negative number will lead to the reverse order. Since we're using all three values and the step is negative, we need to swap the start and end values. Since the start is already included but the end isn't, we'll have to shift indices accordingly:

```
>>> mylist = [1,2,3,4,5]
>>> mylist[-2:0:-1]
[4,3,2]
```

Alternatively, we can do that in two steps:

```
>>> mylist[1: -1][::-1]
[4,3,2]
```

How do we merge two dictionaries, and what happens if some of the keys are the same in both of them?

The best way to merge two dictionaries is to update one with another. In this case, overlapping values will be overwritten by the values of the second dictionary:

```
>>> D1, D2 = {'a':1, 'b':2} {'b':3, 'c':4}
>>> D1.update(D2)
>>> D1
{'a':1, 'b':3, 'c':4}
```

What is the best data structure to check for membership?

The best structure to check for membership is a set.

Can we get the last element of the generator without getting all the others?

No, it is not feasible by definition—to get the last value in a generator, you have to go over all previous ones—and besides, generators can be infinite.

How do we combine elements from N triplets into three arrays of N, one by one?

For that, there is the `zip` function. Consider the following example (*N* is equal to 4):

```
>>> arrays = ((1,2,3), (4,5,6), (7,8,9), (10,11,12))
>>> list(zip(*arrays)) # list is needed for printing
[(1, 4, 7, 10), (2, 5, 8, 11), (3, 6, 9, 12)]
```

What is the short way of generating a list of specific dictionary properties – which are retrieved from a list of dictionaries – if a certain other property of each dictionary is in the set?

Here, we need to execute multiple operations at once – filter dictionaries and get a specific value out of them. The shortest way to do that is via one-liners:

```
>>> dicts = [{'a':1, 'keep':False},
             {'a':2, 'keep':True},
             {'a':3, 'keep':True}]

>>> [D['a'] for D in dicts if D['keep']]
[2,3]
```

That's it!

Chapter 5

Can the if clause work with multiple (more than two) logical branches?

Yes! For that, you can use an additional keyword—elif. This way, you can have an unlimited number of logical branches, though it's recommended to use no more than four to five at a time.

What is the difference between for and while loops?

for loops are explicitly finite—they run for every element in a given iterable (although you can pass an infinite iterable if you need to). They are also meant to use that iterable.

while loops are explicitly infinite until certain criteria are met—so they are good if you don't know the number of iterations it would require to meet them (or want an explicitly infinite loop, which would be stopped from within the loop itself).

How can I loop through multiple (two or more) arrays of the same length? Or of different lengths?

The best way to do that is by using the zip function, which combines those arrays into one array with elements of the same order combined together. If the length is different, zip will cut off the tails of the longer arrays.

Why do we need exceptions? How can I catch one?

Exceptions are the way Python (or any other language) halts execution and returns a corresponding message or error code. If you anticipate that the code will fail, you can catch the exception and define an alternative execution by using `try`/`except`/`finally` statements. This will ensure that the execution of the script as a whole won't be halted. That being said, make sure not to mute exceptions you don't want to – this might cause way more problems in the future!

What is the difference between finally and except?

In the `try`/`except`/`finally` clause, you have to use the first keyword, `try`, but can choose between using `except`, `finally`, or both of them. The difference is simple—code within `finally` is used under any circumstances—even if the exception is raised and not caught before the code halts and exits. Thus, the `finally` clause is invaluable if we need to properly close a certain channel—a database connection, file, or anything else.

When should the with clause be used?

The `with` clause is, to some degree, syntactic sugar for the `try`/`finally` clause. It is used to work with objects that have __enter__ and __exit__ methods and executes them before and after the code within the clause. Once the __enter__ method is run successfully, an execution of __exit__ is guaranteed, even if the code within fails to run—similar to how `finally` behaves. All file objects and many database connections use these methods, as it is a convenient and expressive method to ensure the connection is closed once work has been done. That being said, you can use this keyword in other contexts as well, whenever a similar behavior is desired.

How can I use the with clause on a custom object?

To use the `with` clause on a custom object, all you need is to provide two methods for that object—__enter__ and __exit__. All this statement does is run the former before the code within, and the latter afterward, under any circumstances (even if an exception is raised).

Chapter 6

What is an API? Why would we use it?

An API is a programmatic interface; for example, a way to interact with a given tool or service using code. Generally speaking, any tool can (and many do) have an API; for example, every Python package has some, but usually, it is used in the context of a Web API—in other words, an interface for a certain service that's accessible programmatically via the internet. You use Web APIs all of the time—most applications on your phone communicate with the corresponding servers via their APIs. For us, a Web API is a way to leverage the power and information of web services from within our Python code.

What do the various HTTP(S) response status codes mean?

HTTP response statuses are integers that define the status of interactions and are defined by a server. For example, if routing servers can't find a URL you're passing, they will return a famous status, 404. Similarly, if an interaction with the server is successful, the server will return a code 200, along with the other data. Checking for good status codes is the simplest way to check an interaction status programmatically.

Is there a built-in library for dealing with HTTP? Why do we use requests instead?

Indeed, there is the built-in `urllib` package. It is a good option if you don't want to add extra dependencies. For most use cases, however, it is too low-level and requires some boilerplate—it is way nicer to use the `requests` package, with its clean and beautiful interface.

How do you define command-line interface parameters for Python scripts?

There are quite a few options—such as the lightweight `docopt` and the production-grade `click`. There is also the built-in `argparse`. To use it, you need to create an instance of a parser and add the parameters you need.

What does if __name__ == '__main__' mean and why do we need it at the end of a script?

This is a standard Pythonic way to ensure certain code is executed only when a file is called directly, as a script. On execution, Python assigns a few special variables to the root namespace, including `__name__`. If the script is called directly, its value is equal to `__main__`. Of course, this code can be located anywhere in the code, as long as everything within is defined—but it is easier and cleaner to put it at the end.

Chapter 7

What does the term web scraping mean?

Web scraping is the process of collecting information directly from HTML web pages. Just like mining, we have to first collect ore of the HTML, from which we can then refine the valuable data points.

What are the main differences between scraping and using a web API? What are the challenges?

The main difference is the lack of any guarantees – there is no promise that the web page won't change in terms of its structure, or will be shown at all. In fact, many services actively attempt to prevent web scraping. Another challenge is processing raw HTML into valuable information, as it often requires some custom code.

What exactly does Beautiful Soup do? Can we scrape without it?

In our stack (`requests` and `BeautifulSoup`), the latter allows us to navigate the document and query it, pulling specific values. We can definitely scrape web pages without processing them and, theoretically, we write our own processing code—at the end of the day, every page is just text.

Why do we use recursion for scraping?

Recursion is a technique that's used in scraping, as we often don't know the depth of the links beforehand—for example, a specific page may have links to other pages, which lead to others, and so on. In this case, recursions seem like a natural fit, at least for a relatively modest number of pages.

Should we clean the data during scraping?

No! Often, processing and cleaning are not trivial, and we can't ensure that all the edge cases are working properly until we collect all the data. At runtime, this can halt the whole process, with the possibility of losing some information. It is both safer and cleaner to collect all the data first and then deal with it as the next step.

What is the right approach when it comes to dealing with missing data or broken links?

During the scraping process, it is better not to do anything—just keep the values as they are. You can define an appropriate strategy in the next step while processing the data.

Chapter 8

What are classes? When should we use them?

Classes represent a way in which we can create complex objects, with the corresponding data (attributes) and functions (methods). Classes are a useful concept to represent any entity, such as a database connection, file object, algorithm, and so on. There's also a set of special methods and variables that's used by Python to change the behavior of certain instances.

Can we compare two instances of a class or use arithmetic operations with them?

Yes—this is one of the use cases for special methods. For example, in order for us to check instances for equality, we need to set the __eq__ method of the class. Here, we are checking whether the instance is greater, smaller, and so on—there is a corresponding special method for each operation.

When should we use inheritance?

Inheritance is an important property of classes. By inheriting from another class, you let your class acquire all the methods and attributes of the class you're acquiring from. If there is an overlap in the names, the values of your class are preserved. Inheritance is useful to avoid repetition; for example, if multiple classes have shared attributes or methods, it makes sense for all of them to inherit from the base class. Another frequent case for inheritance is to use a base class with some non-trivial behavior, for example, that's provided by an external framework, and override special attributes and methods that will be executed.

What is the use case for data classes?

Data classes are merely syntactic sugar—they simplify the code that's required to create a class and provide some properties, such as equality, initialization, and hashing, by default. They are extremely useful if your class is mostly required to store data.

Chapter 9

What is a shell? Why and when are command-line interfaces advantageous compared to graphical interfaces?

A shell is a user interface that you use to interact with the operating system of a computer. Usually, people use this term to refer to a command-line shell that allows you to control the OS with a set of textual commands. There are three main advantages of command-line interfaces over GUIs. First, textual commands can be combined and stored and thus form scripts. Second, they require a minimal amount of memory and thus are way more suitable for interacting with remote machines via the internet. Third, command-line interfaces are quite unified across different operating systems—commands on Linux and macOS are identical, and even Windows has either similar or aliased commands.

What exactly does version control mean? Is it suitable for research projects?

Version control (**VC**) is a way you can track changes over multiple versions of your work – a piece of code, a dataset, or any other piece of information. Usually, version control systems allow users to collaborate, split, and merge different versions, and revert to any stored version of the project. The version control of the code is critical for modern development as it allows developers to safely add changes to the same body of code.

What is the difference between Git and GitHub? Is Git owned by GitHub?

Git is an open source technology that allows decentralized version control. It is free and works on any operating system. GitHub, on the other hand, is both a company and a web service, with the main purpose of working as central storage for your code repositories. It allows you to read and provide the overall interaction for the online repository, as well as to provide plenty of social interactions around code. GitHub is free and allows an unlimited number of public repositories; the majority of open source projects are stored and tracked with GitHub. That being said, it is not the only service that provides this functionality.

What are Git branches used for?

Technically, Git branches are just pointer objects, pointing at specific commits. Practically, they represent different parallel flows of code development. As such, they are useful, for example, for when you want to work on adding new functionality without affecting the master version; that is, until this new functionality is ready.

What are the two roles of the Conda tool?

Conda software has two roles. First, it is used as a package manager, allowing you to install and update certain packages and software (not necessarily Python-related) from Conda's cloud. The second role of Conda is to provide virtual environments for development, isolating a specific version of Python and the tools that are required, from other environments. On one hand, this allows you to work on different versions of Python and packages on the same machine, while on the other hand, it allows you to reproduce a specific environment on other machines.

How does Jupyter interact with multiple Conda environments?

Jupyter can work from within an environment. However, we recommend that you run Jupyter from the root environment. With the `nbconda` package installed, Jupyter will see all environments.

Chapter 10

Why should we use a special stack of packages for data analysis?

Data analysis requires a fast and easy way to operate on multiple elements at once—a so-called vectorized approach. Python's scientific stack allows this by using `numpy`—a package for fast array operations.

Why are NumPy computations so fast compared to normal Python?

NumPy is drastically faster than vanilla Python on numerical operations. This is all thanks to a different data representation—NumPy arrays, in contrast to standard Python collections, require all the elements to be of the same data type. Because of that, an array can be passed to a CPU as one entity and computed more effectively.

What is the use case and benefit of using Pandas over NumPy?

NumPy only supports numeric arrays. Pandas, on the other hand, supports datetime, string, and categorical arrays. In addition, it has tons of helpful functions and operations that are useful for everyday data processing, such as groupby aggregation, resampling, and plotting.

What does sklearn stand for?

`sklearn` stands for **SciPy kit for machine learning** and has this name due to its origin as a SciPy subpackage.

Chapter 11

Why, if there is an empty cell in the Pandas column, are integer values in this column converted into floats?

This happens since NumPy (and based on it, Pandas) does not support null integers—every null is a special case of a float. Thus, to keep the datatype consistent across the column, NumPy has to convert all integers into floats.

What is the benefit of plotting missing values?

Often, missing values in a dataset can have a certain pattern—for example, records with a missing value in one column also miss values in others. Having a bird's-eye view allows you to find those patterns and define an appropriate imputation strategy.

What is RegEx? Is it a separate language?

Indeed, Regular Expressions, or regex, is a distinct mini-language for text extraction and search. RegEx is implemented in most programming languages—including Python.

How can we use regex in Python?

There is a dedicated built-in package for this, known as `re`. On top of that, most string operations in pandas, such as `replace` and `match`, accept `regex` as an argument.

How is a RegEx pattern defined? How can we combine and modify patterns dynamically within code?

A RegEx pattern is defined as a simple string (text). In order to dynamically modify a pattern in Python, we can simply manipulate this string as we would any other string.

Is it a good idea to run ordinary Python functions on dataframe cells? What are the pros and cons of that approach? Should we use loops for that?

Generally speaking, no—they will run significantly more slowly than similar vectorized ones. Not everything can be easily defined using built-in vectorized operations, though. In some cases, it is easier—or the only option—to execute normal Python. Don't use loops, though—for that purpose, Pandas has the built-in `apply` method.

Chapter 12

How can we understand some general properties of a dataset with pandas?

Using either specific statistics, such as mean, median, or standard deviation, on specific columns. Alternatively, you can use the `describe` method—it will compute descriptive statistics (the ones above it, plus the minimum/maximum, quartiles, and a few more) for all the columns in a dataframe.

What does the resample function do in pandas? How is it different from aggregation?

This method is meant to be used on a dataframe of time-based records. `resample` works similar to aggregation, except that it groups by a time period and returns rows (with empty values) for missing periods as well.

How does visualization work in pandas?

Pandas has an extensive and simple interface for visualization, but it doesn't create charts on its own; all the actual visual stuff is done by `matplotlib`. Starting with version 0.25, `pandas` allows other visualization engines to be used instead.

What are the benefits of declarative data visualization (for example, with Altair)?

There are multiple benefits to this approach. First, declaration (also known as a specification) is decoupled from the engine – so, in theory, it can be used with different engines. Next, specification is also decoupled from the data, and so it can be used on different datasets with no change. Third, it is decoupled from the aesthetical parts, so colors, fonts, and margins can be defined externally and easily adjusted outside of the specification. As a result, the declarative approach allows for a very flexible and effective workflow, allowing ease of change, iteration, and reuse.

In which cases can big data visualization be useful?

Big data visualization can be extremely useful if you wish to understand the overall distribution of the dataset. This is especially true if you're working with spatial data, networks, or embeddings.

Chapter 13

What is machine learning?

Machine learning is a discipline (a branch of artificial intelligence) that focuses on automatic model building. Machine learning algorithms allow us to automatically find patterns or a hierarchy in data (unsupervised learning), or even predict the property of a given sample after training on the prepared "training" dataset (supervised learning).

What is the difference between supervised and non-supervised learning?

Unsupervised learning algorithms operate on any given dataset with no special preparation required and aim to find patterns or structures without any prior knowledge. Supervised learning models are trained on a properly labeled "training set," which they do by building a generalized model, and then are able to infer values for the new data samples it hasn't seen before.

What are the drawbacks of k-means clustering? Why do we need to use a scaler?

K-means can't define clusters of a non-convex shape since this requires a predefined number of clusters to group by and proper scaling. Scaling is needed to align scales of different units to one scale, but that affects the interpretability of the cluster.

How does the KNN model work? What are the benefits and limitations of such a model?

KNN predicts new records by finding N (hence the name) nearest records in the "training" dataset and inferring value from them (for example, by getting a weighted average). It is very simple, works relatively well on a certain type of data, and needs no time to train—most computations are done in the prediction phase. The limitations of such a model are limited scalability (as it needs access to the whole training set at prediction time), it can't predict beyond the training set, and it has limited accuracy. Most importantly, though, the KNN model makes use of all the features that are provided equally—if it is fed with a non-useful, random feature, it may decrease the performance of the model.

Why does linear regression give more interpretation than KNN? Do we need to scale data in this case?

In contrast to KNN, the linear model generalizes all of the knowledge it gains from training in a simple one-dimensional array of coefficients—one per feature, plus a bias. This is very simple and fast to predict, and provides bird's-eye, simple but relatable interpretability, putting a direct "price tag" on each feature. In this case, scaling is not strictly necessary and will obviously affect interpretation.

How do decision trees work?

The decision trees model is yet another machine learning algorithm. To predict values, the DT model generates a binary tree of "questions," each asking whether a certain feature is greater or smaller than a certain threshold. On each iteration, the algorithm finds a feature and threshold with the maximal difference between the target value. The final "leaves" of this tree are associated with the average/most frequent target variable for the corresponding sample in the training dataset. Decision trees offer good interpretation as they are fast and can perform relatively well, but they are extremely prone to overfitting.

Chapter 14

What is overfitting?

Many ML models (for example, decision trees) actively fit to perform well on the training set at hand, but at some point, this process goes beyond generalizable knowledge that's valuable for the task, with some parts being irrelevant to the test set. This is not only meaningless but will also affect the model's performance on other data. This phenomenon is known as overfitting, and there are ways to overcome it.

Why should we use cross-validation?

Cross-validation is a technique that's aimed at overcoming the issue of overfitting. In its basic form, it splits a training set into multiple folds, trains multiple models with the same settings on different combinations of those folds, and measures their performance on other folds—and then averages the performance across all models. As a result, this sampling and prediction on the data each model never saw prevents it from reporting "better" results on a dataset by addressing its specifics. Thus, using cross-validation allows for safe feature-engineering and model adjustments.

Why can it be bad if our metrics are improving on the test set? Which features are useful for improving model performance on cross-validation?

Improvements on the test set can represent an actual increase in model performance—or overfitting. To improve a model's "actual" performance, you need to either tune the model's parameters, add new features or process existing features to better represent underlying dependencies. One usual trick, for example, is to convert date features into a set of features representing cycles, such as day of the week, time of the day, month/day of the year, and so on.

Why do some features decrease the performance of a decision tree on test data or in cross-validation?

Certain features with little to no value for prediction but a high enough variance "appear" to be useful for decision trees (and other algorithms) on their training sets – and thus lead to a decrease in out-of-sample performance. To prevent that, you need to either filter features thoroughly or use algorithms that have fewer issues with overfitting.

What is the difference between the random search and grid search algorithms for parameter optimization?

Both algorithms are designed to find the best combination of the model's hyperparameters—a set of parameters that can only be optimized by running the model on a specific dataset. GridSearch is the most simple, brute-force solution – all it does is run the model over a finite number of combinations ("grid") of those parameters. Due to dimensionality reduction, even a small, finite number of choices for each quickly leads to huge computations. Random search, on the other hand, is similar, but does not require a finite set of choices, instead deriving from distributions, and attempts to pick each other combination based on the results of the previous runs. As a result, it is a faster and better-resulting solution to use than GridSearch in most cases.

Why is Git not sufficient for data version control?

Git, at its core, is an immutable file-based system – which means that, on each commit, it stores a copy of each file that was changed since the last commit. Thus, any kind of change in any dataset beyond basic metrics will result in a copy of the whole file, which will quickly lead to huge memory consumption. In fact, GitHub prevents uploading files above a certain threshold, so using Git to control data is not an option for data version control.

What are the alternatives to DVC for data version control and experimentation logging?

Currently, there are plenty of alternative solutions to data version control. All of them have different flavors and focus on different aspects. Among the most popular alternatives are MLflow and Sacred, but both are language-specific and require some custom code.

Chapter 15

What are the benefits of packaging code?

Packaging code is a great way to do the following:

- Make certain code available to use from multiple other packages
- Share code with colleagues or make it easy to install for yourself

- Set a project to collaborate on with others
- Add reliability to your code by constantly running tests
- Structure code better and isolate it from your day-to-day work

What is the main difference between Conda and pip as package managers?

At this moment, the difference is not as great as it was before. Historically, pip didn't support adding non-Python code as a binary for various reasons. This is a problem for data analysis projects since many data-related packages, namely NumPy, SciPy, and `sklearn`, use C and even Fortran under the hood.

This is where Conda comes into play—it allows you to install any tool in any language, even one that's totally unrelated to Python. Today, Conda is a well-established package manager and is especially popular among data scientists.

One additional feature of Conda is that it has multiple channels—from personal channels, to shared, and community-driven channels (`conda-forge`), to the most conservative, carefully curated Anaconda channel. If needed, you can also pay for a private channel, dedicated to your company.

What is dependency resolution, and why is it difficult?

Dependency resolution is the process of finding the right versions of all the packages that are required to run software. It is difficult and not always achievable because, for an arbitrary package, there are dozens of direct and indirect dependencies. That's why building a package requires a thorough, sufficiently relaxed, and minimal definition of the required packages.

What are the benefits of poetry over the standard setup tools?

First and foremost, `poetry` supports a new, TOML-based specification for packages. This is fundamentally safer as a client won't be running arbitrary code from the web on installation. Next, `poetry` generates a dedicated virtual environment for the development process and provides a locked specification of that environment for exact replication. Last but not least, it has a powerful dependency resolver and can analyze the depth and status of your dependencies.

Why do we need tests?

Tests are a critical part of any software development. They allow you to ensure that code is behaving as expected, thus allowing for the safe alteration of existing code.

What is the purpose of CI?

CI, or continuous integration, is a term that represents an automated pipeline connected to a version control system. CI usually runs tests and security checks on code and returns a status to the version control system so that developers can safely merge commits and move code to production. CI can also generate and store artifacts (binaries, for example) or trigger updates for live servers. CI plays an important role in the continuous process of rolling out new versions of products to clients. It can also save time by running tests on multiple machines in parallel, compared to running them locally on the developer's machine.

Chapter 16

What are the benefits of writing tasks rather than using simple scripts?

Scripts are great for simple and one-off jobs. If you have a repetitive task to do – or even more so if there is a set of tasks that depend on each other, and you need to ensure that they don't run without a dependency missing, or that they won't override (or append to) existing data—then ETL pipelines and tasks are for you. As a free bonus, frameworks such as Luigi have a lot of utility code that helps to build pipelines – you won't need to write a solution for writing to S3 or a database, or parse a command-line command.

What is the base element of Luigi jobs?

The base element of Luigi jobs (pipelines) is the `Task` class. All the business logic of a task needs to be wrapped in the `run` method. Its output and dependencies are defined within the `output` and `requires` methods.

How are DAGs defined in Luigi? What are the benefits of that architecture?

Luigi forms DAGs (pipelines) automatically; there is no need to set them up explicitly. To define a DAG, you need to run the last task in the pipe—Luigi will check for its dependencies if they are not met, will check for theirs, and so on. Once the queue of tasks to computing is ready, Luigi starts to compute them, one by one, starting with the earliest dependency—and adding others once their requirements are met.

This allows the pipeline to be flexible and easy to build, one step at a time. If something "external" to the pipeline task needs to be dependent, all it needs is to refer to a task.

How can we parameterize a task?

To parameterize a task, all we need to do is set a task attribute to be of the `luigi.Parameter` type, or its derivative. Once set, the parameter can be used as an argument that's passed on class initiation, or passed on the command line. Parameters can be used to run the task on a specific subset of data, or with a specific mode – for example, you can pass a production flag that will direct the dataflow to the production database or staging if the flag is not raised.

What is the best way to run time-based tasks in bulk?

For time-based jobs, Luigi provides built-in functionality for bulk execution – with the main focus on backfill. By using the `DailyRange` (or other ranges) built-in utility, you can pass either the start and end date, or one of those and a number of days to fill. The program will automatically spawn and execute the given task for each day in this range. However, this has one caveat—a task can only have one `DateTime` parameter, which will be used.

How can we schedule a job with Luigi?

Luigi itself does not provide a scheduling mechanism. To schedule a task, an external tool such as cron should be used. Cron is a tool that's used for scheduling arbitrary tasks and is built into all Mac and Linux OS systems. Windows has its own similar tool such as `schtasks` or PyCron.

Chapter 17

What are the main differences between visualizing data in the notebook and on a dashboard?

The main differences are as follows:

1. The audience for the dashboard is meant to be wide—so the dashboard should be easily accessible, for example, via an internet browser, and well-explained. One-off visualizations, on the other hand, are often made for self-consumption, and thus don't need to be self-explanatory.
2. Dashboards are meant to be frequently updated and exploratory. Visualizations are often static and show a specific aspect of data.

Why do we call some dashboards "static"? What are the pros and cons of a static dashboard?

In common terms, *static* web pages are ones that are provided "as-is," as flat files, and there is no active server behind them. Static dashboards are easier to maintain and provide for a wide audience but have some limitations in terms of computation and data access.

What are the benefits of using a dynamic dashboard?

Dynamic dashboards are actively served by dedicated servers and thus have considerable computation power behind them. The servers can also have access to the "raw" data and compute metrics on the fly, allowing for much deeper exploration possibilities.

What are the features of the panel package?

`panel` is a package that was developed by Anaconda (the same company that produces the Conda package manager). Its main feature is that it is agnostic to actual visualization tools—any tool can be used if it produces content that can be present in the Jupyter Notebook.

Chapter 18

What is the REST API?

REST, or REpresentational State Transfer, is a general architecture for APIs interaction that uses the HTTP protocol. The main features of REST-compliant systems are being stateless and their separation of concerns between the client and the server.

What Python packages can be used to build a REST API?

At this point, there are quite a lot of frameworks that can be used to build a REST API in Python. The most popular ones are Flask, Django REST, Hug, Falcon, CherryPy, Quart, and many others. In this book, we're using the FastAPI framework.

What are the key features of the FastAPI framework?

FastAPI has a few unique characteristics. First, it is designed specifically with API in mind, which is different to many others. Second, it fully supports asynchronous execution and can work with a Uvicorn-Gunicorn inspired asynchronous server. Third, it makes use of type annotations, using them to generate interactive documentation (OpenAPI) and, most importantly, to validate passed data automatically. Finally, it provides simple tools for the validation and conversion of data—all that's left is to write the business logic.

Why OpenAPI (Swagger)?

OpenAPI, previously known as Swagger, is an API description specification that allows you to define an API with a simple file and then generate web-based interactive documentation from that file. In fact, while the documentation is autogenerated by FastAPI, this specification can also be used to do the following:

- Autogenerate client libraries in multiple languages, including Python
- Autogenerate API stubs (API-serving server code templates) from the file, also in multiple languages

Why do we need Uvicorn or Gunicorn servers?

Both Uvicorn and Gunicorn are **Web Server Gateway Interface (WSGI)** tools. Their job is to deploy multiple instances of an application, restart them if needed, and pass requests to them and responses back to the client. WSGI servers usually run under a web server, such as nginx, which takes care of requests, returns files, and directs only correct requests to the WSGI (which then passes them to the application). Uvicorn is specifically focused on asynchronous execution and has a slightly different implementation of asynchronous work.

What metrics does the Locust package measure?

Locust is a package that's designed to test the traffic loads of a service (for example, an API). Its main metrics are requests per second, average response time, and the number of errors.

Chapter 19

What does a serverless application mean?

Serverless applications still run on normal servers, but control over the server's behavior and the stack are completely handled by the cloud provider—all that's required from the developer is to write a function that describes the business logic. This function can be set to trigger on a request to a certain API endpoint, on a certain event (for example, a file addition to the S3 bucket), or on a scheduler so that it runs every day.

What are the limitations of the serverless approach?

Serverless applications are mainly bound by the memory they can use and, therefore, the packages that can be installed. For AWS Lambda, the limit is 50 MB.

What are the benefits of serverless APIs?

Serverless APIs have quite a few benefits. First and foremost, you don't need to spend time on the development and maintenance of servers, load balancers, and so on. Serverless APIs are generally paid for each execution, which means that multiple APIs can sit for free, without you paying for a running instance. At the same time, they are scalable – if needed, a vendor will just spawn more machines to work on all the requests!

What role does Chalice play in the development of a serverless application?

Chalice is a Python package for Lambda functions, developed by Amazon. It provides invaluable help with Lambda function development—it handles packaging the code, testing it locally, and uploading it to the server. In other words, it helps with the whole life cycle.

Chapter 20

How can we measure which line in the code took the most time to complete?

The simplest way to do that is via a utility called `line_profiler`. This utility will show each line of the given code and show how much time was spent on each line. Knowing the distribution of the time that was required helps us focus on the right parts of the code.

Does NumPy run faster than Pandas?

In most cases with numeric computations, Pandas uses NumPy under the hood, so the difference is minimal. It does, however, spend certain additional time on building series and dataframes, when needed. So, for a well-scoped and purely numeric task, it makes sense to switch to pure NumPy.

When should we use Numba? What are the challenges and benefits of using Numba?

Numba uses a modern C compiler with some modern techniques to significantly improve performance. It can also be run on a GPU. Its "superpower" is that it's arbitrary Python code with only a few lines of alterations. This makes Numba a great tool of choice if you have a large set of pure Python code that needs to run faster. The challenges of Numba are twofold—first, it requires an LLVM compiler that is relatively large in size. Second, it is not trivial, and in some cases it's impossible to house with existing C code, which means it has problems with SciPy and `sklearn`.

When should we use Dask?

Dask is a powerful and nicely designed library for parallel computations—it can work on multiple cores of a single machine, or on many machines at the same time. Best of all, it has a few different interfaces that "resemble" (actually, just use under the hood) popular libraries, such as NumPy and pandas. As a result, on many occasions, you only need to change a few lines to run the same code in a distributed fashion.

Does code formatting matter? Why is Black better than linters?

It does. Good, standardized formatting helps improve the readability of code, decreases cognitive loads, and helps to avoid syntactic errors and typos. In addition, a unified approach to formatting decreases the number of pointless formatting changes that complicate the use of Git.

Black is an automated formatter—not a linter. Compared to linters, it not only finds code that needs to be edited but also edits it itself. Black is perfect to use on Git pre-commit hooks—it will automatically format the code on every commit.

How does Hypothesis help you test your code?

Standard unit tests provide one of a few cases for code to be tested against. While this is fine most of the time, there are usually plenty of options you wouldn't have thought of beforehand. Hypothesis tries to address that—it allows you to create a probabilistic dataset or set of arguments that follow certain rules—and then will test your code against different data. In doing so, it will use a few known edge cases, such as empty strings or data frames, and some random data. If a certain test fails, Hypothesis will start a new test from the data that led to a failure previously.

Other Books You May Enjoy

If you enjoyed this book, you may be interested in these other books by Packt:

Expert Python Programming - Third Edition
Tarek Ziadé, Michał Jaworski

ISBN: 978-1-78980-889-6

- Explore modern ways of setting up repeatable and consistent development environments
- Package Python code effectively for community and production use
- Learn modern syntax elements of Python programming such as f-strings, enums, and lambda functions
- Demystify metaprogramming in Python with metaclasses
- Write concurrent code in Python
- Extend Python with code written in different languages
- Integrate Python with code written in different languages

Mastering Object-Oriented Python - Second Edition
Steven F. Lott

ISBN: 978-1-78953-136-7

- Explore a variety of different design patterns for the __init__() method
- Learn to use Flask to build a RESTful web service
- Discover SOLID design patterns and principles
- Use the features of Python 3's abstract base
- Create classes for your own applications
- Design testable code using pytest and fixtures
- Understand how to design context managers that leverage the 'with' statement
- Create a new type of collection using standard library and design techniques
- Develop new number types above and beyond the built-in classes of numbers

Leave a review - let other readers know what you think

Please share your thoughts on this book with others by leaving a review on the site that you bought it from. If you purchased the book from Amazon, please leave us an honest review on this book's Amazon page. This is vital so that other potential readers can see and use your unbiased opinion to make purchasing decisions, we can understand what our customers think about our products, and our authors can see your feedback on the title that they have worked with Packt to create. It will only take a few minutes of your time, but is valuable to other potential customers, our authors, and Packt. Thank you!

Index

Made in the USA
Coppell, TX
11 January 2020